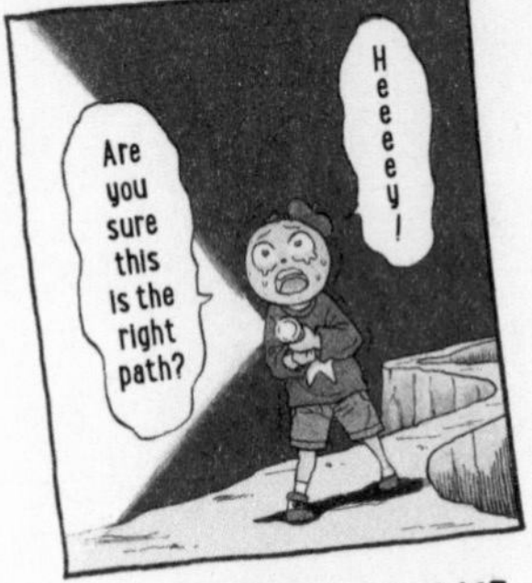
Heeeey!
Are you sure this is the right path?

NOBUAKI ENOKI

Once the warm season starts, I often like to take walks outside. Unfortunately, I have a pretty bad sense of direction, so I get lost a lot. I have been scared on multiple occasions that I would never be able to return home. I also get this feeling while I'm drawing manga.

Nobuaki Enoki received the Jump Treasure New Cartoonist Prize in April 2009 for his work *Rikuo*. *School Judgment: Gakkyu Hotei* was his first work to be serialized in *Weekly Shonen Jump*.

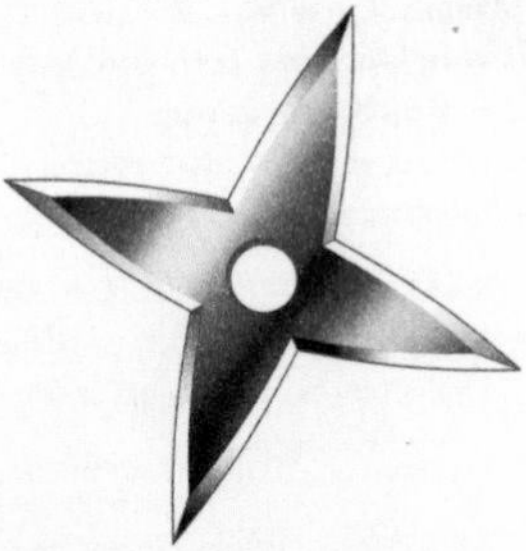

TAKESHI OBATA

Apparently the number one occupation grade-schoolers want is to be a ninja. There's one in this volume.

Takeshi Obata was born in 1969 in Niigata, Japan, and first achieved international recognition as the artist of the wildly popular *Shonen Jump* title *Hikaru no Go*, which won the 2003 Tezuka Osamu Cultural Prize: Shinsei "New Hope" Award and the 2000 Shogakukan Manga Award. He went on to illustrate the smash hit *Death Note* as well as the hugely successful manga *Bakuman*。 and *All You Need Is Kill*.

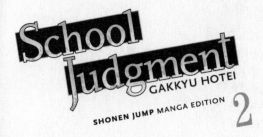

School Judgment

GAKKYU HOTEI

SHONEN JUMP MANGA EDITION 2

STORY BY Nobuaki Enoki
ART BY Takeshi Obata

TRANSLATION Mari Morimoto
TOUCH-UP ART & LETTERING James Gaubatz
DESIGN Shawn Carrico
WEEKLY SHONEN JUMP EDITOR Alexis Kirsch
GRAPHIC NOVEL EDITOR Marlene First

GAKKYU HOTEI © 2014 by Nobuaki Enoki, Takeshi Obata
All rights reserved. First published in Japan in 2014 by SHUEISHA Inc., Tokyo.
English translation rights arranged by SHUEISHA Inc.

Printed in the U.S.A.

Published by VIZ Media, LLC
P.O. Box 77010
San Francisco, CA 94107

10 9 8 7 6 5 4 3 2 1
First printing, April 2016

www.viz.com

www.shonenjump.com

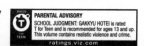

School Judgment

Judgment

GAKKYU HOTEI

2

Civil Trial Arc

STORY BY Nobuaki Enoki
ART BY Takeshi Obata

CHARACTERS

School Judgment
GAKKYU HOTEI

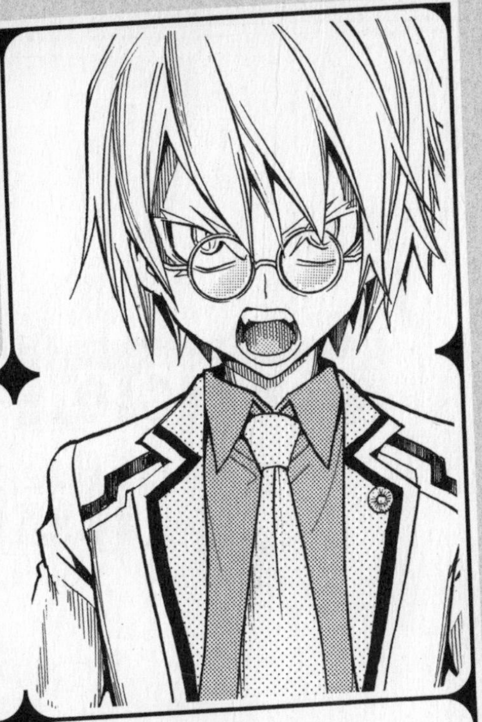

ABAKU INUGAMI

An elementary school attorney who transferred into Tenbin Elementary class 6-3. His hobby is *ronpa*. He is one of the Three Tongues. He previously attended the grade-schoolers' penitentiary Onigashima Elementary, but now...?!

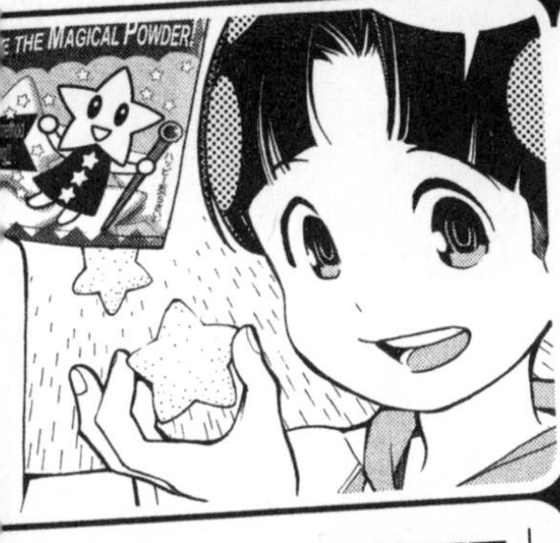
THE MAGICAL POWDER!

TENTO NANAHOSHI

Tenbin Elementary class 6-3 student. Was defended by Abaku in the Suzuki Murder Case and subsequently started assisting him with his work as a lawyer. A fan of fellow classmate Airin.

PINE HANZUKI

A pretty prosecutor who transferred into Tenbin Elementary at the same time as Abaku. She is the daughter of the head of the Hanzuki Conglomerate, which is famous in the legal world. She has nicknamed Abaku "Puppy-gami" and is always at odds with him.

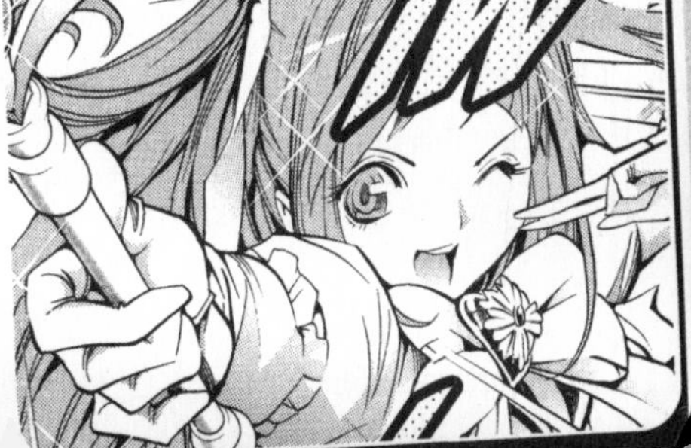

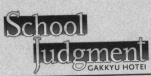

School Judgment
GAKKYU HOTEI

CLASS 6-3 STUDENTS

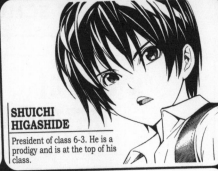

SHUICHI HIGASHIDE

President of class 6-3. He is a prodigy and is at the top of his class.

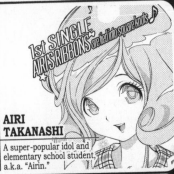

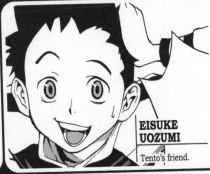

EISUKE UOZUMI

Tento's friend.

1st SINGLE
AIRI'S RIBBONS are tied into square knots♪

AIRI TAKANASHI

A super-popular idol and elementary school student, a.k.a. "Airin."

STORY

School Judgment
GAKKYU HOTEI

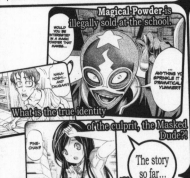

Magical Powder is illegally sold at the school.
WOULD YOU BE INTERESTED IN A MAGIC POWDER THAT MAKES...
... ANYTHING YO SPRINKLE IT DRAMATICAL YUMMIER?
NANA-HOSHI... AND INUGAMI?
What is the true identity of the culprit, the Masked Dude?!
PINE-CHAN?
The story so far...
Miss Shiratori is the suspect?!

The School Judgment System is a new system introduced by the government to resolve problems, such as bullying and punishment in schools.

It is a new form of Classroom Arbitration presided over by children who have answered the call to action to seek the truth under the law. Abaku Inugami, who transferred into Himawari Municipal Tenbin Elementary School, has a hard time fitting in with his class due to his difficult personality and occupation. However, as he works on various cases as an attorney, he starts to develop deep bonds with his classmates.

And today, once again, Abaku is approached to defend someone in this next case...

CLASS SCHEDULE

	MON	TUE	WED	THU	FRI
1		School Judgment GAKKYU HOTEI			2
2	**Chapter 8** Beware of the Magical Powder (2) p. 7	Phys Ed	**Chapter 12** Civil Trial Arc (2): The Courtroom p. 87	Ethics	Social Studies
3	Language	**Chapter 10** The Inu-Saru Reunion p. 47	Science	**Chapter 15** Evil Spirit 5-Meters Deep (2) p. 147	Art
4	**Chapter 9** Beware of the Magical Powder (3) p. 27	Foreign Language	**Chapter 13** Civil Trial Arc (3): The Staircase of Truth p. 107	Math	Art
5	Phys Ed	**Chapter 11** Civil Trial Arc (1): The Investigation p. 67	Classroom Arbitration	**Chapter 16** Evil Spirit 5-Meters Deep (3) p. 167	General Studies
6	Math	Social Studies	**Chapter 14** Evil Spirit 5-Meters Deep (1) p. 127	Phys Ed	**Glossary** p. 188

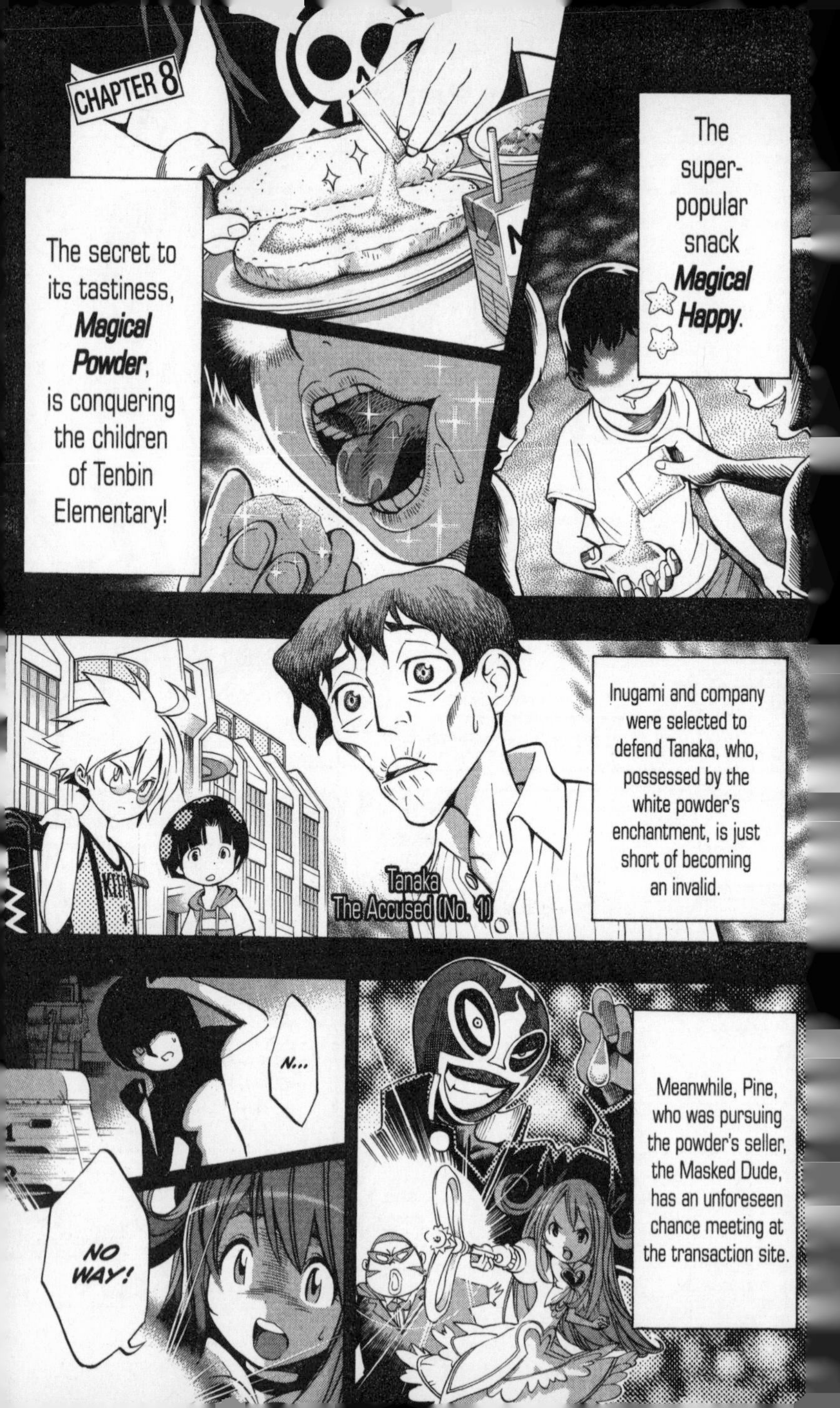
The super-popular snack Magical Happy.
CHAPTER 8
The secret to its tastiness, Magical Powder, is conquering the children of Tenbin Elementary!
Inugami and company were selected to defend Tanaka, who, possessed by the white powder's enchantment, is just short of becoming an invalid.
Tanaka
The Accused (No. 1)
Meanwhile, Pine, who was pursuing the powder's seller, the Masked Dude, has an unforeseen chance meeting at the transaction site.
N...
NO WAY!

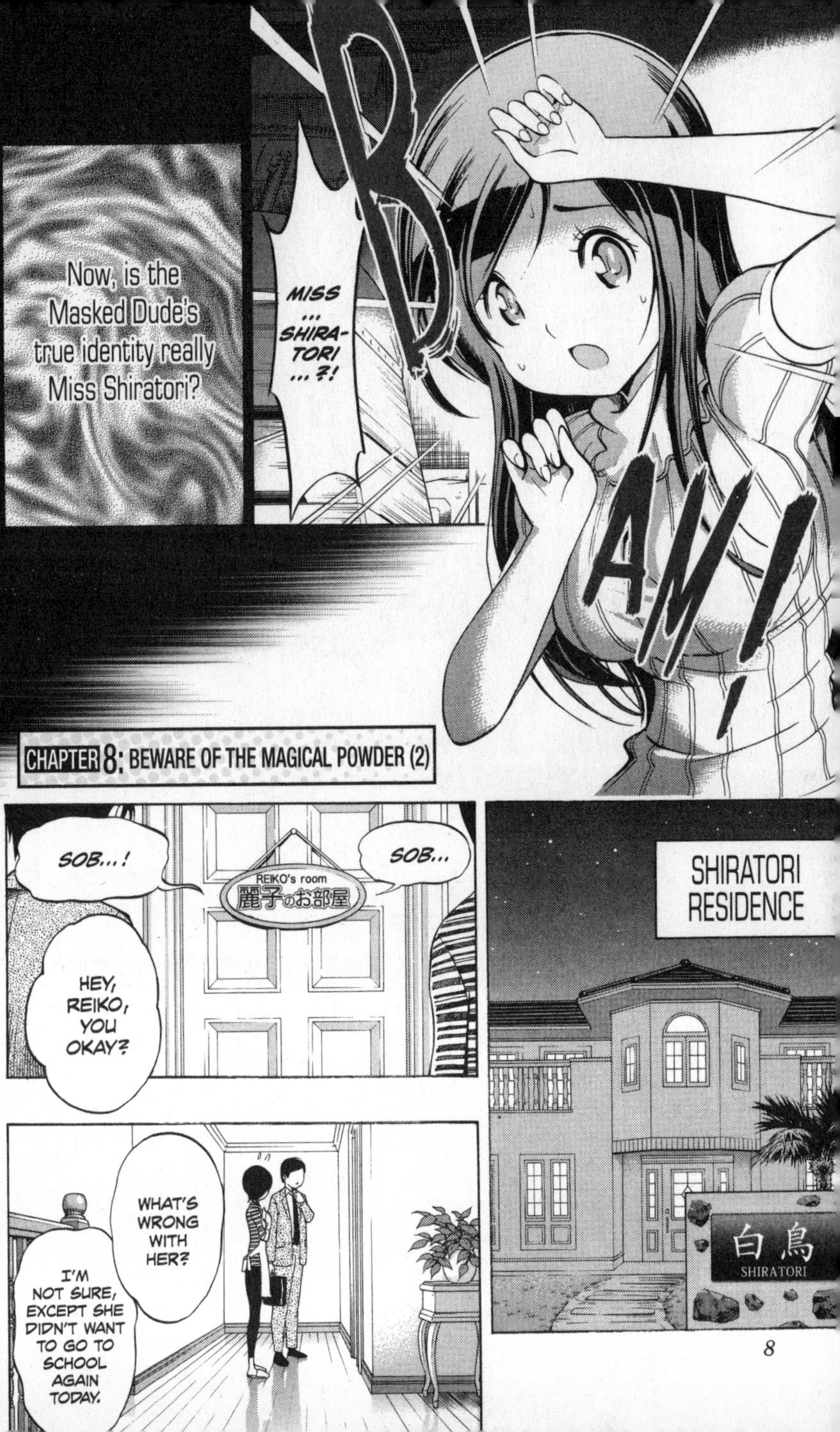

MISS ... SHIRATORI ...?!
AM I
Now, is the Masked Dude's true identity really Miss Shiratori?
CHAPTER 8: BEWARE OF THE MAGICAL POWDER (2)
SHIRATORI RESIDENCE
白鳥
SHIRATORI
SOB...
SOB...!
REIKO's room
麗子のお部屋
HEY, REIKO, YOU OKAY?
WHAT'S WRONG WITH HER?
I'M NOT SURE, EXCEPT SHE DIDN'T WANT TO GO TO SCHOOL AGAIN TODAY.

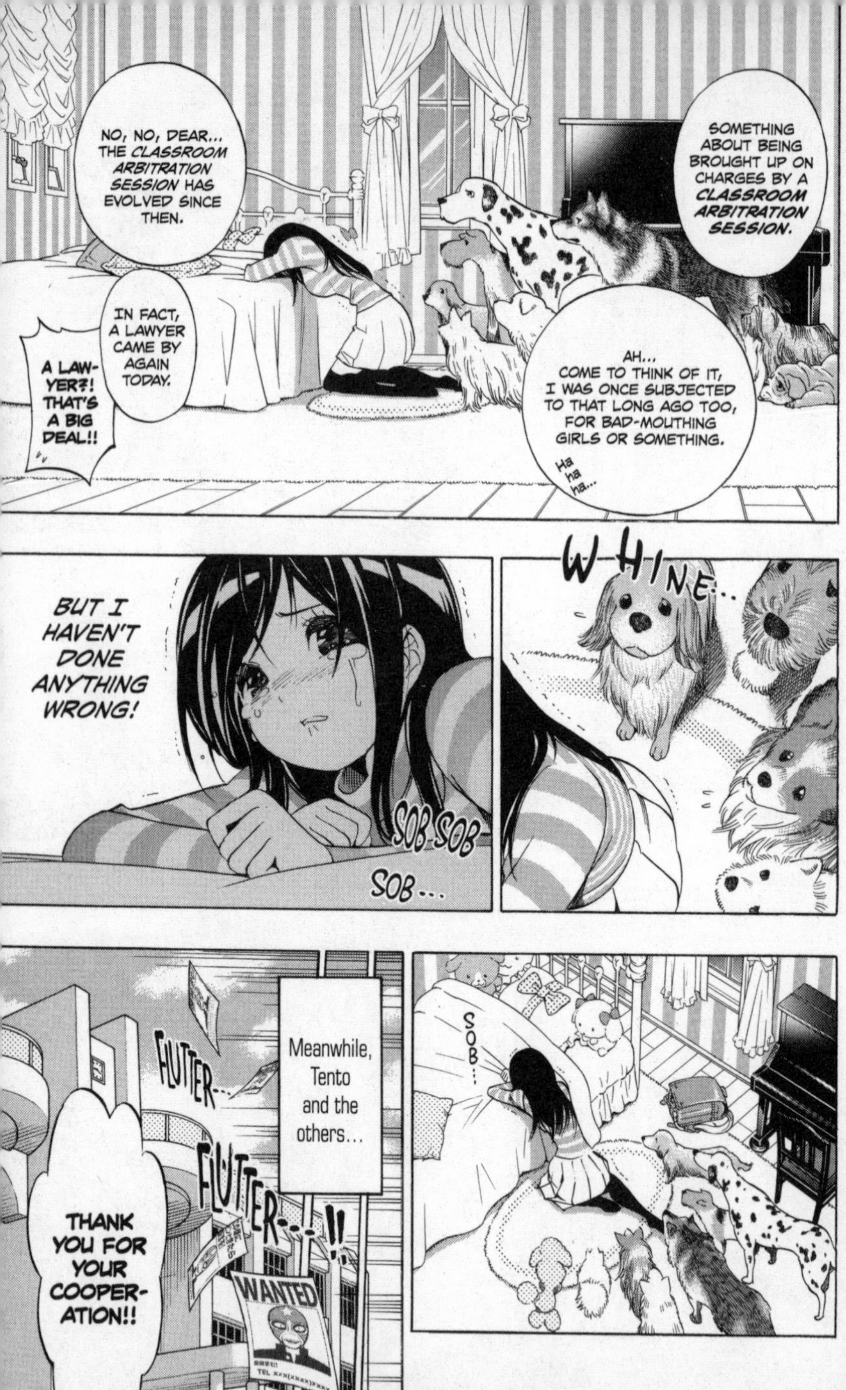
SOMETHING ABOUT BEING BROUGHT UP ON CHARGES BY A *CLASSROOM ARBITRATION SESSION.*
AH... COME TO THINK OF IT, I WAS ONCE SUBJECTED TO THAT LONG AGO TOO, FOR BAD-MOUTHING GIRLS OR SOMETHING.
Ha ha ha...
NO, NO, DEAR... THE *CLASSROOM ARBITRATION SESSION* HAS EVOLVED SINCE THEN.
IN FACT, A LAWYER CAME BY AGAIN TODAY.
A LAW-YER?! THAT'S A BIG DEAL!!
WHINE...
BUT I HAVEN'T DONE ANYTHING WRONG!
SOB SOB
SOB...
SOB...
Meanwhile, Tento and the others...
FLUTTER...
FLUTTER...!!
THANK YOU FOR YOUR COOPER-ATION!!
WANTED

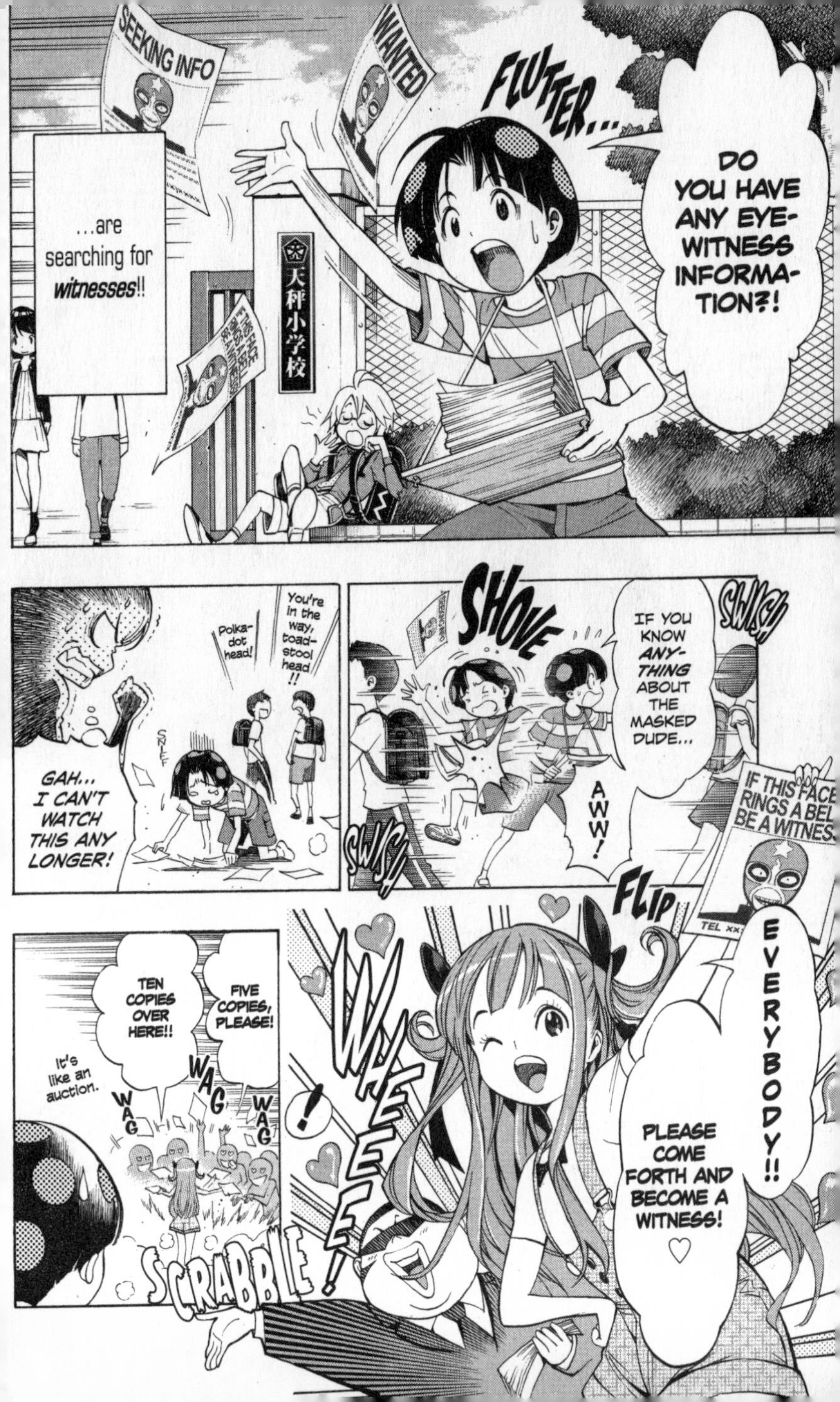
FLUTTER...
DO YOU HAVE ANY EYE-WITNESS INFORMATION?!
WANTED
SEEKING INFO
天秤小学校
...are searching for *witnesses*!!
SHOVE
SWISH
IF YOU KNOW ANYTHING ABOUT THE MASKED DUDE...
AWW!
SWISH
IF THIS FACE RINGS A BEL
BE A WITNES
You're in the way, toadstool head!!
Polka-dot head!
SNIFF
GAH... I CAN'T WATCH THIS ANY LONGER!
FLIP
EVERYBODY!!
PLEASE COME FORTH AND BECOME A WITNESS! ♡
WHEEEEE!
SCRABBLE!
FIVE COPIES, PLEASE!
TEN COPIES OVER HERE!!
WAG
WAG
WAG
It's like an auction.

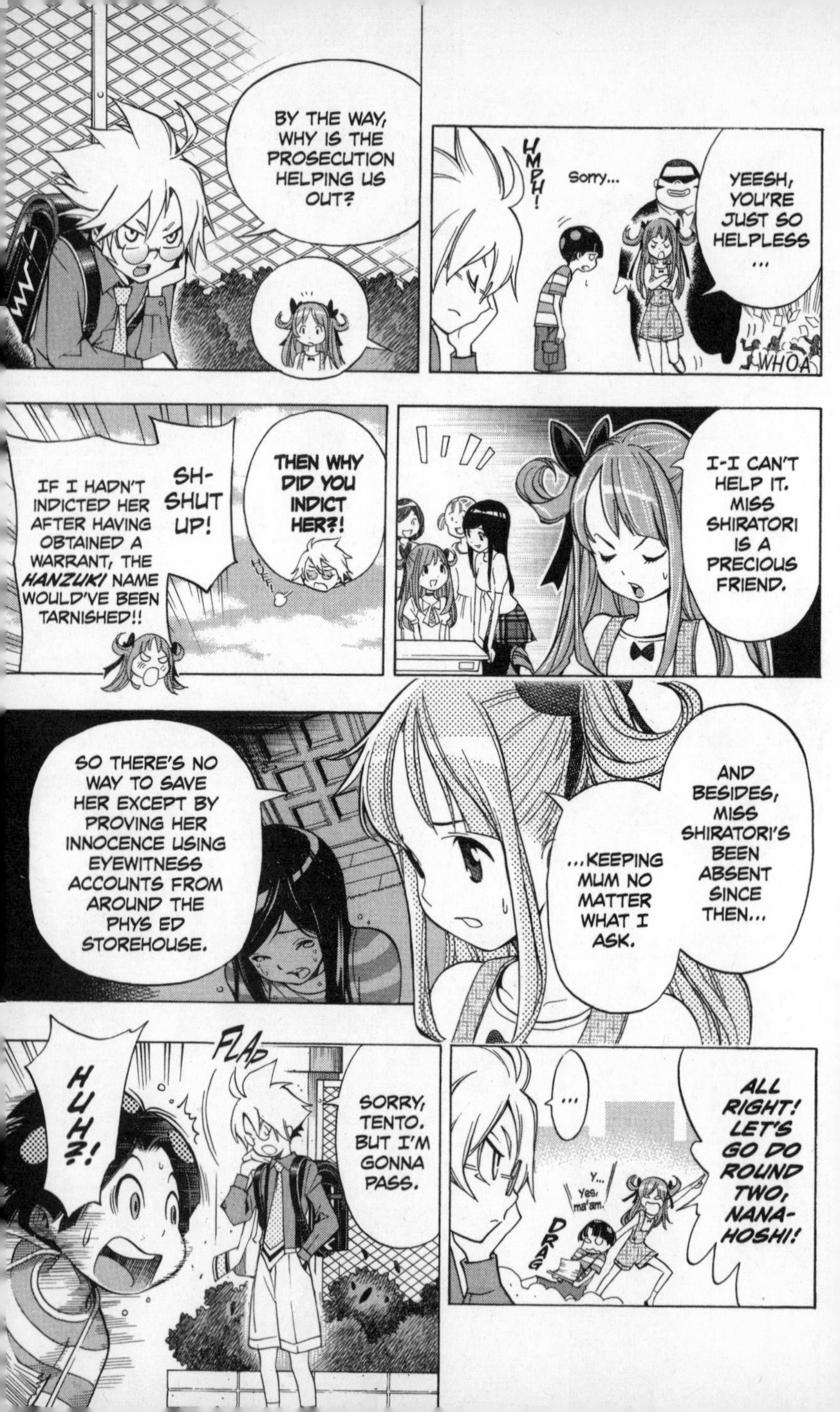
YEESH, YOU'RE JUST SO HELPLESS ...
Sorry...
HMPH!
WHOA
BY THE WAY, WHY IS THE PROSECUTION HELPING US OUT?
I-I CAN'T HELP IT. MISS SHIRATORI IS A PRECIOUS FRIEND.
THEN WHY DID YOU INDICT HER?!
SH-SHUT UP!
IF I HADN'T INDICTED HER AFTER HAVING OBTAINED A WARRANT, THE *HANZUKI* NAME WOULD'VE BEEN TARNISHED!!
AND BESIDES, MISS SHIRATORI'S BEEN ABSENT SINCE THEN...
...KEEPING MUM NO MATTER WHAT I ASK.
SO THERE'S NO WAY TO SAVE HER EXCEPT BY PROVING HER INNOCENCE USING EYEWITNESS ACCOUNTS FROM AROUND THE PHYS ED STOREHOUSE.
ALL RIGHT! LET'S GO DO ROUND TWO, NANAHOSHI!
...
Y... Yes, ma'am!
DRAG
SORRY, TENTO. BUT I'M GONNA PASS.
FLAP
HUH?!

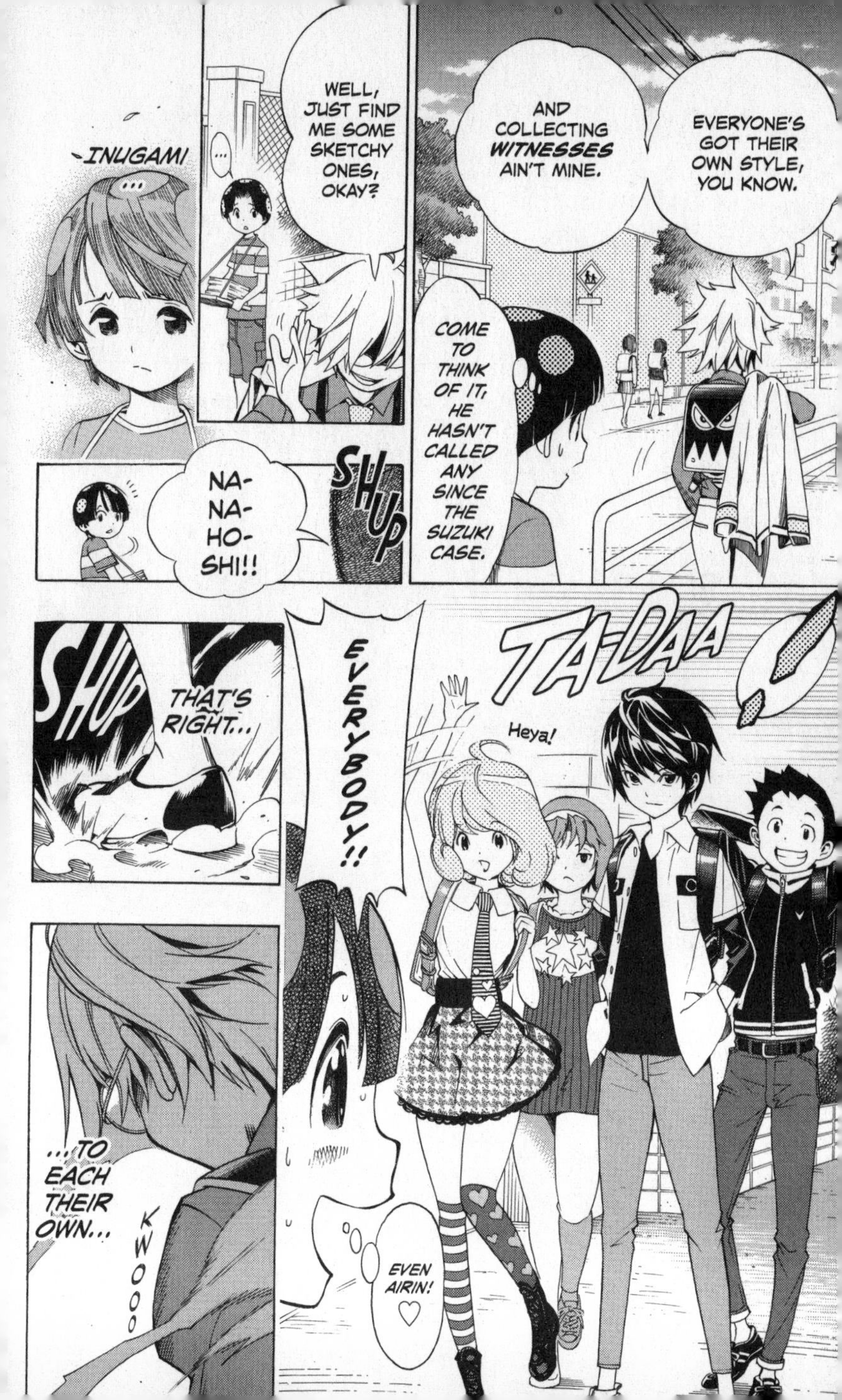

EVERYONE'S GOT THEIR OWN STYLE, YOU KNOW.
AND COLLECTING *WITNESSES* AIN'T MINE.
COME TO THINK OF IT, HE HASN'T CALLED ANY SINCE THE SUZUKI CASE.
SHUP
WELL, JUST FIND ME SOME SKETCHY ONES, OKAY?
...
-INUGAMI
...
NA-NA-HO-SHI!!
TA-DAA
Heya!
EVERYBODY!!
EVEN AIRIN! ♡
SHUP
THAT'S RIGHT...
...TO EACH THEIR OWN...
KWOOO

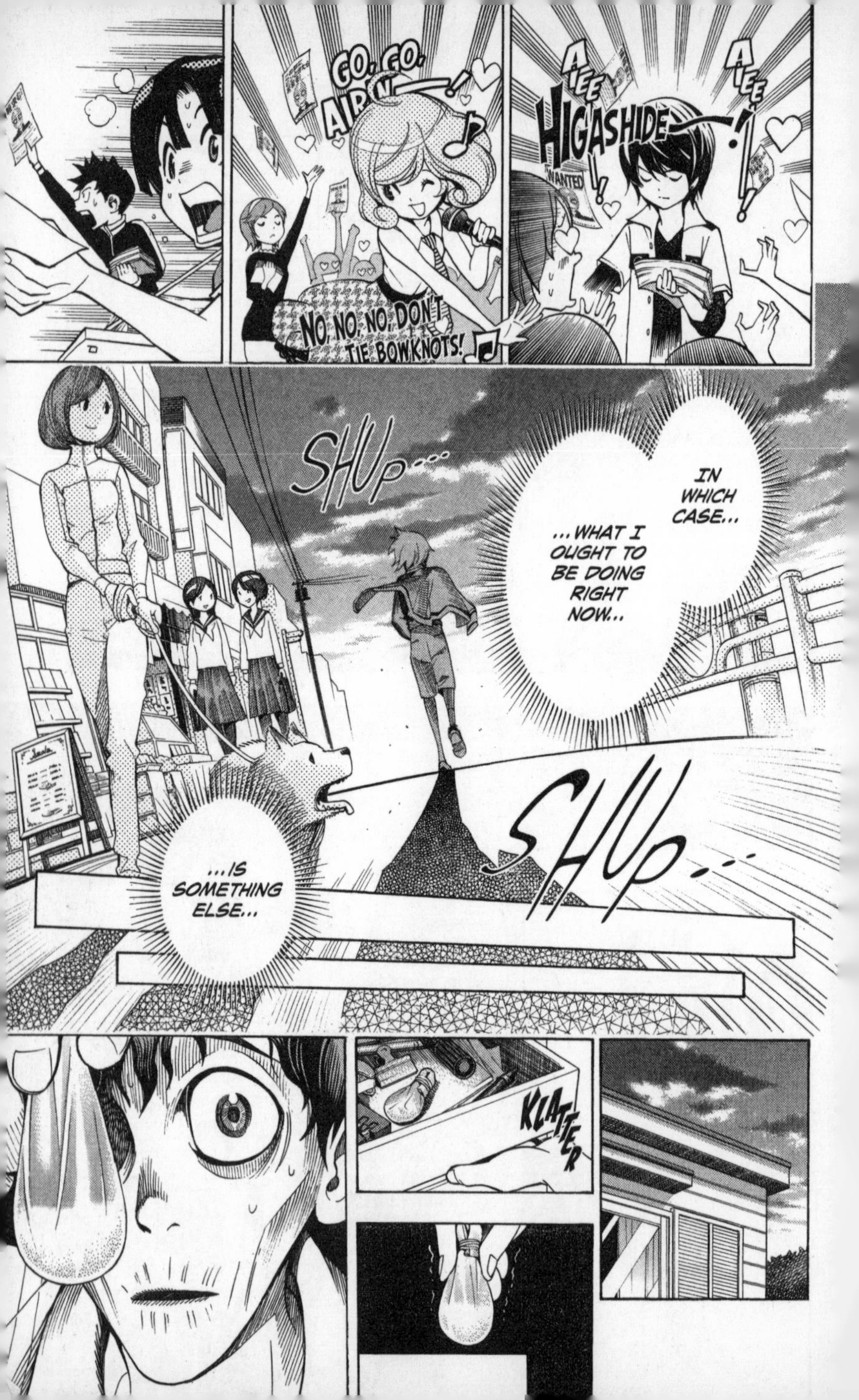
AIEE
HIGASHIDE—!
AIEE—!
WANTED
GO, GO, AIRIN—!
NO, NO, NO, DON'T TIE BOWKNOTS!
IN WHICH CASE...
...WHAT I OUGHT TO BE DOING RIGHT NOW...
SHUP...
SHUP...
...IS SOMETHING ELSE...
KLATTER

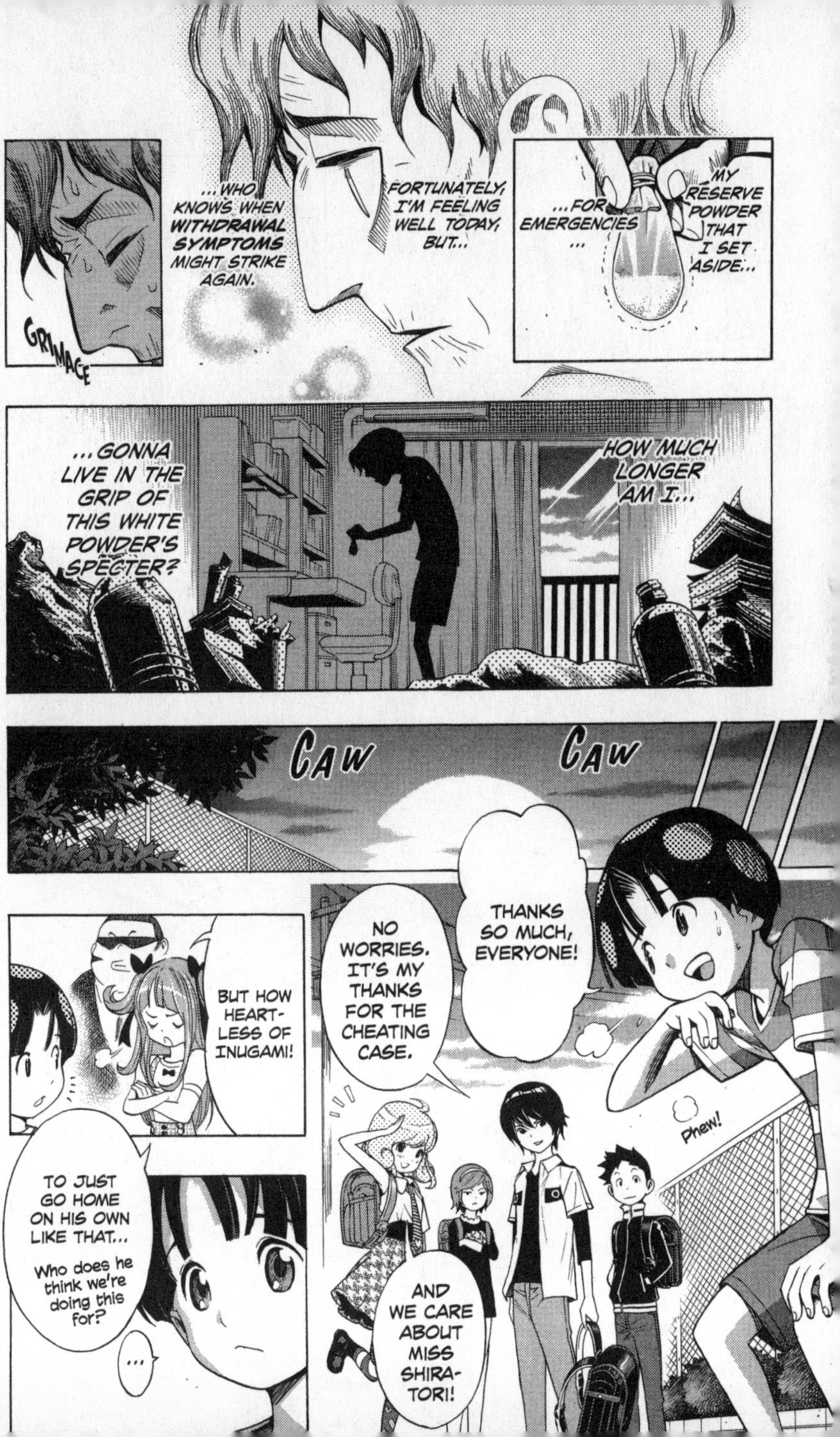
MY RESERVE POWDER THAT I SET ASIDE...
...FOR EMERGENCIES...
FORTUNATELY, I'M FEELING WELL TODAY, BUT...
...WHO KNOWS WHEN WITHDRAWAL SYMPTOMS MIGHT STRIKE AGAIN.
GRIMACE
HOW MUCH LONGER AM I...
...GONNA LIVE IN THE GRIP OF THIS WHITE POWDER'S SPECTER?
CAW
CAW
THANKS SO MUCH, EVERYONE!
Phew!
NO WORRIES. IT'S MY THANKS FOR THE CHEATING CASE.
AND WE CARE ABOUT MISS SHIRATORI!
BUT HOW HEARTLESS OF INUGAMI!
TO JUST GO HOME ON HIS OWN LIKE THAT... Who does he think we're doing this for?
...

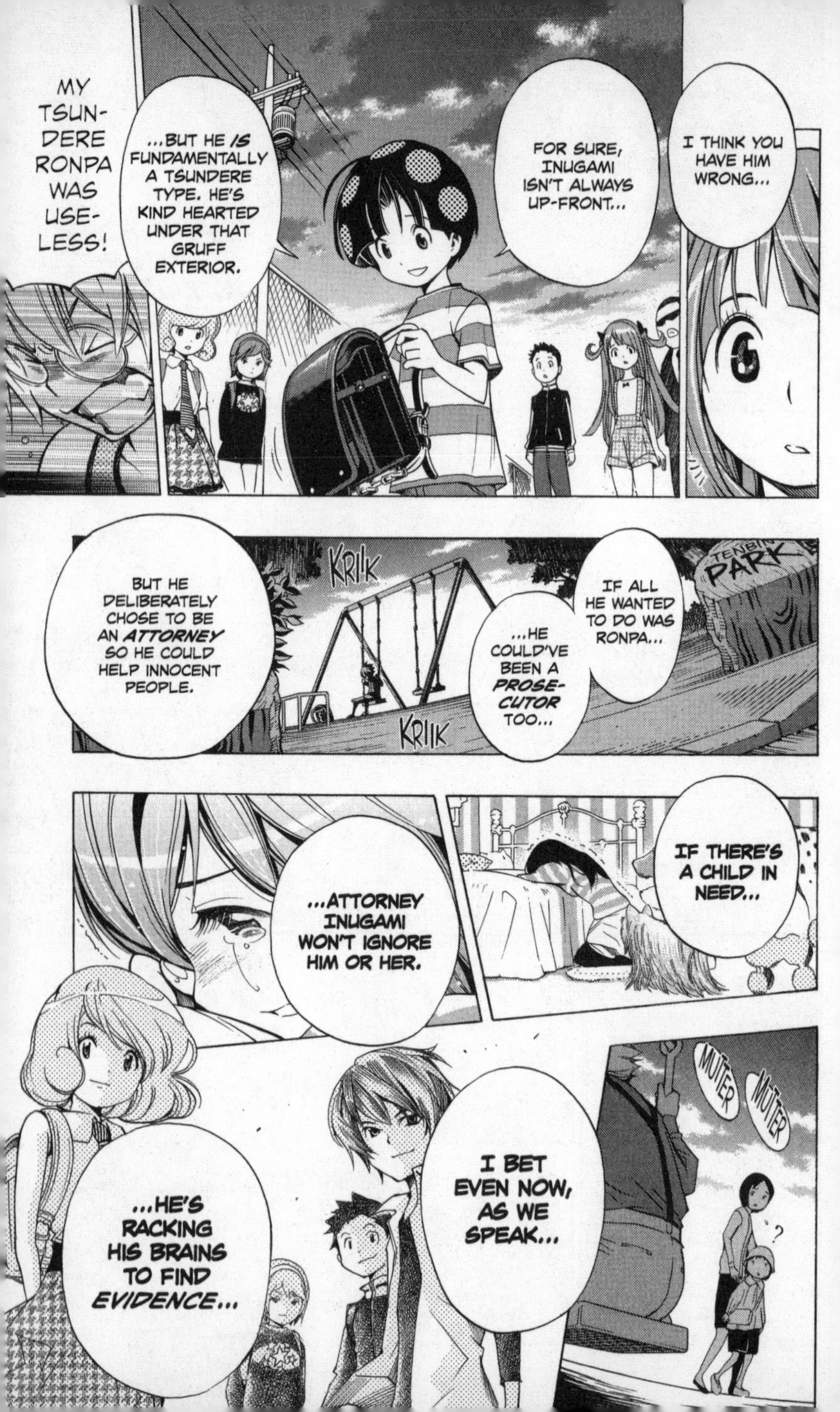
I THINK YOU HAVE HIM WRONG...
FOR SURE, INUGAMI ISN'T ALWAYS UP-FRONT...
...BUT HE *IS* FUNDAMENTALLY A TSUNDERE TYPE. HE'S KIND HEARTED UNDER THAT GRUFF EXTERIOR.
MY TSUN-DERE RONPA WAS USE-LESS!
TENBIN PARK
IF ALL HE WANTED TO DO WAS RONPA...
...HE COULD'VE BEEN A *PROSE-CUTOR* TOO...
KRIK
KRIK
BUT HE DELIBERATELY CHOSE TO BE AN *ATTORNEY* SO HE COULD HELP INNOCENT PEOPLE.
IF THERE'S A CHILD IN NEED...
...ATTORNEY INUGAMI WON'T IGNORE HIM OR HER.
MUTTER
MUTTER
?
I BET EVEN NOW, AS WE SPEAK...
...HE'S RACKING HIS BRAINS TO FIND *EVIDENCE*...

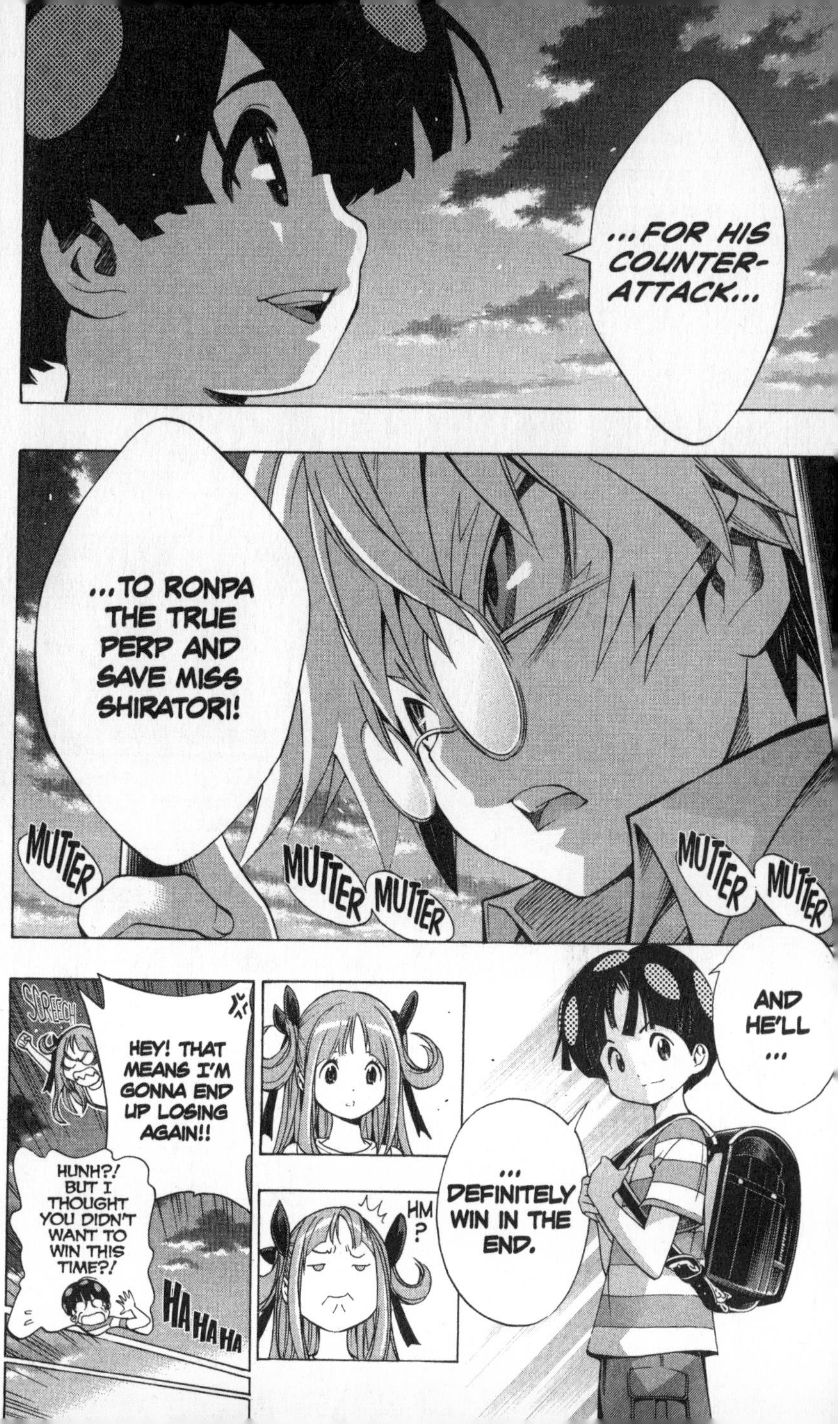
...FOR HIS COUNTER-ATTACK...
...TO RONPA THE TRUE PERP AND SAVE MISS SHIRATORI!
MUTTER
MUTTER
MUTTER
MUTTER
MUTTER
AND HE'LL ...
... DEFINITELY WIN IN THE END.
HM?
SCREECH
HEY! THAT MEANS I'M GONNA END UP LOSING AGAIN!!
HUNH?! BUT I THOUGHT YOU DIDN'T WANT TO WIN THIS TIME?!
HAHAHAHA

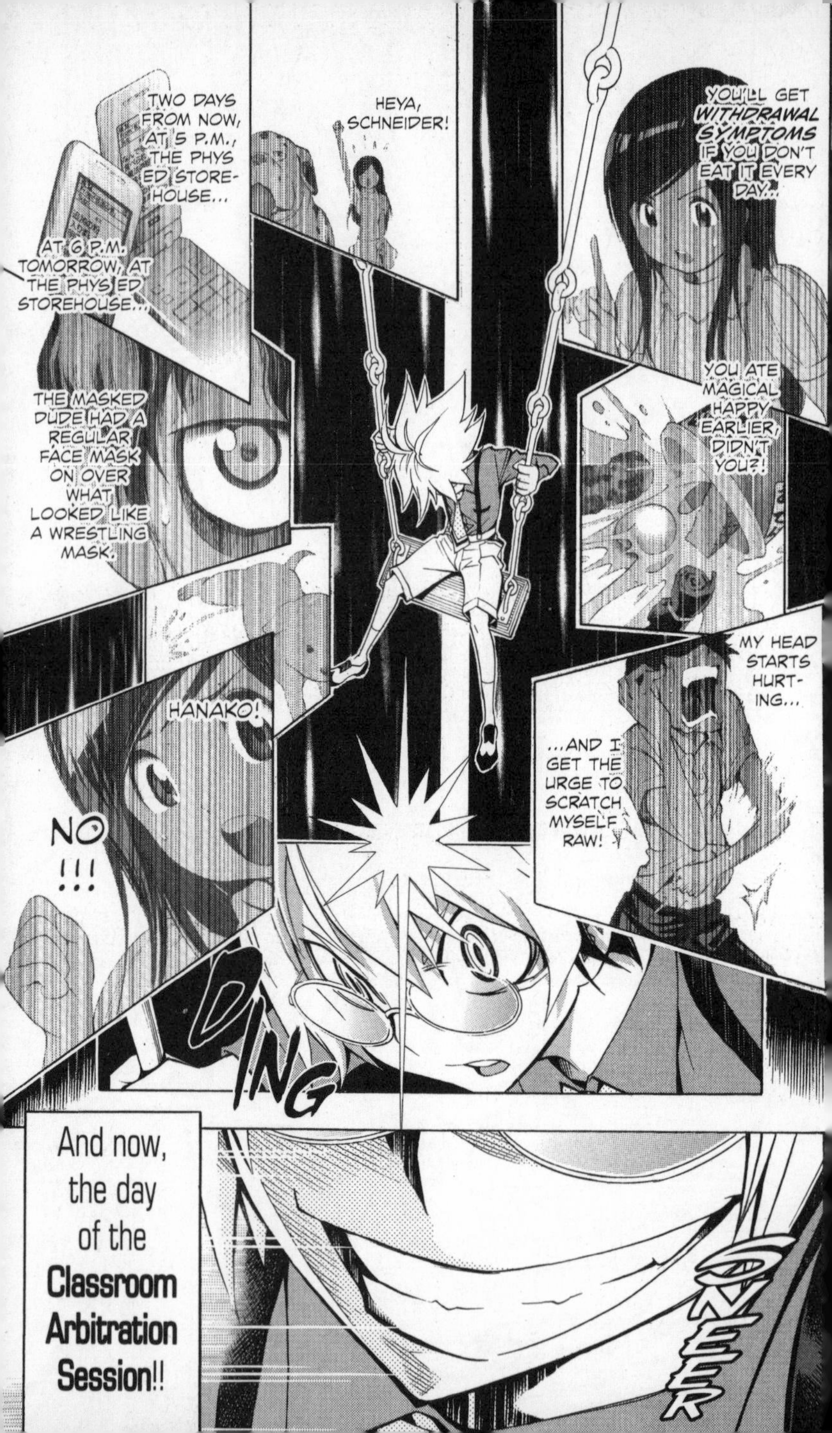
YOU'LL GET WITHDRAWAL SYMPTOMS IF YOU DON'T EAT IT EVERY DAY...
HEYA, SCHNEIDER!
TWO DAYS FROM NOW, AT 5 P.M., THE PHYS ED STORE-HOUSE...
AT 6 P.M. TOMORROW, AT THE PHYS ED STOREHOUSE...
YOU ATE MAGICAL HAPPY EARLIER, DIDN'T YOU?!
THE MASKED DUDE HAD A REGULAR FACE MASK ON OVER WHAT LOOKED LIKE A WRESTLING MASK.
MY HEAD STARTS HURT-ING...
...AND I GET THE URGE TO SCRATCH MYSELF RAW!
HANAKO!
NO!!!
DING
And now, the day of the Classroom Arbitration Session!!
SNEER

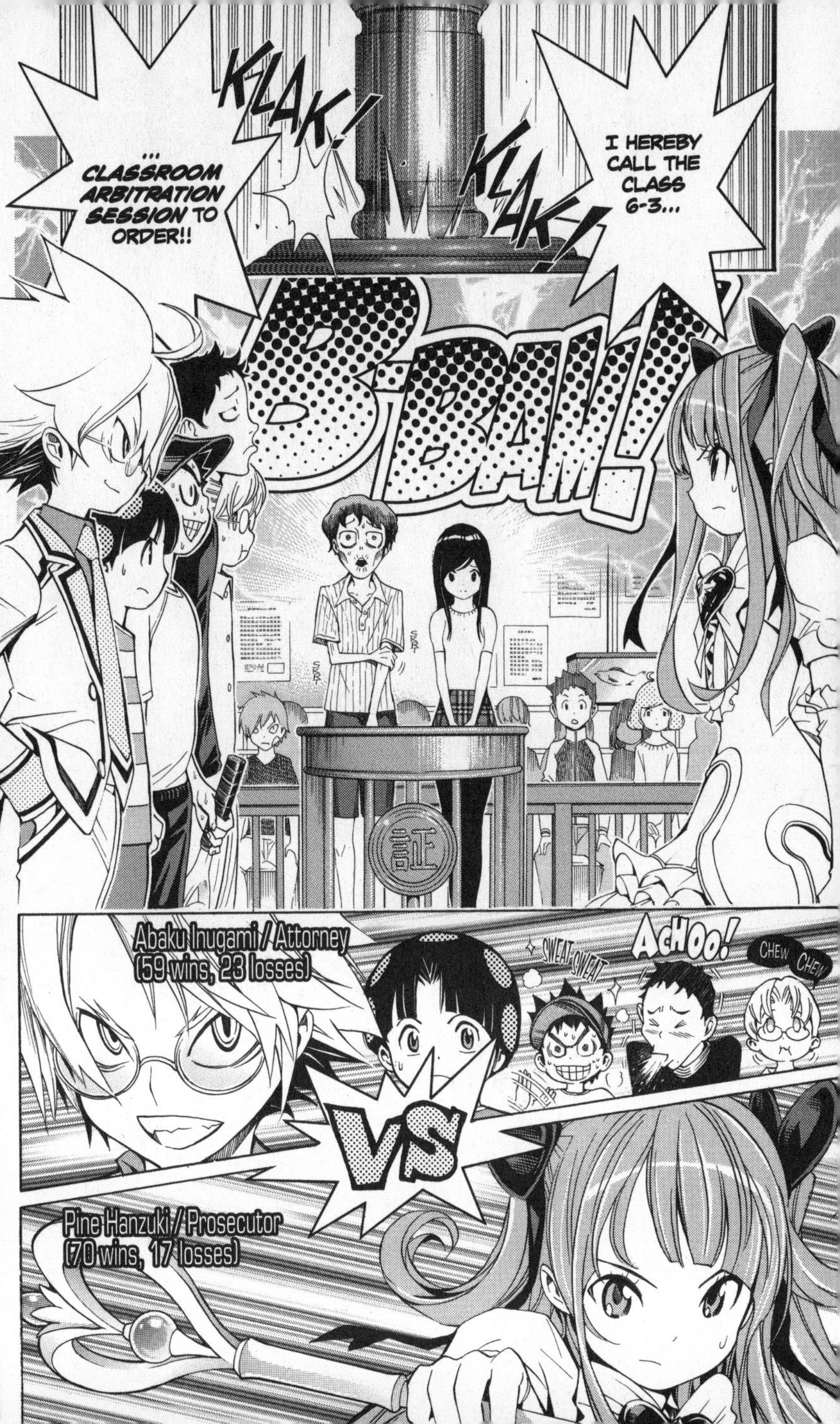
I HEREBY CALL THE CLASS 6-3...
KLAK! KLAK!
... CLASSROOM ARBITRATION SESSION TO ORDER!!
B-BAM!
SRT SRT
CHEW CHEW
ACHOO!
SWEAT SWEAT
Abaku Inugami / Attorney (59 wins, 23 losses)
VS
Pine Hanzuki / Prosecutor (70 wins, 17 losses)

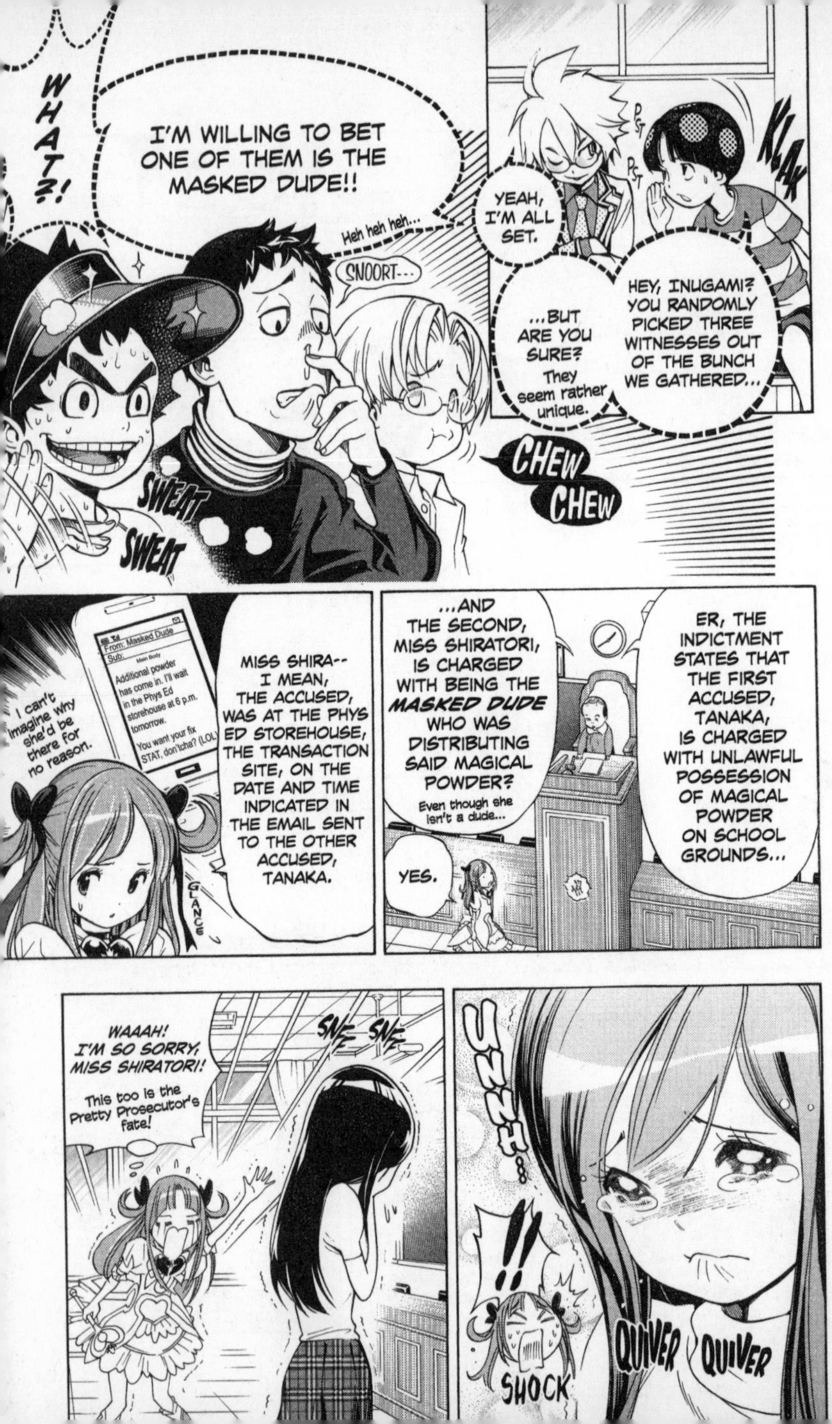
PST PST
KLAK
HEY, INUGAMI? YOU RANDOMLY PICKED THREE WITNESSES OUT OF THE BUNCH WE GATHERED...
...BUT ARE YOU SURE? They seem rather unique.
YEAH, I'M ALL SET.
WHAT?!
I'M WILLING TO BET ONE OF THEM IS THE MASKED DUDE!!
Heh heh heh...
SNOORT...
CHEW CHEW
SWEAT SWEAT
ER, THE INDICTMENT STATES THAT THE FIRST ACCUSED, TANAKA, IS CHARGED WITH UNLAWFUL POSSESSION OF MAGICAL POWDER ON SCHOOL GROUNDS...
...AND THE SECOND, MISS SHIRATORI, IS CHARGED WITH BEING THE *MASKED DUDE* WHO WAS DISTRIBUTING SAID MAGICAL POWDER?
Even though she isn't a dude...
YES.
MISS SHIRA-- I MEAN, THE ACCUSED, WAS AT THE PHYS ED STOREHOUSE, THE TRANSACTION SITE, ON THE DATE AND TIME INDICATED IN THE EMAIL SENT TO THE OTHER ACCUSED, TANAKA.
From: Masked Dude
Sub:
Main Body
Additional powder has come in. I'll wait in the Phys Ed storehouse at 6 p.m. tomorrow.
You want your fix STAT, don'tcha? (LOL)
I can't imagine why she'd be there for no reason.
GLANCE
UNNH...
!!
SHOCK
QUIVER QUIVER
SNF SNF
WAAAH! I'M SO SORRY, MISS SHIRATORI!
This too is the Pretty Prosecutor's fate!

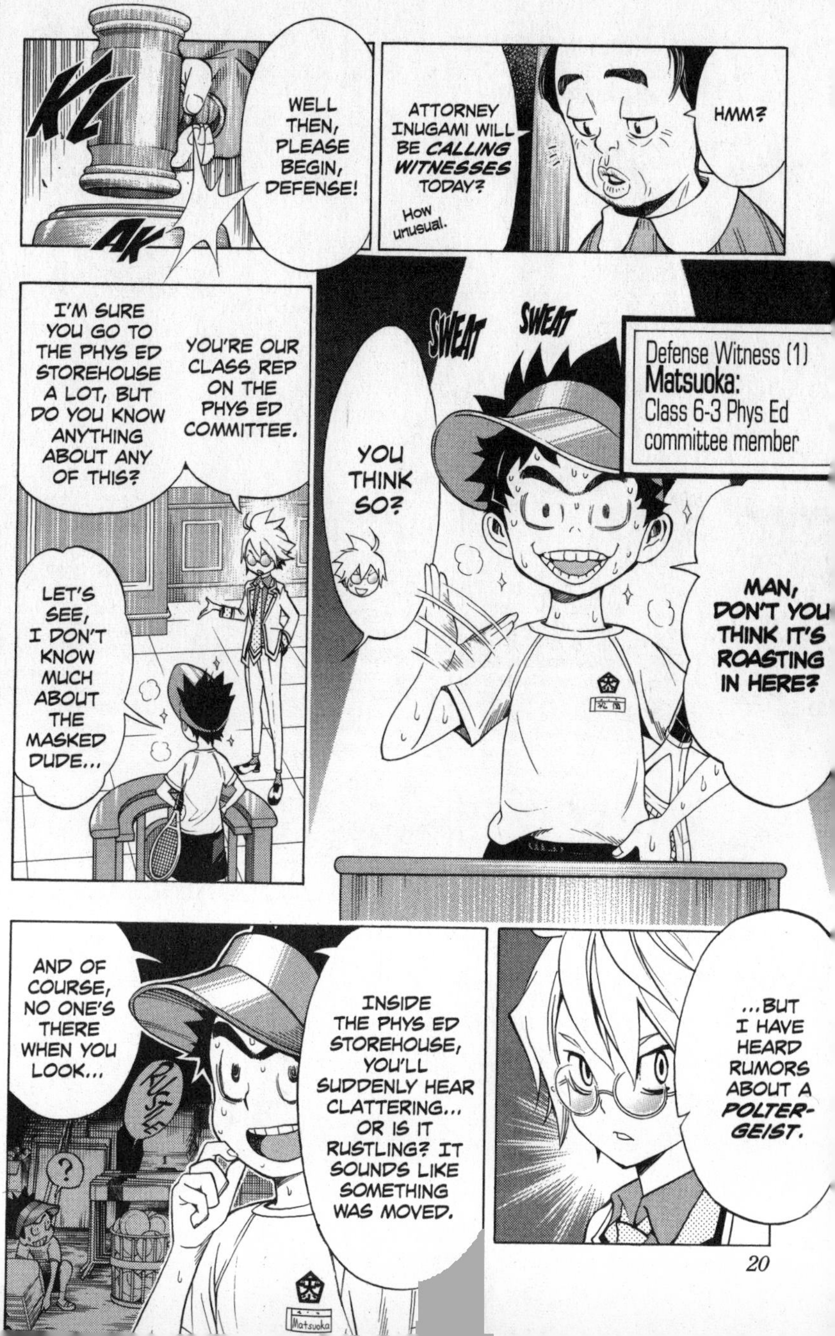
HMM?
ATTORNEY INUGAMI WILL BE *CALLING WITNESSES* TODAY?
How unusual.
KL
AK
WELL THEN, PLEASE BEGIN, DEFENSE!
SWEAT
SWEAT
Defense Witness (1) **Matsuoka:** Class 6-3 Phys Ed committee member
MAN, DON'T YOU THINK IT'S ROASTING IN HERE?
YOU THINK SO?
YOU'RE OUR CLASS REP ON THE PHYS ED COMMITTEE.
I'M SURE YOU GO TO THE PHYS ED STOREHOUSE A LOT, BUT DO YOU KNOW ANYTHING ABOUT ANY OF THIS?
LET'S SEE, I DON'T KNOW MUCH ABOUT THE MASKED DUDE...
...BUT I HAVE HEARD RUMORS ABOUT A *POLTERGEIST*.
INSIDE THE PHYS ED STOREHOUSE, YOU'LL SUDDENLY HEAR CLATTERING... OR IS IT RUSTLING? IT SOUNDS LIKE SOMETHING WAS MOVED.
AND OF COURSE, NO ONE'S THERE WHEN YOU LOOK...
?
Matsuoka

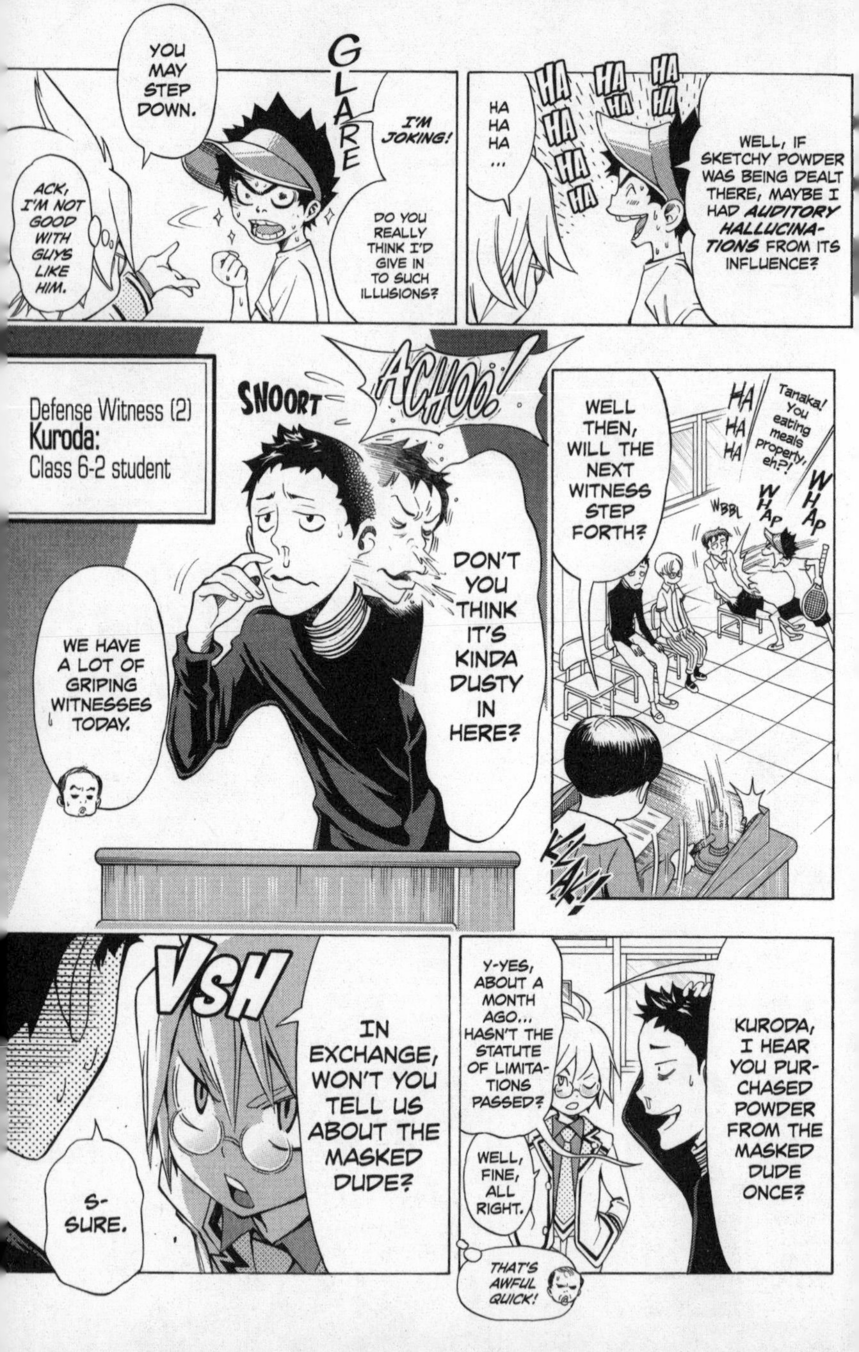

WELL, IF SKETCHY POWDER WAS BEING DEALT THERE, MAYBE I HAD AUDITORY HALLUCINATIONS FROM ITS INFLUENCE?
HA HA HA HA HA HA HA HA HA HA
HA HA HA ...
GLARE
I'M JOKING!
DO YOU REALLY THINK I'D GIVE IN TO SUCH ILLUSIONS?
YOU MAY STEP DOWN.
ACK, I'M NOT GOOD WITH GUYS LIKE HIM.
WELL THEN, WILL THE NEXT WITNESS STEP FORTH?
HA HA HA
Tanaka! You eating meals properly, eh?!
WBBL
WHAP WHAP
KLAK!
ACHOO!
SNOORT
Defense Witness (2)
Kuroda:
Class 6-2 student
DON'T YOU THINK IT'S KINDA DUSTY IN HERE?
WE HAVE A LOT OF GRIPING WITNESSES TODAY.
KURODA, I HEAR YOU PURCHASED POWDER FROM THE MASKED DUDE ONCE?
Y-YES, ABOUT A MONTH AGO... HASN'T THE STATUTE OF LIMITATIONS PASSED?
WELL, FINE, ALL RIGHT.
THAT'S AWFUL QUICK!
VSH
IN EXCHANGE, WON'T YOU TELL US ABOUT THE MASKED DUDE?
S-SURE.

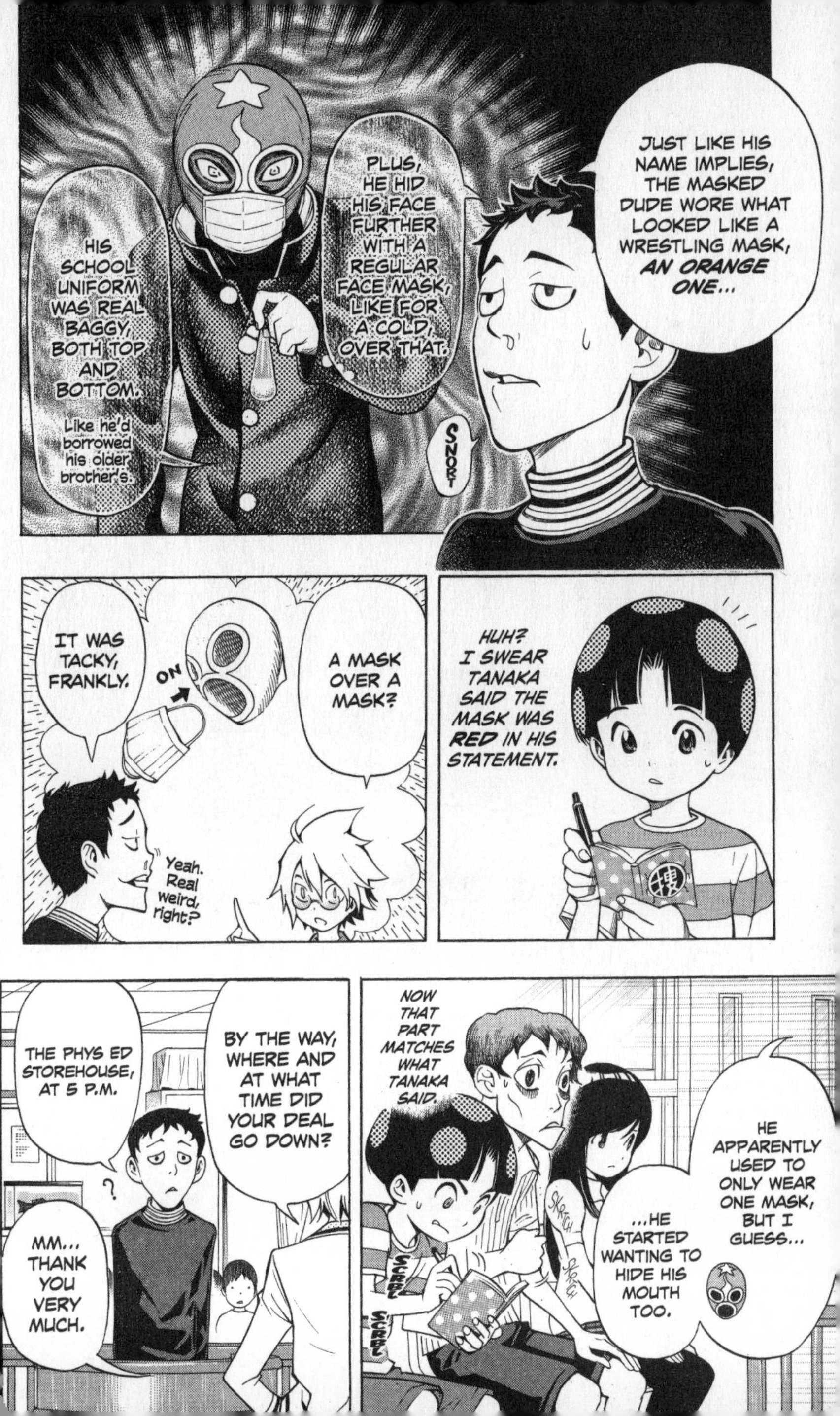
JUST LIKE HIS NAME IMPLIES, THE MASKED DUDE WORE WHAT LOOKED LIKE A WRESTLING MASK, AN ORANGE ONE...
SNORT
PLUS, HE HID HIS FACE FURTHER WITH A REGULAR FACE MASK, LIKE FOR A COLD, OVER THAT.
HIS SCHOOL UNIFORM WAS REAL BAGGY, BOTH TOP AND BOTTOM.
Like he'd borrowed his older brother's.
HUH? I SWEAR TANAKA SAID THE MASK WAS RED IN HIS STATEMENT.
A MASK OVER A MASK?
ON
IT WAS TACKY, FRANKLY.
Yeah. Real weird, right?
HE APPARENTLY USED TO ONLY WEAR ONE MASK, BUT I GUESS...
...HE STARTED WANTING TO HIDE HIS MOUTH TOO.
NOW THAT PART MATCHES WHAT TANAKA SAID.
SKRTCH
SKRTCH
SCRBL
SCRBL
BY THE WAY, WHERE AND AT WHAT TIME DID YOUR DEAL GO DOWN?
THE PHYS ED STOREHOUSE, AT 5 P.M.
MM... THANK YOU VERY MUCH.

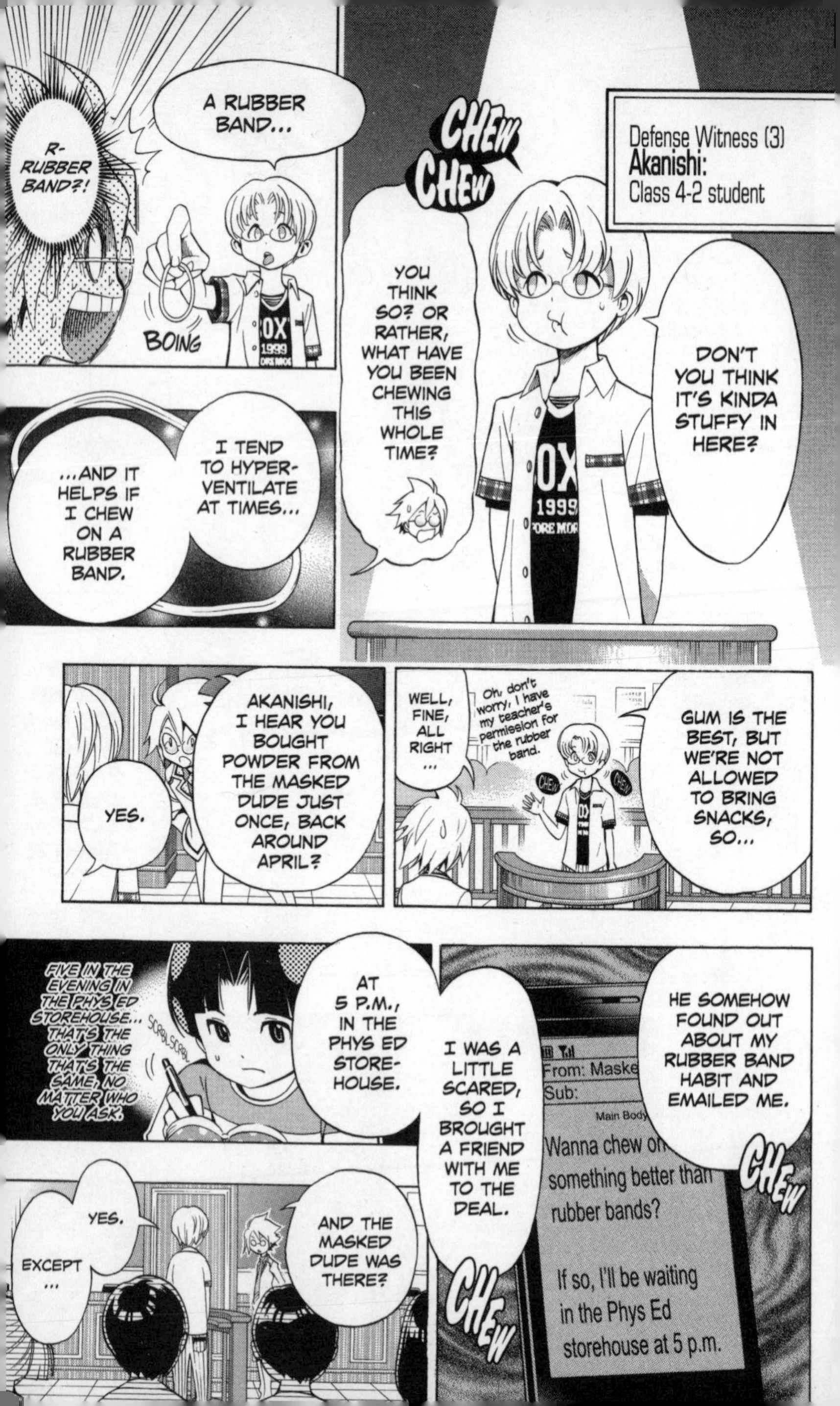
CHEW CHEW
Defense Witness (3)
Akanishi:
Class 4-2 student
DON'T YOU THINK IT'S KINDA STUFFY IN HERE?
YOU THINK SO? OR RATHER, WHAT HAVE YOU BEEN CHEWING THIS WHOLE TIME?
A RUBBER BAND...
R-RUBBER BAND?!
BOING
I TEND TO HYPER-VENTILATE AT TIMES...
...AND IT HELPS IF I CHEW ON A RUBBER BAND.
GUM IS THE BEST, BUT WE'RE NOT ALLOWED TO BRING SNACKS, SO...
Oh, don't worry, I have my teacher's permission for the rubber band.
CHEW CHEW
WELL, FINE, ALL RIGHT...
AKANISHI, I HEAR YOU BOUGHT POWDER FROM THE MASKED DUDE JUST ONCE, BACK AROUND APRIL?
YES.
HE SOMEHOW FOUND OUT ABOUT MY RUBBER BAND HABIT AND EMAILED ME.
From:
Sub:
Main Body
Wanna chew
something better than
rubber bands?
If so, I'll be waiting in the Phys Ed storehouse at 5 p.m.
CHEW
I WAS A LITTLE SCARED, SO I BROUGHT A FRIEND WITH ME TO THE DEAL.
CHEW
AT 5 P.M., IN THE PHYS ED STOREHOUSE.
FIVE IN THE EVENING IN THE PHYS ED STOREHOUSE... THAT'S THE ONLY THING THAT'S THE SAME, NO MATTER WHO YOU ASK.
SCRBL SCRBL
AND THE MASKED DUDE WAS THERE?
YES.
EXCEPT...

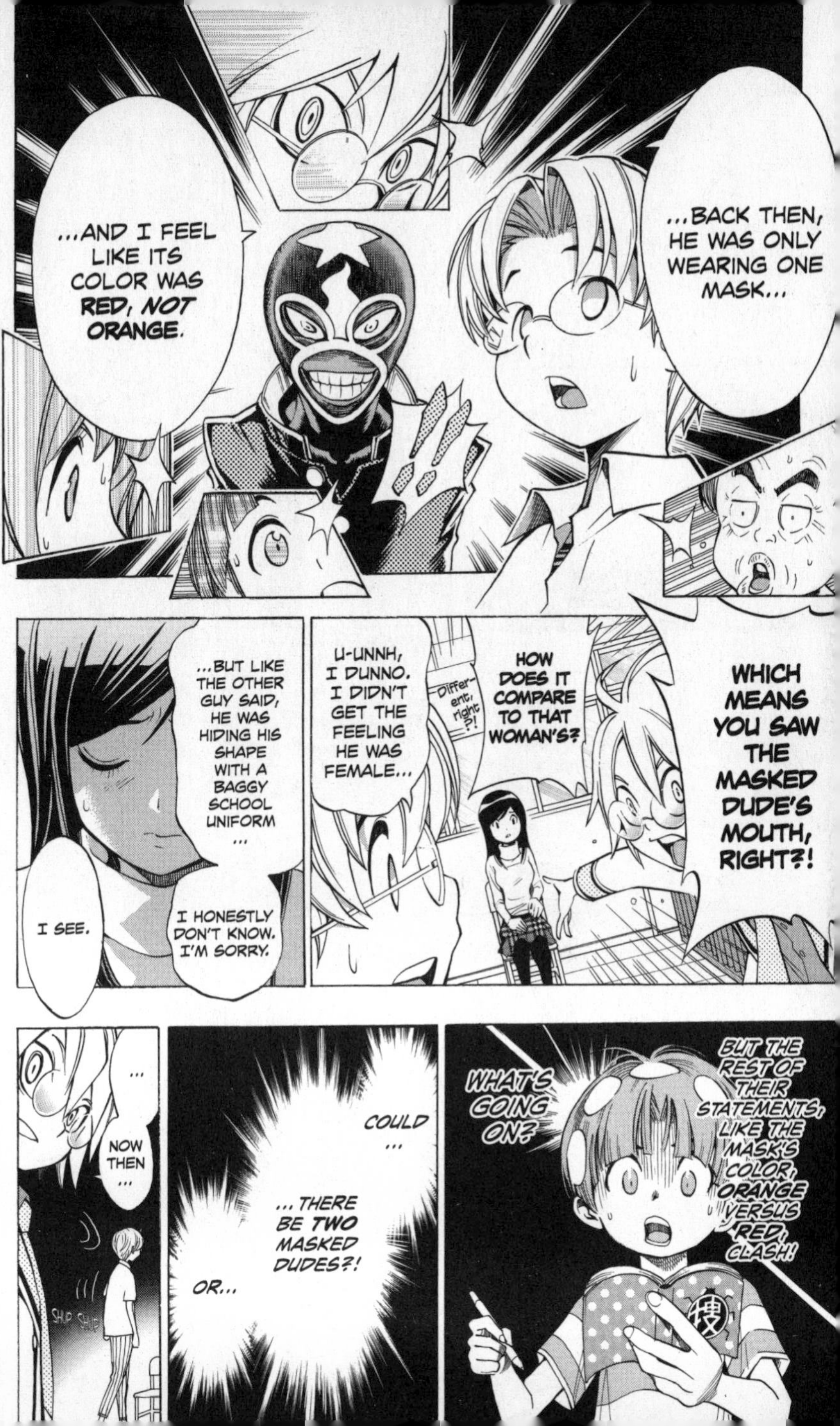
...BACK THEN, HE WAS ONLY WEARING ONE MASK...
...AND I FEEL LIKE ITS COLOR WAS RED, NOT ORANGE.
WHICH MEANS YOU SAW THE MASKED DUDE'S MOUTH, RIGHT?!
HOW DOES IT COMPARE TO THAT WOMAN'S?
Differ-ent, right?!
U-UNNH, I DUNNO. I DIDN'T GET THE FEELING HE WAS FEMALE...
...BUT LIKE THE OTHER GUY SAID, HE WAS HIDING HIS SHAPE WITH A BAGGY SCHOOL UNIFORM ...
I HONESTLY DON'T KNOW. I'M SORRY.
I SEE.
BUT THE REST OF THEIR STATEMENTS, LIKE THE MASK'S COLOR, ORANGE VERSUS RED, CLASH!
WHAT'S GOING ON?
COULD ...
...THERE BE TWO MASKED DUDES?!
OR...
...
NOW THEN ...
SHUP SHUP

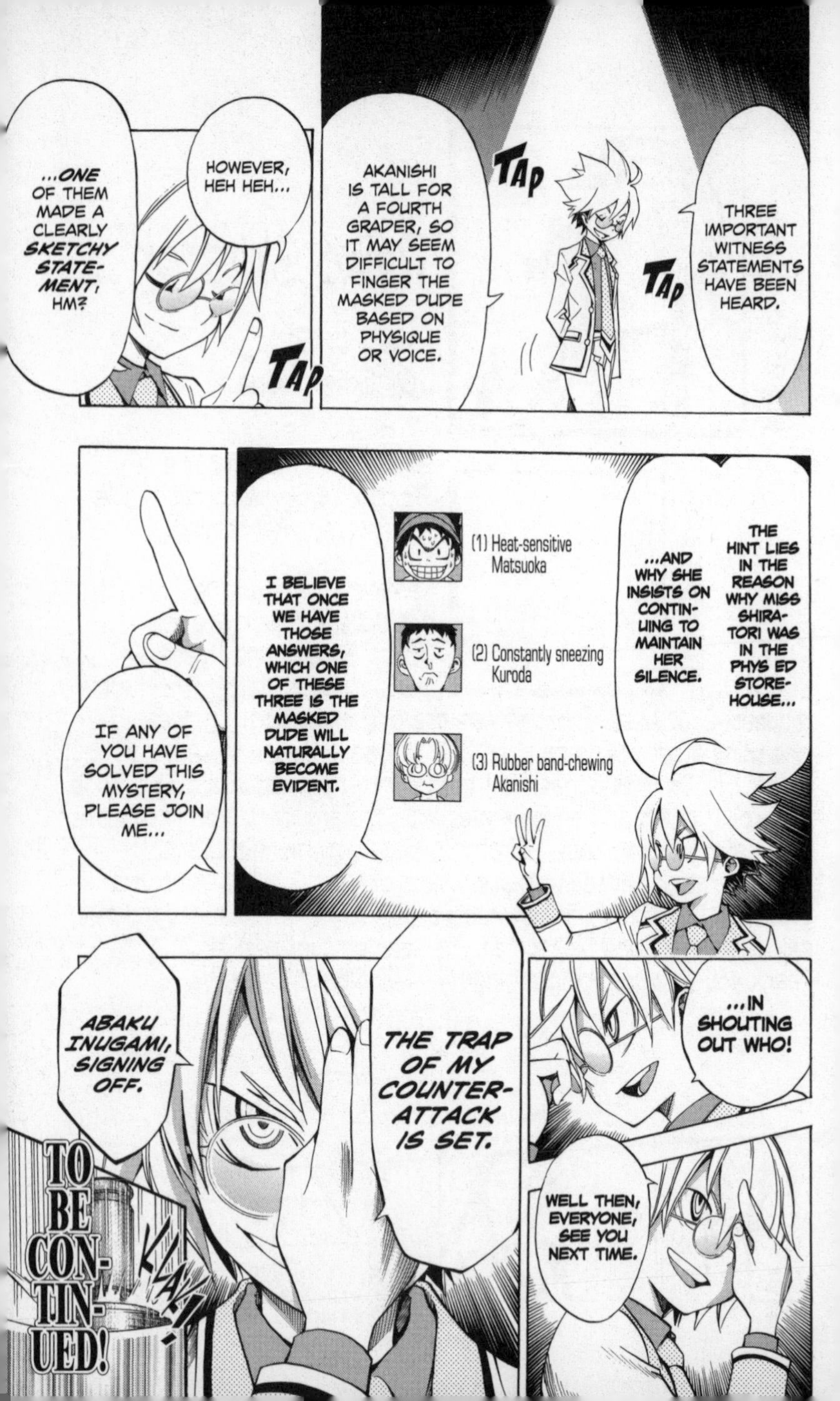
THREE IMPORTANT WITNESS STATEMENTS HAVE BEEN HEARD.
TAP
TAP
AKANISHI IS TALL FOR A FOURTH GRADER, SO IT MAY SEEM DIFFICULT TO FINGER THE MASKED DUDE BASED ON PHYSIQUE OR VOICE.
TAP
HOWEVER, HEH HEH...
...ONE OF THEM MADE A CLEARLY SKETCHY STATEMENT, HM?
THE HINT LIES IN THE REASON WHY MISS SHIRATORI WAS IN THE PHYS ED STOREHOUSE...
...AND WHY SHE INSISTS ON CONTINUING TO MAINTAIN HER SILENCE.
(1) Heat-sensitive Matsuoka
(2) Constantly sneezing Kuroda
(3) Rubber band-chewing Akanishi
I BELIEVE THAT ONCE WE HAVE THOSE ANSWERS, WHICH ONE OF THESE THREE IS THE MASKED DUDE WILL NATURALLY BECOME EVIDENT.
IF ANY OF YOU HAVE SOLVED THIS MYSTERY, PLEASE JOIN ME...
...IN SHOUTING OUT WHO!
WELL THEN, EVERYONE, SEE YOU NEXT TIME.
THE TRAP OF MY COUNTER-ATTACK IS SET.
ABAKU INUGAMI, SIGNING OFF.
KLAK!
TO BE CONTINUED!

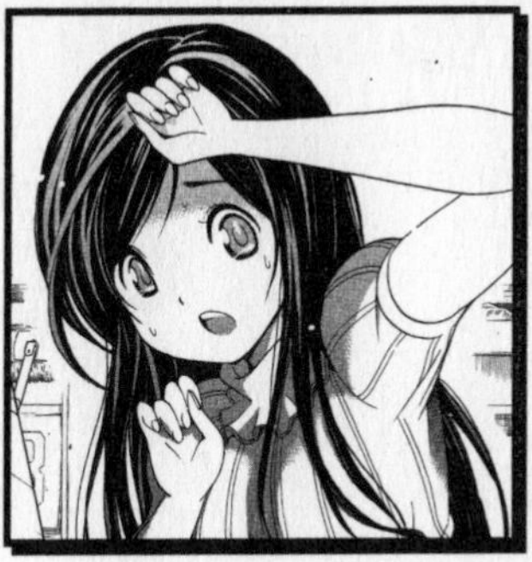

(Obata's final version)

Reiko Shiratori

Height: 5'
Dislikes: None

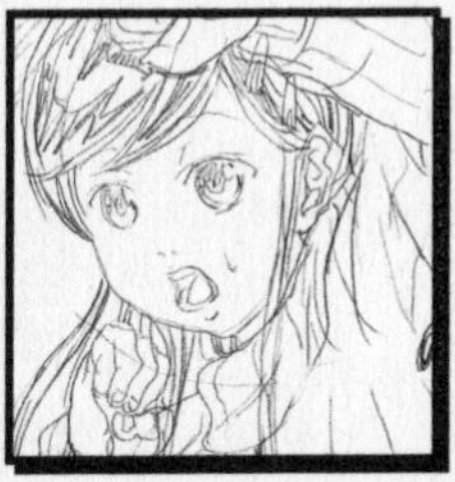

(Enoki's draft version)

She's the official heroine of *School Judgment*, but that's just my personal opinion.

I always entrusted the characters' final looks to Obata Sensei, and I generally didn't make any after-the-fact requests, but Miss Shiratori was the only exception. I requested one thing after seeing chapter 1. That was..."Please make her boobs bigger...!" On that occasion, I even earnestly created a dingy "boob hierarchy" chart and armed myself with the argument that it ought to be all right that Miss Shiratori's body undergoes a dramatic transformation between chapter 1 and chapter 7 since she's in a growth spurt, and thus, her precipitously ample bosoms, secondary sex characteristics blossomed...as seen on the lower left.
Thank you so much for granting my wish, Obata Sensei!!!

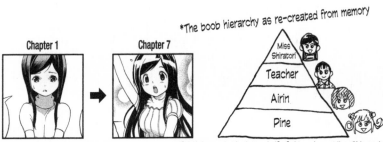

*The boob hierarchy as re-created from memory

Chapter 1

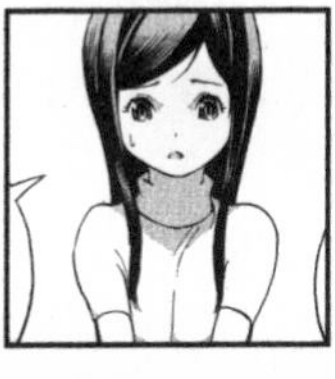

Chapter 7

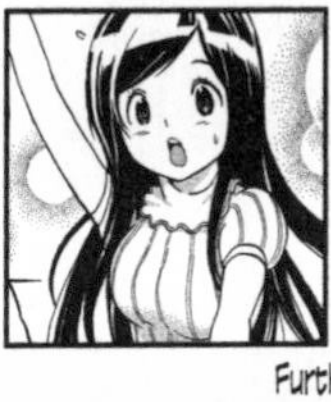

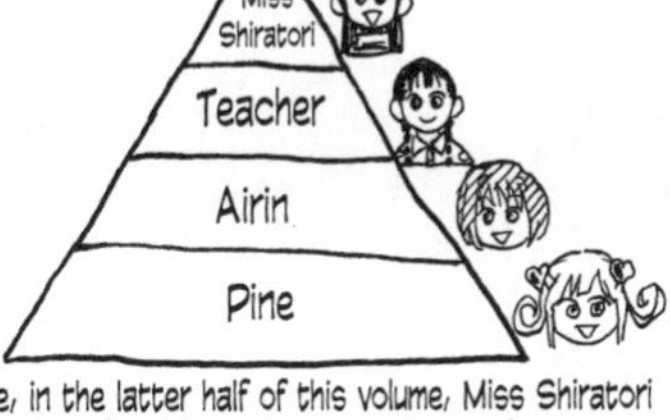
Miss Shiratori
Teacher
Airin
Pine

Furthermore, in the latter half of this volume, Miss Shiratori will be surpassed by an even stronger contender!

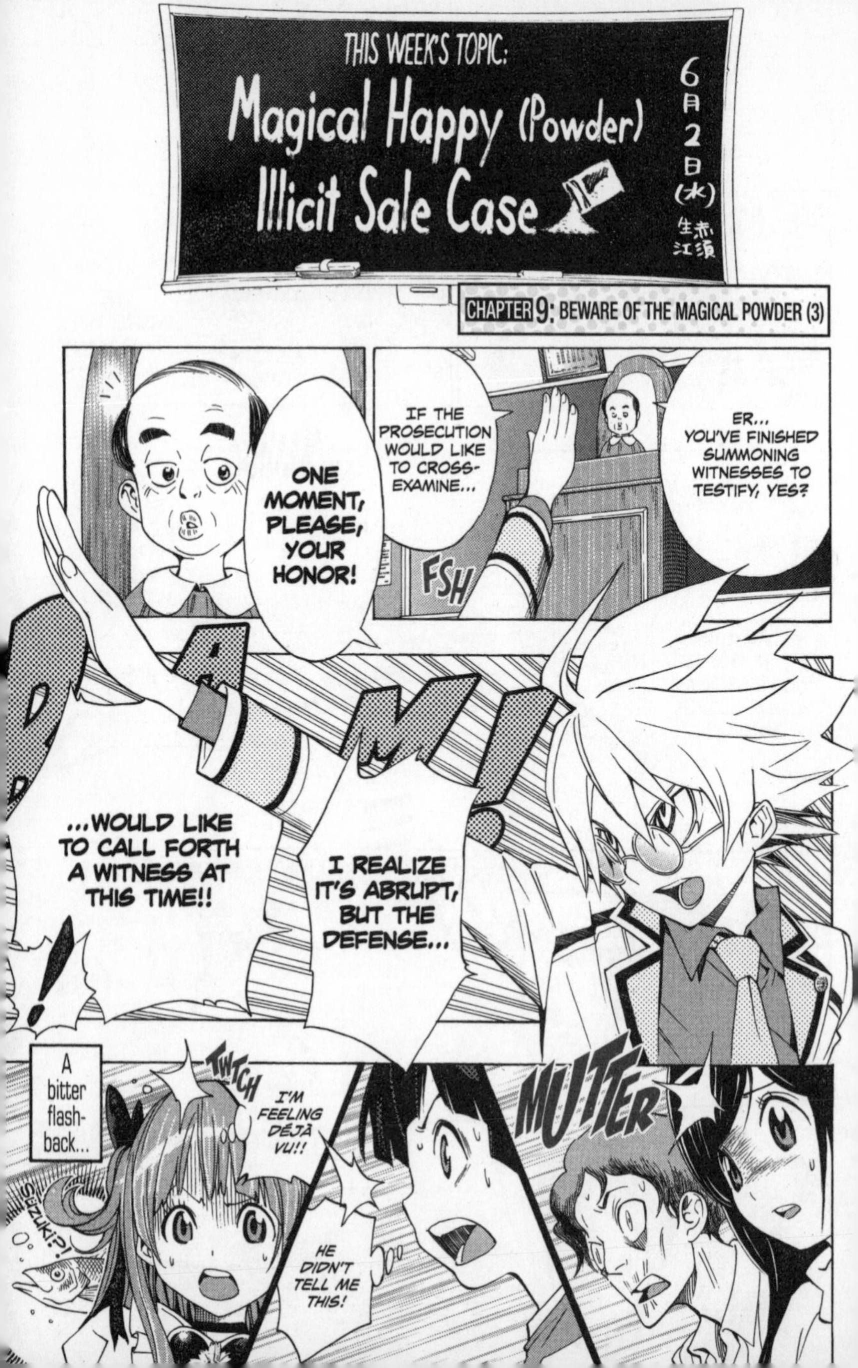
THIS WEEK'S TOPIC:
Magical Happy (Powder) Illicit Sale Case
6月2日(水)
赤須
生江
CHAPTER 9: BEWARE OF THE MAGICAL POWDER (3)
ER... YOU'VE FINISHED SUMMONING WITNESSES TO TESTIFY, YES?
IF THE PROSECUTION WOULD LIKE TO CROSS-EXAMINE...
FSH
ONE MOMENT, PLEASE, YOUR HONOR!
I REALIZE IT'S ABRUPT, BUT THE DEFENSE...
...WOULD LIKE TO CALL FORTH A WITNESS AT THIS TIME!!
MUTTER
HE DIDN'T TELL ME THIS!
A bitter flash-back...
TWITCH
I'M FEELING DÉJÀ VU!!
SUZUKI?!

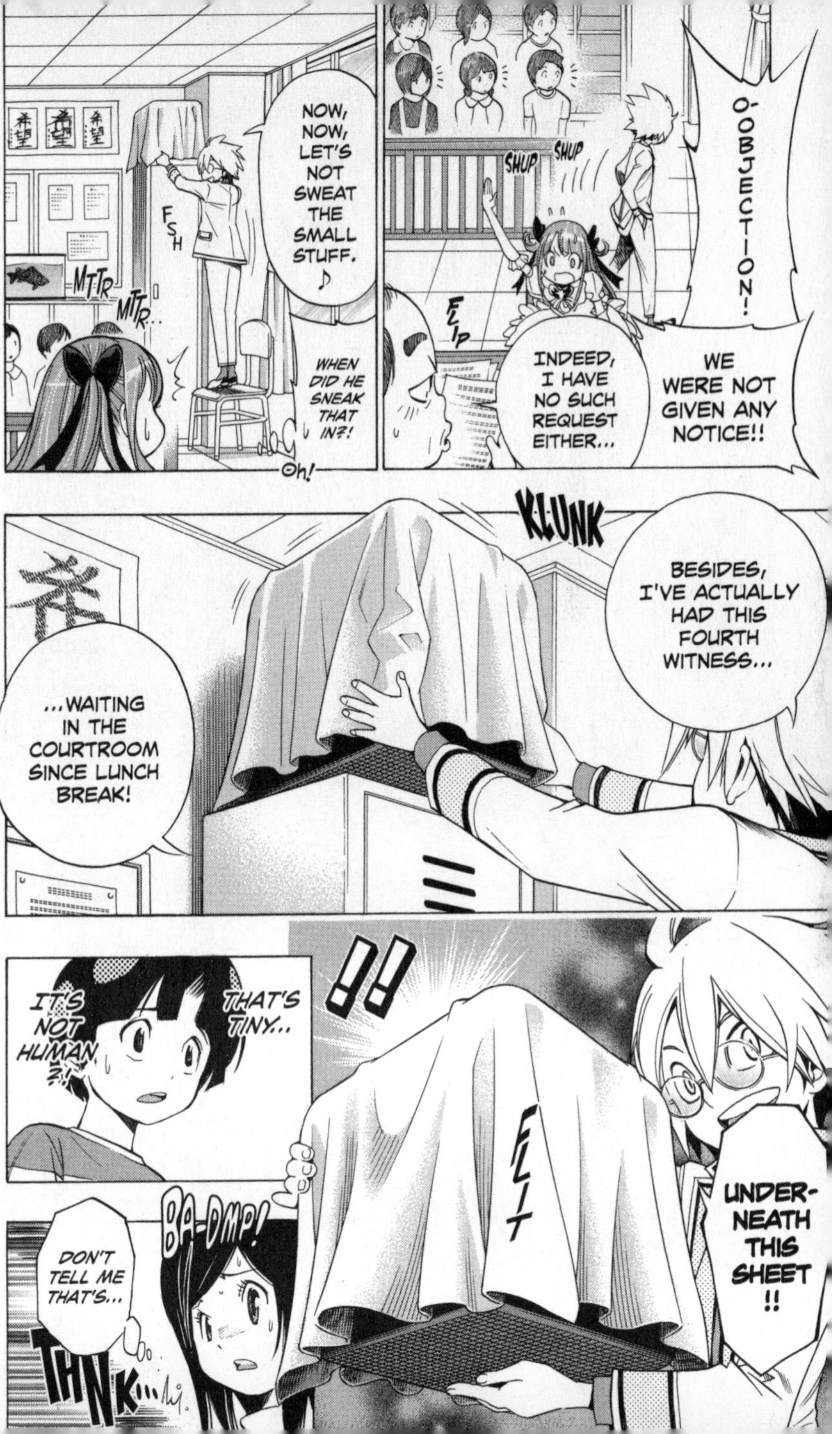
O-OBJECTION!
WE WERE NOT GIVEN ANY NOTICE!!
SHUP
SHUP
FLIP
INDEED, I HAVE NO SUCH REQUEST EITHER...
NOW, NOW, LET'S NOT SWEAT THE SMALL STUFF. ♪
FSH
MTTR
MTTR...
WHEN DID HE SNEAK THAT IN?!
Oh!
KLUNK
BESIDES, I'VE ACTUALLY HAD THIS FOURTH WITNESS...
...WAITING IN THE COURTROOM SINCE LUNCH BREAK!
!!
UNDER-NEATH THIS SHEET!!
FLIT
THAT'S TINY...
IT'S NOT HUMAN?!
BA-DMP!
DON'T TELL ME THAT'S...
THNK...

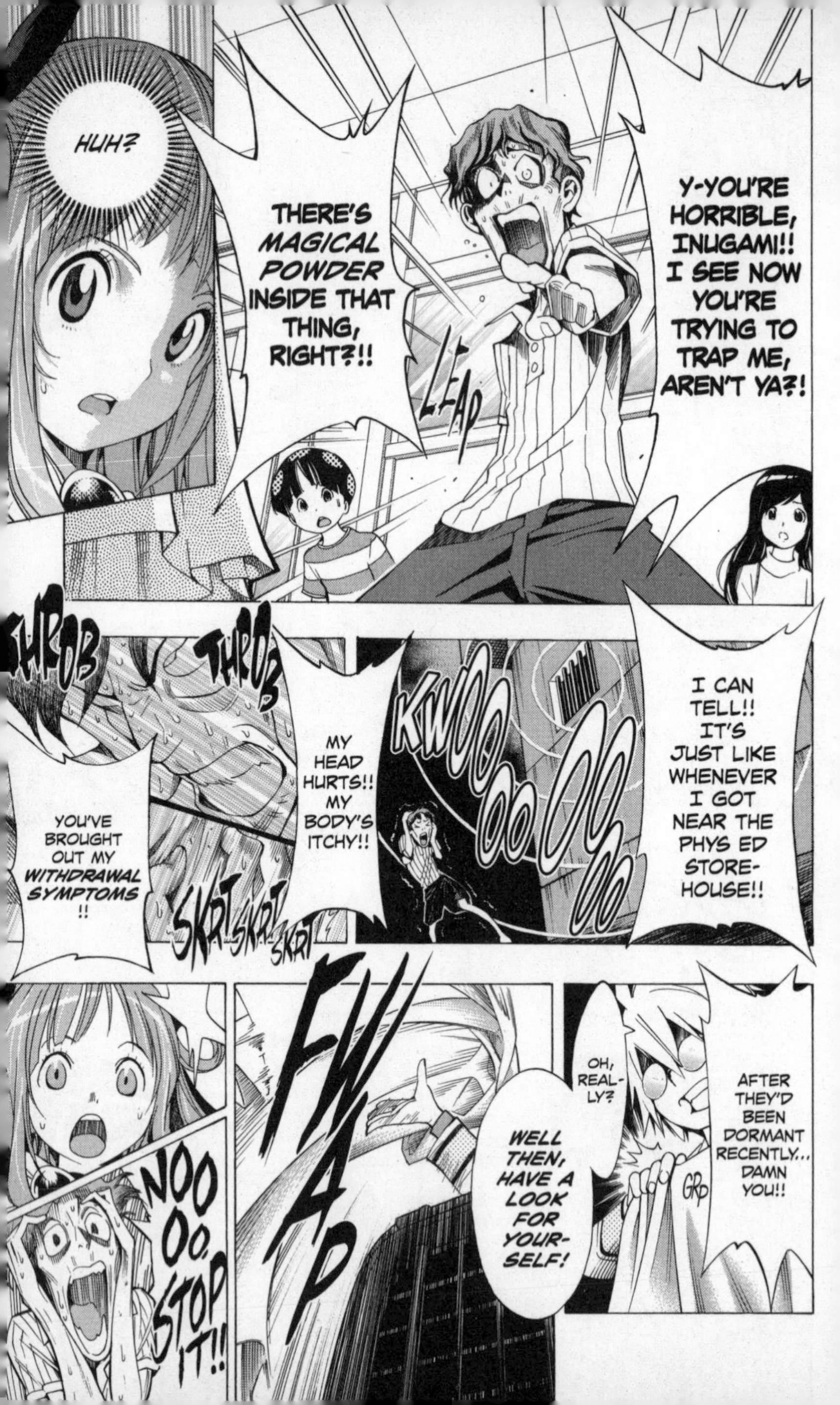
Y-YOU'RE HORRIBLE, INUGAMI!! I SEE NOW YOU'RE TRYING TO TRAP ME, AREN'T YA?!
THERE'S MAGICAL POWDER INSIDE THAT THING, RIGHT?!!
LEAP
HUH?
I CAN TELL!! IT'S JUST LIKE WHENEVER I GOT NEAR THE PHYS ED STOREHOUSE!!
KWOOOOOOOO
MY HEAD HURTS!! MY BODY'S ITCHY!!
THROB THROB
YOU'VE BROUGHT OUT MY WITHDRAWAL SYMPTOMS!!
SKRT SKRT SKRT
AFTER THEY'D BEEN DORMANT RECENTLY... DAMN YOU!!
GRP
OH, REALLY?
WELL THEN, HAVE A LOOK FOR YOURSELF!
FWAP
NOOOOO, STOP IT!!

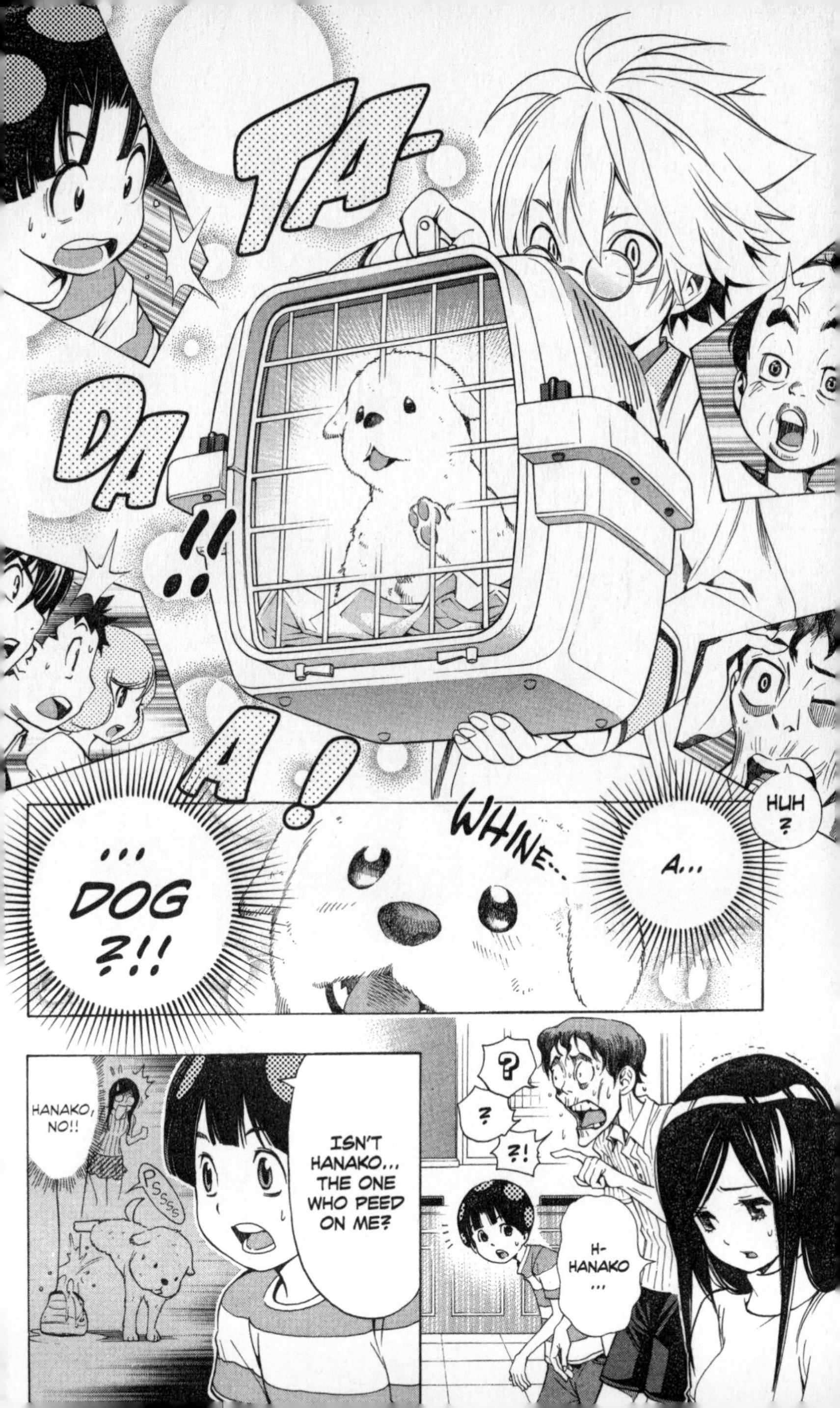
TA- DA- A!!
HUH?
A...
WHINE...
...DOG?!!
?
?
?!
H-HANAKO...
ISN'T HANAKO... THE ONE WHO PEED ON ME?
HANAKO, NO!!
PSSSS

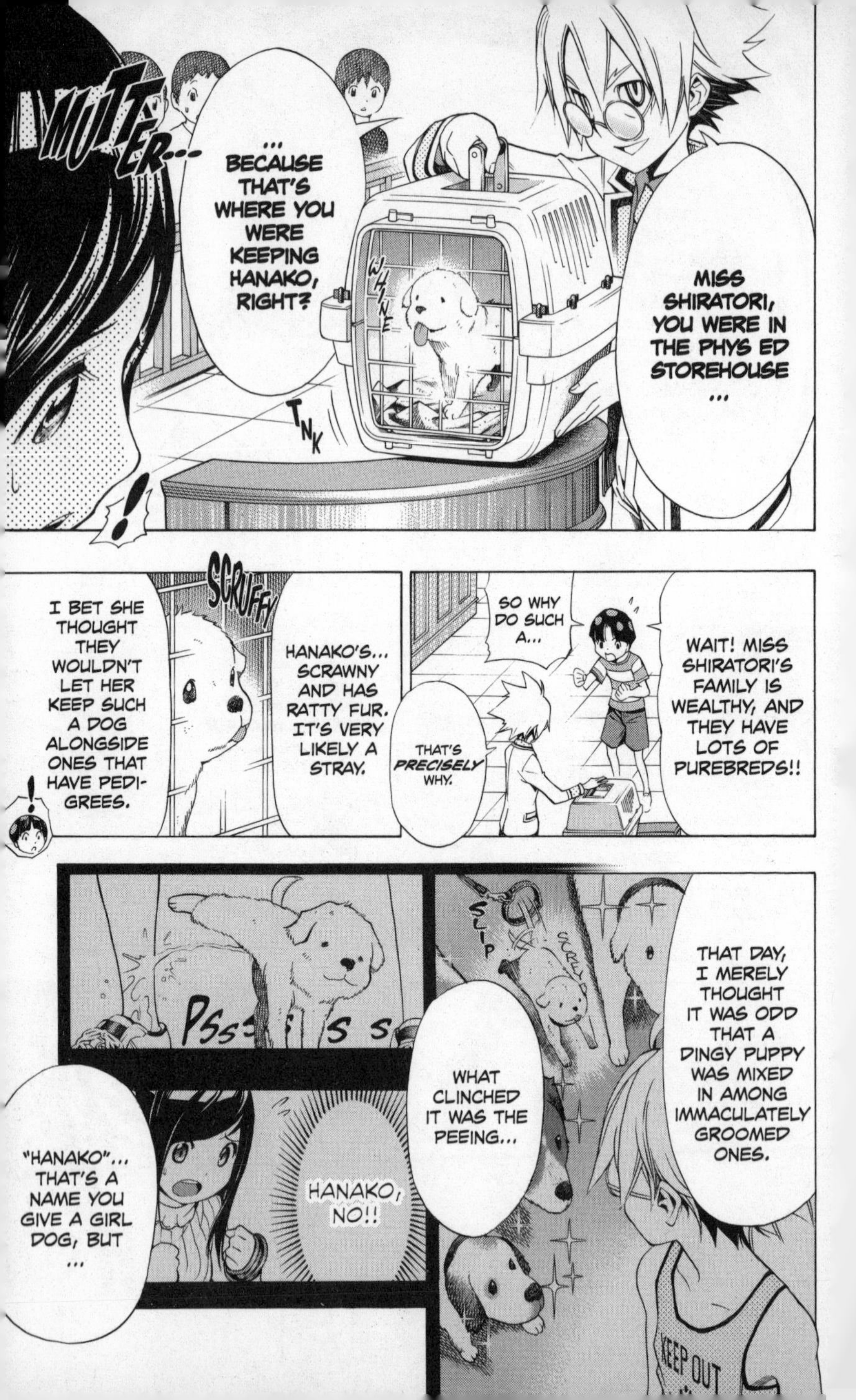
MISS SHIRATORI, YOU WERE IN THE PHYS ED STOREHOUSE ...
... BECAUSE THAT'S WHERE YOU WERE KEEPING HANAKO, RIGHT?
WHINE
TNK
MUTTER...
!
WAIT! MISS SHIRATORI'S FAMILY IS WEALTHY, AND THEY HAVE LOTS OF PUREBREDS!!
SO WHY DO SUCH A...
THAT'S *PRECISELY* WHY.
SCRUFFY
HANAKO'S... SCRAWNY AND HAS RATTY FUR. IT'S VERY LIKELY A STRAY.
I BET SHE THOUGHT THEY WOULDN'T LET HER KEEP SUCH A DOG ALONGSIDE ONES THAT HAVE PEDI-GREES.
!
THAT DAY, I MERELY THOUGHT IT WAS ODD THAT A DINGY PUPPY WAS MIXED IN AMONG IMMACULATELY GROOMED ONES.
SLIP
WHAT CLINCHED IT WAS THE PEEING...
KEEP OUT
PSSSSSS
HANAKO, NO!!
"HANAKO"... THAT'S A NAME YOU GIVE A GIRL DOG, BUT ...

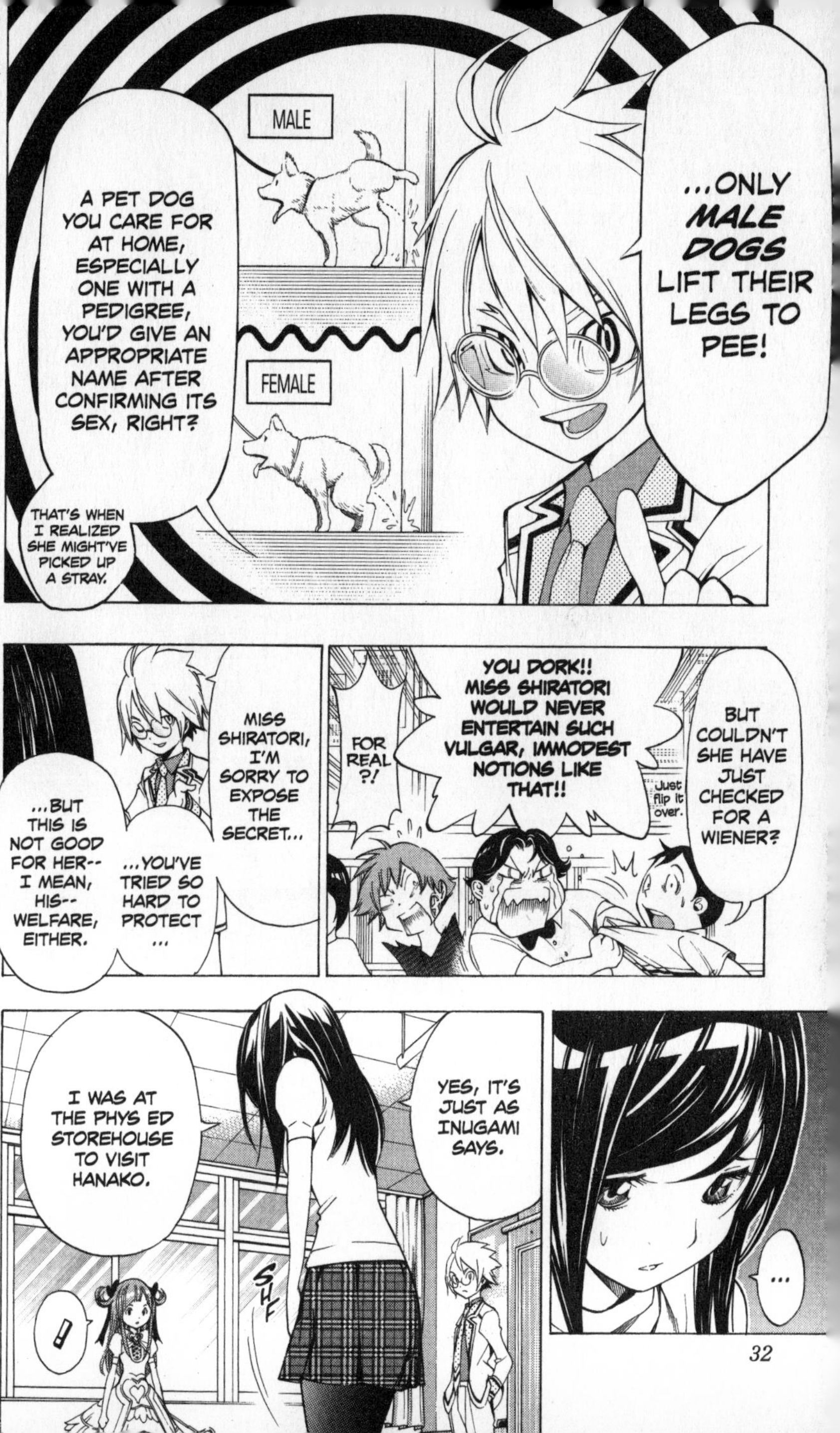
...ONLY *MALE DOGS* LIFT THEIR LEGS TO PEE!
A PET DOG YOU CARE FOR AT HOME, ESPECIALLY ONE WITH A PEDIGREE, YOU'D GIVE AN APPROPRIATE NAME AFTER CONFIRMING ITS SEX, RIGHT?
MALE
FEMALE
THAT'S WHEN I REALIZED SHE MIGHT'VE PICKED UP A STRAY.
BUT COULDN'T SHE HAVE JUST CHECKED FOR A WIENER?
Just flip it over.
YOU DORK!! MISS SHIRATORI WOULD NEVER ENTERTAIN SUCH VULGAR, IMMODEST NOTIONS LIKE THAT!!
FOR REAL?!
MISS SHIRATORI, I'M SORRY TO EXPOSE THE SECRET...
...YOU'VE TRIED SO HARD TO PROTECT...
...BUT THIS IS NOT GOOD FOR HER-- I MEAN, HIS-- WELFARE, EITHER.
...
YES, IT'S JUST AS INUGAMI SAYS.
I WAS AT THE PHYS ED STOREHOUSE TO VISIT HANAKO.
SHF
!

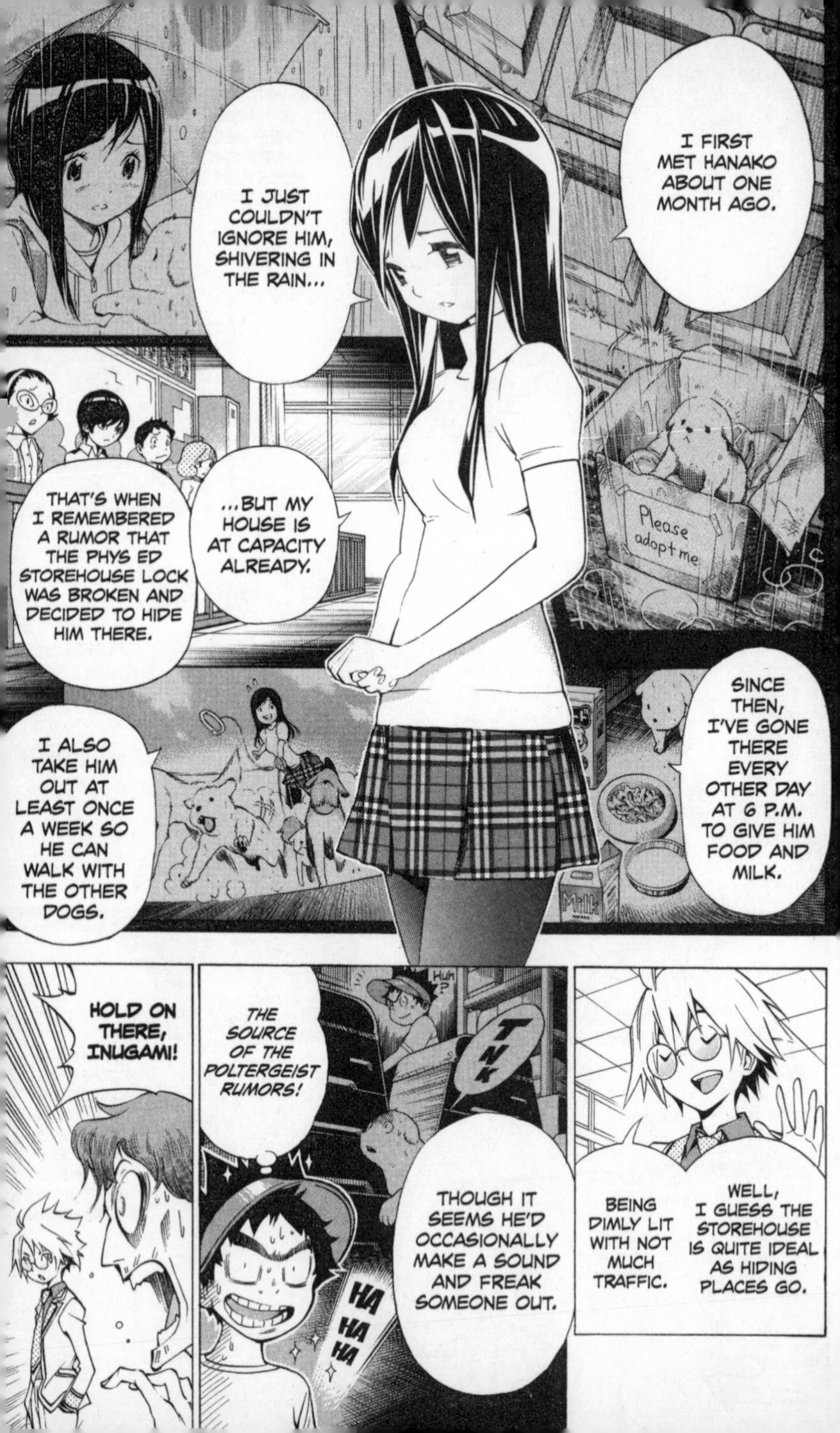
I FIRST MET HANAKO ABOUT ONE MONTH AGO.
Please adopt me
I JUST COULDN'T IGNORE HIM, SHIVERING IN THE RAIN...
...BUT MY HOUSE IS AT CAPACITY ALREADY.
THAT'S WHEN I REMEMBERED A RUMOR THAT THE PHYS ED STOREHOUSE LOCK WAS BROKEN AND DECIDED TO HIDE HIM THERE.
SINCE THEN, I'VE GONE THERE EVERY OTHER DAY AT 6 P.M. TO GIVE HIM FOOD AND MILK.
Milk
I ALSO TAKE HIM OUT AT LEAST ONCE A WEEK SO HE CAN WALK WITH THE OTHER DOGS.
WELL, I GUESS THE STOREHOUSE IS QUITE IDEAL AS HIDING PLACES GO.
BEING DIMLY LIT WITH NOT MUCH TRAFFIC.
Huh?
TNK
THE SOURCE OF THE POLTERGEIST RUMORS!
THOUGH IT SEEMS HE'D OCCASIONALLY MAKE A SOUND AND FREAK SOMEONE OUT.
HA HA HA
HOLD ON THERE, INUGAMI!

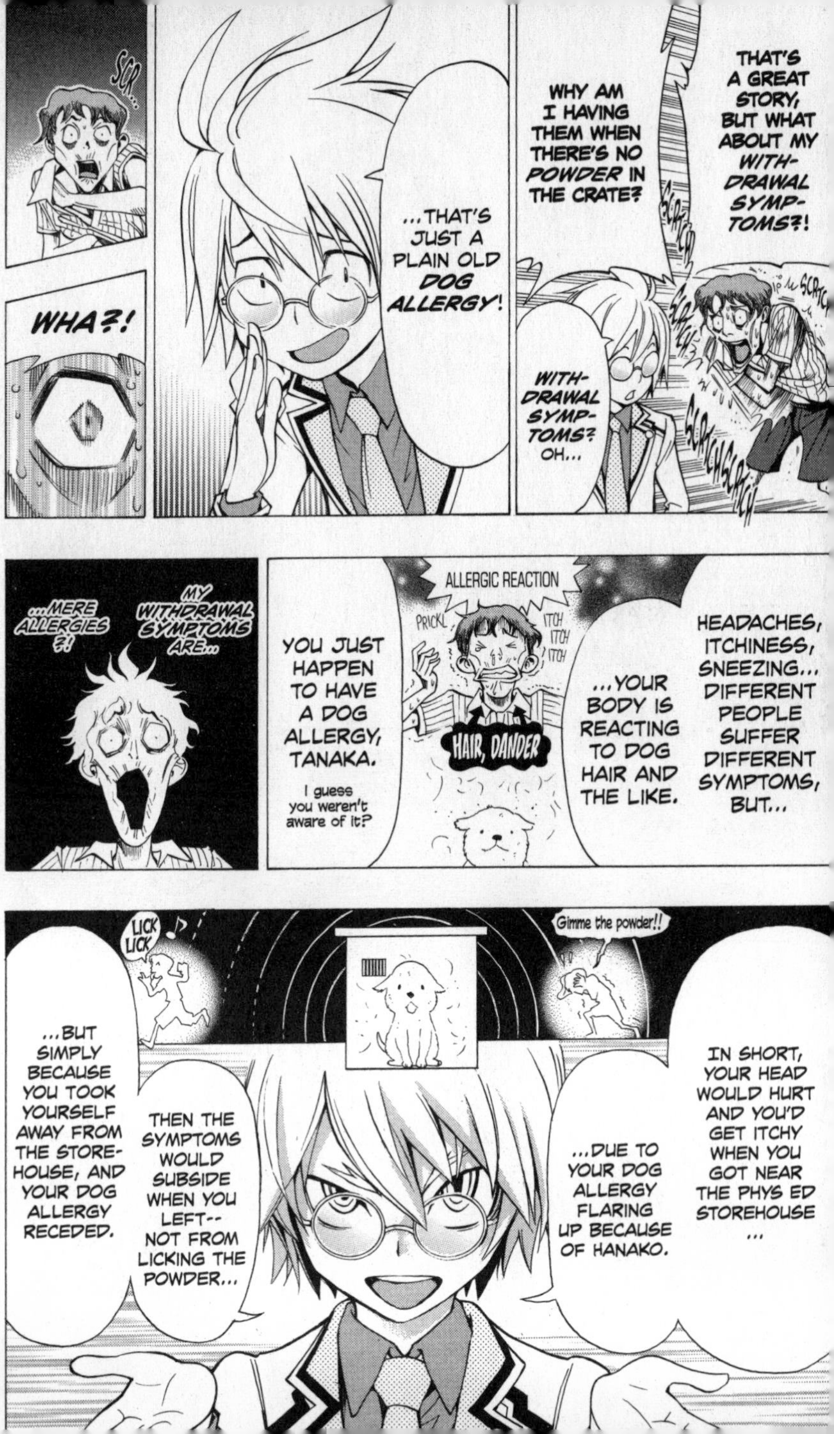
THAT'S A GREAT STORY, BUT WHAT ABOUT MY WITH-DRAWAL SYMP-TOMS?!
SCRATCH
WHY AM I HAVING THEM WHEN THERE'S NO POWDER IN THE CRATE?
SCRATCH
SCRATCH
SCRATCHSCRATCH
WITH-DRAWAL SYMP-TOMS? OH...
...THAT'S JUST A PLAIN OLD DOG ALLERGY!
SCR...
WHA?!
HEADACHES, ITCHINESS, SNEEZING... DIFFERENT PEOPLE SUFFER DIFFERENT SYMPTOMS, BUT...
...YOUR BODY IS REACTING TO DOG HAIR AND THE LIKE.
ALLERGIC REACTION
ITCH ITCH ITCH
PRICKL
HAIR, DANDER
YOU JUST HAPPEN TO HAVE A DOG ALLERGY, TANAKA.
I guess you weren't aware of it?
MY WITHDRAWAL SYMPTOMS ARE...
...MERE ALLERGIES?!
IN SHORT, YOUR HEAD WOULD HURT AND YOU'D GET ITCHY WHEN YOU GOT NEAR THE PHYS ED STOREHOUSE ...
...DUE TO YOUR DOG ALLERGY FLARING UP BECAUSE OF HANAKO.
Gimme the powder!!
THEN THE SYMPTOMS WOULD SUBSIDE WHEN YOU LEFT-- NOT FROM LICKING THE POWDER...
LICK LICK
...BUT SIMPLY BECAUSE YOU TOOK YOURSELF AWAY FROM THE STORE-HOUSE, AND YOUR DOG ALLERGY RECEDED.

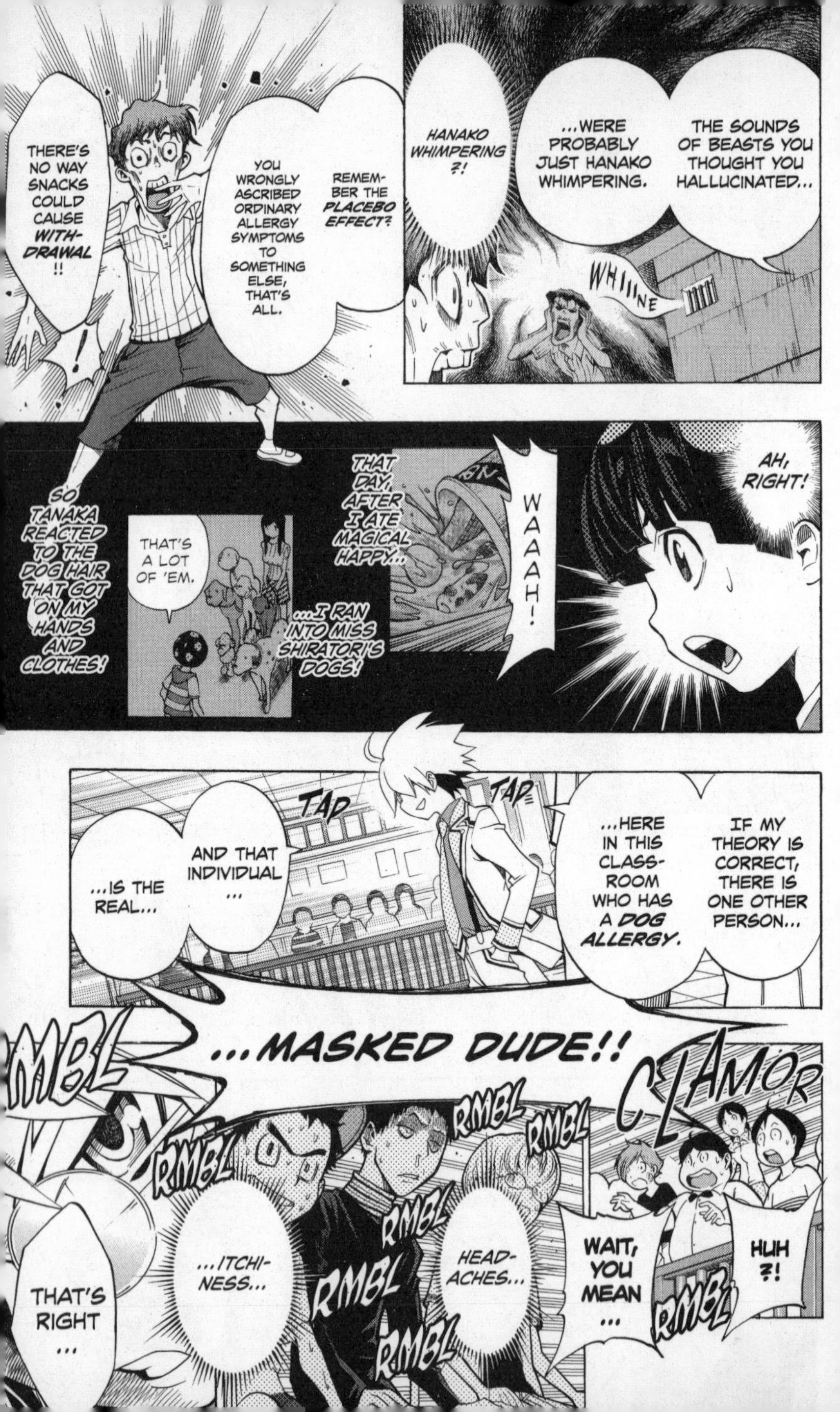
THE SOUNDS OF BEASTS YOU THOUGHT YOU HALLUCINATED...
...WERE PROBABLY JUST HANAKO WHIMPERING.
WHIIINE
HANAKO WHIMPERING?!
REMEMBER THE PLACEBO EFFECT?
YOU WRONGLY ASCRIBED ORDINARY ALLERGY SYMPTOMS TO SOMETHING ELSE, THAT'S ALL.
THERE'S NO WAY SNACKS COULD CAUSE WITHDRAWAL!!
AH, RIGHT!
WAAAAH!
THAT DAY, AFTER I ATE MAGICAL HAPPY...
...I RAN INTO MISS SHIRATORI'S DOGS!
THAT'S A LOT OF 'EM.
SO TANAKA REACTED TO THE DOG HAIR THAT GOT ON MY HANDS AND CLOTHES!
IF MY THEORY IS CORRECT, THERE IS ONE OTHER PERSON...
...HERE IN THIS CLASSROOM WHO HAS A DOG ALLERGY.
TAP
TAP
AND THAT INDIVIDUAL...
...IS THE REAL...
...MASKED DUDE!!
CLAMOR
RMBL
HUH?!
WAIT, YOU MEAN...
HEADACHES...
...ITCHINESS...
THAT'S RIGHT...

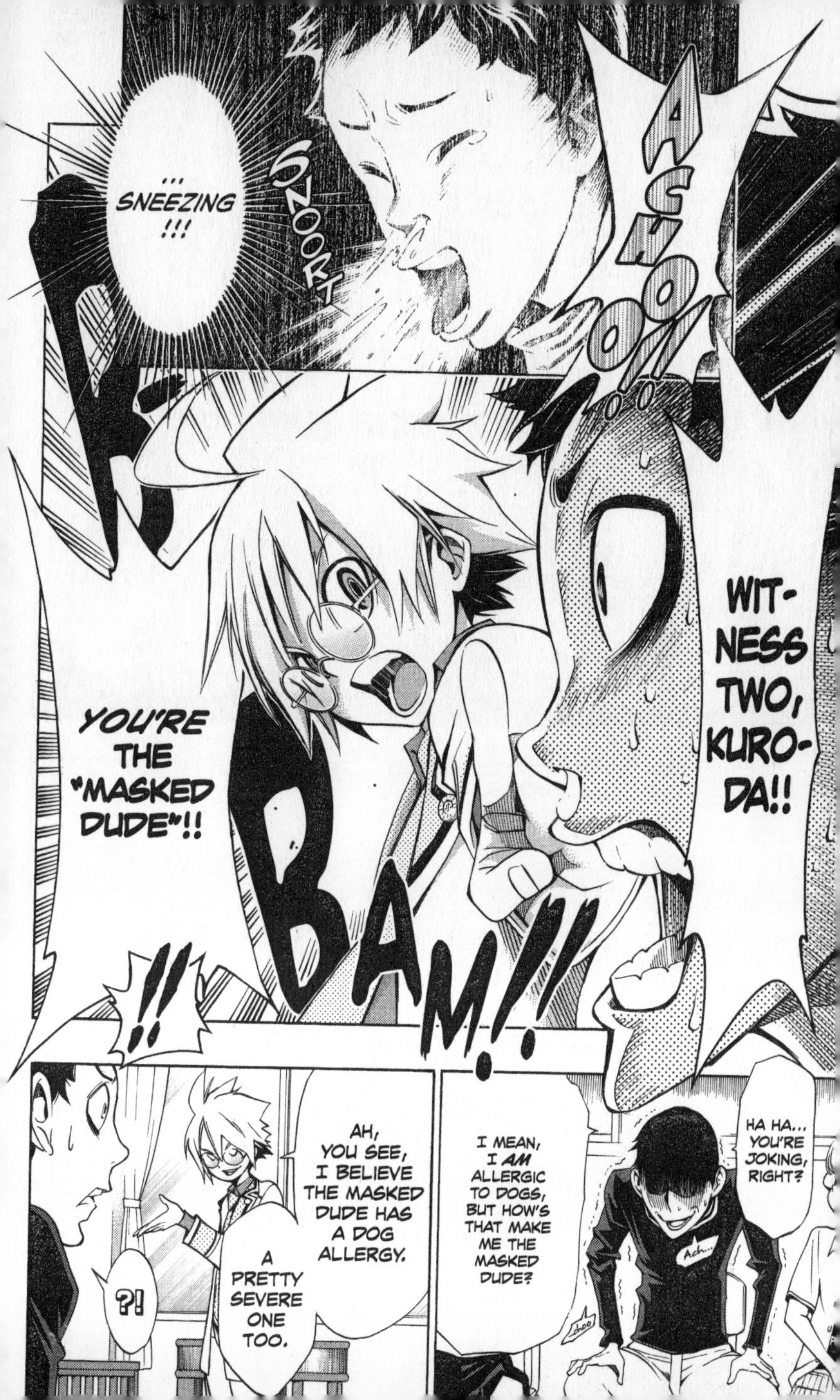
ACHOO!!
SNOORT
...SNEEZING!!!
WIT-NESS TWO, KURO-DA!!
BAM!!
YOU'RE THE "MASKED DUDE"!!
!!
HA HA... YOU'RE JOKING, RIGHT?
Ach...
choo
I MEAN, I *AM* ALLERGIC TO DOGS, BUT HOW'S THAT MAKE ME THE MASKED DUDE?
AH, YOU SEE, I BELIEVE THE MASKED DUDE HAS A DOG ALLERGY.
A PRETTY SEVERE ONE TOO.
?!

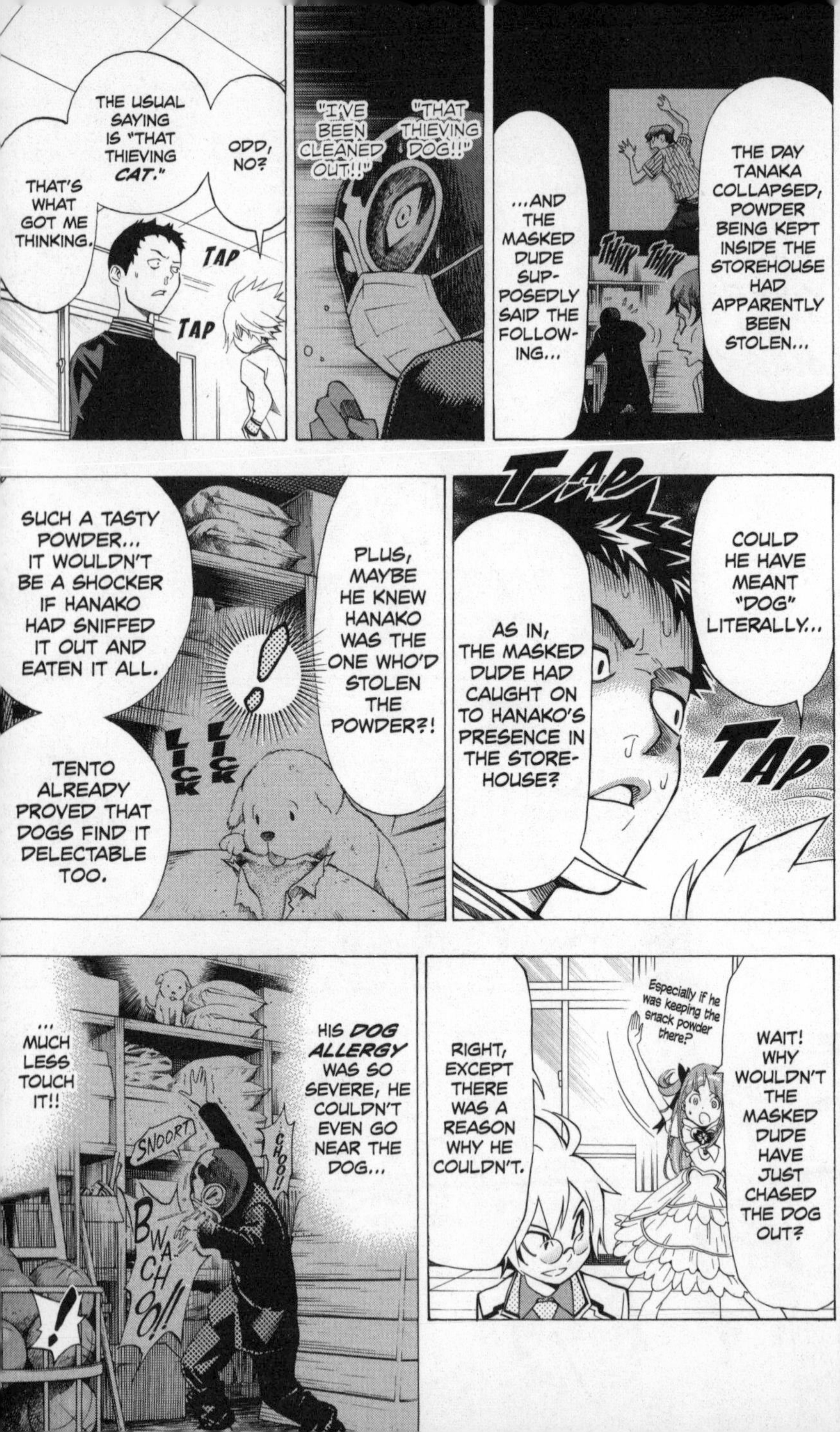
THE DAY TANAKA COLLAPSED, POWDER BEING KEPT INSIDE THE STOREHOUSE HAD APPARENTLY BEEN STOLEN...
THNK THNK
...AND THE MASKED DUDE SUPPOSEDLY SAID THE FOLLOWING...
"THAT THIEVING DOG!!"
"I'VE BEEN CLEANED OUT!!"
ODD, NO?
THE USUAL SAYING IS "THAT THIEVING *CAT*."
THAT'S WHAT GOT ME THINKING.
TAP
TAP
TAP
COULD HE HAVE MEANT "DOG" LITERALLY...
AS IN, THE MASKED DUDE HAD CAUGHT ON TO HANAKO'S PRESENCE IN THE STOREHOUSE?
TAP
PLUS, MAYBE HE KNEW HANAKO WAS THE ONE WHO'D STOLEN THE POWDER?!
SUCH A TASTY POWDER... IT WOULDN'T BE A SHOCKER IF HANAKO HAD SNIFFED IT OUT AND EATEN IT ALL.
LICK LICK
TENTO ALREADY PROVED THAT DOGS FIND IT DELECTABLE TOO.
WAIT! WHY WOULDN'T THE MASKED DUDE HAVE JUST CHASED THE DOG OUT?
Especially if he was keeping the snack powder there?
RIGHT, EXCEPT THERE WAS A REASON WHY HE COULDN'T.
HIS *DOG ALLERGY* WAS SO SEVERE, HE COULDN'T EVEN GO NEAR THE DOG...
...MUCH LESS TOUCH IT!!
SNOORT
CHOO!!
BWACHOO!!

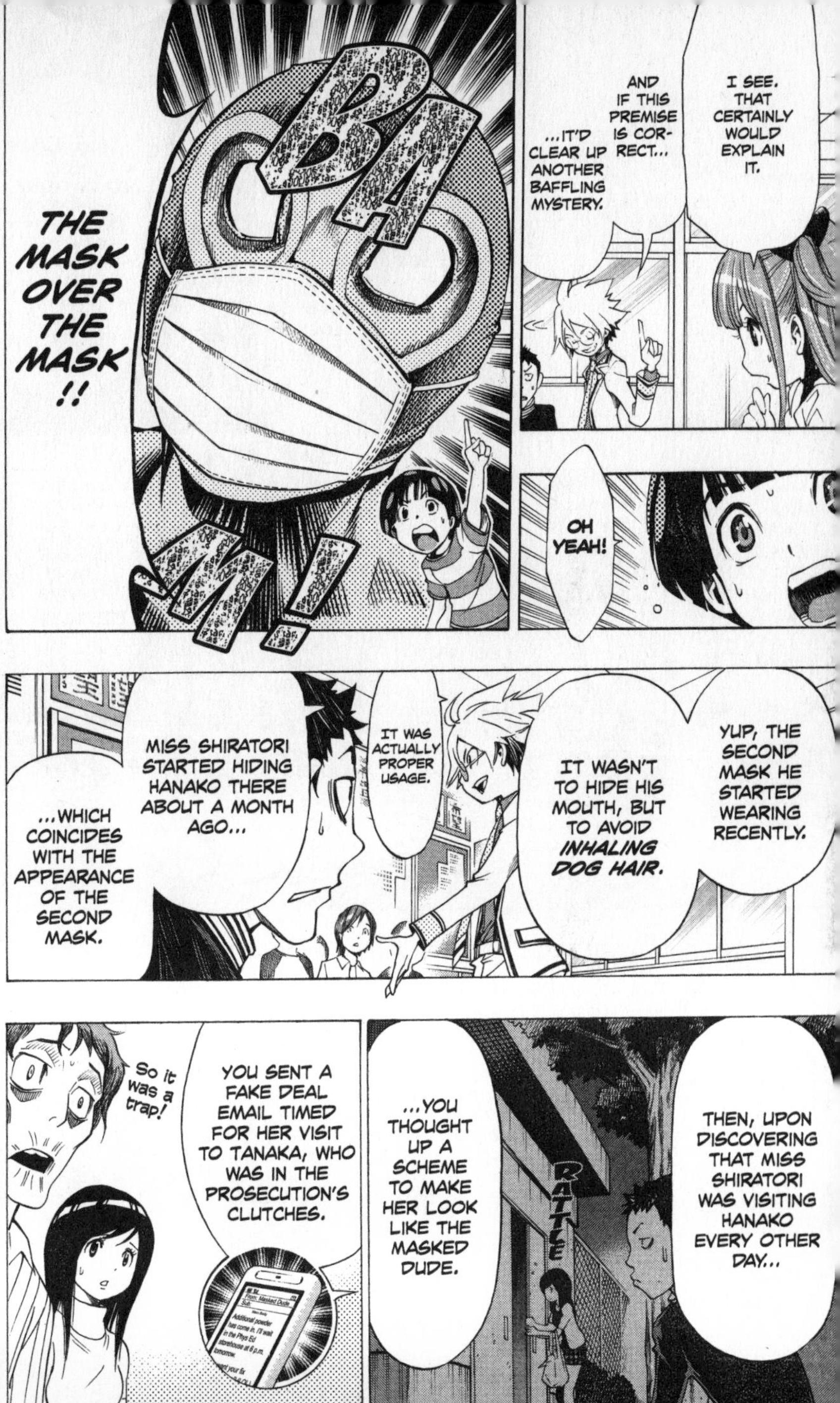
I SEE. THAT CERTAINLY WOULD EXPLAIN IT.
AND IF THIS PREMISE IS CORRECT...
...IT'D CLEAR UP ANOTHER BAFFLING MYSTERY.
OH YEAH!
BAM!
THE MASK OVER THE MASK!!
YUP, THE SECOND MASK HE STARTED WEARING RECENTLY.
IT WASN'T TO HIDE HIS MOUTH, BUT TO AVOID *INHALING DOG HAIR*.
IT WAS ACTUALLY PROPER USAGE.
MISS SHIRATORI STARTED HIDING HANAKO THERE ABOUT A MONTH AGO...
...WHICH COINCIDES WITH THE APPEARANCE OF THE SECOND MASK.
THEN, UPON DISCOVERING THAT MISS SHIRATORI WAS VISITING HANAKO EVERY OTHER DAY...
RATTLE
...YOU THOUGHT UP A SCHEME TO MAKE HER LOOK LIKE THE MASKED DUDE.
YOU SENT A FAKE DEAL EMAIL TIMED FOR HER VISIT TO TANAKA, WHO WAS IN THE PROSECUTION'S CLUTCHES.
So it was a trap!

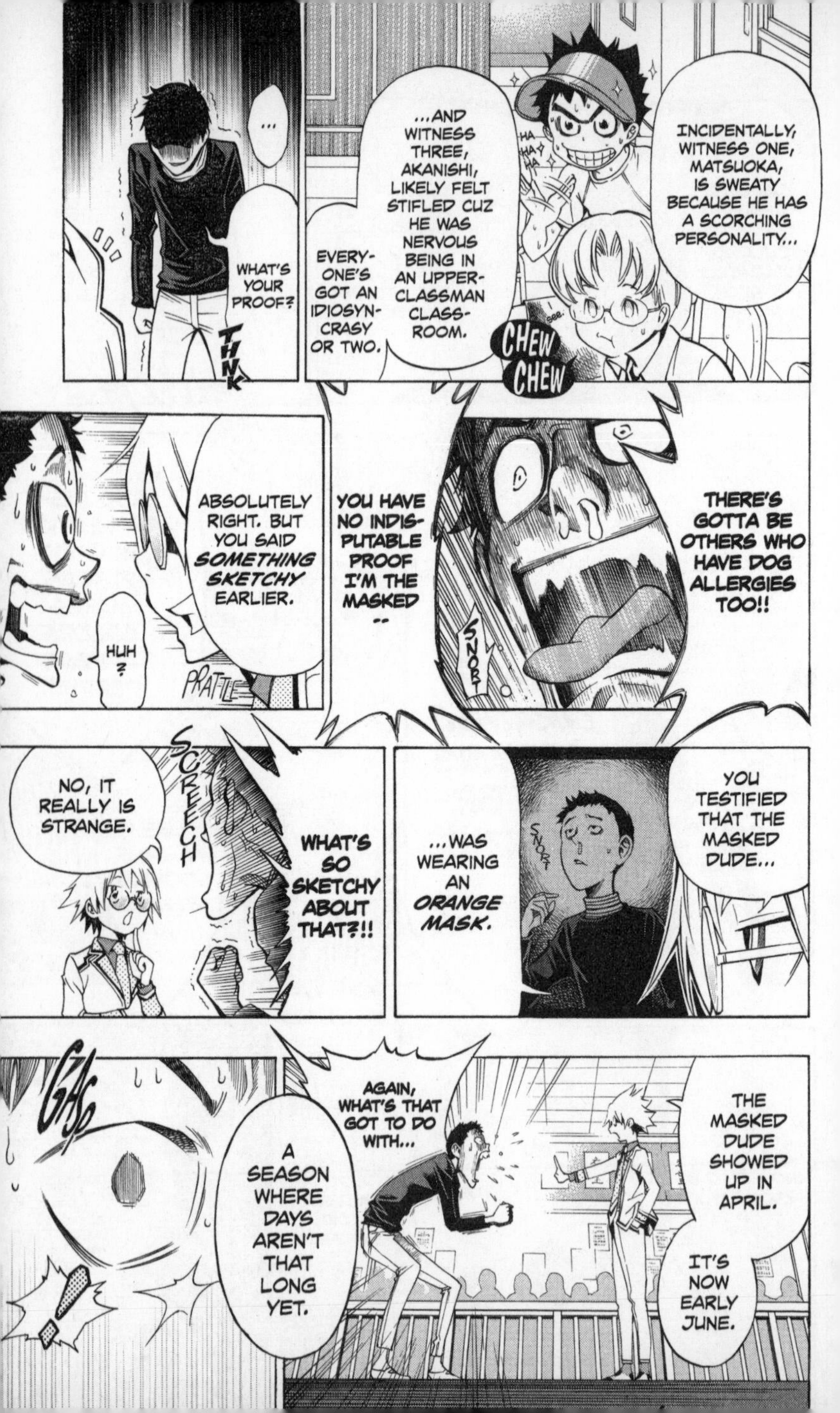
INCIDENTALLY, WITNESS ONE, MATSUOKA, IS SWEATY BECAUSE HE HAS A SCORCHING PERSONALITY...
HA HA HA
...AND WITNESS THREE, AKANISHI, LIKELY FELT STIFLED CUZ HE WAS NERVOUS BEING IN AN UPPER-CLASSMAN CLASS-ROOM.
I see.
CHEW CHEW
EVERY-ONE'S GOT AN IDIOSYN-CRASY OR TWO.
...
WHAT'S YOUR PROOF?
THNK
THERE'S GOTTA BE OTHERS WHO HAVE DOG ALLERGIES TOO!!
SNORT
YOU HAVE NO INDIS-PUTABLE PROOF I'M THE MASKED --
ABSOLUTELY RIGHT. BUT YOU SAID *SOMETHING SKETCHY* EARLIER.
HUH?
PRATTLE
YOU TESTIFIED THAT THE MASKED DUDE...
SNORT
...WAS WEARING AN *ORANGE MASK.*
WHAT'S SO SKETCHY ABOUT THAT?!!
SCREECH
NO, IT REALLY IS STRANGE.
THE MASKED DUDE SHOWED UP IN APRIL.
IT'S NOW EARLY JUNE.
AGAIN, WHAT'S THAT GOT TO DO WITH...
A SEASON WHERE DAYS AREN'T THAT LONG YET.
GASP

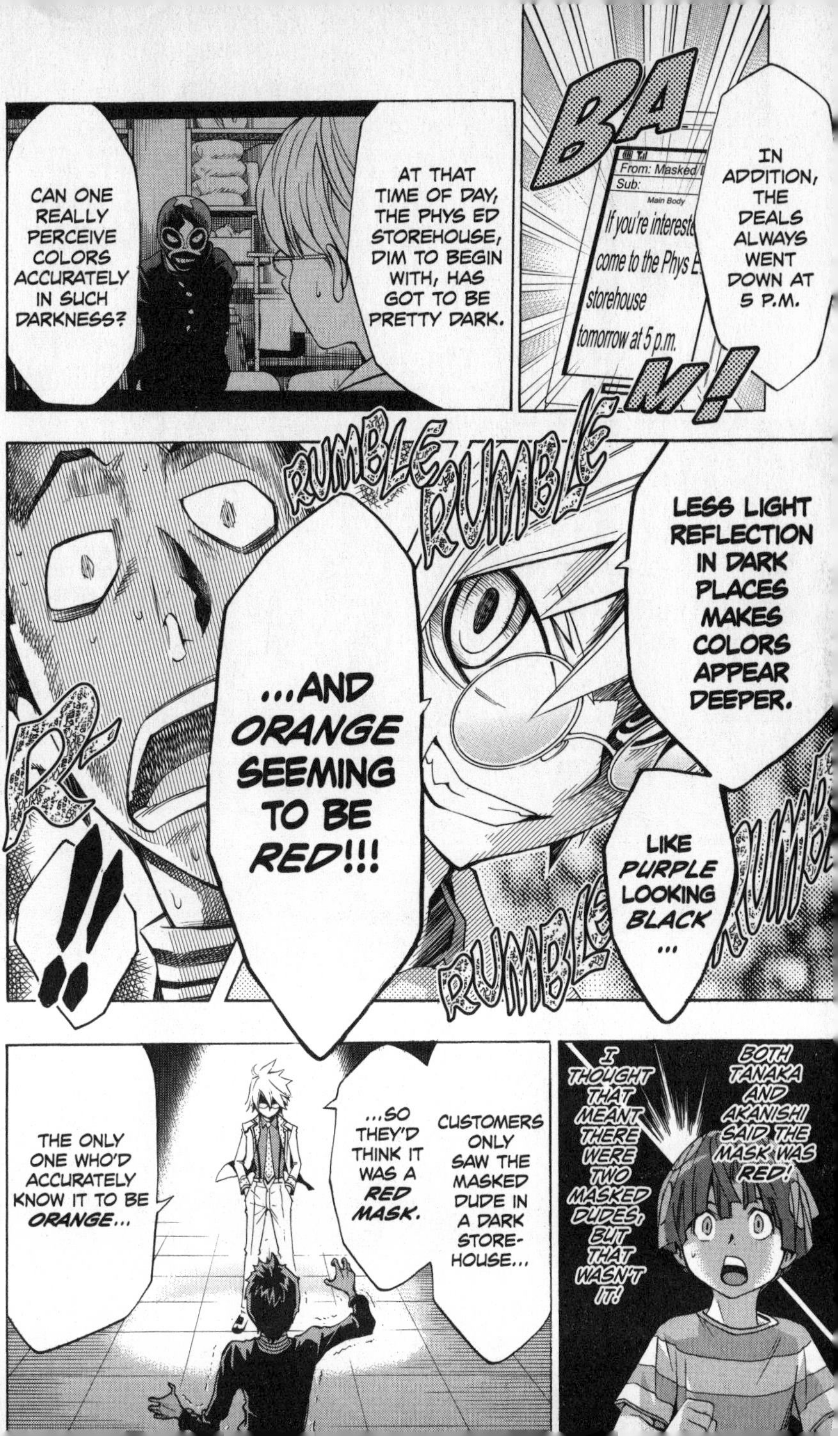
BA-
From: Masked
Sub:
Main Body
If you're intereste
come to the Phys E
storehouse
tomorrow at 5 p.m.
-M!
IN ADDITION, THE DEALS ALWAYS WENT DOWN AT 5 P.M.
AT THAT TIME OF DAY, THE PHYS ED STOREHOUSE, DIM TO BEGIN WITH, HAS GOT TO BE PRETTY DARK.
CAN ONE REALLY PERCEIVE COLORS ACCURATELY IN SUCH DARKNESS?
RUMBLE RUMBLE
LESS LIGHT REFLECTION IN DARK PLACES MAKES COLORS APPEAR DEEPER.
LIKE *PURPLE* LOOKING *BLACK*...
...AND *ORANGE* SEEMING TO BE *RED*!!!
RUMBLE RUMBLE
!!
BOTH TANAKA AND AKANISHI SAID THE MASK WAS RED!
I THOUGHT THAT MEANT THERE WERE TWO MASKED DUDES, BUT THAT WASN'T IT!
CUSTOMERS ONLY SAW THE MASKED DUDE IN A DARK STOREHOUSE...
...SO THEY'D THINK IT WAS A *RED MASK*.
THE ONLY ONE WHO'D ACCURATELY KNOW IT TO BE *ORANGE*...

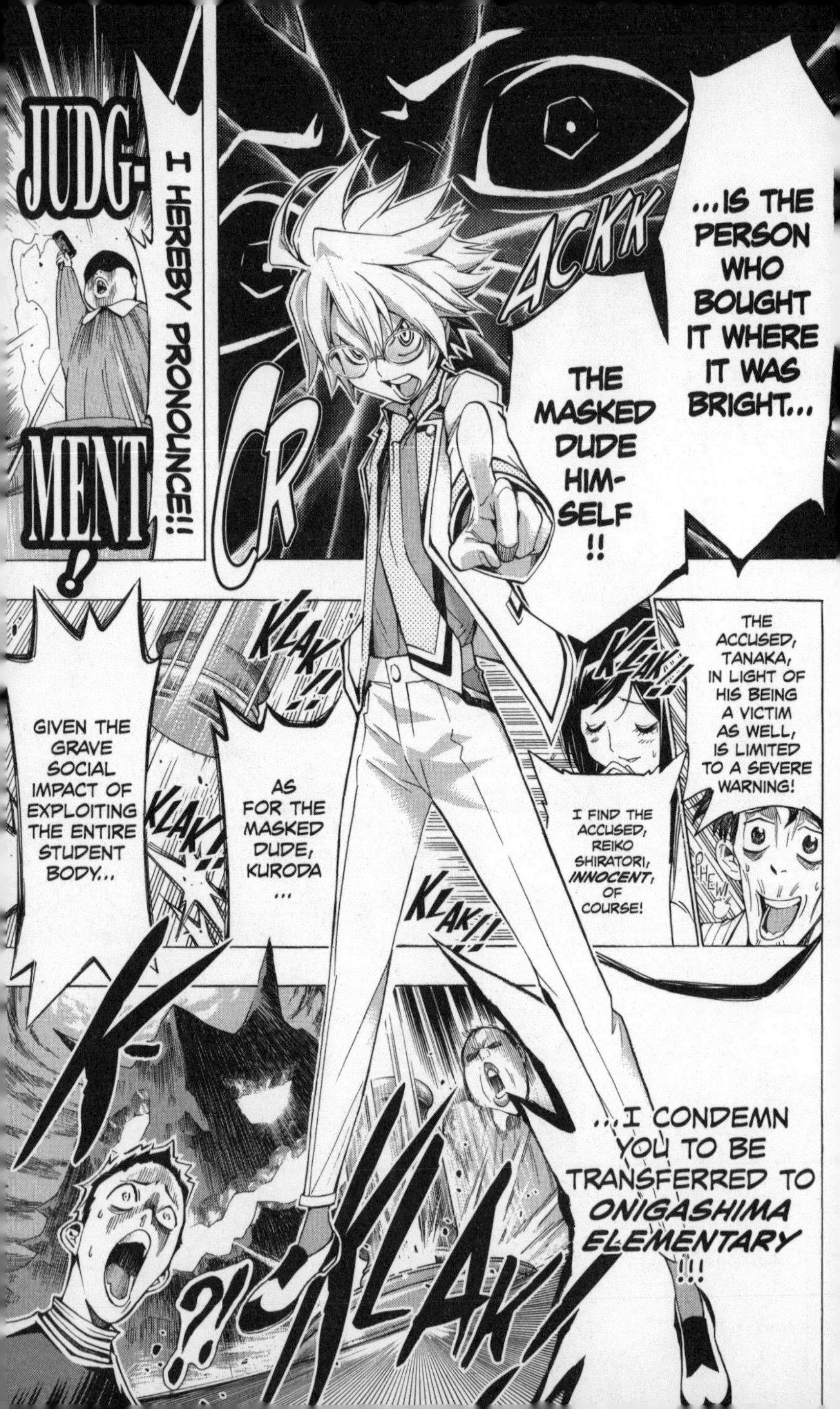
...IS THE PERSON WHO BOUGHT IT WHERE IT WAS BRIGHT...
THE MASKED DUDE HIMSELF!!
ACKK
CR
I HEREBY PRONOUNCE!!
JUDG-MENT!
THE ACCUSED, TANAKA, IN LIGHT OF HIS BEING A VICTIM AS WELL, IS LIMITED TO A SEVERE WARNING!
KLAK!!
I FIND THE ACCUSED, REIKO SHIRATORI, *INNOCENT*, OF COURSE!
PHEW!
KLAK!!
KLAK!!
AS FOR THE MASKED DUDE, KURODA...
KLAK!!
GIVEN THE GRAVE SOCIAL IMPACT OF EXPLOITING THE ENTIRE STUDENT BODY...
...I CONDEMN YOU TO BE TRANSFERRED TO *ONIGASHIMA ELEMENTARY*!!!
K-KLAK!
?!

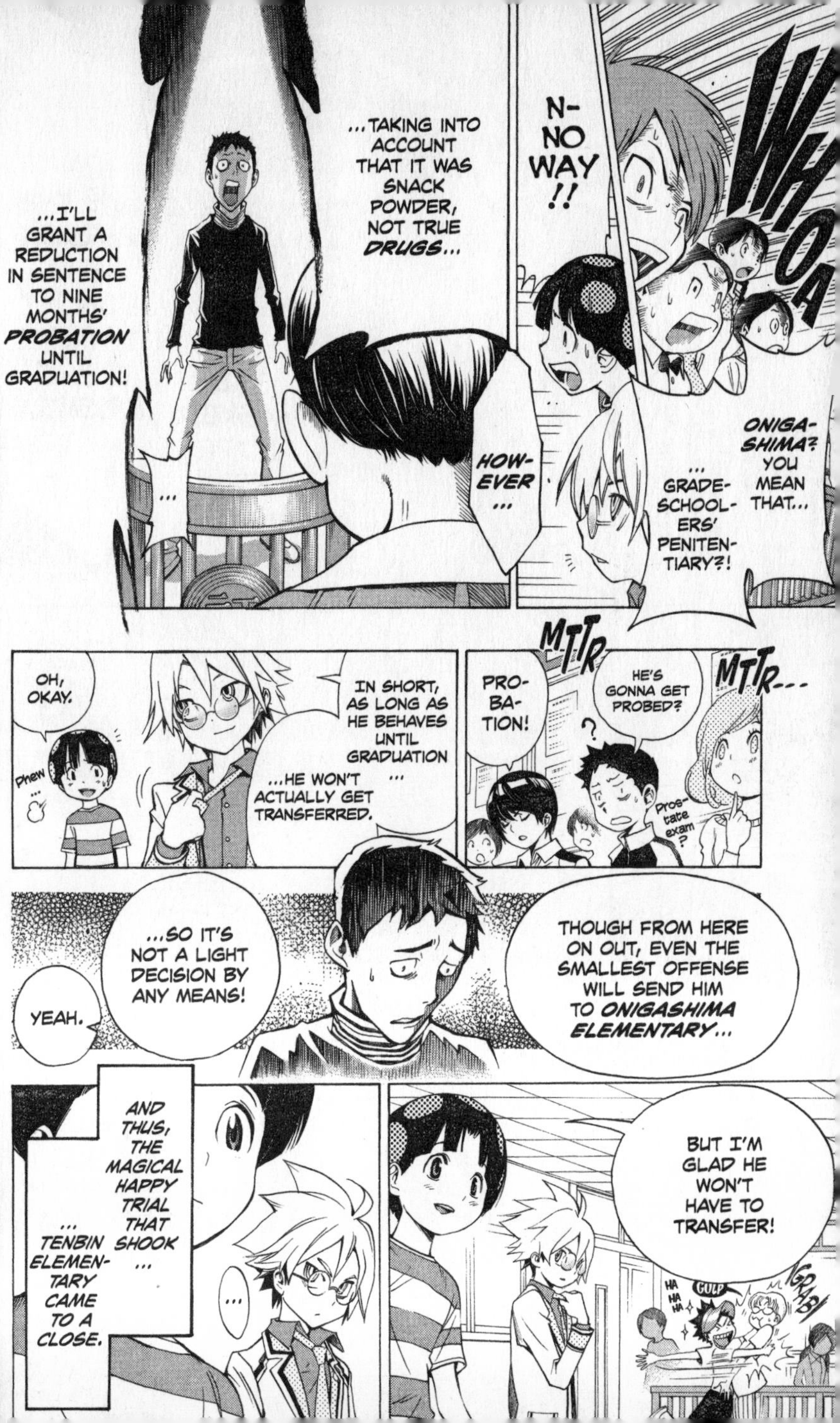
WHOA
N-NO WAY!!
ONIGASHIMA? YOU MEAN THAT...
...GRADE-SCHOOLERS' PENITENTIARY?!
HOW-EVER...
...TAKING INTO ACCOUNT THAT IT WAS SNACK POWDER, NOT TRUE DRUGS...
...I'LL GRANT A REDUCTION IN SENTENCE TO NINE MONTHS' PROBATION UNTIL GRADUATION!
...
MTTR
PRO-BA-TION!
HE'S GONNA GET PROBED?
MTTR...
Pros-tate exam?
IN SHORT, AS LONG AS HE BEHAVES UNTIL GRADUATION...
...HE WON'T ACTUALLY GET TRANSFERRED.
OH, OKAY.
Phew...
THOUGH FROM HERE ON OUT, EVEN THE SMALLEST OFFENSE WILL SEND HIM TO ONIGASHIMA ELEMENTARY...
...SO IT'S NOT A LIGHT DECISION BY ANY MEANS!
YEAH.
BUT I'M GLAD HE WON'T HAVE TO TRANSFER!
HA HA HA
GULP
GRAB!
AND THUS, THE MAGICAL HAPPY TRIAL THAT SHOOK...
...TENBIN ELEMENTARY CAME TO A CLOSE.
...

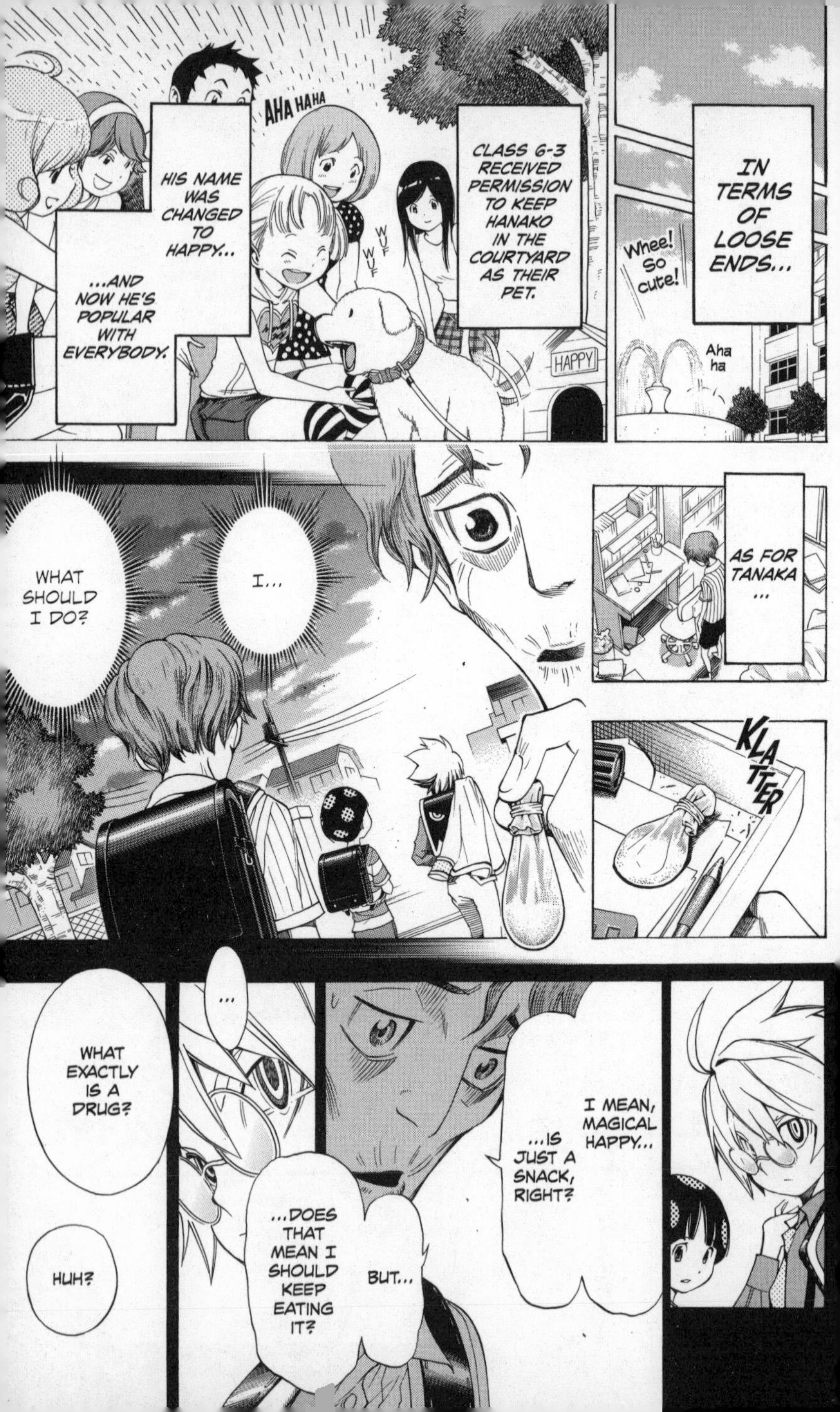
IN TERMS OF LOOSE ENDS...
Whee! So cute!
Aha ha
CLASS 6-3 RECEIVED PERMISSION TO KEEP HANAKO IN THE COURTYARD AS THEIR PET.
AHA HAHA
HAPPY
WUF WUF
HIS NAME WAS CHANGED TO HAPPY...
...AND NOW HE'S POPULAR WITH EVERYBODY.
AS FOR TANAKA...
KLATTER
I...
WHAT SHOULD I DO?
I MEAN, MAGICAL HAPPY...
...IS JUST A SNACK, RIGHT?
BUT...
...DOES THAT MEAN I SHOULD KEEP EATING IT?
...
WHAT EXACTLY IS A DRUG?
HUH?

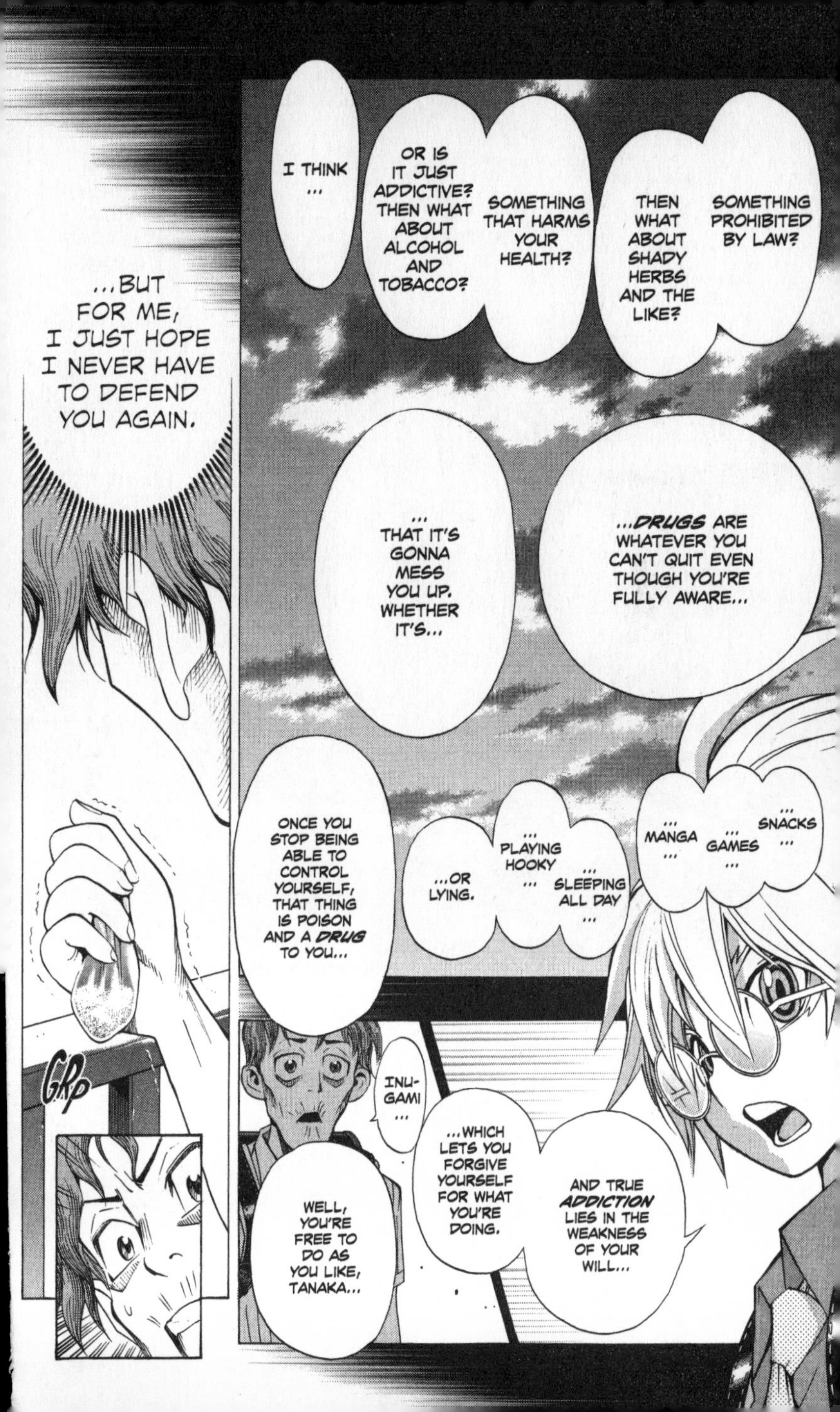
SOMETHING PROHIBITED BY LAW?
THEN WHAT ABOUT SHADY HERBS AND THE LIKE?
SOMETHING THAT HARMS YOUR HEALTH?
OR IS IT JUST ADDICTIVE? THEN WHAT ABOUT ALCOHOL AND TOBACCO?
I THINK ...
...*DRUGS* ARE WHATEVER YOU CAN'T QUIT EVEN THOUGH YOU'RE FULLY AWARE...
... THAT IT'S GONNA MESS YOU UP. WHETHER IT'S...
... SNACKS ...
... GAMES ...
... MANGA ...
... SLEEPING ALL DAY ...
... PLAYING HOOKY ...
...OR LYING.
ONCE YOU STOP BEING ABLE TO CONTROL YOURSELF, THAT THING IS POISON AND A *DRUG* TO YOU...
AND TRUE *ADDICTION* LIES IN THE WEAKNESS OF YOUR WILL...
...WHICH LETS YOU FORGIVE YOURSELF FOR WHAT YOU'RE DOING.
INU-GAMI ...
WELL, YOU'RE FREE TO DO AS YOU LIKE, TANAKA...
...BUT FOR ME, I JUST HOPE I NEVER HAVE TO DEFEND YOU AGAIN.
GRP

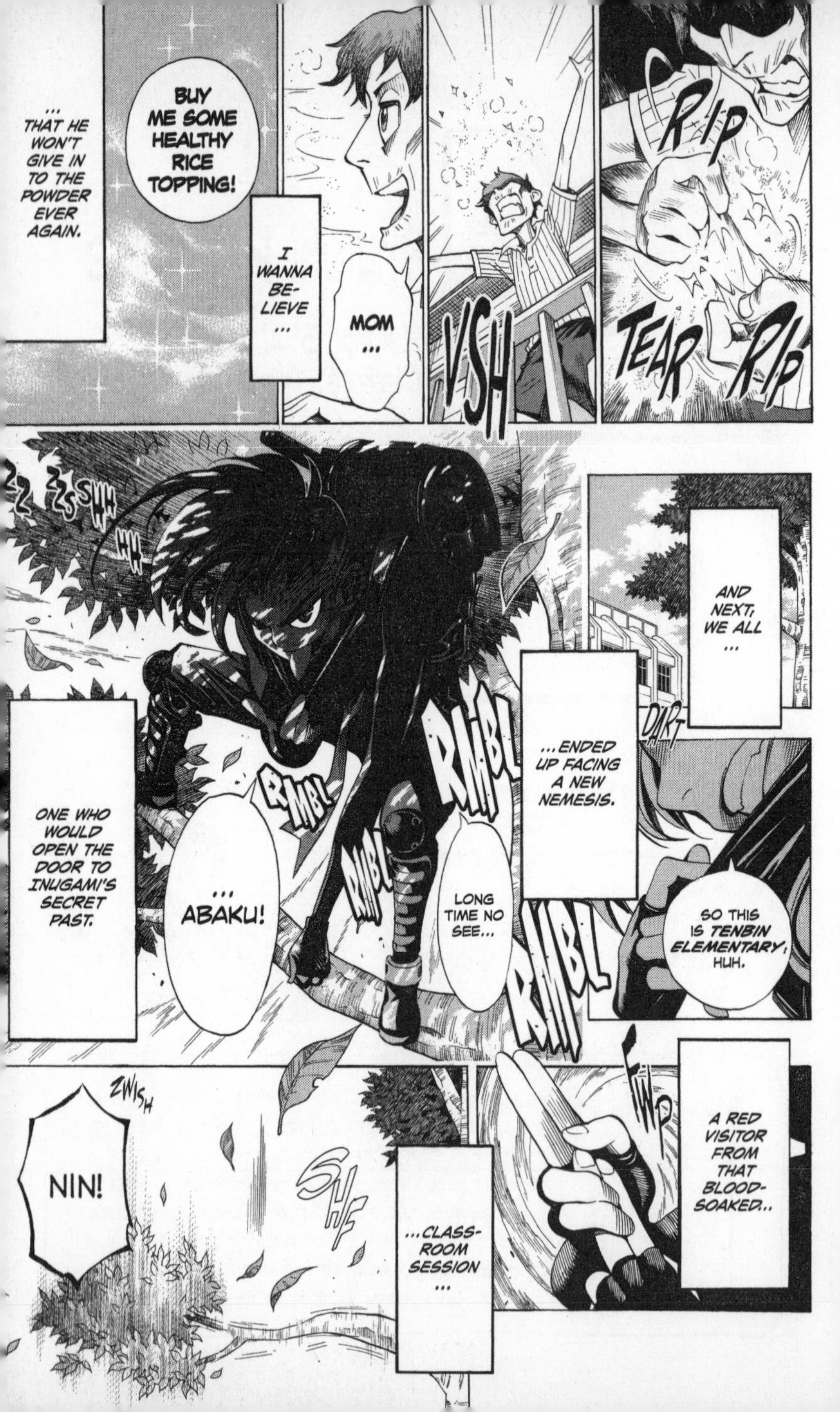

RIP
TEAR
RIP
VSH
MOM ...
I WANNA BE-LIEVE ...
BUY ME SOME HEALTHY RICE TOPPING!
... THAT HE WON'T GIVE IN TO THE POWDER EVER AGAIN.
AND NEXT, WE ALL ...
... ENDED UP FACING A NEW NEMESIS.
DART
SO THIS IS *TENBIN ELEMENTARY*, HUH.
ZZ ZZSSHH HH
RMBL
RMBL
RMBL
RMBL
LONG TIME NO SEE...
... ABAKU!
ONE WHO WOULD OPEN THE DOOR TO INUGAMI'S SECRET PAST.
FWP
A RED VISITOR FROM THAT BLOOD-SOAKED...
...CLASS-ROOM SESSION ...
SHF
ZWISH
NIN!

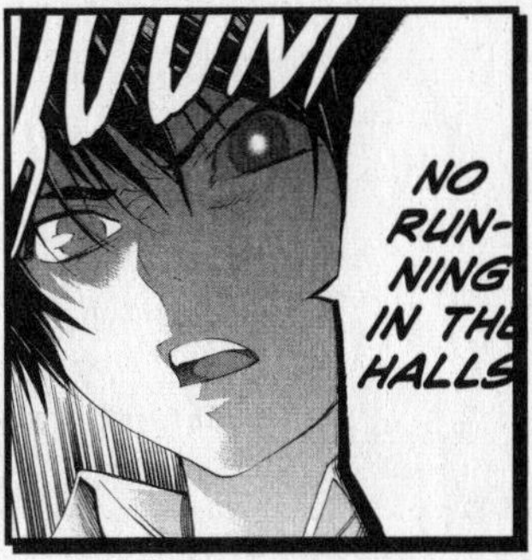
JUUN
NO RUNNING IN THE HALLS

(Obata's final version)

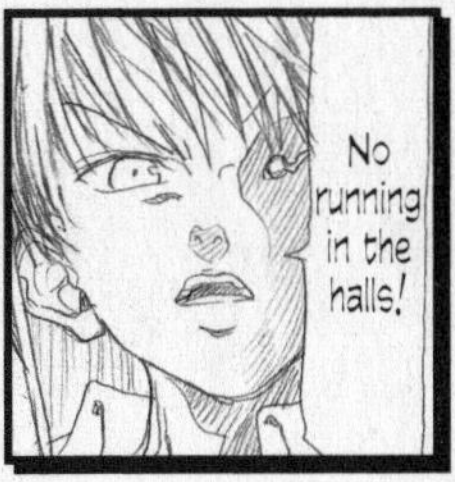
No running in the halls!

(Enoki's draft version)

Shuichi Higashide

Height: 5'2"
Dislikes: Those who break rules

Class 6-3 class president. **Black hair** and **super handsome** were the two key phrases I put in my request to Obata Sensei. As you can see, an indisputably black-haired handsome boy was born.

Honestly, he's my favorite character!

What could his true identity be...?!

When I was tidying up, I found an early drawing of Higashide.

I am wholeheartedly glad he didn't end up like this.

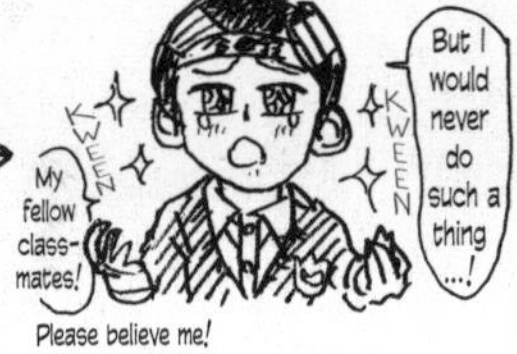
KWEEN
My fellow class-mates!
KWEEN
But I would never do such a thing...!
Please believe me!

☆School Judgment Backstory④☆

"Magical Happy" The basis for this was, of course, a certain famous, yummy snack covered in a mysterious powder. I was a bit nervous that we might receive complaints from the manufacturer because I made the powder out to be a sketchy substance. When I was told that my editor received an "editorial call" after the chapter was published, I thought to myself, "That's it, I'm finished!" It turned out to be a dog breeder letting us know that "some female dogs **do** lift their leg to urinate." (As a general rule, it seems it's male dogs mostly...)

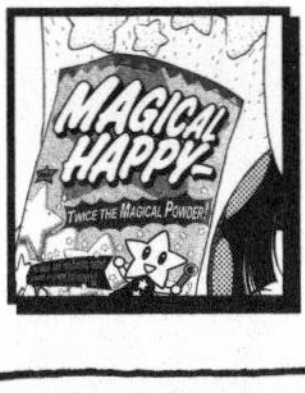
MAGICAL HAPPY
TWICE THE MAGICAL POWDER!

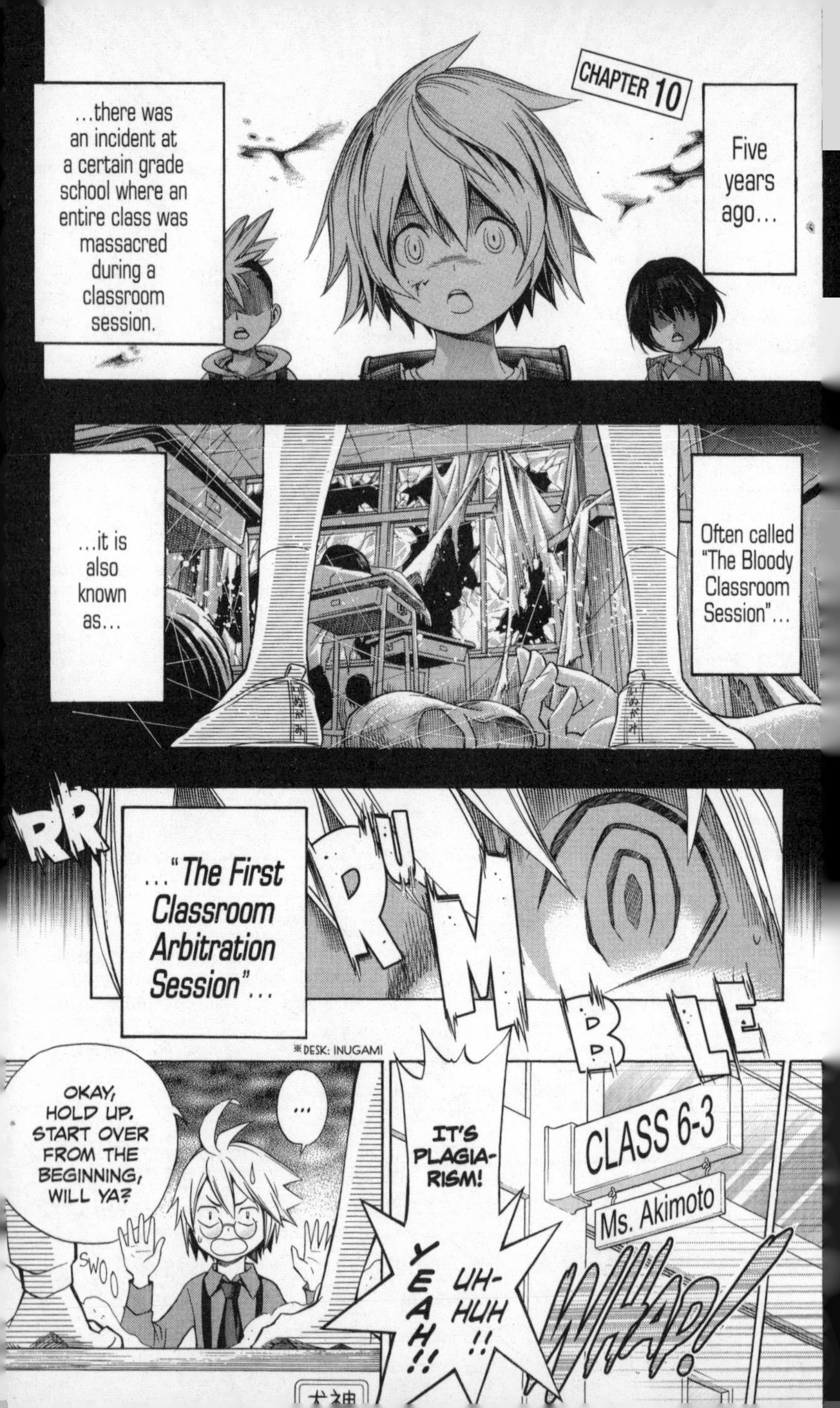
CHAPTER 10
Five years ago…
…there was an incident at a certain grade school where an entire class was massacred during a classroom session.
Often called "The Bloody Classroom Session"…
…it is also known as…
RRRUMBLE
…"The First Classroom Arbitration Session"…
※DESK: INUGAMI
CLASS 6-3
Ms. Akimoto
WHAP!
IT'S PLAGIA-RISM!
UH-HUH!!
YEAH!!
…
OKAY, HOLD UP. START OVER FROM THE BEGINNING, WILL YA?
SWOO

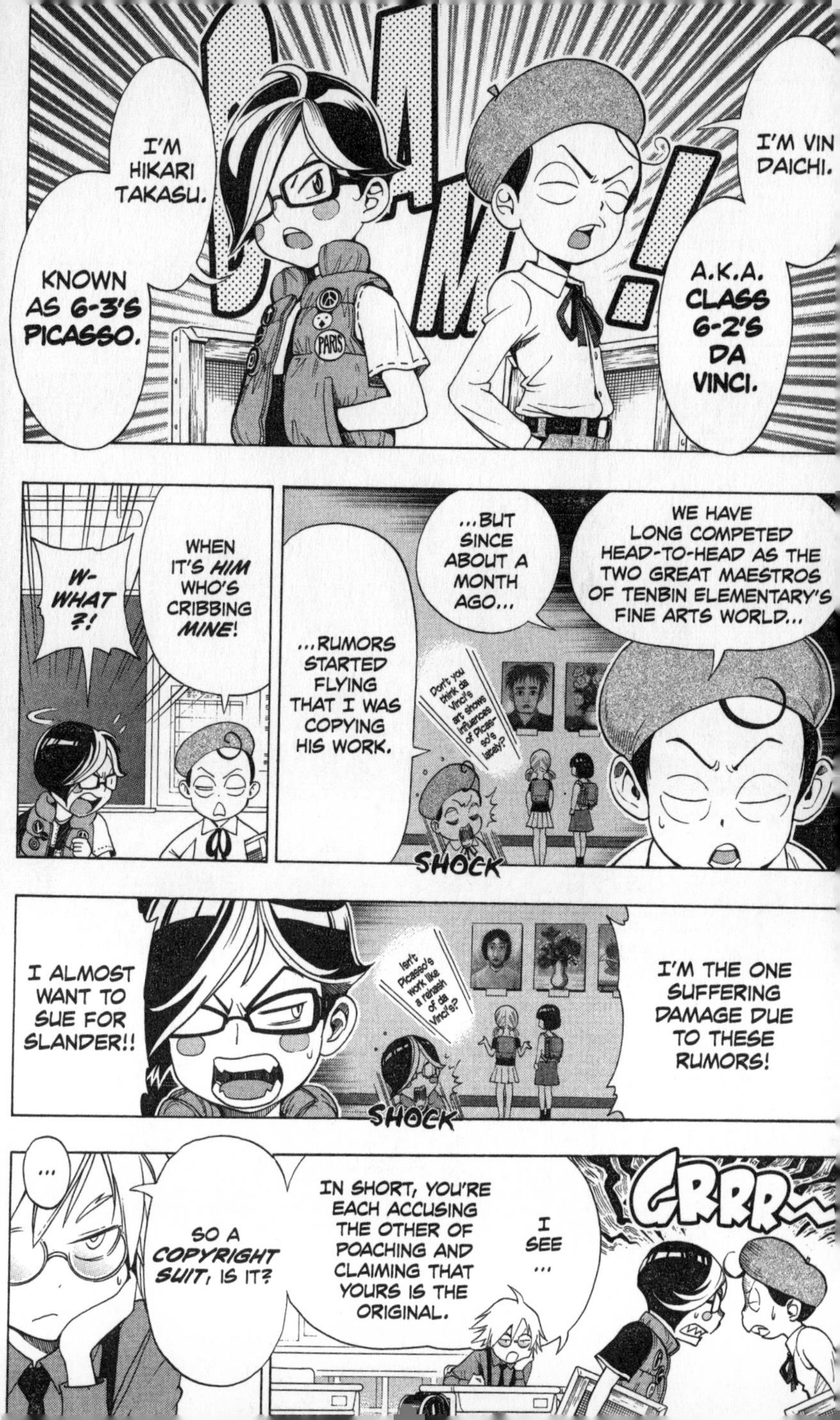
I'M VIN DAICHI.
A.K.A. CLASS 6-2'S DA VINCI.
I'M HIKARI TAKASU.
KNOWN AS 6-3'S PICASSO.
WE HAVE LONG COMPETED HEAD-TO-HEAD AS THE TWO GREAT MAESTROS OF TENBIN ELEMENTARY'S FINE ARTS WORLD...
...BUT SINCE ABOUT A MONTH AGO...
...RUMORS STARTED FLYING THAT I WAS COPYING HIS WORK.
Don't you think da Vinci's art shows influences of Picasso's lately?
SHOCK
WHEN IT'S HIM WHO'S CRIBBING MINE!
W-WHAT?!
I'M THE ONE SUFFERING DAMAGE DUE TO THESE RUMORS!
Isn't Picasso's work like a rehash of da Vinci's?
SHOCK
I ALMOST WANT TO SUE FOR SLANDER!!
GRRR~
I SEE...
IN SHORT, YOU'RE EACH ACCUSING THE OTHER OF POACHING AND CLAIMING THAT YOURS IS THE ORIGINAL.
SO A COPYRIGHT SUIT, IS IT?
...

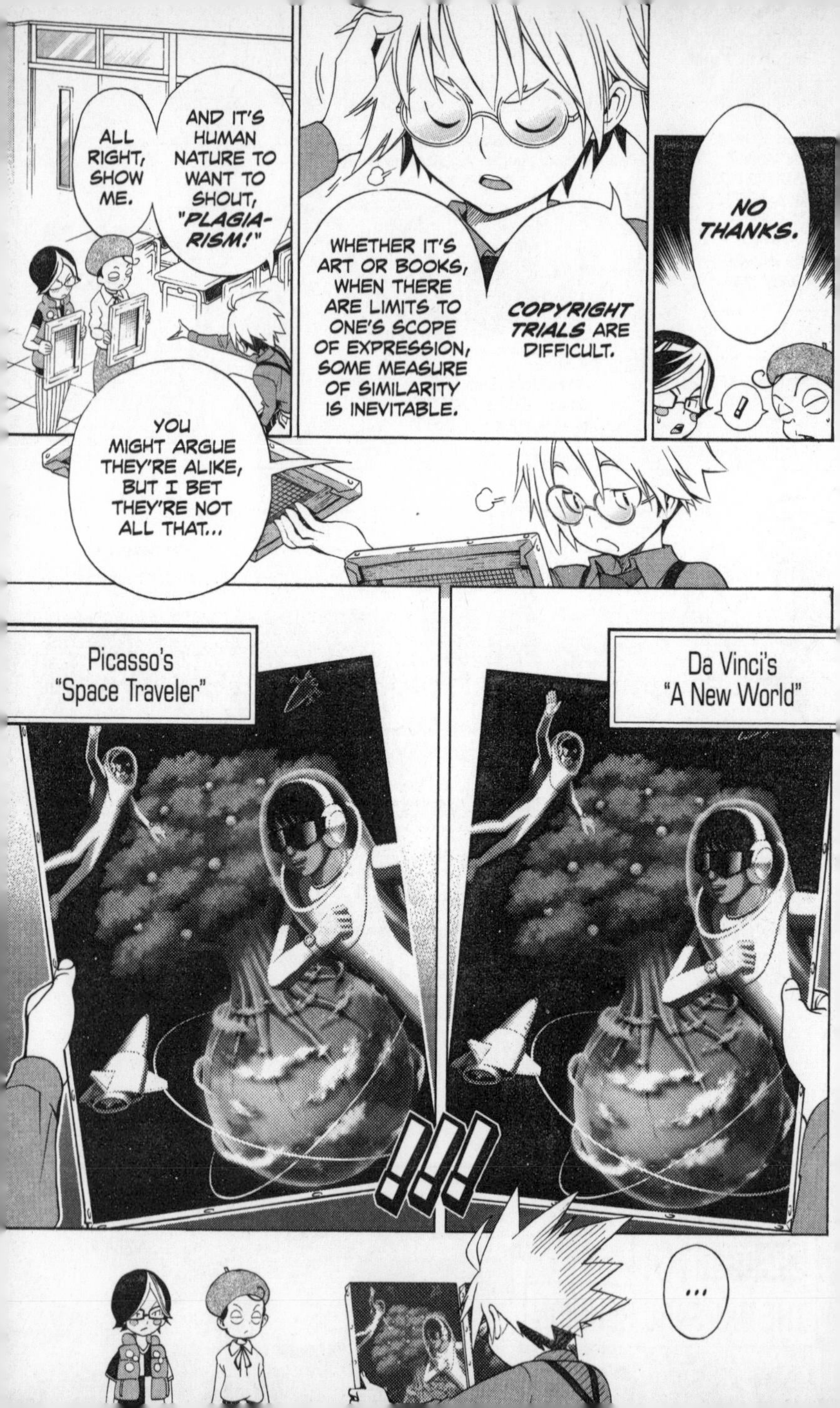
NO THANKS.
!
WHETHER IT'S ART OR BOOKS, WHEN THERE ARE LIMITS TO ONE'S SCOPE OF EXPRESSION, SOME MEASURE OF SIMILARITY IS INEVITABLE.
COPYRIGHT TRIALS ARE DIFFICULT.
AND IT'S HUMAN NATURE TO WANT TO SHOUT, "PLAGIA-RISM!"
ALL RIGHT, SHOW ME.
YOU MIGHT ARGUE THEY'RE ALIKE, BUT I BET THEY'RE NOT ALL THAT...
Da Vinci's "A New World"
Picasso's "Space Traveler"
!!!
...

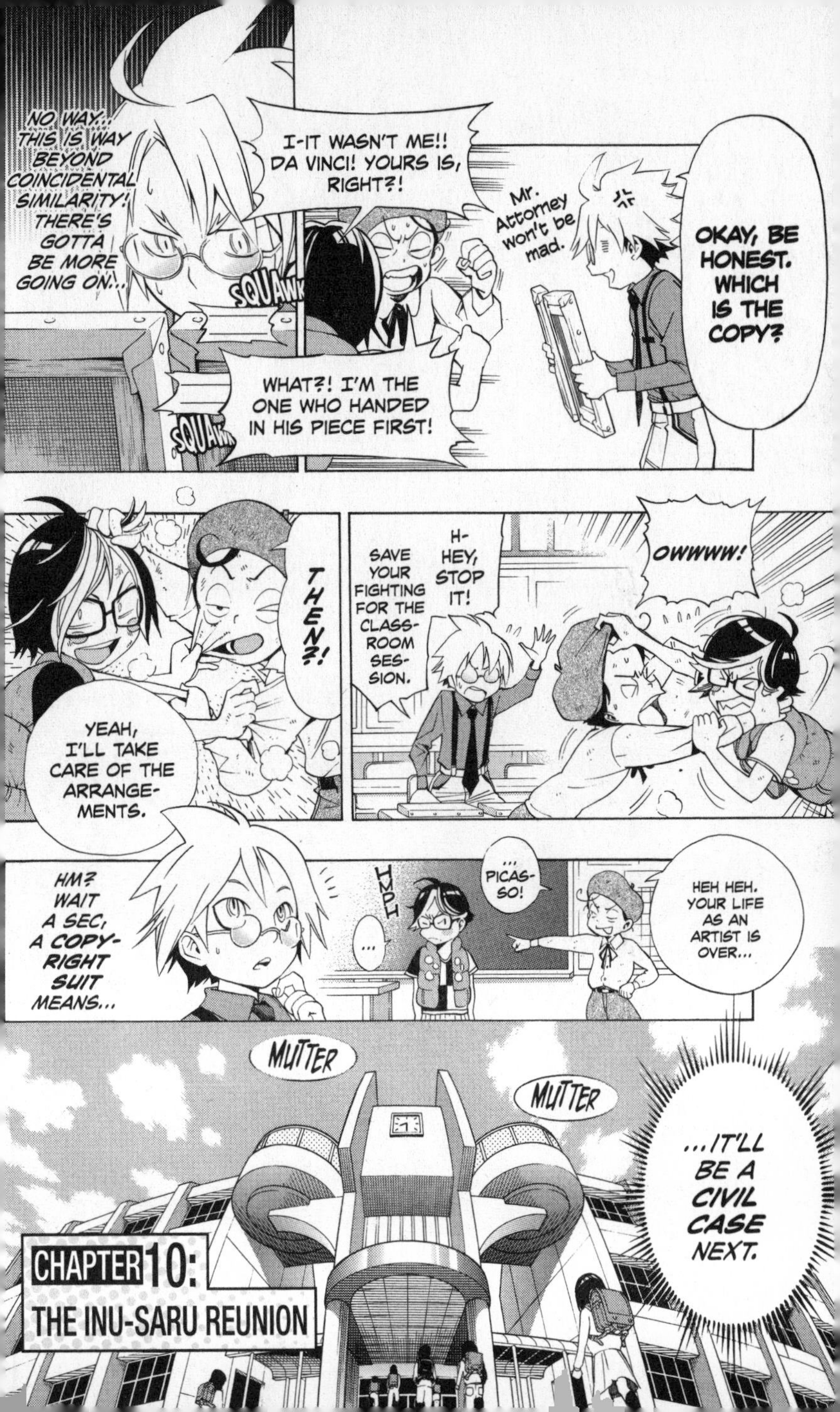

OKAY, BE HONEST. WHICH IS THE COPY?
Mr. Attorney won't be mad.
I-IT WASN'T ME!! DA VINCI! YOURS IS, RIGHT?!
NO WAY... THIS IS WAY BEYOND COINCIDENTAL SIMILARITY! THERE'S GOTTA BE MORE GOING ON...
SQUAWK
WHAT?! I'M THE ONE WHO HANDED IN HIS PIECE FIRST!
SQUAWK
OWWWW!
H-HEY, STOP IT!
SAVE YOUR FIGHTING FOR THE CLASS-ROOM SES-SION.
THEN?!
YEAH, I'LL TAKE CARE OF THE ARRANGE-MENTS.
HEH HEH. YOUR LIFE AS AN ARTIST IS OVER...
...PICAS-SO!
HMPH
...
HM? WAIT A SEC, A COPY-RIGHT SUIT MEANS...
MUTTER
MUTTER
...IT'LL BE A CIVIL CASE NEXT.
CHAPTER 10:
THE INU-SARU REUNION

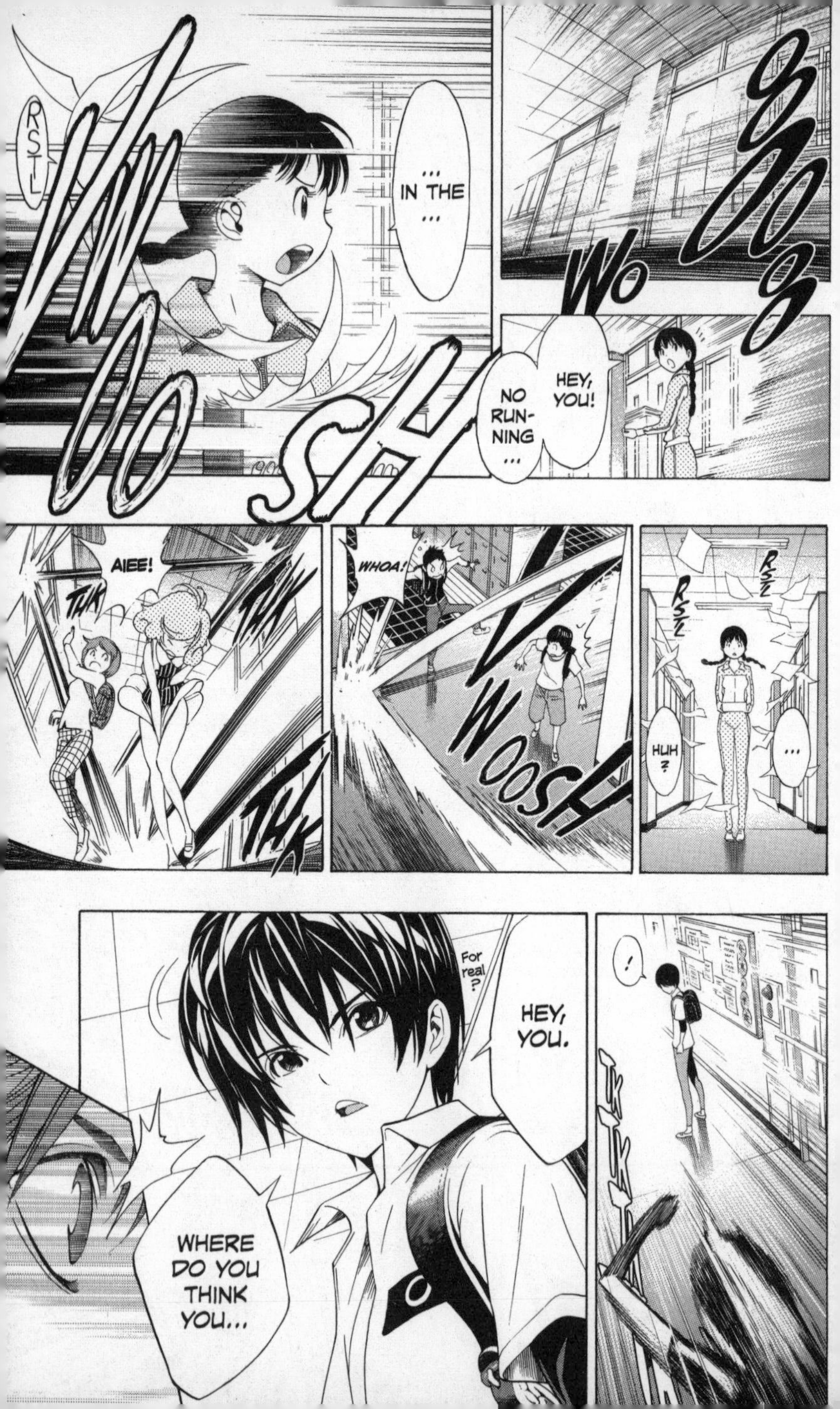
WOOOOO
HEY, YOU!
NO RUN-NING ...
... IN THE ...
RSTL
WHOOSH
RSTL
RSTL
HUH?
...
WHOA!
WOOSH
AIEE!
TAK
TAK
TAK
!
TK TK TK
For real?
HEY, YOU.
WHERE DO YOU THINK YOU...

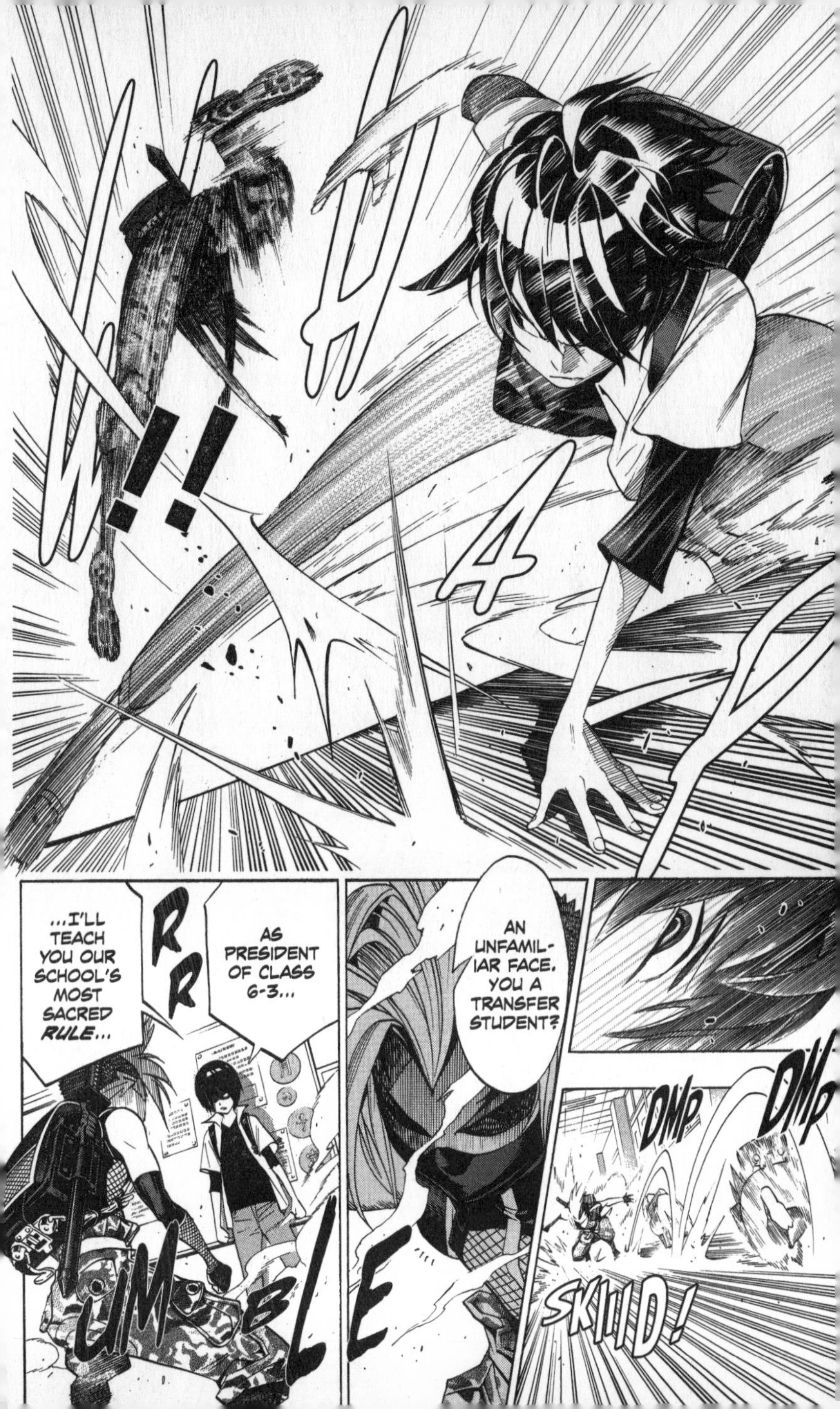
DMP
DMP
SKIIID!
AN UNFAMILIAR FACE. YOU A TRANSFER STUDENT?
AS PRESIDENT OF CLASS 6-3...
...I'LL TEACH YOU OUR SCHOOL'S MOST SACRED *RULE*...
RRUMBLE

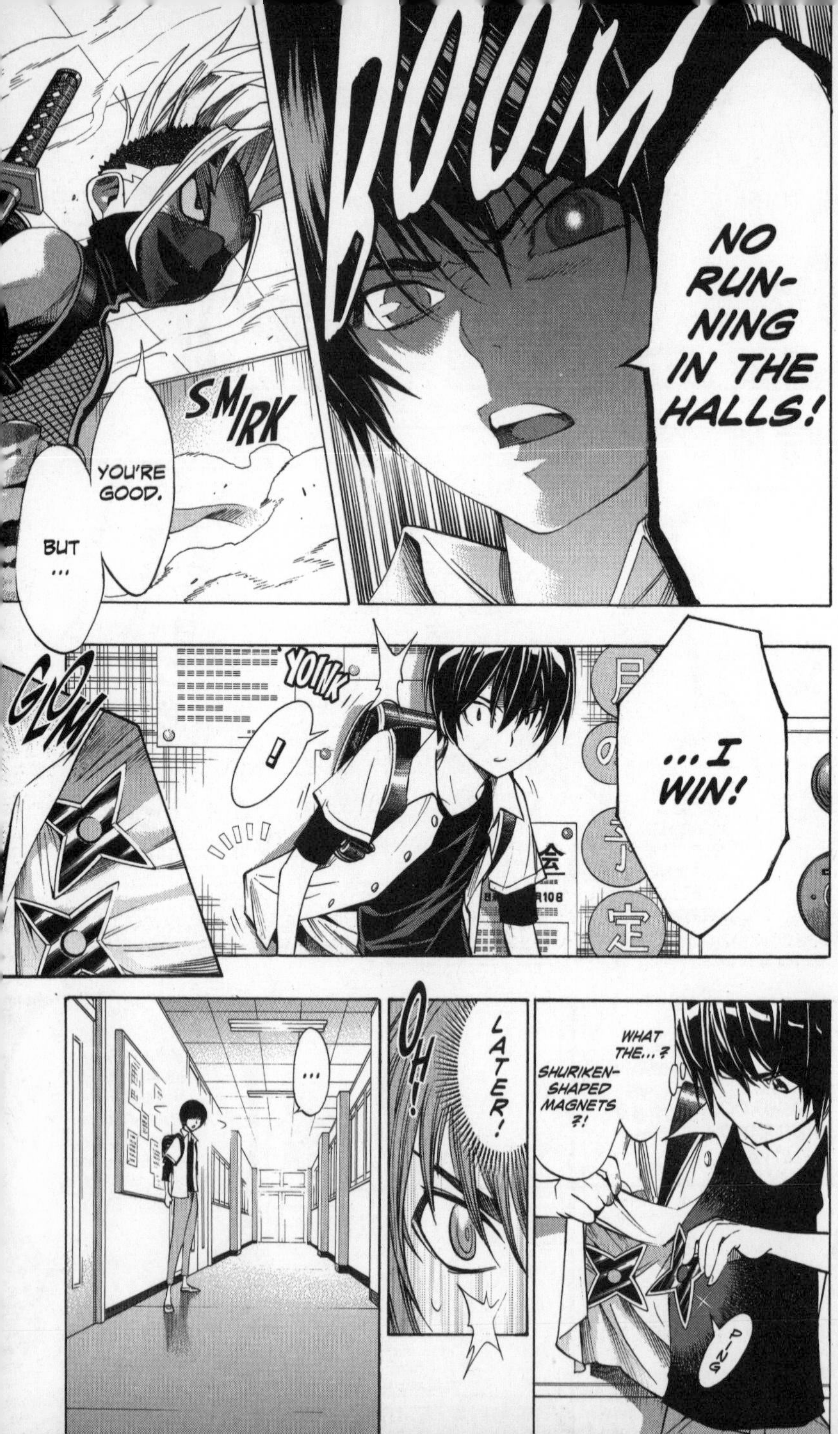
BOOM
NO RUNNING IN THE HALLS!
SMIRK
YOU'RE GOOD.
BUT ...
...I WIN!
YOINK
!
GLOM
WHAT THE...?
SHURIKEN-SHAPED MAGNETS?!
PING
OH!
LATER!
...

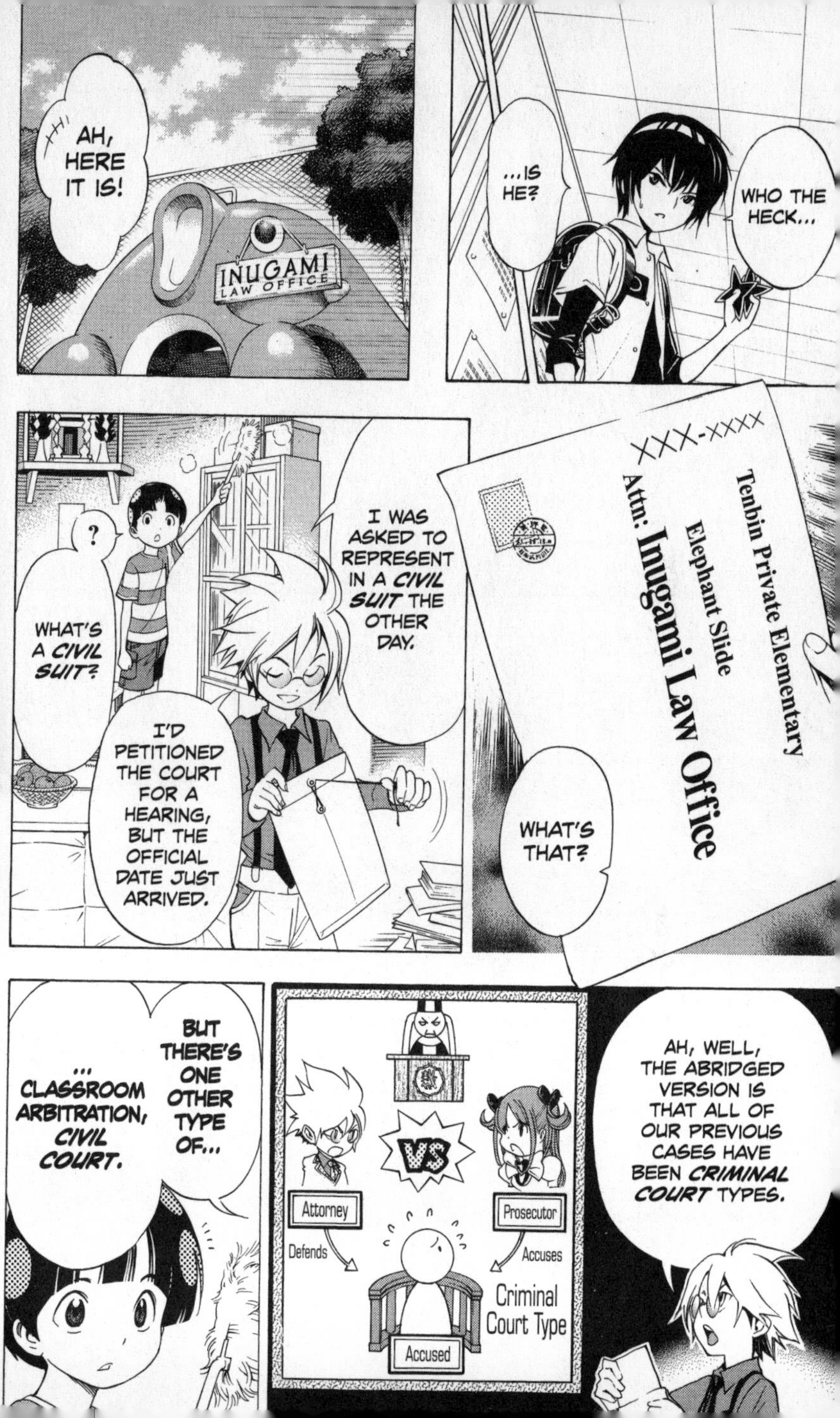
WHO THE HECK...
...IS HE?
AH, HERE IT IS!
INUGAMI LAW OFFICE
XXX-XXXX
Tenbin Private Elementary
Elephant Slide
Attn: Inugami Law Office
WHAT'S THAT?
I WAS ASKED TO REPRESENT IN A *CIVIL SUIT* THE OTHER DAY.
I'D PETITIONED THE COURT FOR A HEARING, BUT THE OFFICIAL DATE JUST ARRIVED.
?
WHAT'S A *CIVIL SUIT?*
AH, WELL, THE ABRIDGED VERSION IS THAT ALL OF OUR PREVIOUS CASES HAVE BEEN *CRIMINAL COURT* TYPES.
VS
Attorney
Prosecutor
Defends
Accuses
Criminal Court Type
Accused
BUT THERE'S ONE OTHER TYPE OF...
...CLASSROOM ARBITRATION, *CIVIL COURT.*

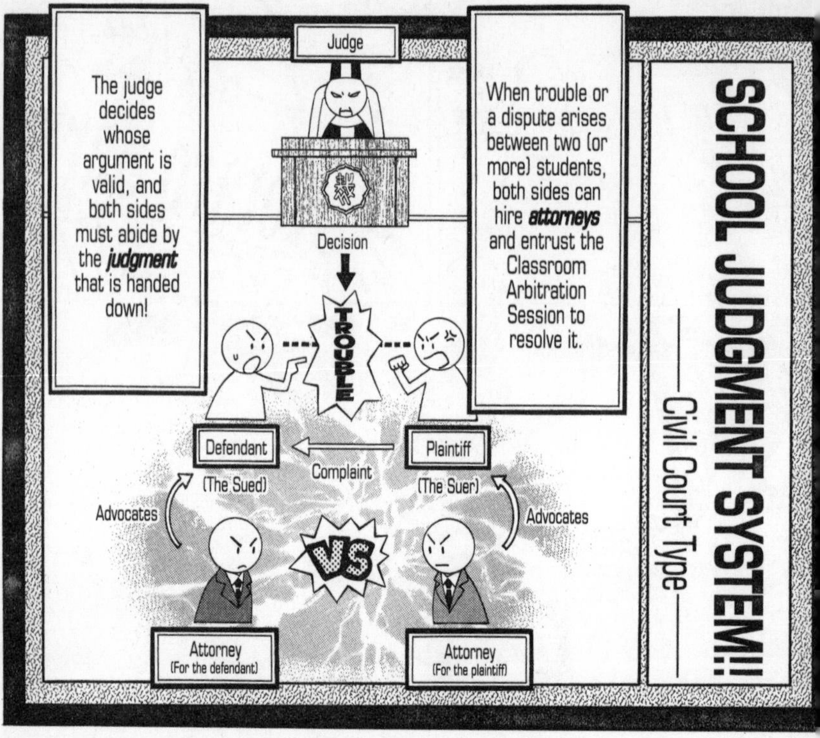
SCHOOL JUDGMENT SYSTEM!!!
—Civil Court Type—
When trouble or a dispute arises between two (or more) students, both sides can hire ***attorneys*** and entrust the Classroom Arbitration Session to resolve it.
Judge
The judge decides whose argument is valid, and both sides must abide by the ***judgment*** that is handed down!
Decision
TROUBLE
Plaintiff
(The Suer)
Complaint
Defendant
(The Sued)
Advocates
Advocates
VS
Attorney (For the plaintiff)
Attorney (For the defendant)

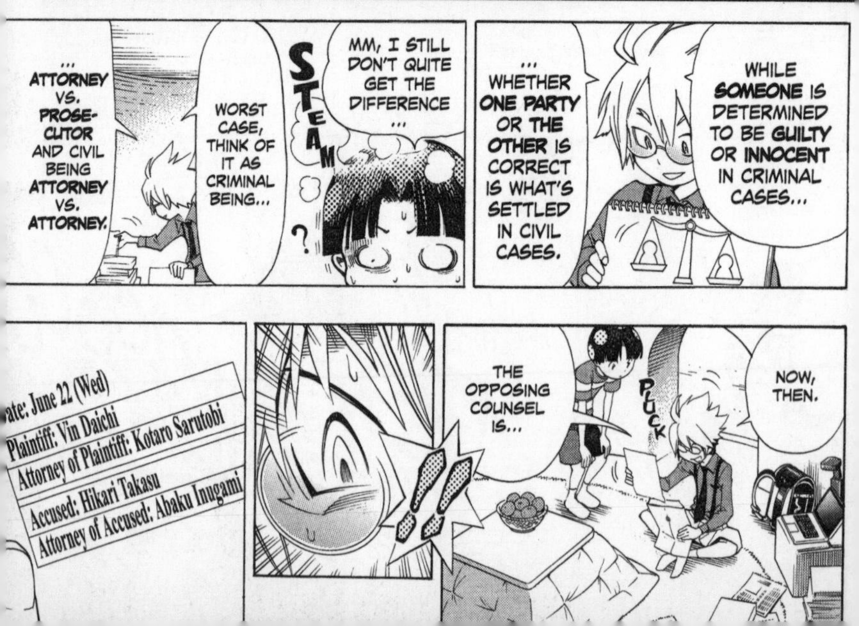
WHILE SOMEONE IS DETERMINED TO BE GUILTY OR INNOCENT IN CRIMINAL CASES...
...WHETHER ONE PARTY OR THE OTHER IS CORRECT IS WHAT'S SETTLED IN CIVIL CASES.
MM, I STILL DON'T QUITE GET THE DIFFERENCE...
STEAM
WORST CASE, THINK OF IT AS CRIMINAL BEING...
...ATTORNEY VS. PROSECUTOR AND CIVIL BEING ATTORNEY VS. ATTORNEY.
NOW, THEN.
PLUCK
THE OPPOSING COUNSEL IS...
!!
ate: June 22 (Wed)
Plaintiff: Vin Daichi
Attorney of Plaintiff: Kotaro Sarutobi
Accused: Hikari Takasu
Attorney of Accused: Abaku Inugami

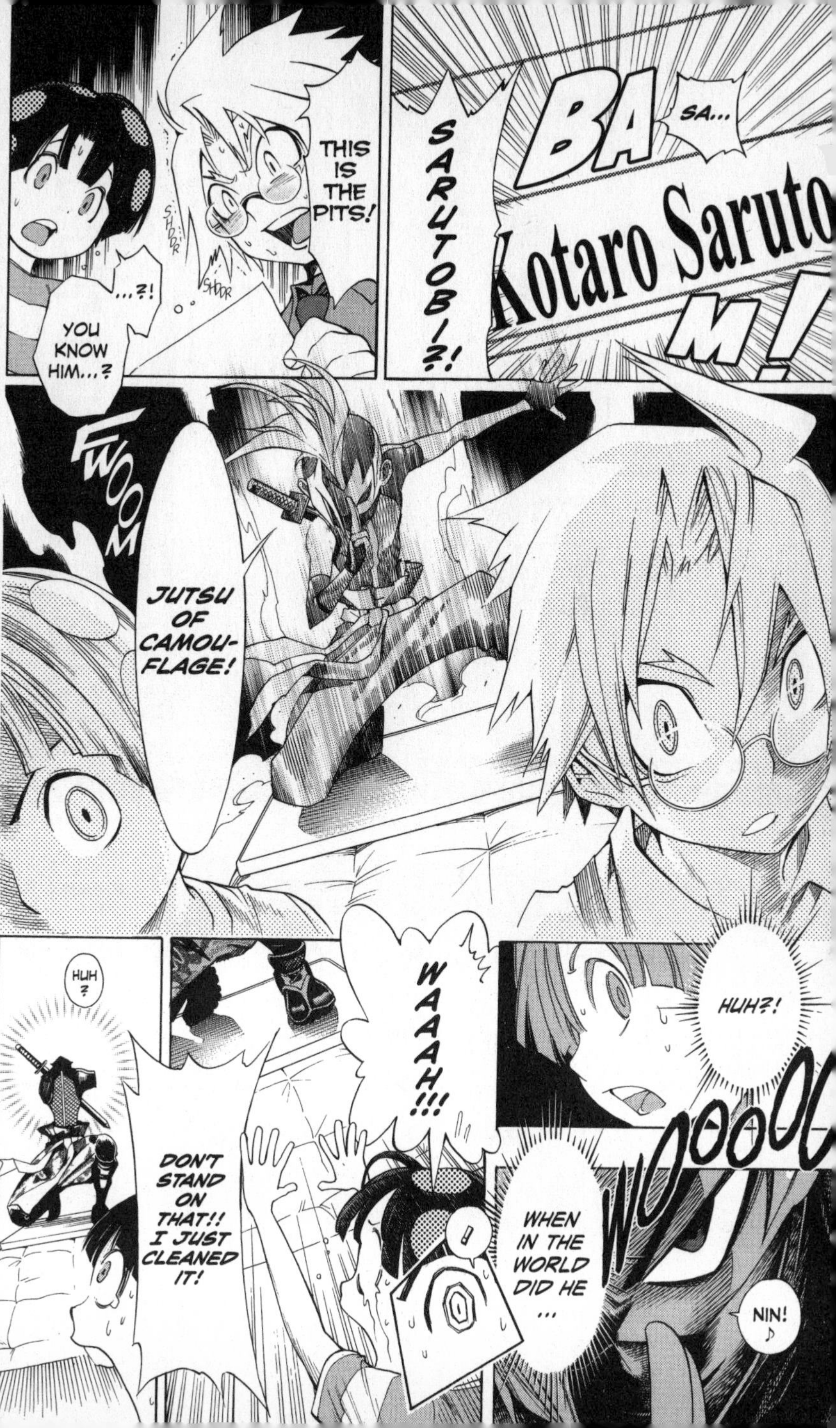
SA...
BA
Kotaro Saruto
M!
SARUTOBI?!
THIS IS THE PITS!
SHDDR
SHDDR
...?!
YOU KNOW HIM...?
FWOOM
JUTSU OF CAMOUFLAGE!
HUH?!
WOOOOO
WHEN IN THE WORLD DID HE ...
NIN! ♪
WAAAAH!!!
!
HUH?
DON'T STAND ON THAT!! I JUST CLEANED IT!

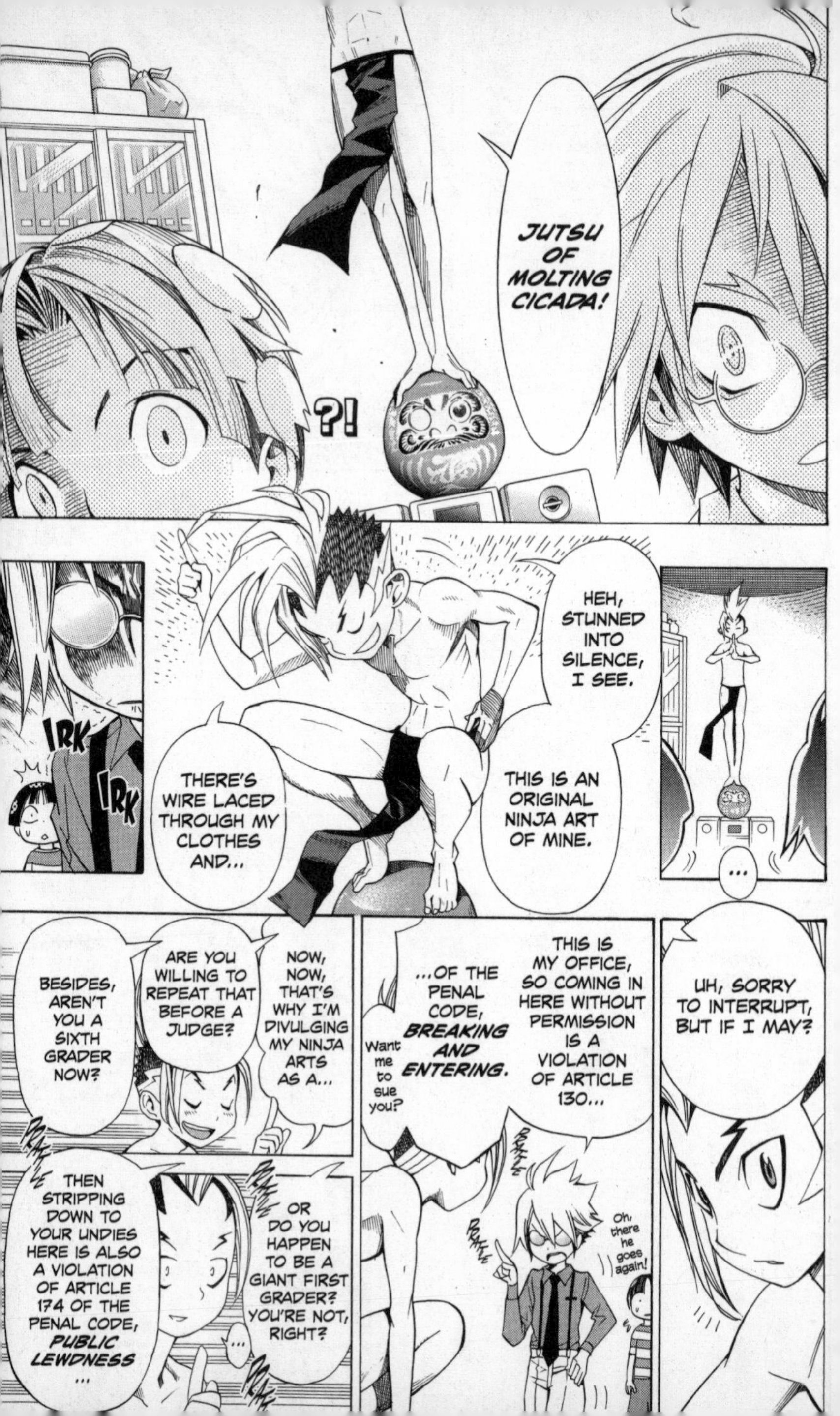
JUTSU OF MOLTING CICADA!
?!
...
HEH, STUNNED INTO SILENCE, I SEE.
THIS IS AN ORIGINAL NINJA ART OF MINE.
THERE'S WIRE LACED THROUGH MY CLOTHES AND...
IRK
IRK
UH, SORRY TO INTERRUPT, BUT IF I MAY?
THIS IS MY OFFICE, SO COMING IN HERE WITHOUT PERMISSION IS A VIOLATION OF ARTICLE 130...
...OF THE PENAL CODE, BREAKING AND ENTERING.
Want me to sue you?
Oh, there he goes again!
NOW, NOW, THAT'S WHY I'M DIVULGING MY NINJA ARTS AS A...
ARE YOU WILLING TO REPEAT THAT BEFORE A JUDGE?
BESIDES, AREN'T YOU A SIXTH GRADER NOW?
OR DO YOU HAPPEN TO BE A GIANT FIRST GRADER? YOU'RE NOT, RIGHT?
THEN STRIPPING DOWN TO YOUR UNDIES HERE IS ALSO A VIOLATION OF ARTICLE 174 OF THE PENAL CODE, PUBLIC LEWDNESS...
...

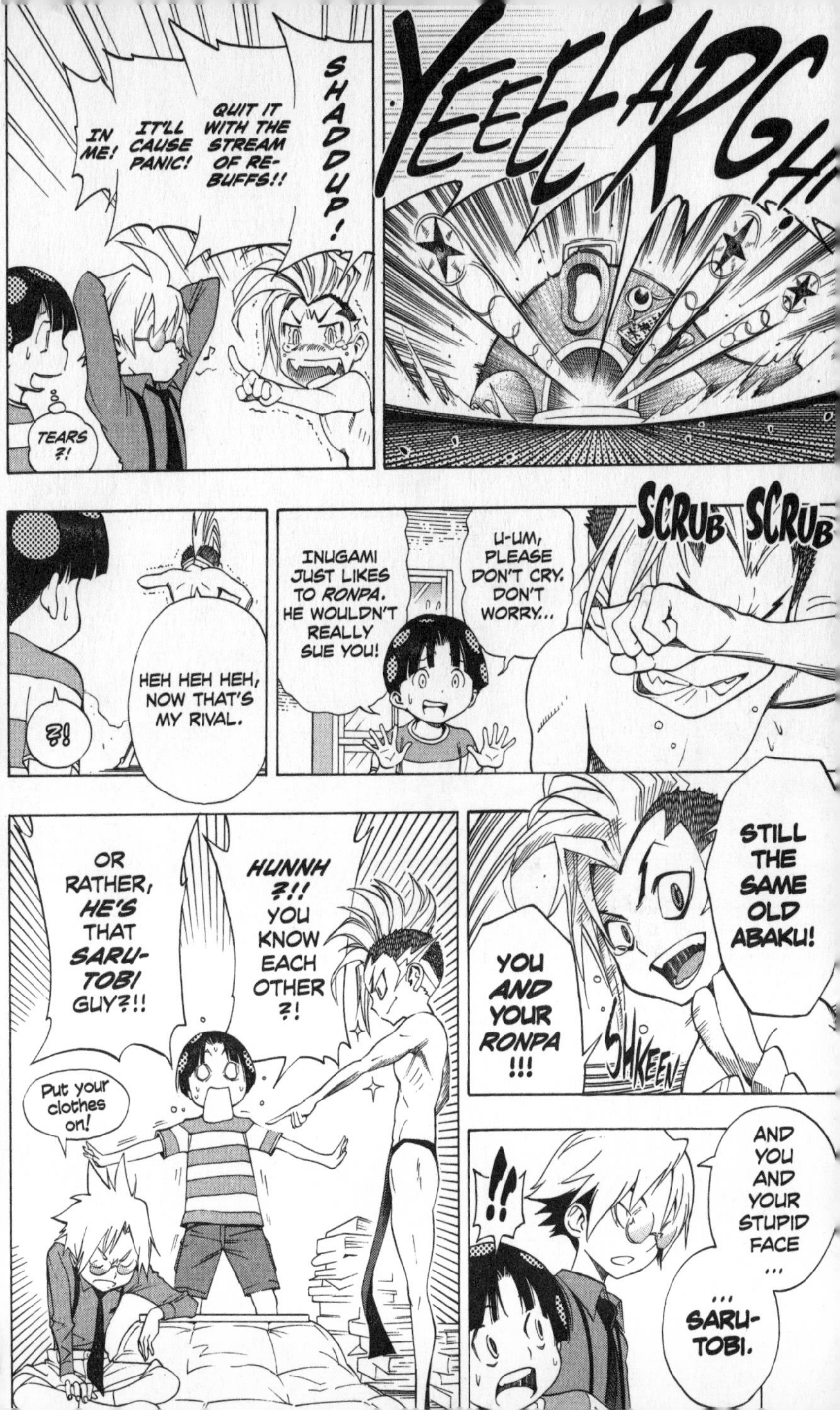

YEEEARGH!!
SHADDUP!
QUIT IT WITH THE STREAM OF RE-BUFFS!!
IT'LL CAUSE PANIC!
IN ME!
TEARS ?!
SCRUB SCRUB
U-UM, PLEASE DON'T CRY. DON'T WORRY...
INUGAMI JUST LIKES TO RONPA. HE WOULDN'T REALLY SUE YOU!
HEH HEH HEH, NOW THAT'S MY RIVAL.
?!
STILL THE SAME OLD ABAKU!
YOU AND YOUR RONPA!!!
SHKEEN
AND YOU AND YOUR STUPID FACE ...
... SARU-TOBI.
!!
HUNNH ?!! YOU KNOW EACH OTHER ?!
OR RATHER, HE'S THAT SARU-TOBI GUY?!!
Put your clothes on!

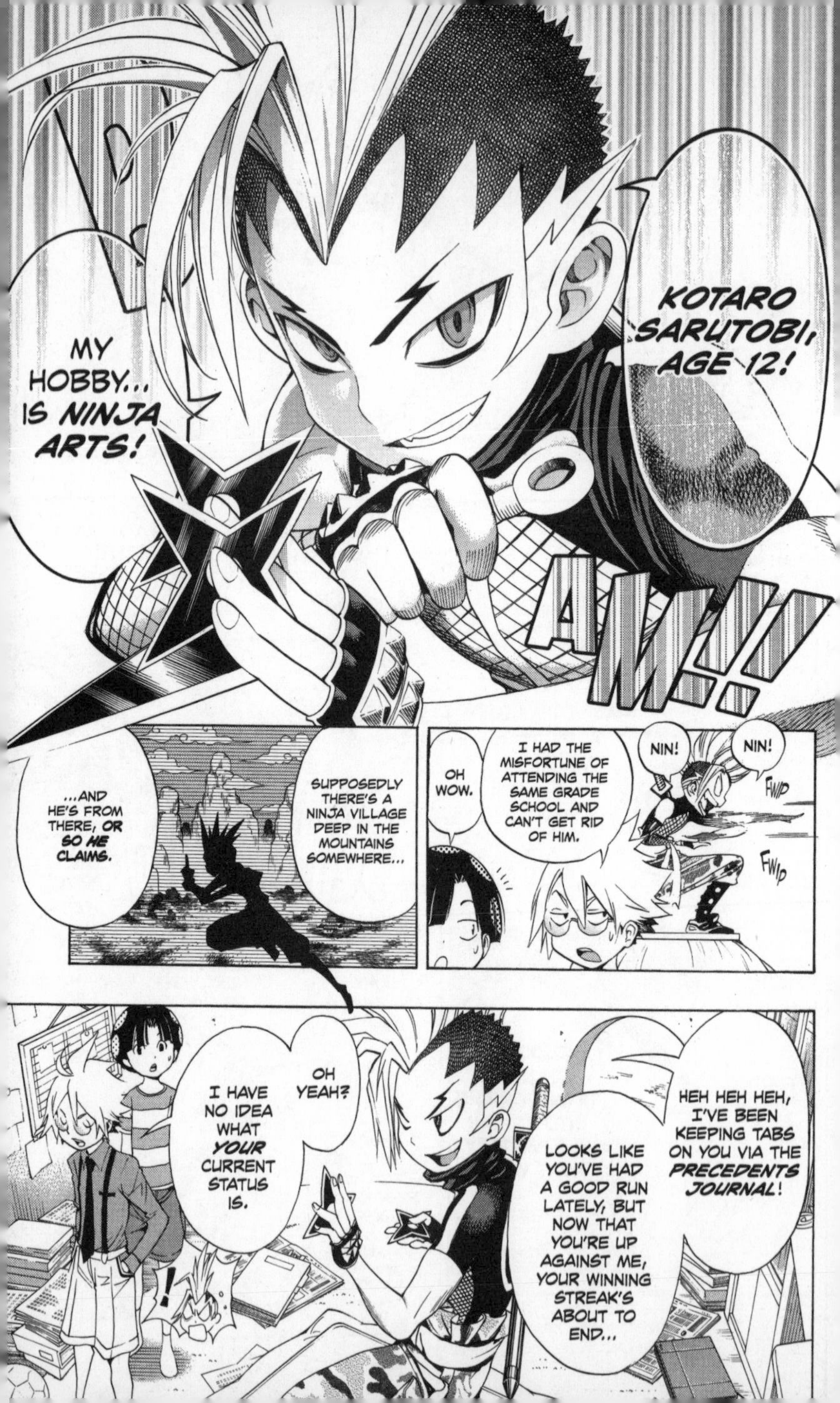
KOTARO SARUTOBI, AGE 12!
AM!!
MY HOBBY... IS NINJA ARTS!
NIN!
NIN!
FWIP
FWIP
I HAD THE MISFORTUNE OF ATTENDING THE SAME GRADE SCHOOL AND CAN'T GET RID OF HIM.
OH WOW.
SUPPOSEDLY THERE'S A NINJA VILLAGE DEEP IN THE MOUNTAINS SOMEWHERE...
...AND HE'S FROM THERE, OR SO HE CLAIMS.
HEH HEH HEH, I'VE BEEN KEEPING TABS ON YOU VIA THE PRECEDENTS JOURNAL!
LOOKS LIKE YOU'VE HAD A GOOD RUN LATELY, BUT NOW THAT YOU'RE UP AGAINST ME, YOUR WINNING STREAK'S ABOUT TO END...
!
OH YEAH?
I HAVE NO IDEA WHAT YOUR CURRENT STATUS IS.

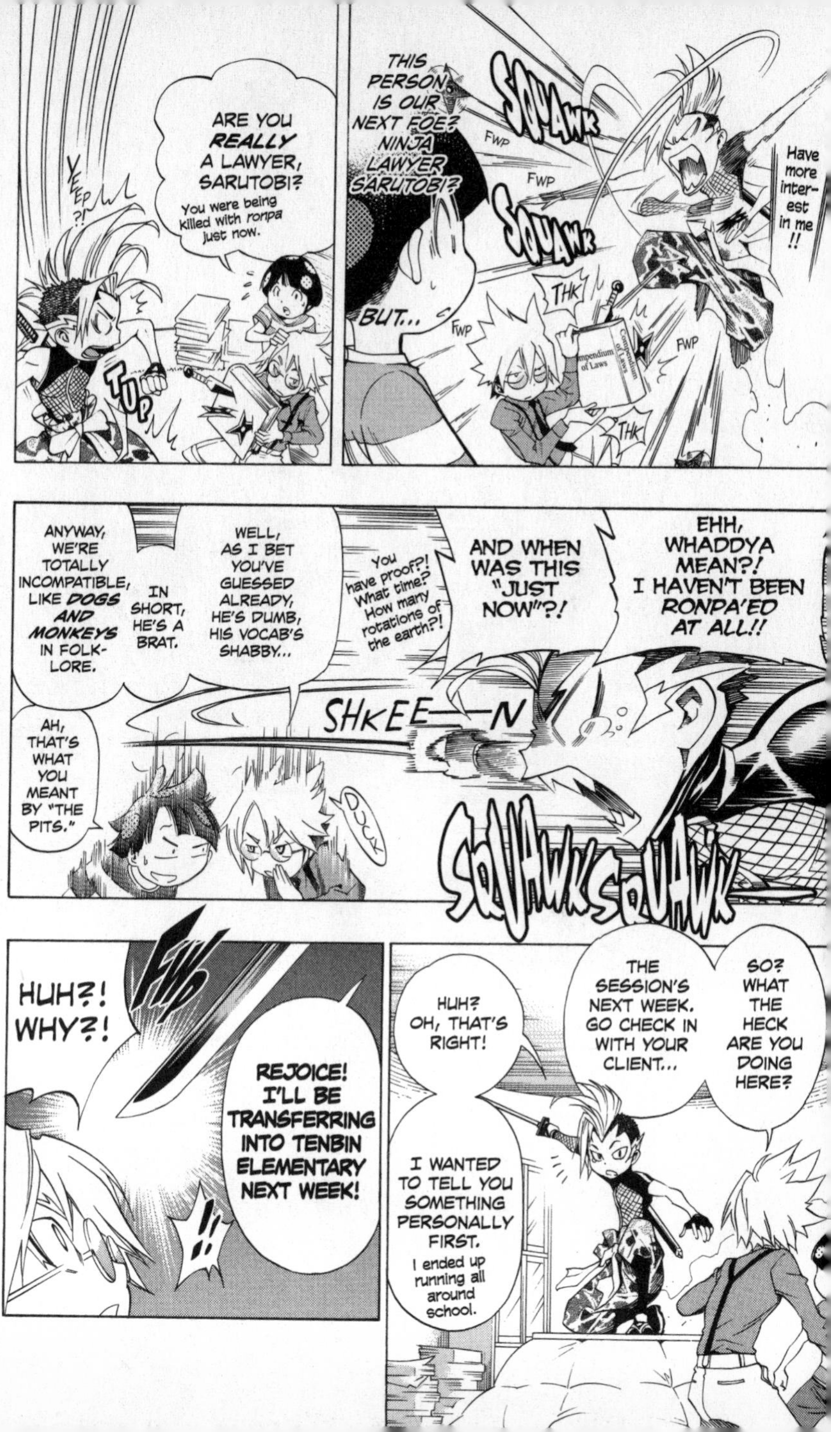
Have more interest in me!!
SQUAWK
SQUAWK
FWP
FWP
THIS PERSON IS OUR NEXT FOE? NINJA LAWYER SARUTOBI?
THK
FWP
Compendium of Laws
FWP
THK
BUT...
ARE YOU ***REALLY*** A LAWYER, SARUTOBI?
You were being killed with *ronpa* just now.
YEEP?!
TUP
EHH, WHADDYA MEAN?! I HAVEN'T BEEN *RONPA'ED* AT ALL!!
AND WHEN WAS THIS "JUST NOW"?!
You have proof?! What time? How many rotations of the earth?!
SHKEE—N
WELL, AS I BET YOU'VE GUESSED ALREADY, HE'S DUMB, HIS VOCAB'S SHABBY...
IN SHORT, HE'S A BRAT.
ANYWAY, WE'RE TOTALLY INCOMPATIBLE, LIKE ***DOGS AND MONKEYS*** IN FOLKLORE.
SQUAWK SQUAWK
DUCK
AH, THAT'S WHAT YOU MEANT BY "THE PITS."
SO? WHAT THE HECK ARE YOU DOING HERE?
THE SESSION'S NEXT WEEK. GO CHECK IN WITH YOUR CLIENT...
HUH? OH, THAT'S RIGHT!
I WANTED TO TELL YOU SOMETHING PERSONALLY FIRST.
I ended up running all around school.
FWP
REJOICE! I'LL BE TRANSFERRING INTO TENBIN ELEMENTARY NEXT WEEK!
HUH?! WHY?!
!!

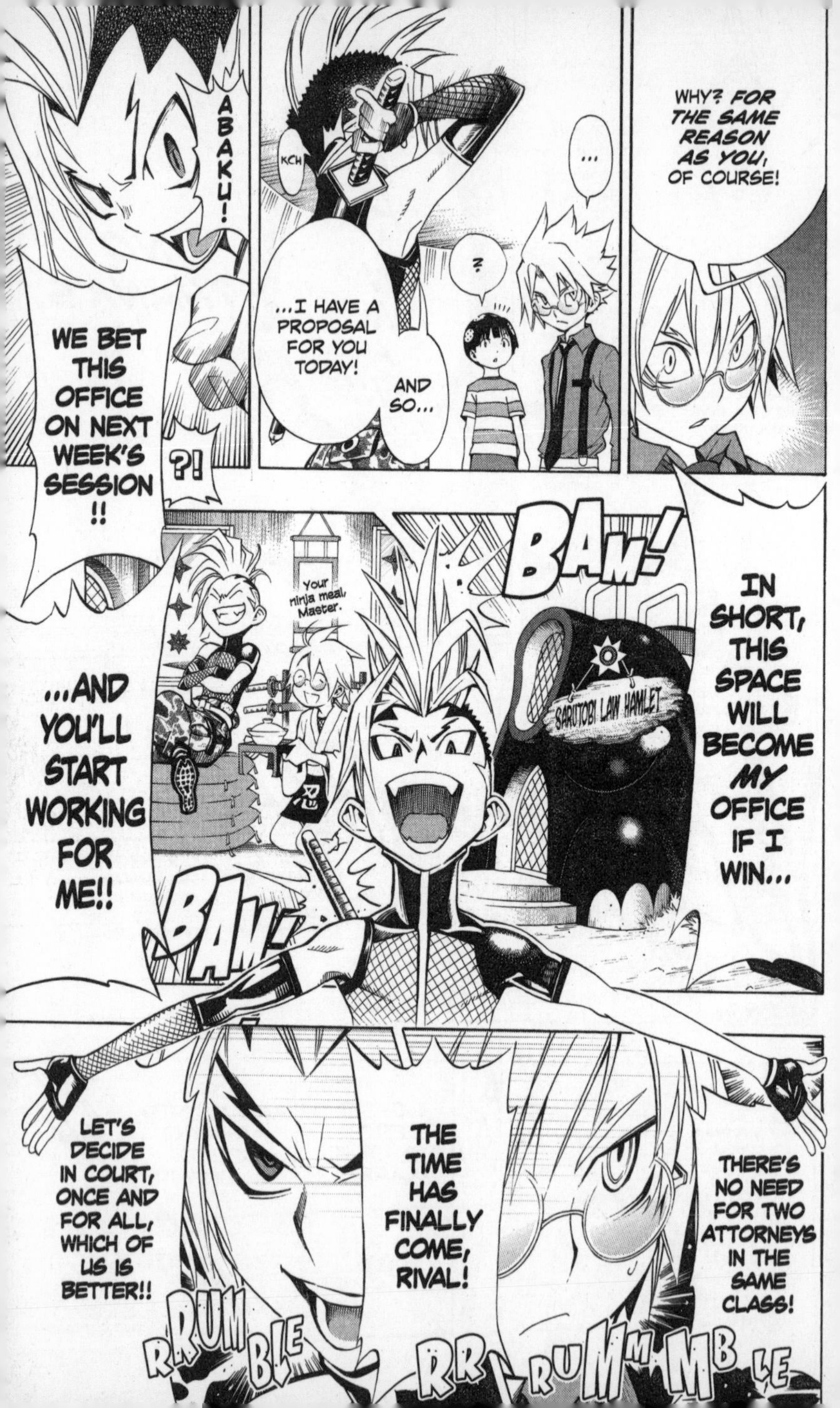
WHY? FOR THE SAME REASON AS YOU, OF COURSE!
...
?
KCH
AND SO...
...I HAVE A PROPOSAL FOR YOU TODAY!
ABAKU!
?!
WE BET THIS OFFICE ON NEXT WEEK'S SESSION!!
IN SHORT, THIS SPACE WILL BECOME MY OFFICE IF I WIN...
BAM!
SARUTOBI LAW HAMLET
Your ninja meal, Master.
...AND YOU'LL START WORKING FOR ME!!
BAM!
THERE'S NO NEED FOR TWO ATTORNEYS IN THE SAME CLASS!
THE TIME HAS FINALLY COME, RIVAL!
LET'S DECIDE IN COURT, ONCE AND FOR ALL, WHICH OF US IS BETTER!!
RR-RUMMMMBLE
RRUMBLE

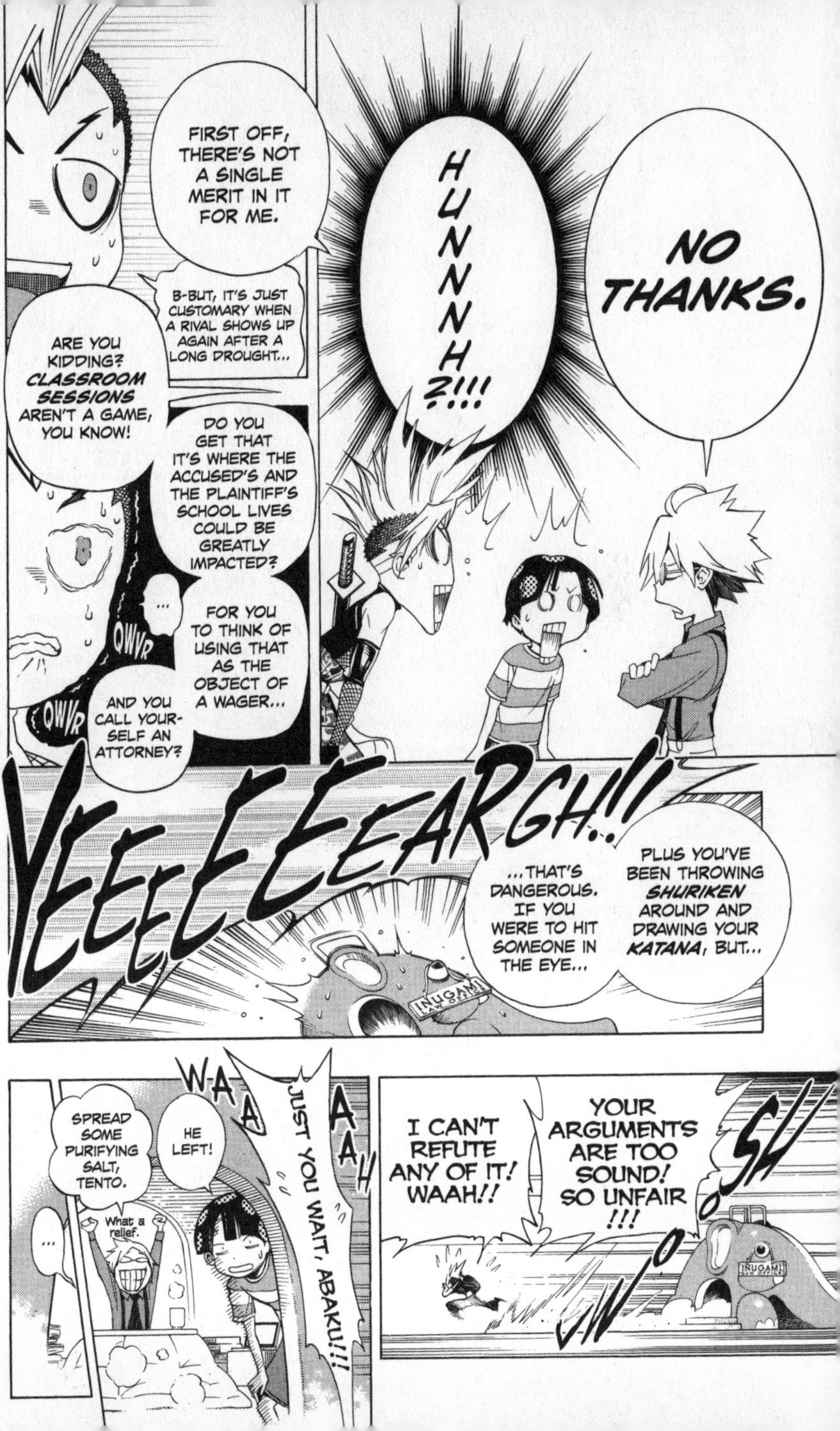
NO THANKS.
HUNNNNH?!!!
FIRST OFF, THERE'S NOT A SINGLE MERIT IN IT FOR ME.
B-BUT, IT'S JUST CUSTOMARY WHEN A RIVAL SHOWS UP AGAIN AFTER A LONG DROUGHT...
ARE YOU KIDDING? *CLASSROOM SESSIONS* AREN'T A GAME, YOU KNOW!
DO YOU GET THAT IT'S WHERE THE ACCUSED'S AND THE PLAINTIFF'S SCHOOL LIVES COULD BE GREATLY IMPACTED?
...
FOR YOU TO THINK OF USING THAT AS THE OBJECT OF A WAGER...
AND YOU CALL YOURSELF AN ATTORNEY?
QWVR
QWVR
YEEEEEEARGH!!
PLUS YOU'VE BEEN THROWING *SHURIKEN* AROUND AND DRAWING YOUR *KATANA*, BUT...
...THAT'S DANGEROUS. IF YOU WERE TO HIT SOMEONE IN THE EYE...
INUGAMI LAW OFFICE
YOUR ARGUMENTS ARE TOO SOUND! SO UNFAIR!!!
I CAN'T REFUTE ANY OF IT! WAAH!!
WHOOSH
INUGAMI
WAAAAH
JUST YOU WAIT, ABAKU!!!
HE LEFT!
SPREAD SOME PURIFYING SALT, TENTO.
What a relief.
...

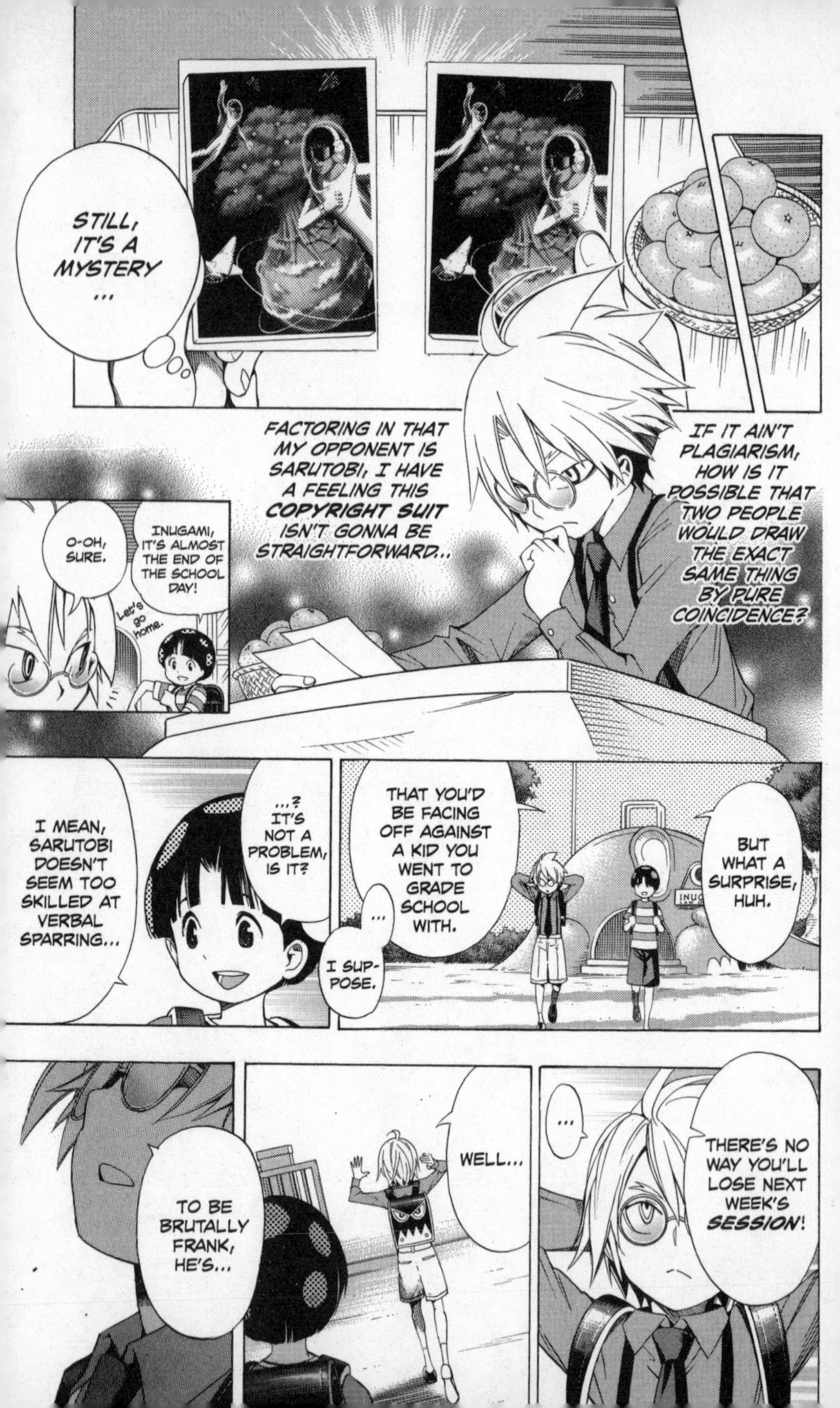
STILL, IT'S A MYSTERY ...
IF IT AIN'T PLAGIARISM, HOW IS IT POSSIBLE THAT TWO PEOPLE WOULD DRAW THE EXACT SAME THING BY PURE COINCIDENCE?
FACTORING IN THAT MY OPPONENT IS SARUTOBI, I HAVE A FEELING THIS COPYRIGHT SUIT ISN'T GONNA BE STRAIGHTFORWARD...
INUGAMI, IT'S ALMOST THE END OF THE SCHOOL DAY!
Let's go home.
O-OH, SURE.
BUT WHAT A SURPRISE, HUH.
THAT YOU'D BE FACING OFF AGAINST A KID YOU WENT TO GRADE SCHOOL WITH.
...
I SUP-POSE.
...? IT'S NOT A PROBLEM, IS IT?
I MEAN, SARUTOBI DOESN'T SEEM TOO SKILLED AT VERBAL SPARRING...
...
THERE'S NO WAY YOU'LL LOSE NEXT WEEK'S SESSION!
WELL...
TO BE BRUTALLY FRANK, HE'S...

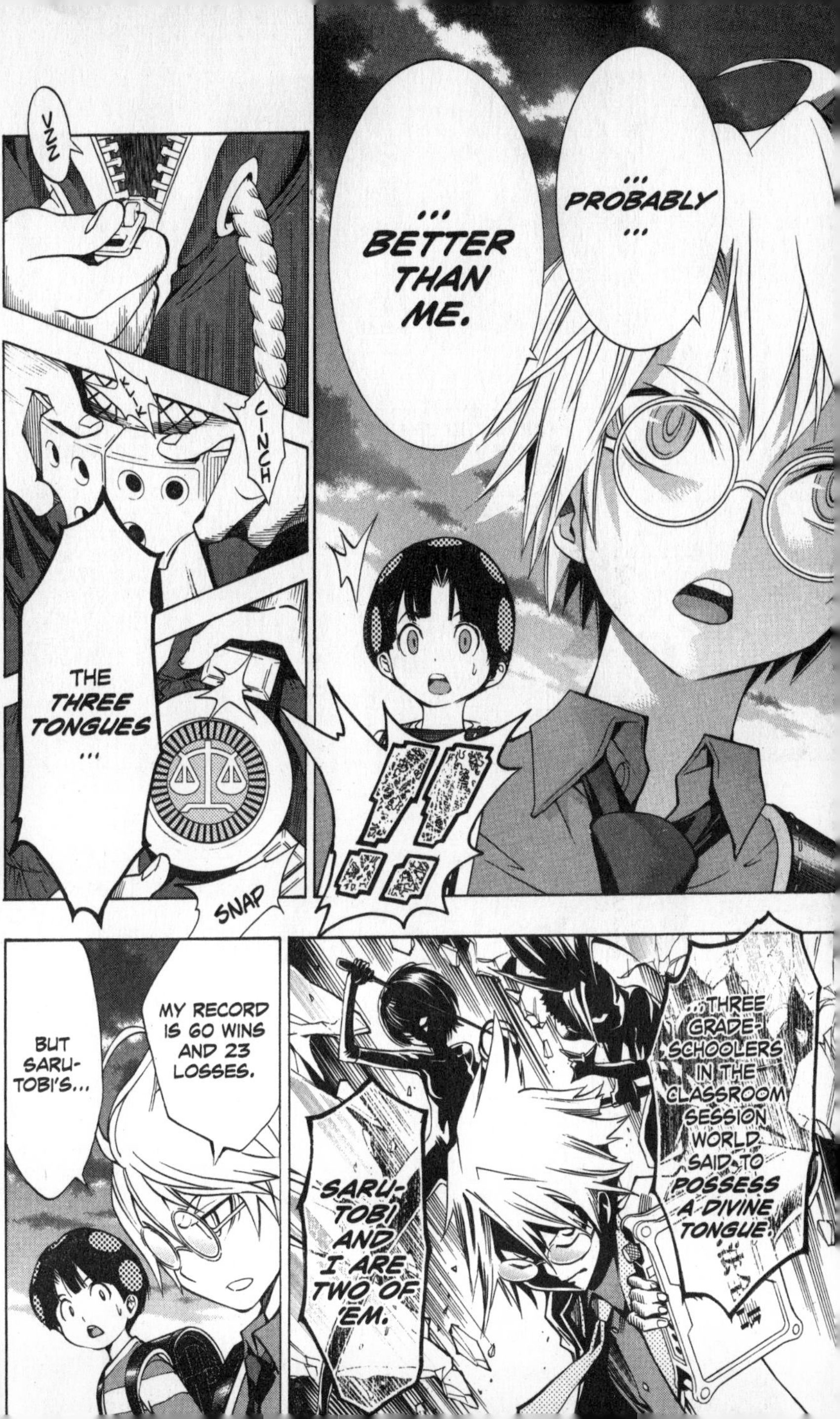
...PROBABLY...
...BETTER THAN ME.
VZZ
CINCH
THE THREE TONGUES...
SNAP
...THREE GRADE-SCHOOLERS IN THE CLASSROOM SESSION WORLD SAID TO POSSESS A DIVINE TONGUE.
SARUTOBI AND I ARE TWO OF 'EM.
MY RECORD IS 60 WINS AND 23 LOSSES.
BUT SARUTOBI'S...

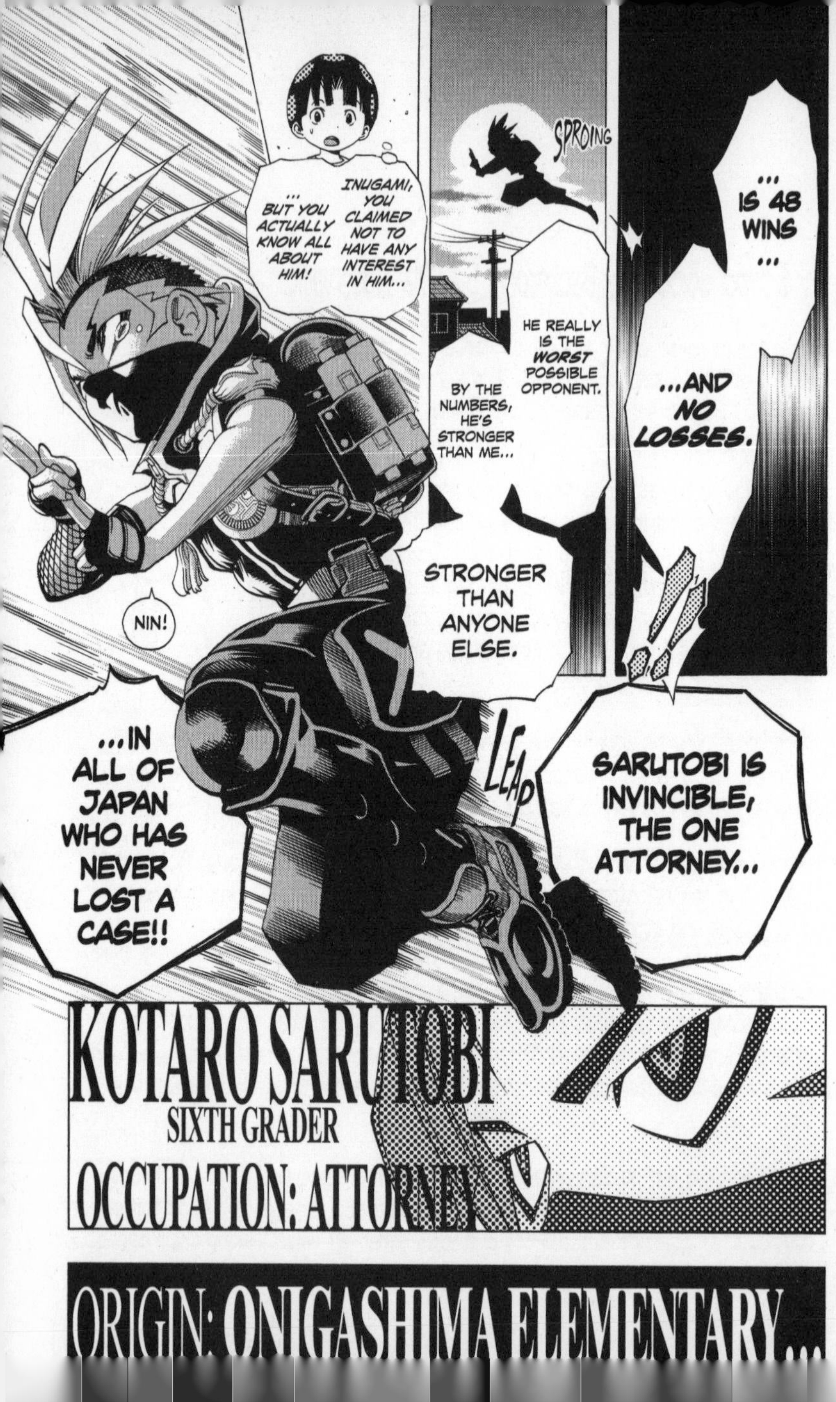
... IS 48 WINS ...
...AND NO LOSSES.
SPROING
HE REALLY IS THE WORST POSSIBLE OPPONENT.
BY THE NUMBERS, HE'S STRONGER THAN ME...
INUGAMI, YOU CLAIMED NOT TO HAVE ANY INTEREST IN HIM...
... BUT YOU ACTUALLY KNOW ALL ABOUT HIM!
SARUTOBI IS INVINCIBLE, THE ONE ATTORNEY...
STRONGER THAN ANYONE ELSE.
LEAP
NIN!
...IN ALL OF JAPAN WHO HAS NEVER LOST A CASE!!
KOTARO SARUTOBI
SIXTH GRADER
OCCUPATION: ATTORNEY
ORIGIN: ONIGASHIMA ELEMENTARY...

School Judgment Backstory ⑤ "Trial Observation"

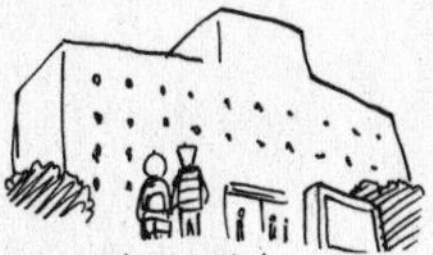

This comes up briefly in the next chapter, but anyone can go watch a trial whenever they want to. (Though, if it's a popular trial, there may be a lottery to get in...) Before serialization, I, along with my editor, actually did go to observe a real trial for research.

When you arrive at a courthouse, you receive a ticket at the entrance and have your bag checked before going inside. Then, prior to being admitted into the courtroom, you check your bag(s) and are patted down by security. This thorough inspection is to make sure no one brings anything dangerous into the courtroom.

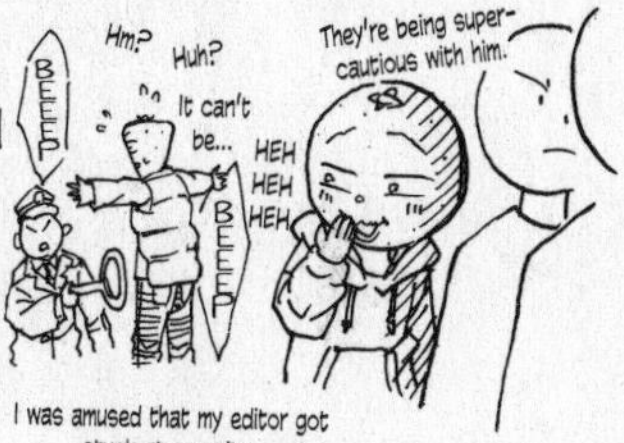
They're being super-cautious with him.
HEH HEH HEH
Hm?
Huh?
It can't be...
BEEEP
BEEEP
I was amused that my editor got stuck at security.

After that, you sit down in the gallery, wait a few minutes...and then the defense attorney(s), prosecutor(s) and accused file in. Then the trial finally begins. (What I observed was a criminal trial.)

Because there was an actual person involved, I can't mention specifics, but just like in television dramas and movies, a war of words unfolded between the prosecutor and attorney, occasionally getting quite heated.

Furthermore, it was interesting how the attorney and prosecutor each had a distinct personality. What I saw was "a young, logic-driven prosecutor vs. a veteran, empathetic attorney." I think that trials would be really fun if you went just to see the different personalities of various attorneys and prosecutors over time.

However, that well-known phrase from television dramas and games, "Objection!" was not used at all. Basically, both the defense and prosecution took turns stating their opinions and did not cut each other off when making their cases...

⇦ Continued on p. 86

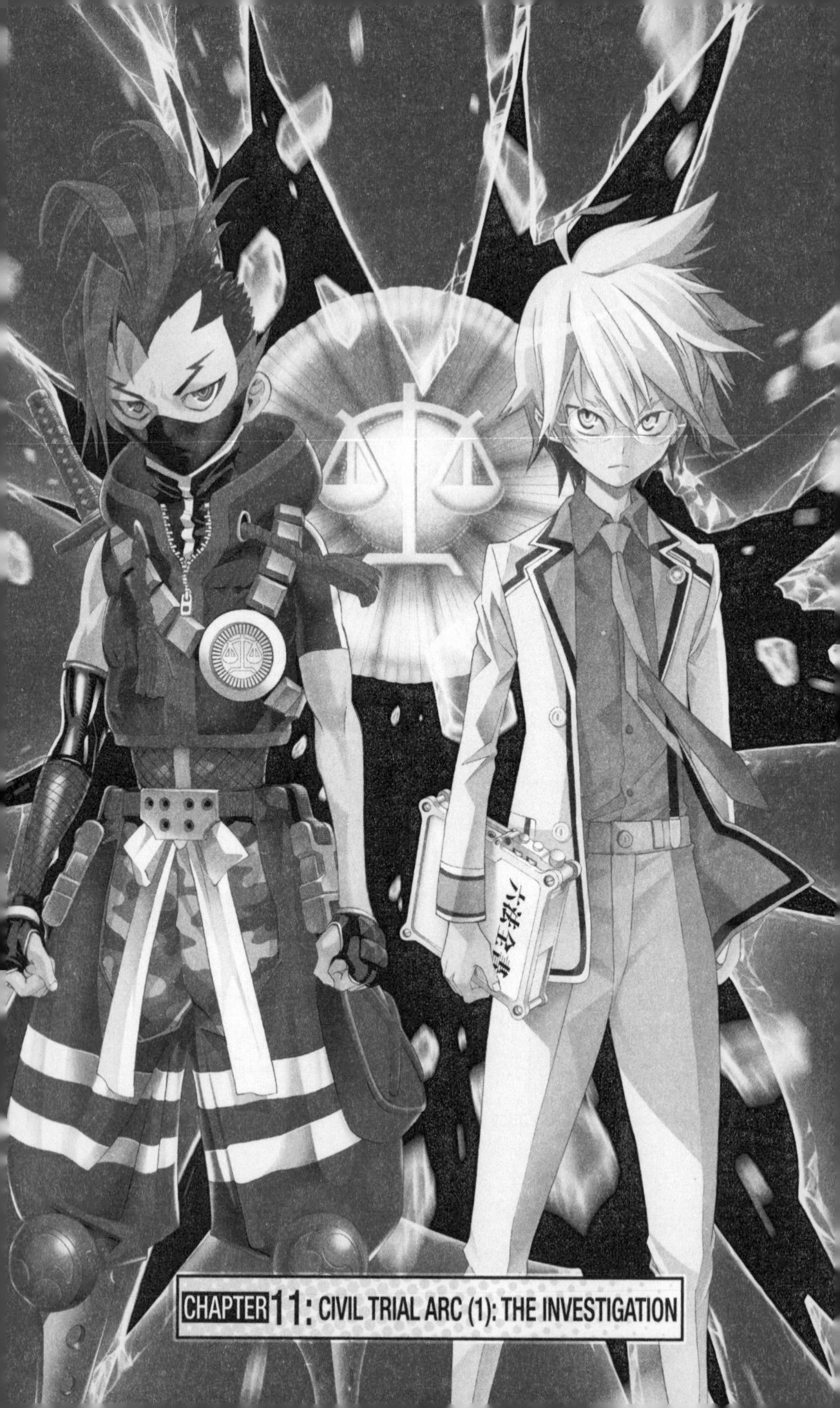
CHAPTER 11: CIVIL TRIAL ARC (1): THE INVESTIGATION

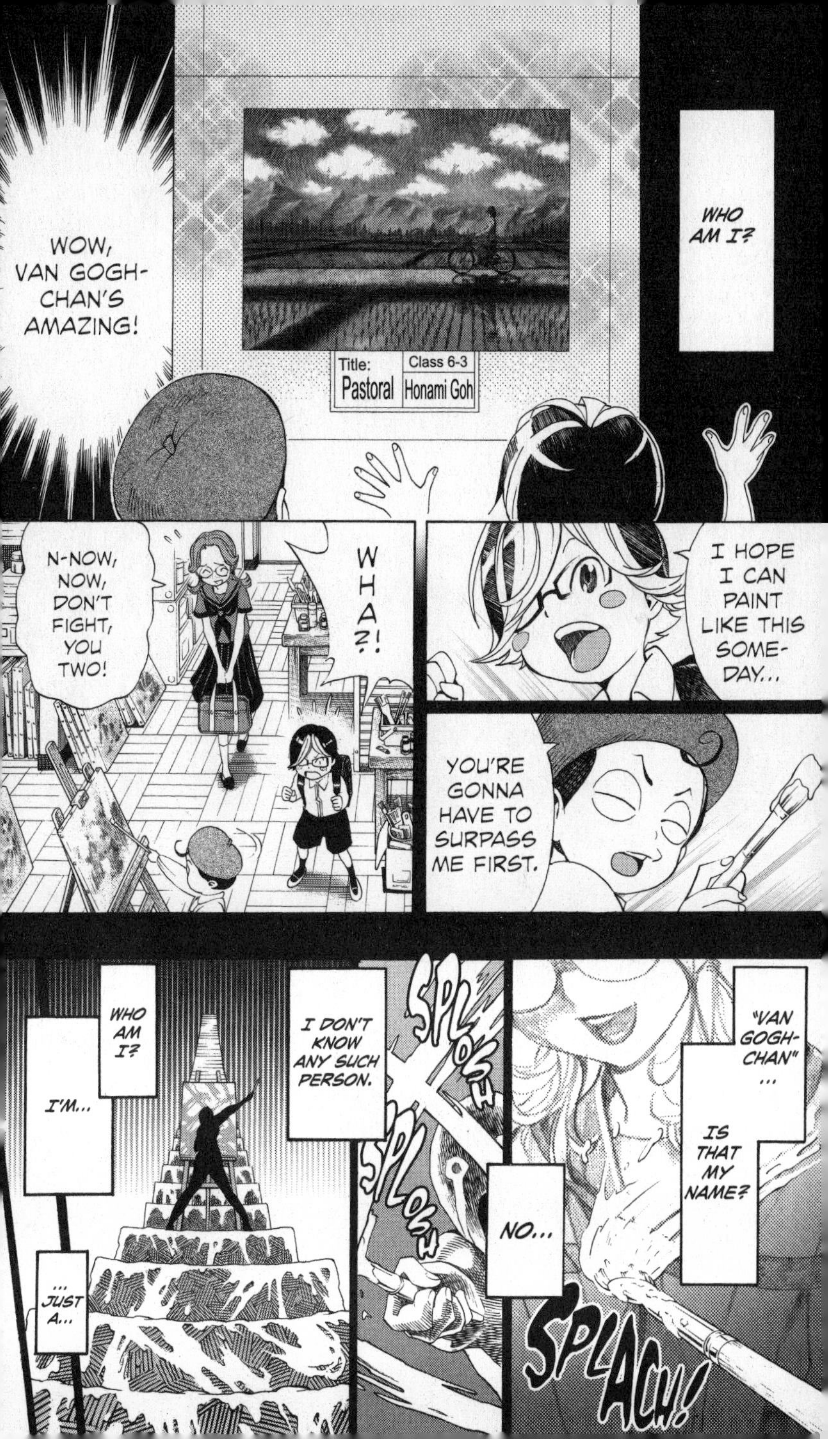
WHO AM I?
Title: Pastoral
Class 6-3
Honami Goh
WOW, VAN GOGH-CHAN'S AMAZING!
I HOPE I CAN PAINT LIKE THIS SOMEDAY...
YOU'RE GONNA HAVE TO SURPASS ME FIRST.
WHA?!
N-NOW, NOW, DON'T FIGHT, YOU TWO!
"VAN GOGH-CHAN"...
IS THAT MY NAME?
NO...
SPLACH!
SPLOSH
SPLOSH
I DON'T KNOW ANY SUCH PERSON.
WHO AM I?
I'M...
...JUST A...

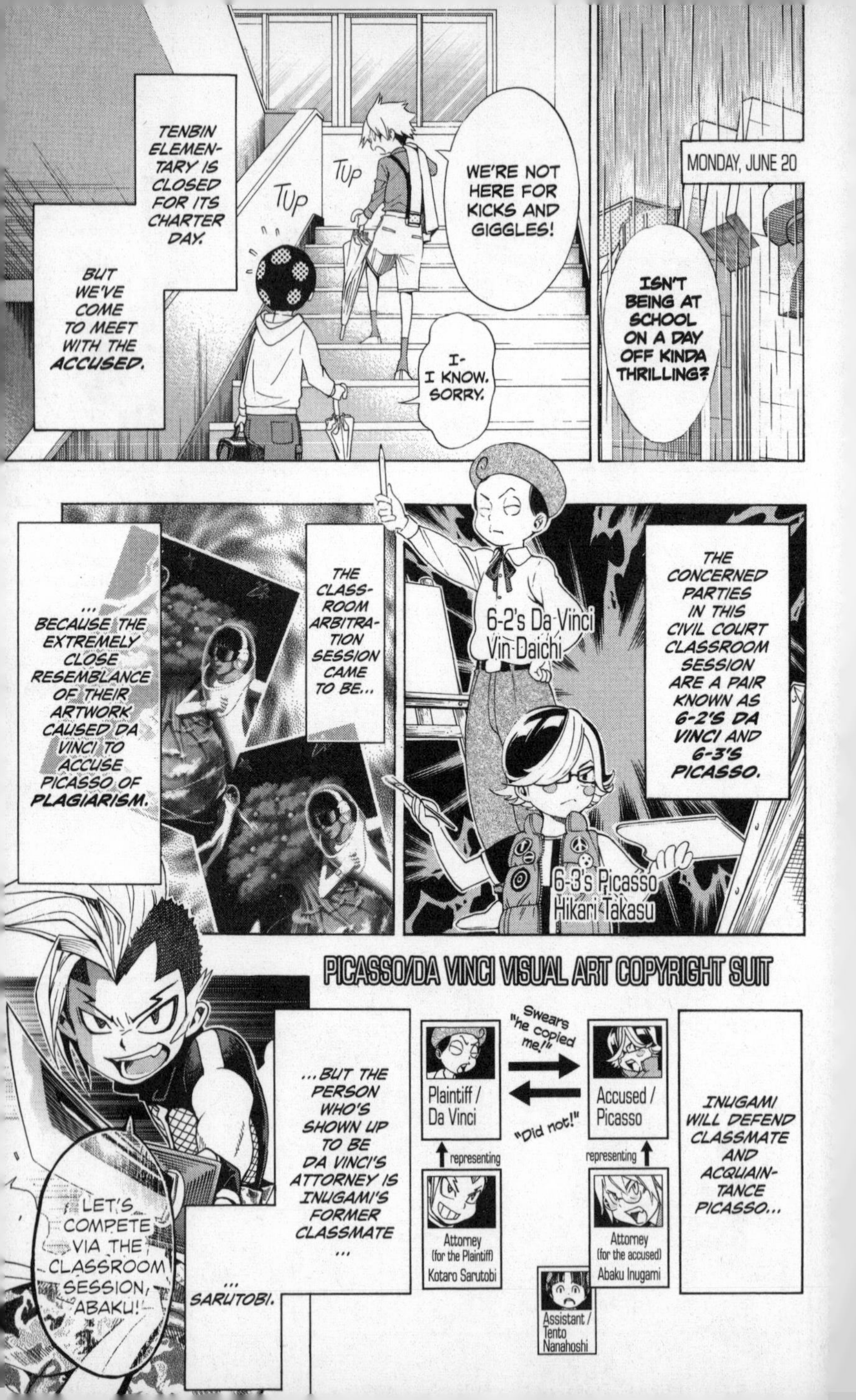
MONDAY, JUNE 20
ISN'T BEING AT SCHOOL ON A DAY OFF KINDA THRILLING?
WE'RE NOT HERE FOR KICKS AND GIGGLES!
I- I KNOW. SORRY.
TUP
TUP
TENBIN ELEMENTARY IS CLOSED FOR ITS CHARTER DAY.
BUT WE'VE COME TO MEET WITH THE ACCUSED.
THE CONCERNED PARTIES IN THIS CIVIL COURT CLASSROOM SESSION ARE A PAIR KNOWN AS 6-2'S DA VINCI AND 6-3'S PICASSO.
6-2's Da Vinci Vin Daichi
6-3's Picasso Hikari Takasu
THE CLASSROOM ARBITRATION SESSION CAME TO BE...
...BECAUSE THE EXTREMELY CLOSE RESEMBLANCE OF THEIR ARTWORK CAUSED DA VINCI TO ACCUSE PICASSO OF PLAGIARISM.
PICASSO/DA VINCI VISUAL ART COPYRIGHT SUIT
INUGAMI WILL DEFEND CLASSMATE AND ACQUAINTANCE PICASSO...
Accused / Picasso
Swears "he copied me!"
"Did not!"
Plaintiff / Da Vinci
representing
Attorney (for the accused) Abaku Inugami
representing
Attorney (for the Plaintiff) Kotaro Sarutobi
Assistant / Tento Nanahoshi
...BUT THE PERSON WHO'S SHOWN UP TO BE DA VINCI'S ATTORNEY IS INUGAMI'S FORMER CLASSMATE...
...SARUTOBI.
LET'S COMPETE VIA THE CLASSROOM SESSION, ABAKU!

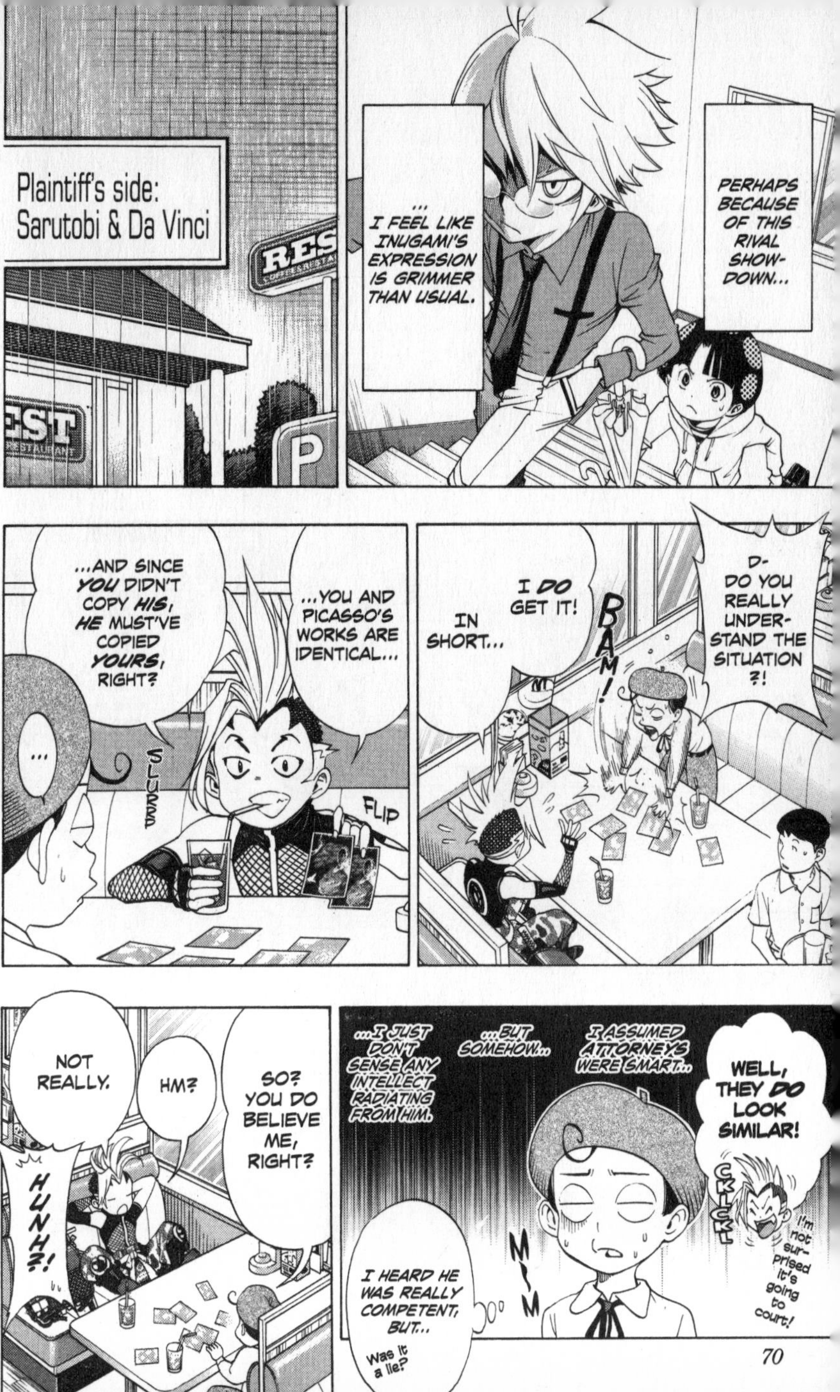
PERHAPS BECAUSE OF THIS RIVAL SHOW-DOWN...
... I FEEL LIKE INUGAMI'S EXPRESSION IS GRIMMER THAN USUAL.
Plaintiff's side: Sarutobi & Da Vinci
REST
REST
P
D- DO YOU REALLY UNDER-STAND THE SITUATION ?!
BAM!
I DO GET IT!
IN SHORT...
...YOU AND PICASSO'S WORKS ARE IDENTICAL...
...AND SINCE YOU DIDN'T COPY HIS, HE MUST'VE COPIED YOURS, RIGHT?
FLIP
SLURRP
...
I ASSUMED ATTORNEYS WERE SMART...
...BUT SOMEHOW...
...I JUST DON'T SENSE ANY INTELLECT RADIATING FROM HIM.
WELL, THEY DO LOOK SIMILAR!
I'm not surprised it's going to court!
I HEARD HE WAS REALLY COMPETENT, BUT...
Was it a lie?
SO? YOU DO BELIEVE ME, RIGHT?
HM?
NOT REALLY.
HUNH?!

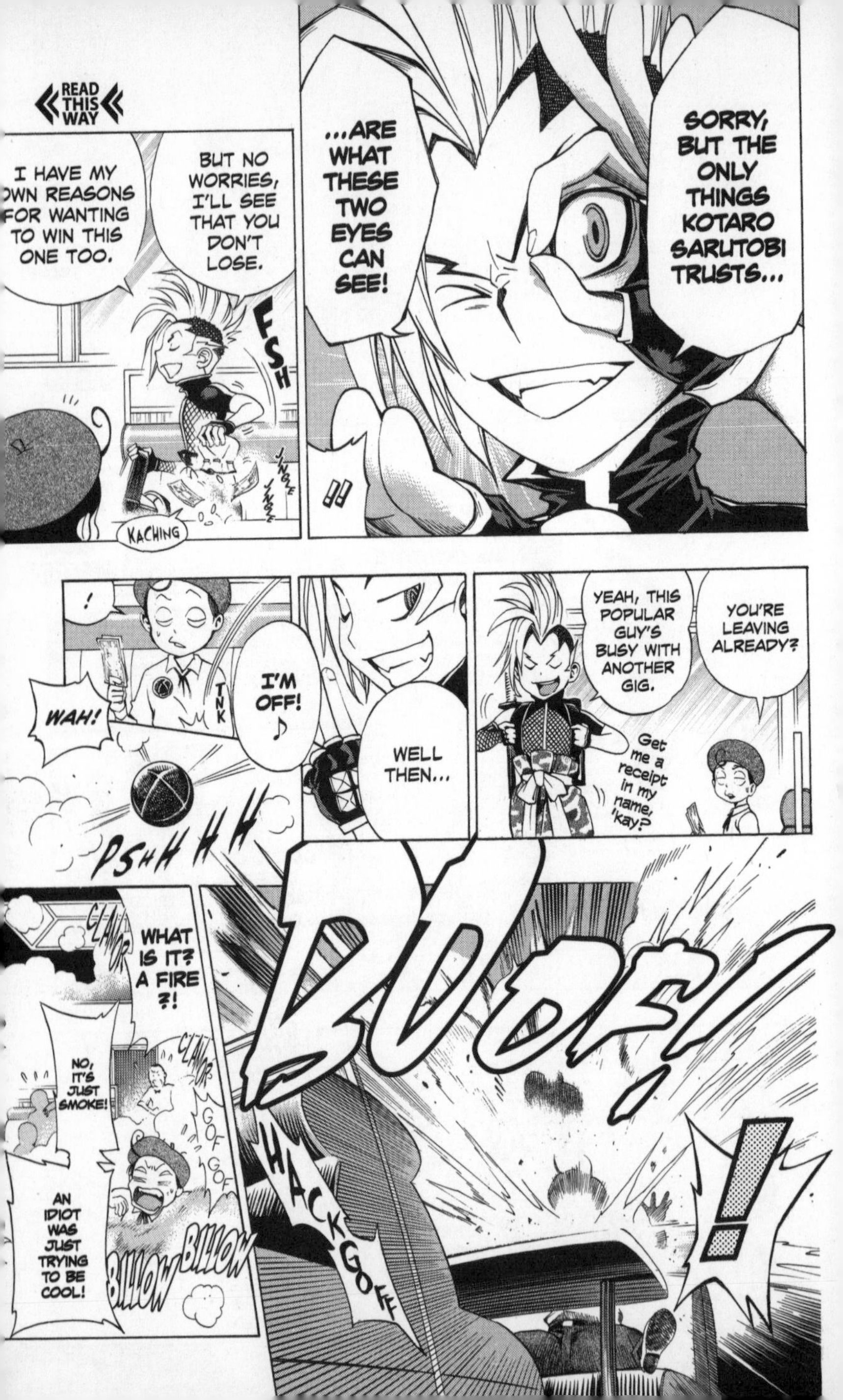
READ THIS WAY
SORRY, BUT THE ONLY THINGS KOTARO SARUTOBI TRUSTS...
...ARE WHAT THESE TWO EYES CAN SEE!
!!
BUT NO WORRIES, I'LL SEE THAT YOU DON'T LOSE.
I HAVE MY OWN REASONS FOR WANTING TO WIN THIS ONE TOO.
FSH
JINGLE JINGLE
KACHING
YOU'RE LEAVING ALREADY?
YEAH, THIS POPULAR GUY'S BUSY WITH ANOTHER GIG.
Get me a receipt in my name, 'kay?
WELL THEN...
I'M OFF! ♪
!
TNK
WAH!
PSHHHH
BOOF!
HACK GOFF
!
WHAT IS IT? A FIRE?!
CLAMOR
NO, IT'S JUST SMOKE!
CLAMOR
GOF GOF
AN IDIOT WAS JUST TRYING TO BE COOL!
BILLOW BILLOW

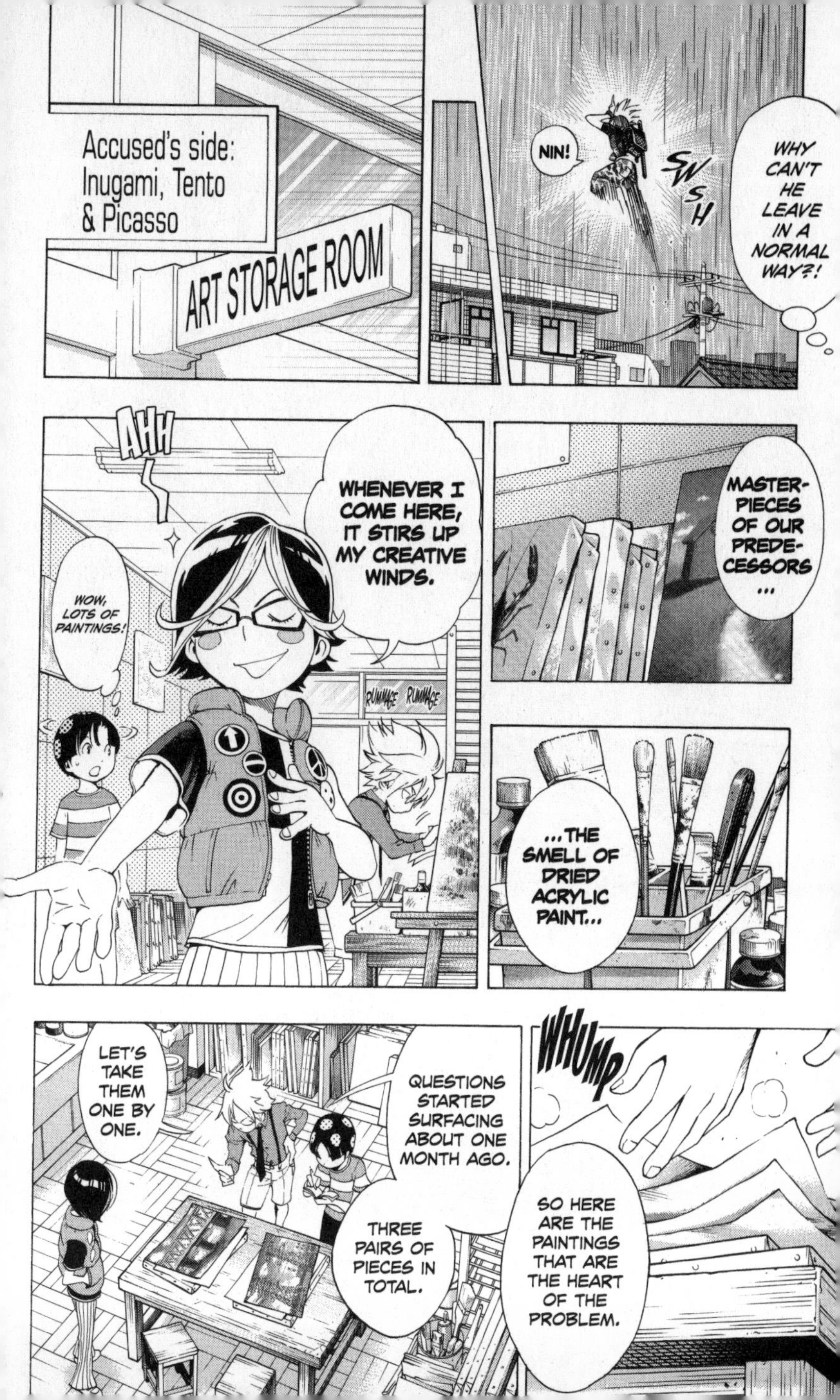
WHY CAN'T HE LEAVE IN A NORMAL WAY?!
SWSH
NIN!
Accused's side: Inugami, Tento & Picasso
ART STORAGE ROOM
MASTER-PIECES OF OUR PREDE-CESSORS...
...THE SMELL OF DRIED ACRYLIC PAINT...
AHH
WHENEVER I COME HERE, IT STIRS UP MY CREATIVE WINDS.
WOW, LOTS OF PAINTINGS!
RUMMAGE RUMMAGE
WHUMP
SO HERE ARE THE PAINTINGS THAT ARE THE HEART OF THE PROBLEM.
QUESTIONS STARTED SURFACING ABOUT ONE MONTH AGO.
THREE PAIRS OF PIECES IN TOTAL.
LET'S TAKE THEM ONE BY ONE.

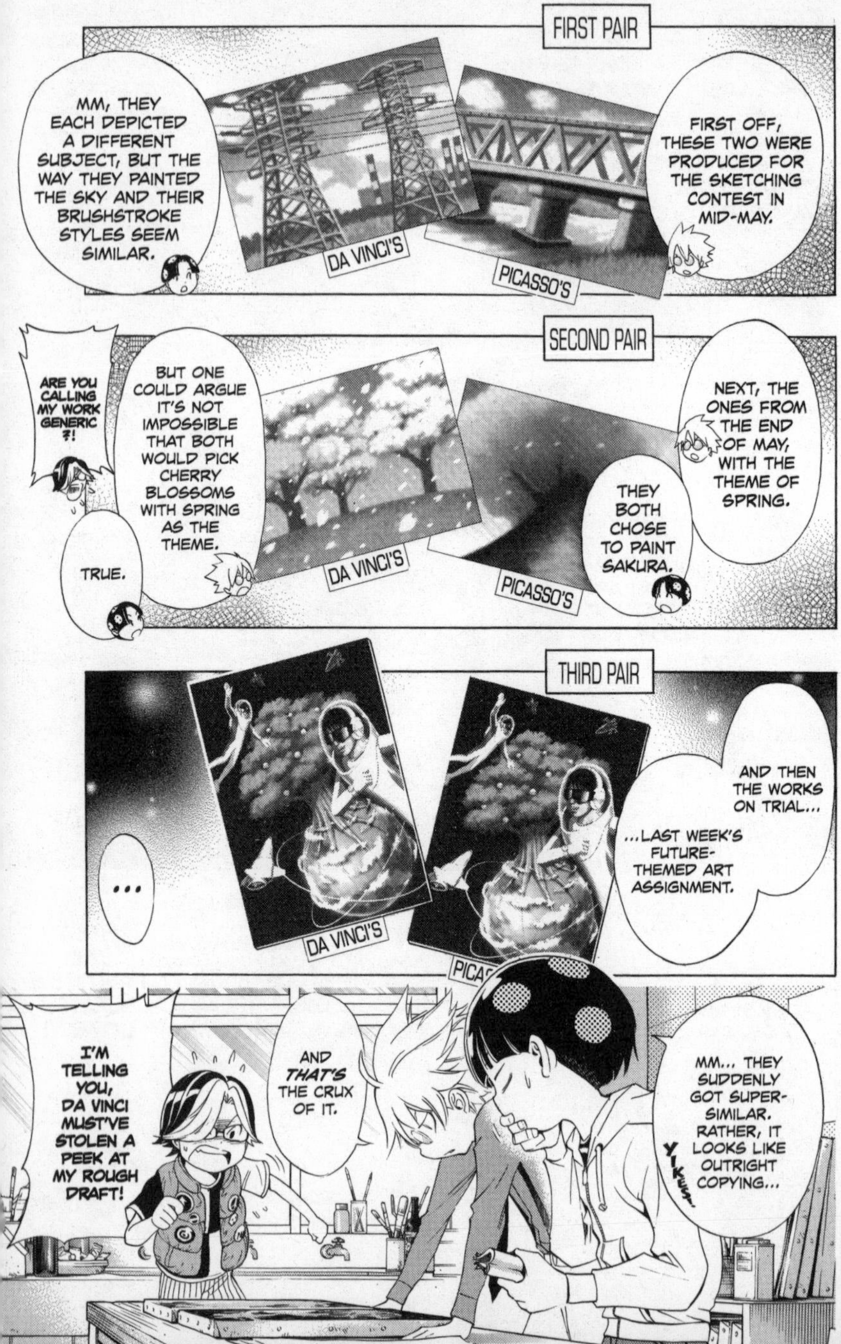
FIRST PAIR
FIRST OFF, THESE TWO WERE PRODUCED FOR THE SKETCHING CONTEST IN MID-MAY.
PICASSO'S
DA VINCI'S
MM, THEY EACH DEPICTED A DIFFERENT SUBJECT, BUT THE WAY THEY PAINTED THE SKY AND THEIR BRUSHSTROKE STYLES SEEM SIMILAR.
SECOND PAIR
NEXT, THE ONES FROM THE END OF MAY, WITH THE THEME OF SPRING.
THEY BOTH CHOSE TO PAINT SAKURA.
PICASSO'S
DA VINCI'S
BUT ONE COULD ARGUE IT'S NOT IMPOSSIBLE THAT BOTH WOULD PICK CHERRY BLOSSOMS WITH SPRING AS THE THEME.
TRUE.
ARE YOU CALLING MY WORK GENERIC?!
THIRD PAIR
AND THEN THE WORKS ON TRIAL...
...LAST WEEK'S FUTURE-THEMED ART ASSIGNMENT.
DA VINCI'S
...
MM... THEY SUDDENLY GOT SUPER-SIMILAR. RATHER, IT LOOKS LIKE OUTRIGHT COPYING...
YIKES!
AND *THAT'S* THE CRUX OF IT.
I'M TELLING YOU, DA VINCI MUST'VE STOLEN A PEEK AT MY ROUGH DRAFT!

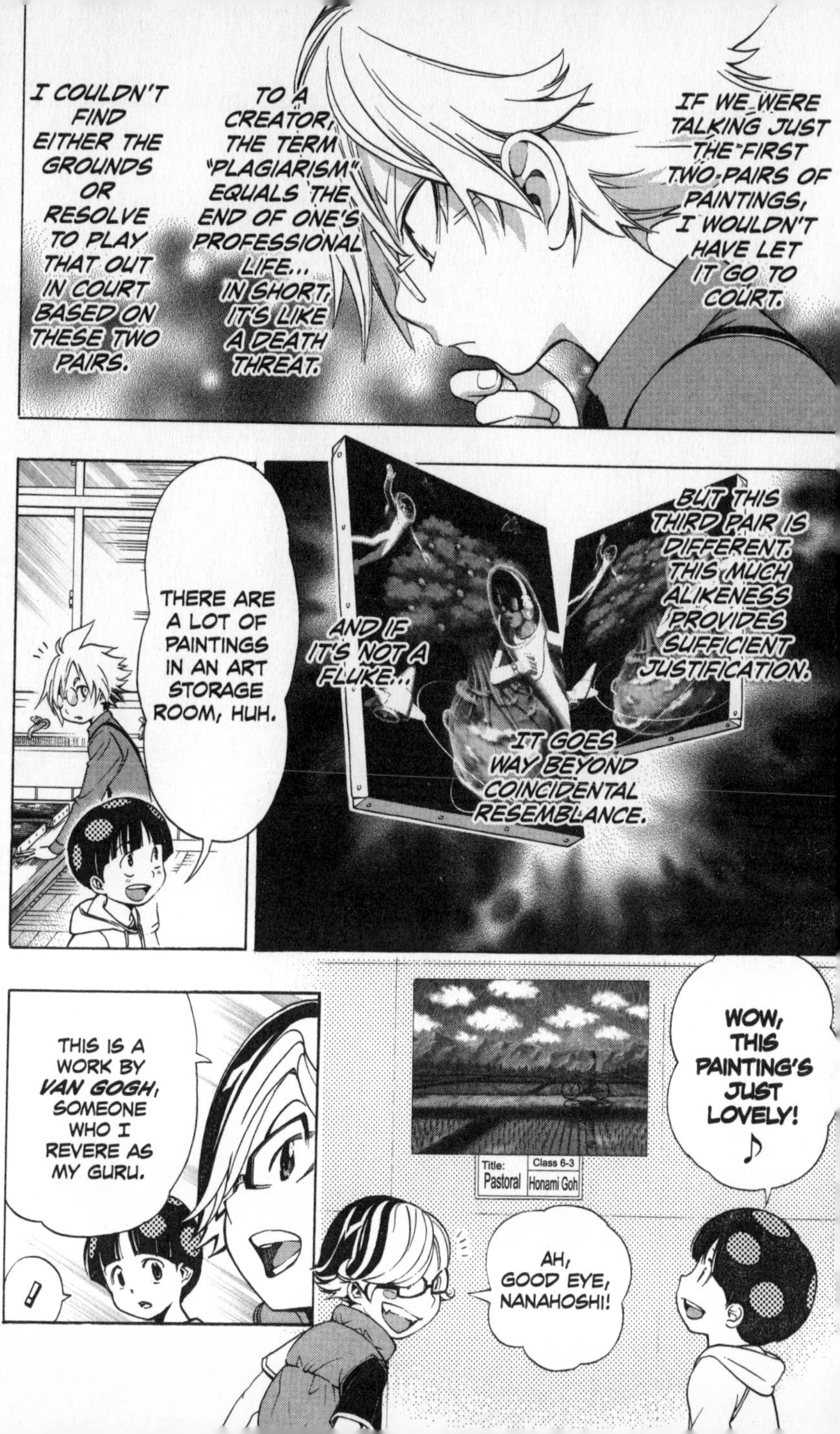
IF WE WERE TALKING JUST THE FIRST TWO PAIRS OF PAINTINGS, I WOULDN'T HAVE LET IT GO TO COURT.
TO A CREATOR, THE TERM "PLAGIARISM" EQUALS THE END OF ONE'S PROFESSIONAL LIFE... IN SHORT, IT'S LIKE A DEATH THREAT.
I COULDN'T FIND EITHER THE GROUNDS OR RESOLVE TO PLAY THAT OUT IN COURT BASED ON THESE TWO PAIRS.
BUT THIS THIRD PAIR IS DIFFERENT. THIS MUCH ALIKENESS PROVIDES SUFFICIENT JUSTIFICATION.
AND IF IT'S NOT A FLUKE...
IT GOES WAY BEYOND COINCIDENTAL RESEMBLANCE.
THERE ARE A LOT OF PAINTINGS IN AN ART STORAGE ROOM, HUH.
WOW, THIS PAINTING'S JUST LOVELY! ♪
Title: Pastoral
Class 6-3 Honami Goh
AH, GOOD EYE, NANAHOSHI!
THIS IS A WORK BY VAN GOGH, SOMEONE WHO I REVERE AS MY GURU.
!

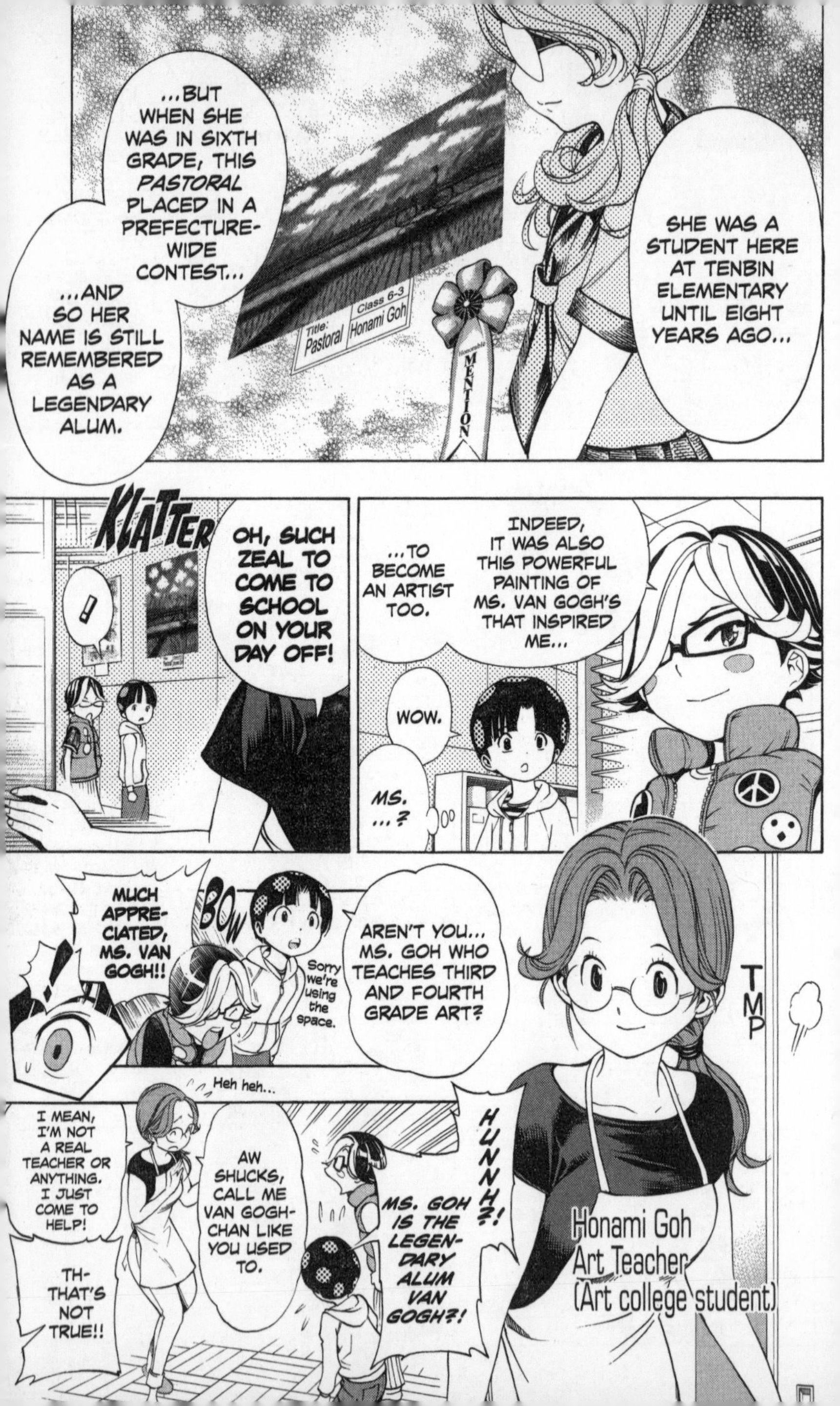
SHE WAS A STUDENT HERE AT TENBIN ELEMENTARY UNTIL EIGHT YEARS AGO...
...BUT WHEN SHE WAS IN SIXTH GRADE, THIS PASTORAL PLACED IN A PREFECTURE-WIDE CONTEST...
...AND SO HER NAME IS STILL REMEMBERED AS A LEGENDARY ALUM.
Class 6-3
Honami Goh
Title: Pastoral
Honorable MENTION
INDEED, IT WAS ALSO THIS POWERFUL PAINTING OF MS. VAN GOGH'S THAT INSPIRED ME...
...TO BECOME AN ARTIST TOO.
WOW.
MS. ...?
KLATTER
OH, SUCH ZEAL TO COME TO SCHOOL ON YOUR DAY OFF!
!
TMP
AREN'T YOU... MS. GOH WHO TEACHES THIRD AND FOURTH GRADE ART?
Sorry we're using the space.
BOW
MUCH APPRECIATED, MS. VAN GOGH!!
!
Honami Goh
Art Teacher
(Art college student)
HUNNH?!
MS. GOH IS THE LEGENDARY ALUM VAN GOGH?!
AW SHUCKS, CALL ME VAN GOGH-CHAN LIKE YOU USED TO.
Heh heh...
I MEAN, I'M NOT A REAL TEACHER OR ANYTHING. I JUST COME TO HELP!
TH-THAT'S NOT TRUE!!

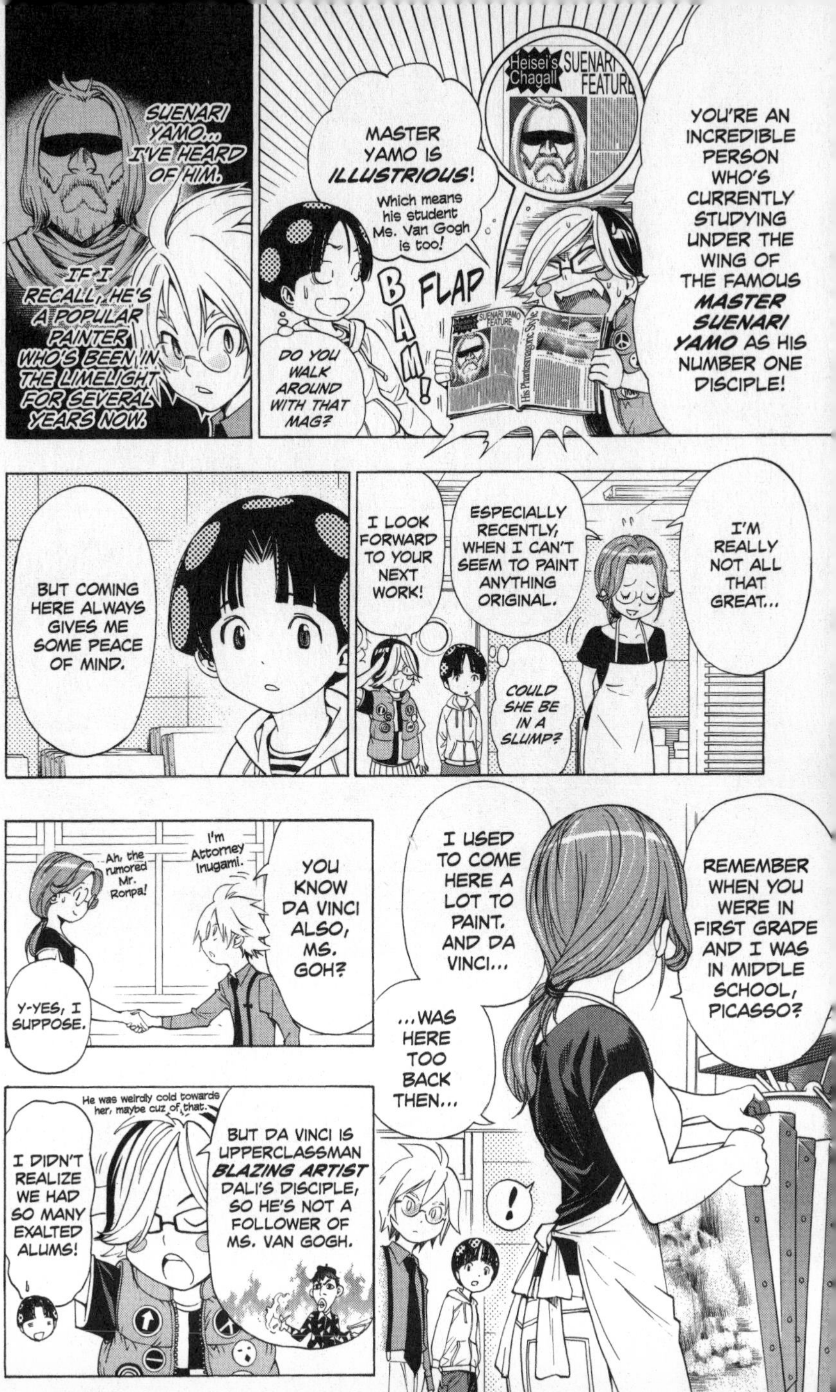
YOU'RE AN INCREDIBLE PERSON WHO'S CURRENTLY STUDYING UNDER THE WING OF THE FAMOUS MASTER SUENARI YAMO AS HIS NUMBER ONE DISCIPLE!
Heisei's Chagall
SUENARI FEATURE
MASTER YAMO IS ILLUSTRIOUS!
Which means his student Ms. Van Gogh is too!
FLAP
BAM!
SUENARI YAMO FEATURE
His Phantasmagoric Style
DO YOU WALK AROUND WITH THAT MAG?
SUENARI YAMO... I'VE HEARD OF HIM.
IF I RECALL, HE'S A POPULAR PAINTER WHO'S BEEN IN THE LIMELIGHT FOR SEVERAL YEARS NOW.
I'M REALLY NOT ALL THAT GREAT...
ESPECIALLY RECENTLY, WHEN I CAN'T SEEM TO PAINT ANYTHING ORIGINAL.
I LOOK FORWARD TO YOUR NEXT WORK!
COULD SHE BE IN A SLUMP?
BUT COMING HERE ALWAYS GIVES ME SOME PEACE OF MIND.
REMEMBER WHEN YOU WERE IN FIRST GRADE AND I WAS IN MIDDLE SCHOOL, PICASSO?
I USED TO COME HERE A LOT TO PAINT. AND DA VINCI...
...WAS HERE TOO BACK THEN...
!
YOU KNOW DA VINCI ALSO, MS. GOH?
I'm Attorney Inugami.
Ah, the rumored Mr. Ronpa!
Y-YES, I SUPPOSE.
BUT DA VINCI IS UPPERCLASSMAN BLAZING ARTIST DALI'S DISCIPLE, SO HE'S NOT A FOLLOWER OF MS. VAN GOGH.
He was weirdly cold towards her, maybe cuz of that.
I DIDN'T REALIZE WE HAD SO MANY EXALTED ALUMS!

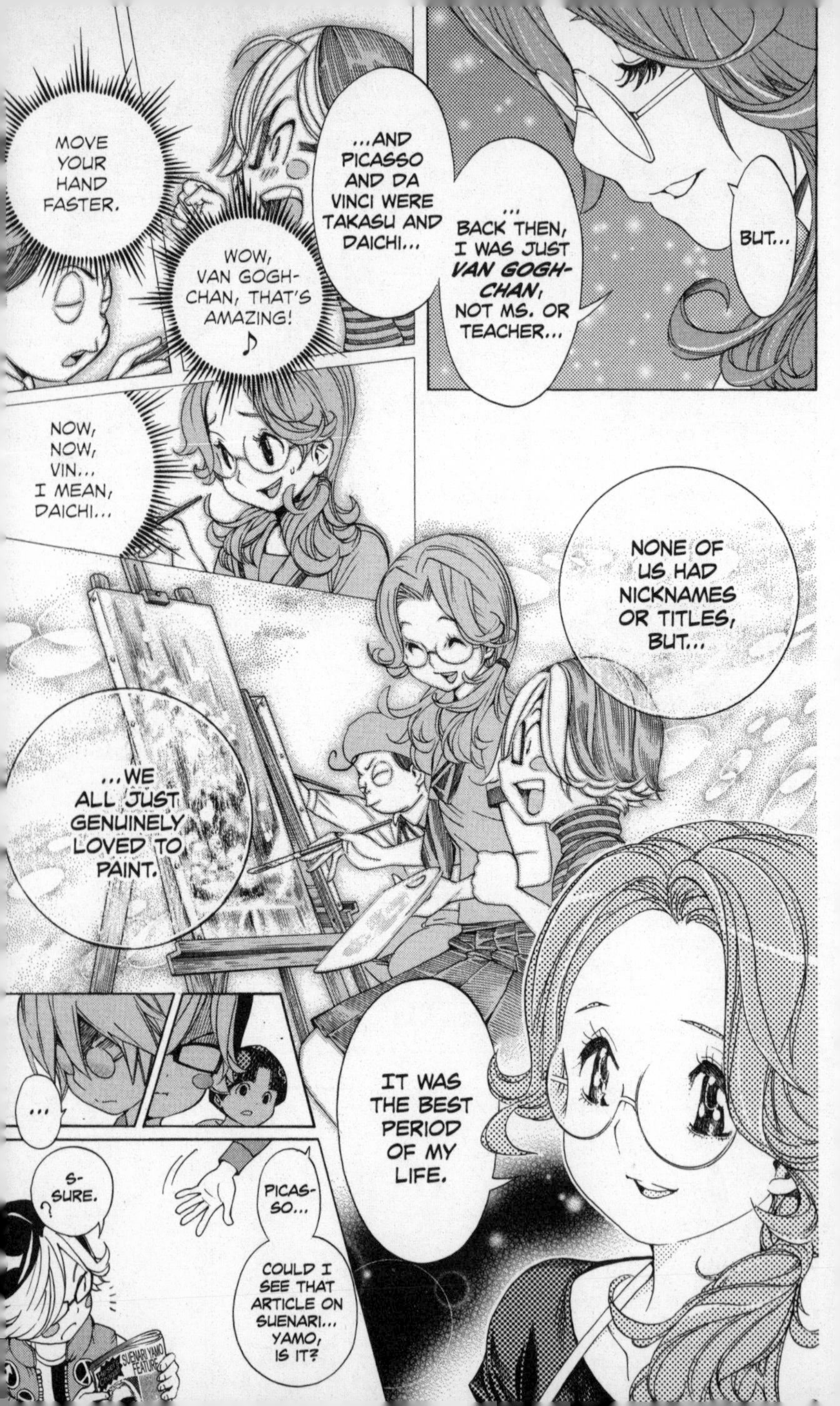
BUT...
... BACK THEN, I WAS JUST *VAN GOGH-CHAN*, NOT MS. OR TEACHER...
...AND PICASSO AND DA VINCI WERE TAKASU AND DAICHI...
MOVE YOUR HAND FASTER.
WOW, VAN GOGH-CHAN, THAT'S AMAZING! ♪
NOW, NOW, VIN... I MEAN, DAICHI...
NONE OF US HAD NICKNAMES OR TITLES, BUT...
...WE ALL JUST GENUINELY LOVED TO PAINT.
IT WAS THE BEST PERIOD OF MY LIFE.
...
PICAS-SO...
COULD I SEE THAT ARTICLE ON SUENARI... YAMO, IS IT?
S-SURE.
SUENARI YAMO FEATURE

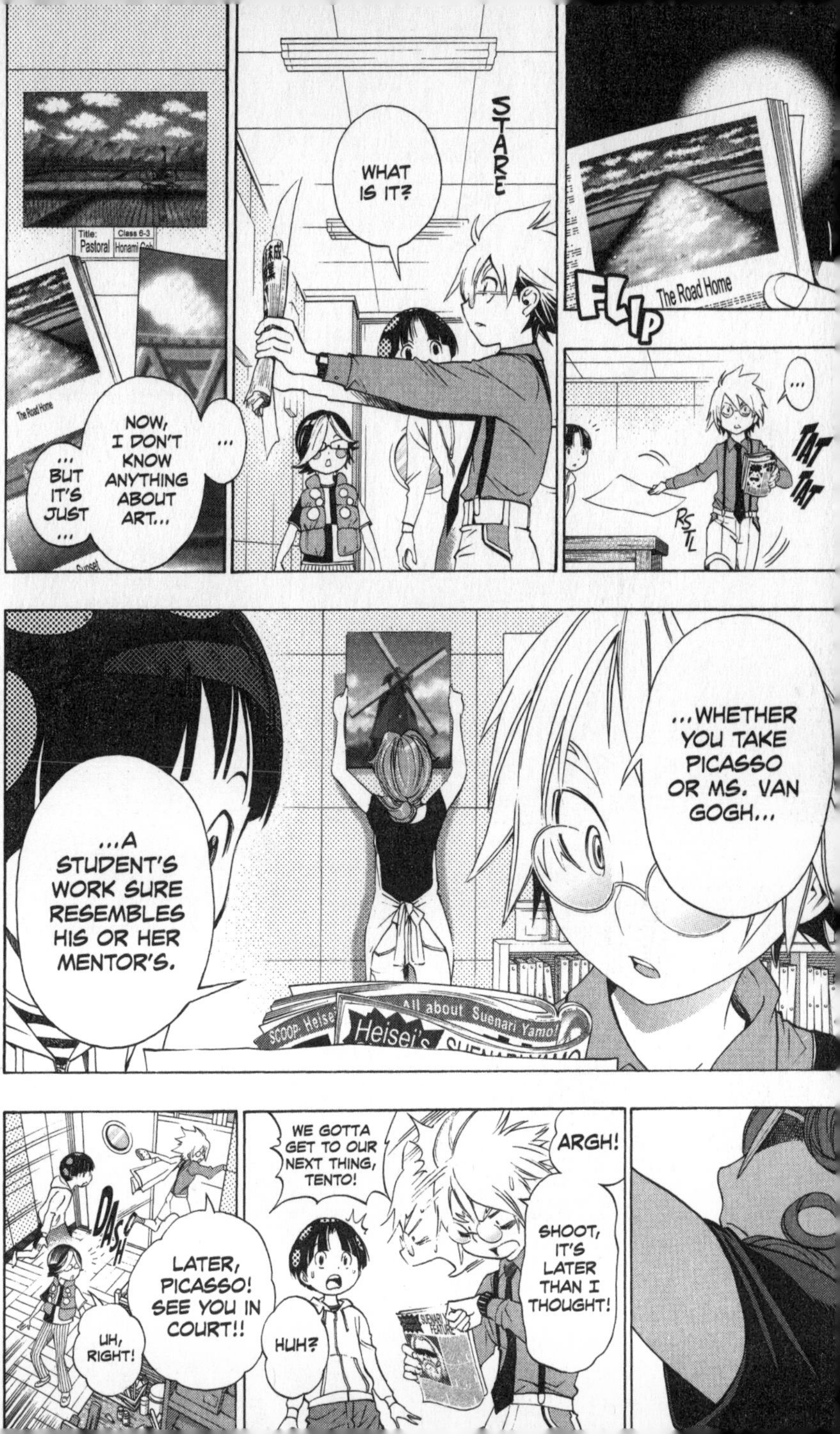
The Road Home
FLIP
...
TAT TAT
RSTL
STARE
WHAT IS IT?
Title: Pastoral
Class 6-3
The Road Home
...
NOW, I DON'T KNOW ANYTHING ABOUT ART...
...BUT IT'S JUST...
Sunset
...WHETHER YOU TAKE PICASSO OR MS. VAN GOGH...
...A STUDENT'S WORK SURE RESEMBLES HIS OR HER MENTOR'S.
All about Suenari Yamo!
ARGH!
SHOOT, IT'S LATER THAN I THOUGHT!
WE GOTTA GET TO OUR NEXT THING, TENTO!
HUH?
LATER, PICASSO! SEE YOU IN COURT!!
DASH
UH, RIGHT!

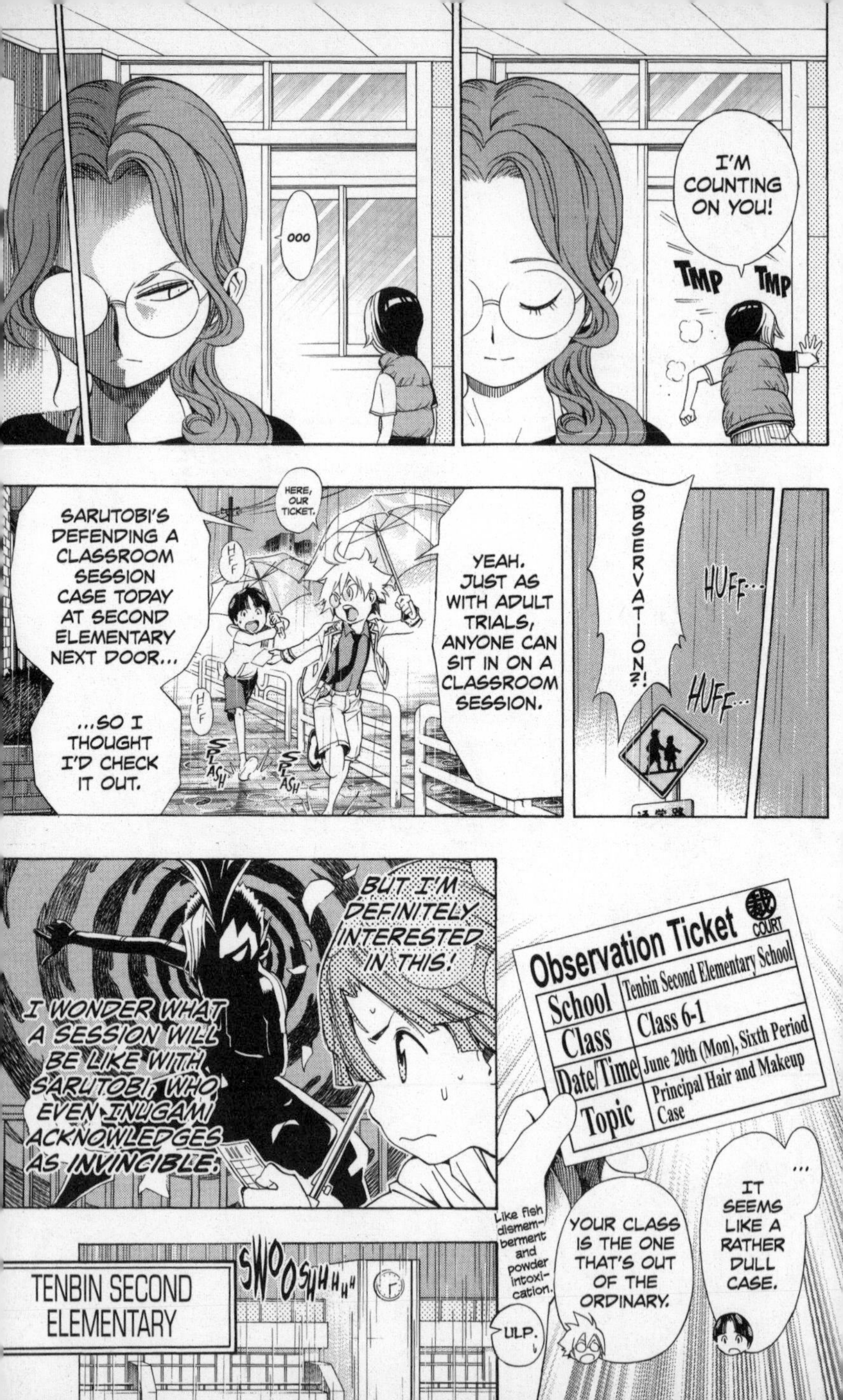
I'M COUNTING ON YOU!
TMP
TMP
ooo
OBSERVATION?!
HUFF...
HUFF...
HERE, OUR TICKET.
YEAH. JUST AS WITH ADULT TRIALS, ANYONE CAN SIT IN ON A CLASSROOM SESSION.
SARUTOBI'S DEFENDING A CLASSROOM SESSION CASE TODAY AT SECOND ELEMENTARY NEXT DOOR...
HFF
HFF
...SO I THOUGHT I'D CHECK IT OUT.
SPLASH
SPLASH
Observation Ticket
COURT
School
Tenbin Second Elementary School
Class
Class 6-1
Date/Time
June 20th (Mon), Sixth Period
Topic
Principal Hair and Makeup Case
...
IT SEEMS LIKE A RATHER DULL CASE.
YOUR CLASS IS THE ONE THAT'S OUT OF THE ORDINARY.
Like fish dismemberment and powder intoxication.
ULP.
BUT I'M DEFINITELY INTERESTED IN THIS!
I WONDER WHAT A SESSION WILL BE LIKE WITH SARUTOBI, WHO EVEN INUGAMI ACKNOWLEDGES AS INVINCIBLE.
SWOOSHHHHH
TENBIN SECOND ELEMENTARY

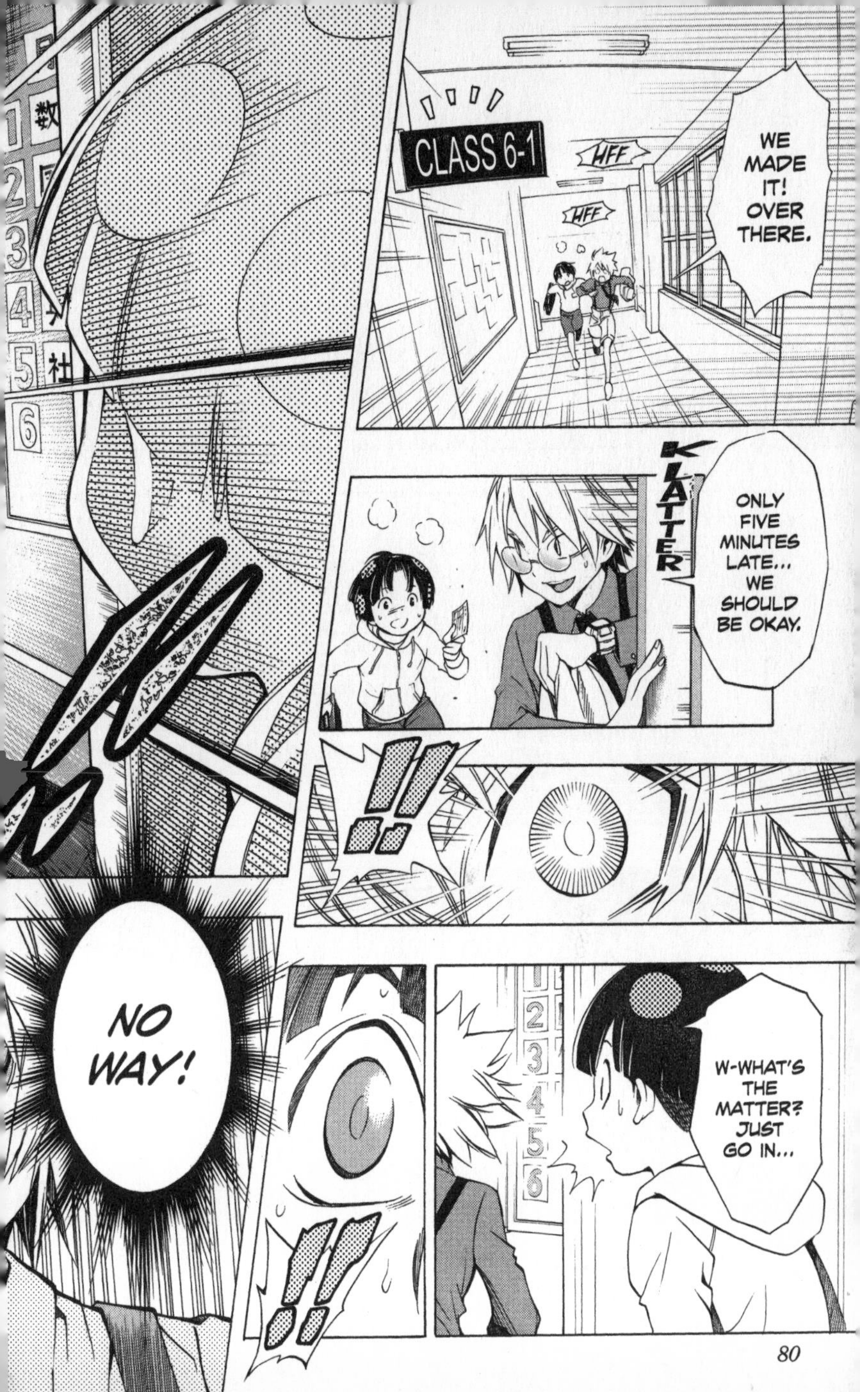
WE MADE IT! OVER THERE.
CLASS 6-1
HFF
HFF
KLATTER
ONLY FIVE MINUTES LATE... WE SHOULD BE OKAY.
!!
W-WHAT'S THE MATTER? JUST GO IN...
!!
NO WAY!

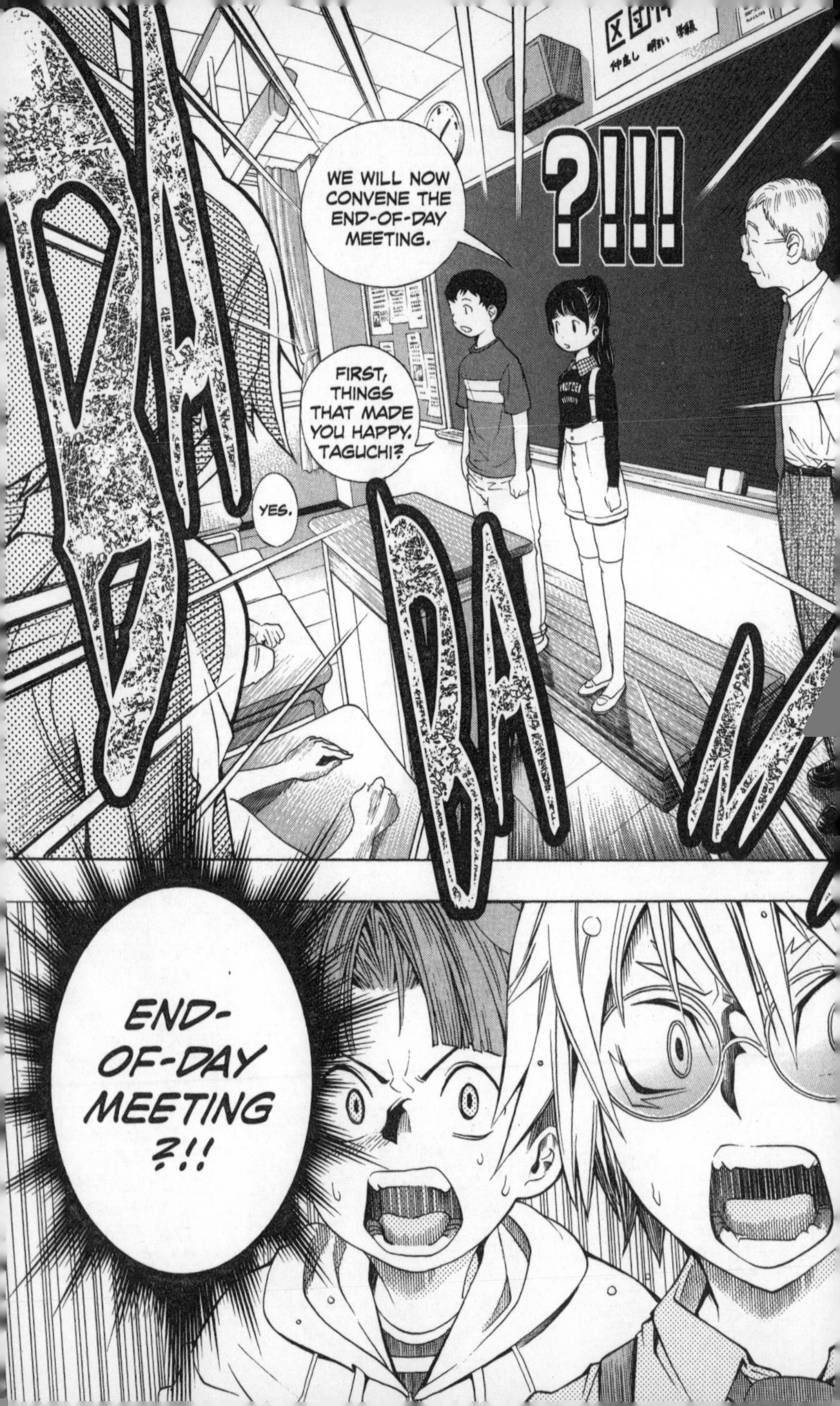
?!!!
WE WILL NOW CONVENE THE END-OF-DAY MEETING.
FIRST, THINGS THAT MADE YOU HAPPY. TAGUCHI?
YES.
END-OF-DAY MEETING?!!

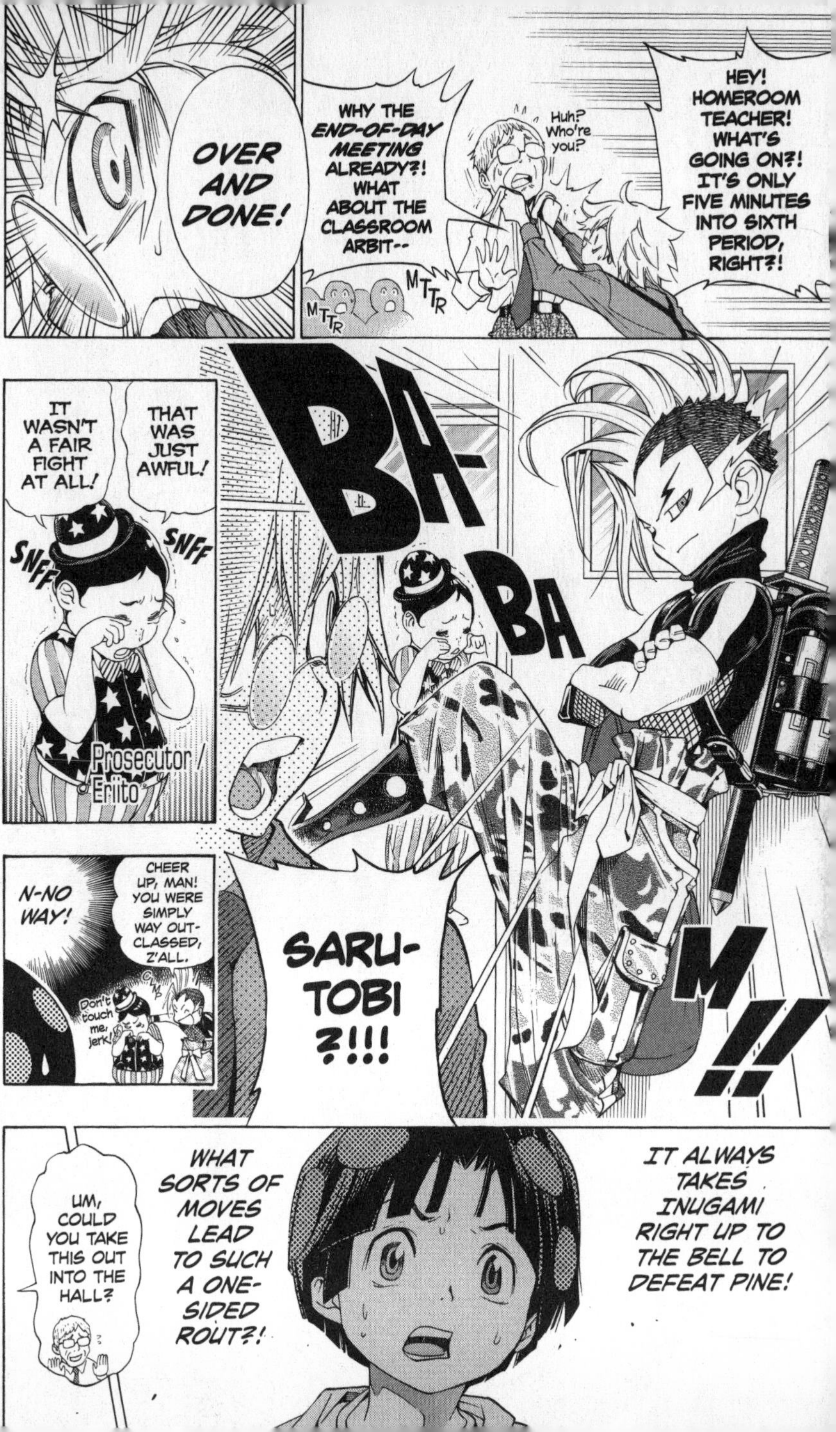
HEY! HOMEROOM TEACHER! WHAT'S GOING ON?! IT'S ONLY FIVE MINUTES INTO SIXTH PERIOD, RIGHT?!
Huh? Who're you?
WHY THE END-OF-DAY MEETING ALREADY?! WHAT ABOUT THE CLASSROOM ARBIT--
MTTR
MTTR
OVER AND DONE!
BA-BA
M!!
SARU-TOBI?!!!
THAT WAS JUST AWFUL!
IT WASN'T A FAIR FIGHT AT ALL!
SNFF
SNFF
Prosecutor / Eriito
CHEER UP, MAN! YOU WERE SIMPLY WAY OUT-CLASSED, Z'ALL.
N-NO WAY!
Don't touch me, jerk!
IT ALWAYS TAKES INUGAMI RIGHT UP TO THE BELL TO DEFEAT PINE!
WHAT SORTS OF MOVES LEAD TO SUCH A ONE-SIDED ROUT?!
UM, COULD YOU TAKE THIS OUT INTO THE HALL?

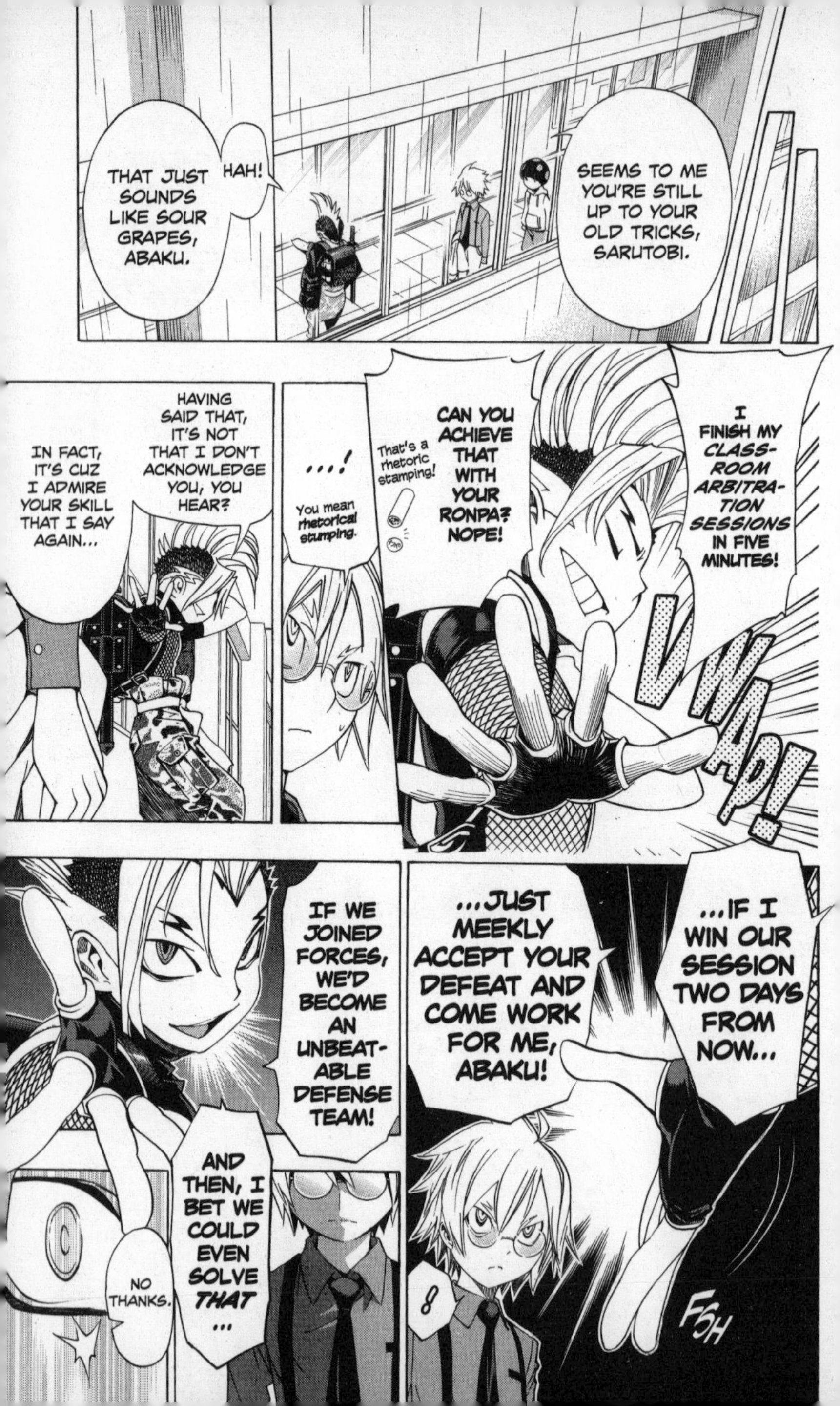
SEEMS TO ME YOU'RE STILL UP TO YOUR OLD TRICKS, SARUTOBI.
HAH!
THAT JUST SOUNDS LIKE SOUR GRAPES, ABAKU.
I FINISH MY *CLASSROOM ARBITRATION SESSIONS* IN FIVE MINUTES!
CAN YOU ACHIEVE THAT WITH YOUR RONPA? NOPE!
VWAP!!
That's a rhetoric stamping!
You mean *rhetorical stumping*.
...!
HAVING SAID THAT, IT'S NOT THAT I DON'T ACKNOWLEDGE YOU, YOU HEAR?
IN FACT, IT'S CUZ I ADMIRE YOUR SKILL THAT I SAY AGAIN...
...IF I WIN OUR SESSION TWO DAYS FROM NOW...
...JUST MEEKLY ACCEPT YOUR DEFEAT AND COME WORK FOR ME, ABAKU!
FSH
IF WE JOINED FORCES, WE'D BECOME AN UNBEATABLE DEFENSE TEAM!
AND THEN, I BET WE COULD EVEN SOLVE *THAT*...
NO THANKS.

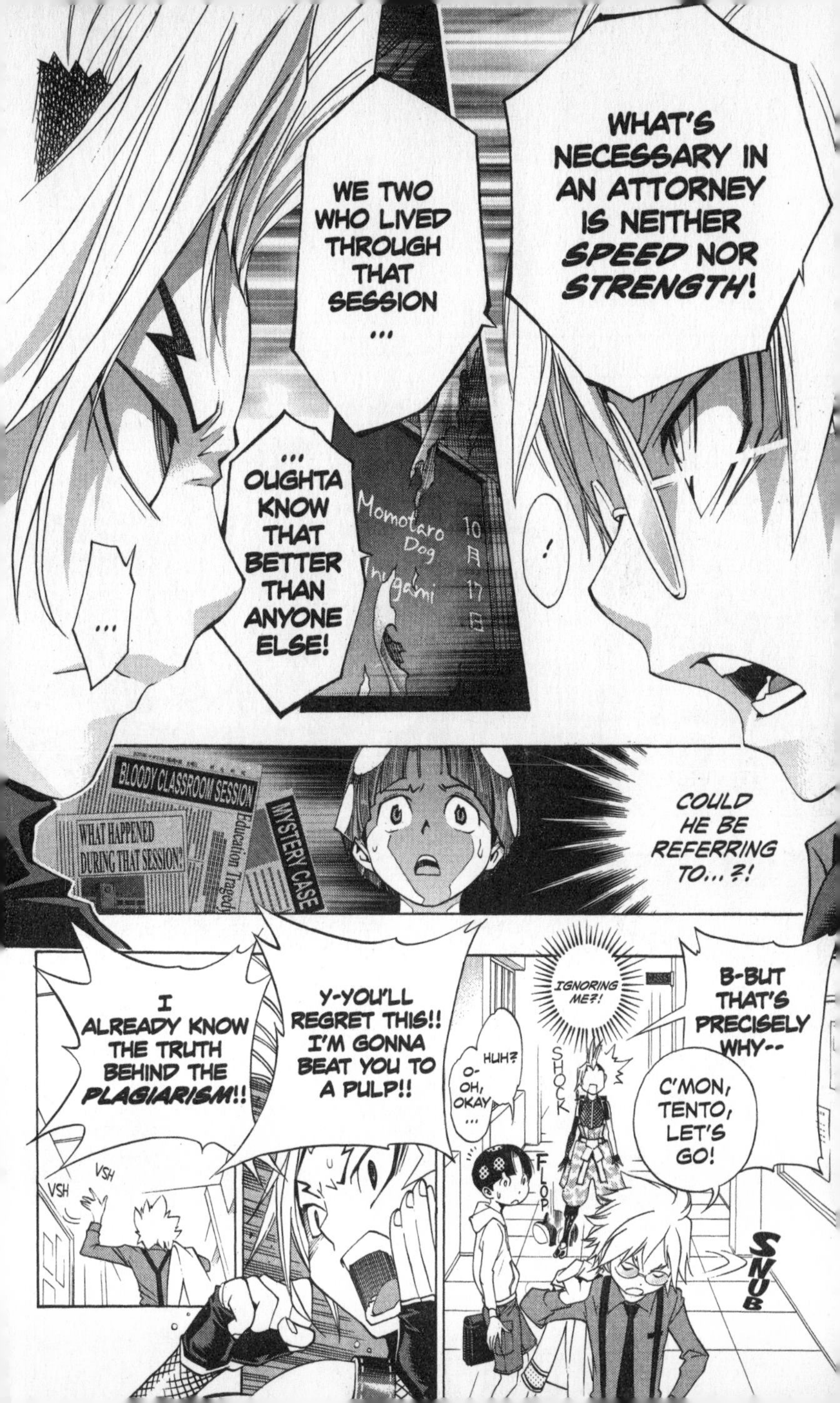
WHAT'S NECESSARY IN AN ATTORNEY IS NEITHER *SPEED* NOR *STRENGTH*!
WE TWO WHO LIVED THROUGH THAT SESSION ...
!
... OUGHTA KNOW THAT BETTER THAN ANYONE ELSE!
Momotaro Dog Inugami
10 月 17 日
...
COULD HE BE REFERRING TO...?!
MYSTERY CASE
Education Traged
BLOODY CLASSROOM SESSION
WHAT HAPPENED DURING THAT SESSION?!
B-BUT THAT'S PRECISELY WHY--
IGNORING ME?!
C'MON, TENTO, LET'S GO!
SHOCK
HUH?
O-OH, OKAY ...
FLOP
SNUB
Y-YOU'LL REGRET THIS!! I'M GONNA BEAT YOU TO A PULP!!
I ALREADY KNOW THE TRUTH BEHIND THE *PLAGIARISM*!!
VSH
VSH

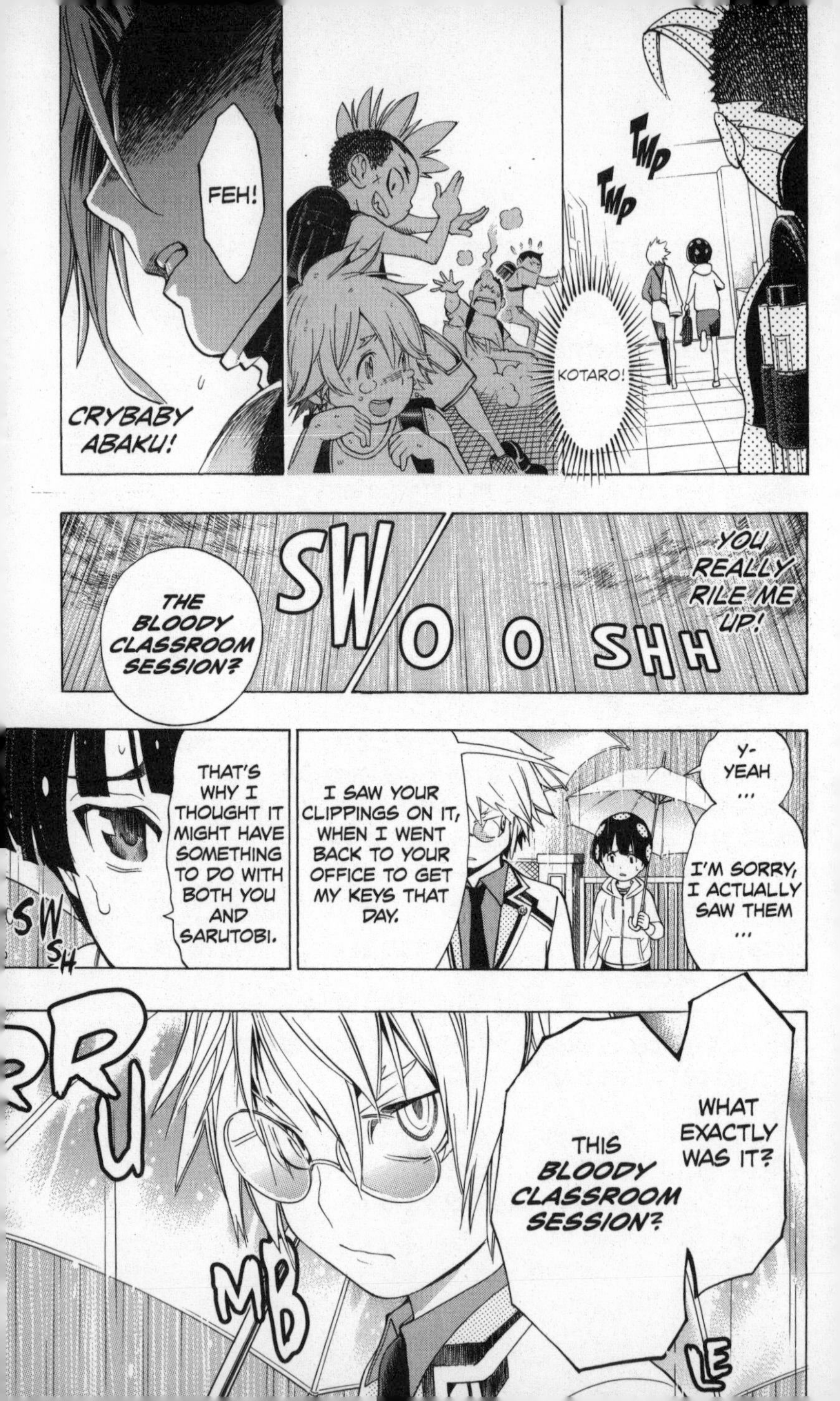
TMP
TMP
KOTARO!
FEH!
CRYBABY ABAKU!
YOU REALLY RILE ME UP!
SWOOSHH
THE BLOODY CLASSROOM SESSION?
Y-YEAH ...
I'M SORRY, I ACTUALLY SAW THEM ...
I SAW YOUR CLIPPINGS ON IT, WHEN I WENT BACK TO YOUR OFFICE TO GET MY KEYS THAT DAY.
THAT'S WHY I THOUGHT IT MIGHT HAVE SOMETHING TO DO WITH BOTH YOU AND SARUTOBI.
SWSH
WHAT EXACTLY WAS IT?
THIS BLOODY CLASSROOM SESSION?
RRUMBLE

Continued from p. 66 ⇦

To a simple person such as myself, the prosecution speaks like 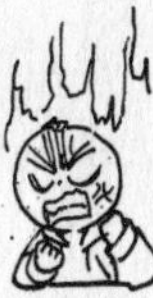 "Accused, you jerk!"

But...

When the defense starts talking, the prosecution is then easily moved to empathize and be like 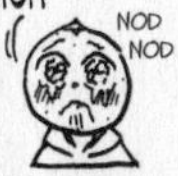
NOD
NOD
"It's okay, accused..."

It made me realize just how difficult it must be to be a judge who must coolly weigh both sides' sentimental arguments without being swayed by them and then hand down an appropriate sentence.
(It's no wonder the Babies age so fast!)

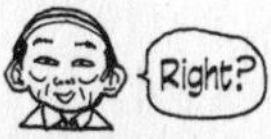
Right?

However, for those of us who are not judges, even if we observe the same trial, our perception of it may not be the same...
On the way home, my editor was totally raging at the accused, but I felt sorry for him.

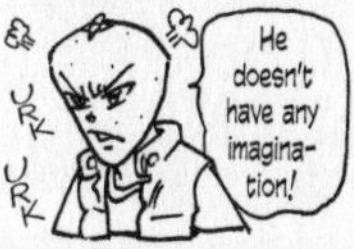
URK
URK
He doesn't have any imagination!

Of course, no matter what the circumstances or context, the moment that the accused committed the crime, that person was wrong. But just by being on the wrong side of a railing only a few inches thick and being deprived of freedom with handcuffs and a waist rope makes that person seems so distant and alone...

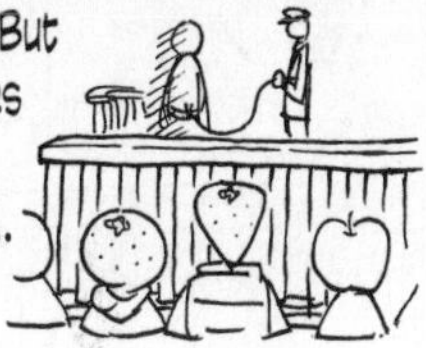

And at the same time, I also think this....

That person must have had an ordinary **sixth grade life** just like Tento and the others, and also probably friends...
So the truly insurmountable, heartless railing may not be the one between the gallery and the accused's seat, but one that is lying unnoticed between such an innocent past and the crushing present.

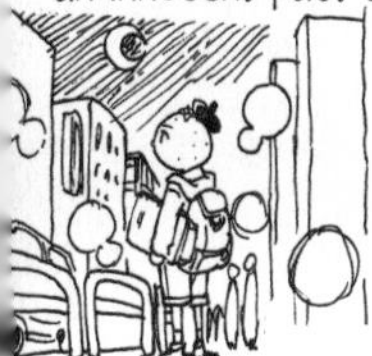

The generally lenient rulings in *School Judgment* are likely proof that the children in this story are still on the outside of the railing.

CHAPTER 12

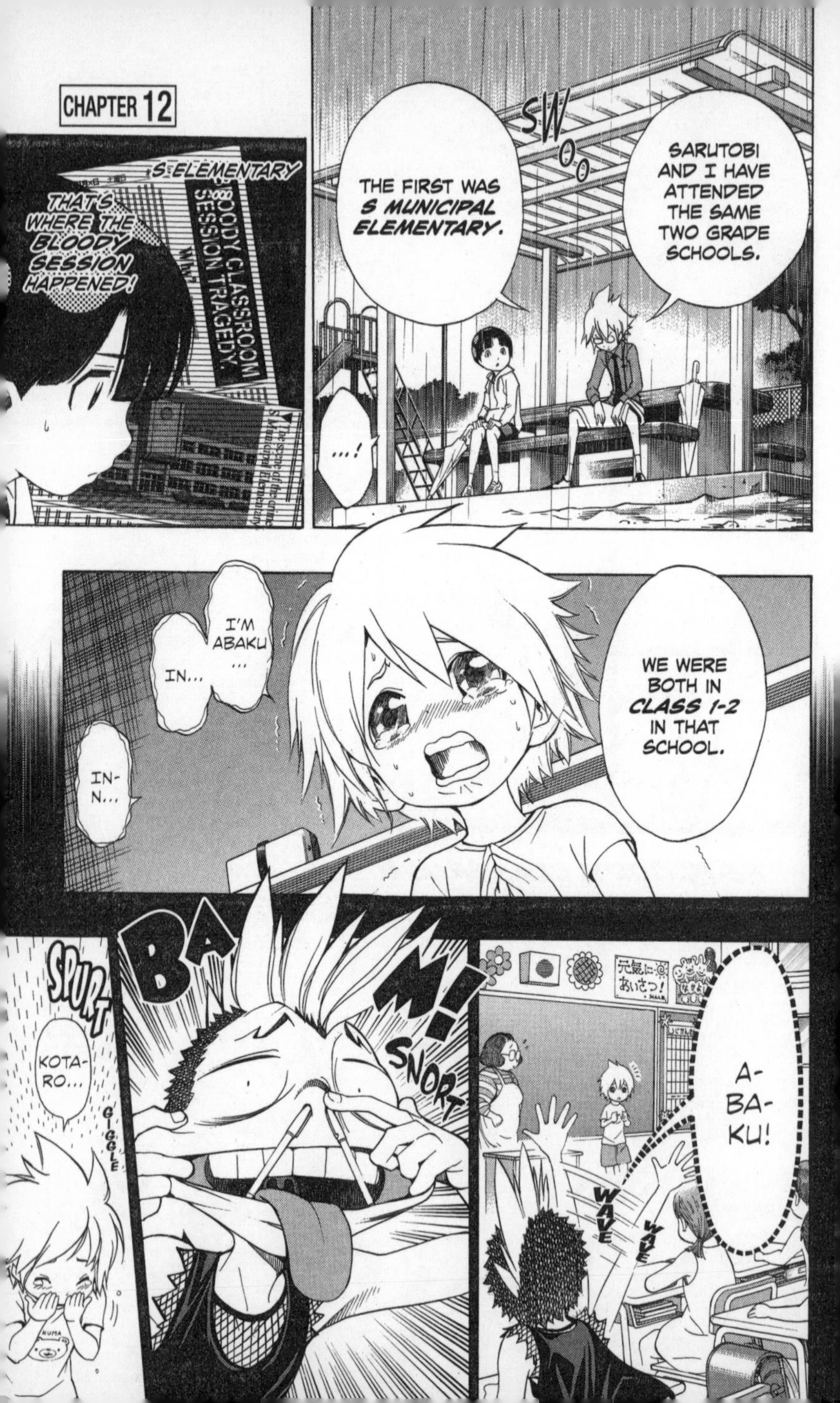
SWOOO
SARUTOBI AND I HAVE ATTENDED THE SAME TWO GRADE SCHOOLS.
THE FIRST WAS *S MUNICIPAL ELEMENTARY*.
...!
S ELEMENTARY
BLOODY CLASSROOM SESSION TRAGEDY.
THAT'S WHERE THE BLOODY SESSION HAPPENED!
WE WERE BOTH IN *CLASS 1-2* IN THAT SCHOOL.
I'M ABAKU ...
IN...
IN-N...
A-BA-KU!
元気に あいさつ!
WAVE
WAVE
BAM!
SNORT
SPURT
KOTARO...
GIGGLE

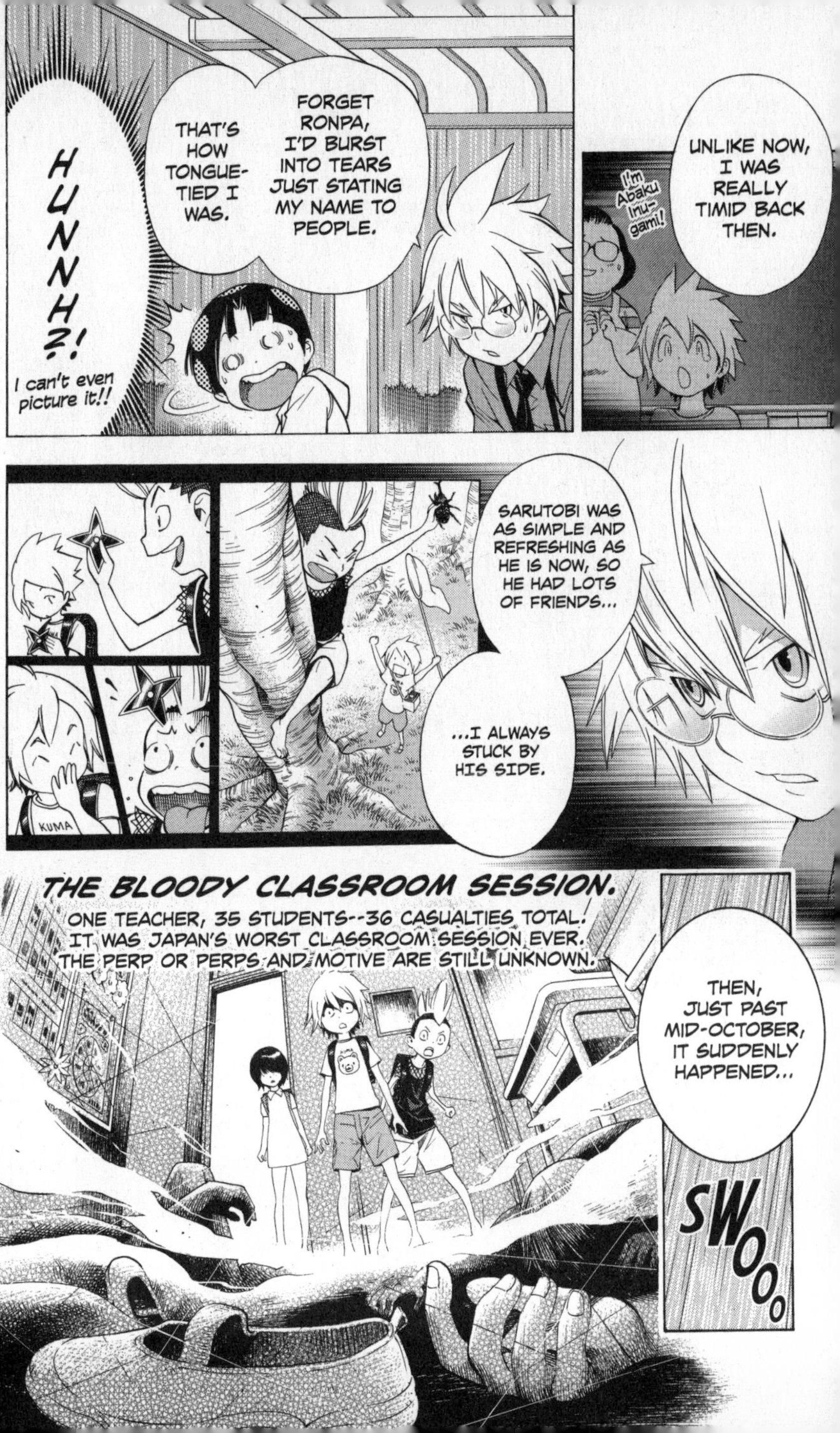
UNLIKE NOW, I WAS REALLY TIMID BACK THEN.
I'm Abaku Inugami!
FORGET RONPA, I'D BURST INTO TEARS JUST STATING MY NAME TO PEOPLE.
THAT'S HOW TONGUE-TIED I WAS.
HUNNNH?!
I can't even picture it!!
SARUTOBI WAS AS SIMPLE AND REFRESHING AS HE IS NOW, SO HE HAD LOTS OF FRIENDS...
...I ALWAYS STUCK BY HIS SIDE.
KUMA
THEN, JUST PAST MID-OCTOBER, IT SUDDENLY HAPPENED...
THE BLOODY CLASSROOM SESSION.
ONE TEACHER, 35 STUDENTS--36 CASUALTIES TOTAL. IT WAS JAPAN'S WORST CLASSROOM SESSION EVER. THE PERP OR PERPS AND MOTIVE ARE STILL UNKNOWN.
SWOOO

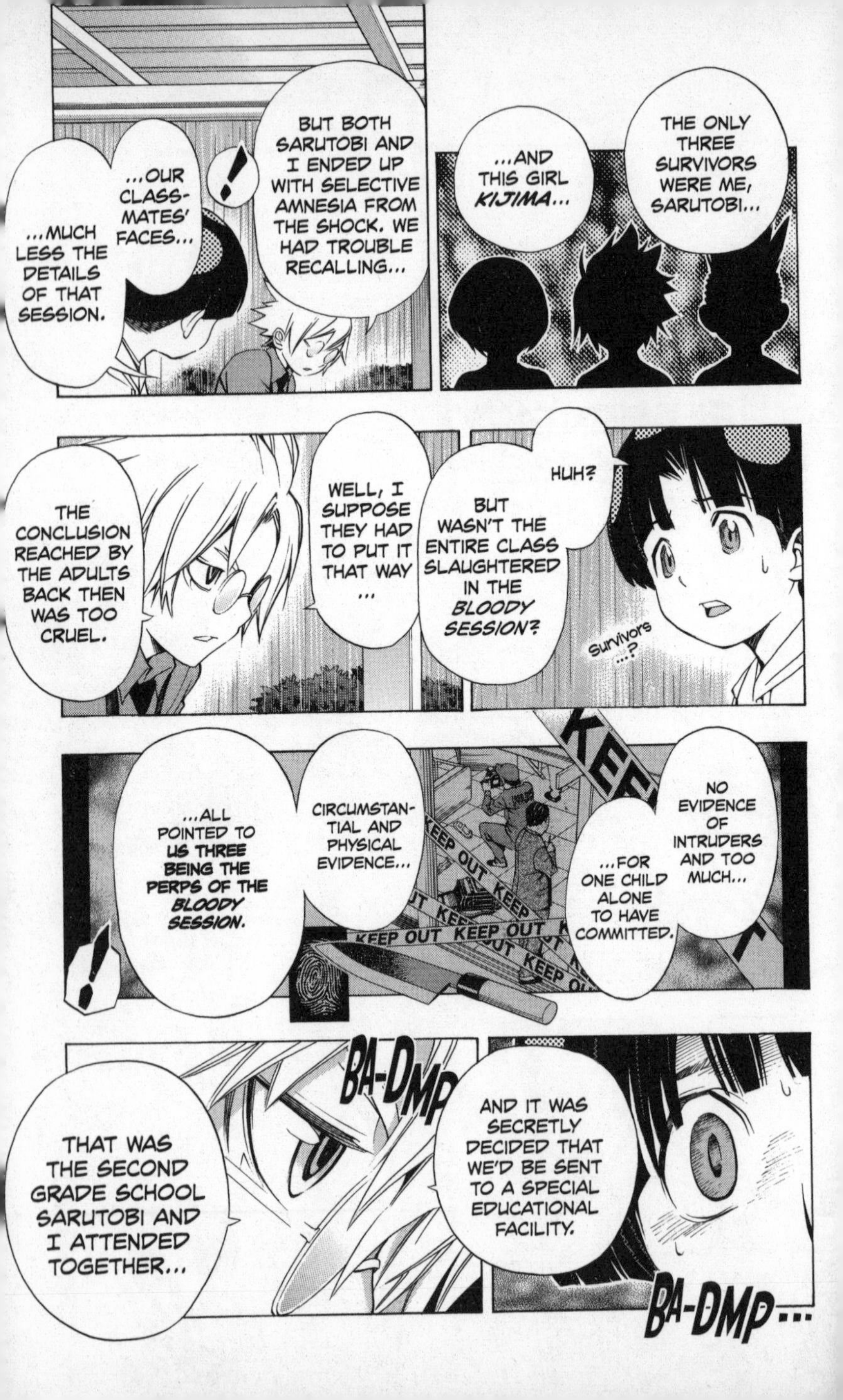
THE ONLY THREE SURVIVORS WERE ME, SARUTOBI...
...AND THIS GIRL *KIJIMA*...
BUT BOTH SARUTOBI AND I ENDED UP WITH SELECTIVE AMNESIA FROM THE SHOCK. WE HAD TROUBLE RECALLING...
!
...OUR CLASSMATES' FACES...
...MUCH LESS THE DETAILS OF THAT SESSION.
HUH?
BUT WASN'T THE ENTIRE CLASS SLAUGHTERED IN THE *BLOODY SESSION*?
Survivors ...?
WELL, I SUPPOSE THEY HAD TO PUT IT THAT WAY...
THE CONCLUSION REACHED BY THE ADULTS BACK THEN WAS TOO CRUEL.
NO EVIDENCE OF INTRUDERS AND TOO MUCH...
...FOR ONE CHILD ALONE TO HAVE COMMITTED.
KEEP OUT KEEP OUT
CIRCUMSTANTIAL AND PHYSICAL EVIDENCE...
...ALL POINTED TO **US THREE** BEING THE PERPS OF THE *BLOODY SESSION*.
!
AND IT WAS SECRETLY DECIDED THAT WE'D BE SENT TO A SPECIAL EDUCATIONAL FACILITY.
BA-DMP...
BA-DMP
THAT WAS THE SECOND GRADE SCHOOL SARUTOBI AND I ATTENDED TOGETHER...

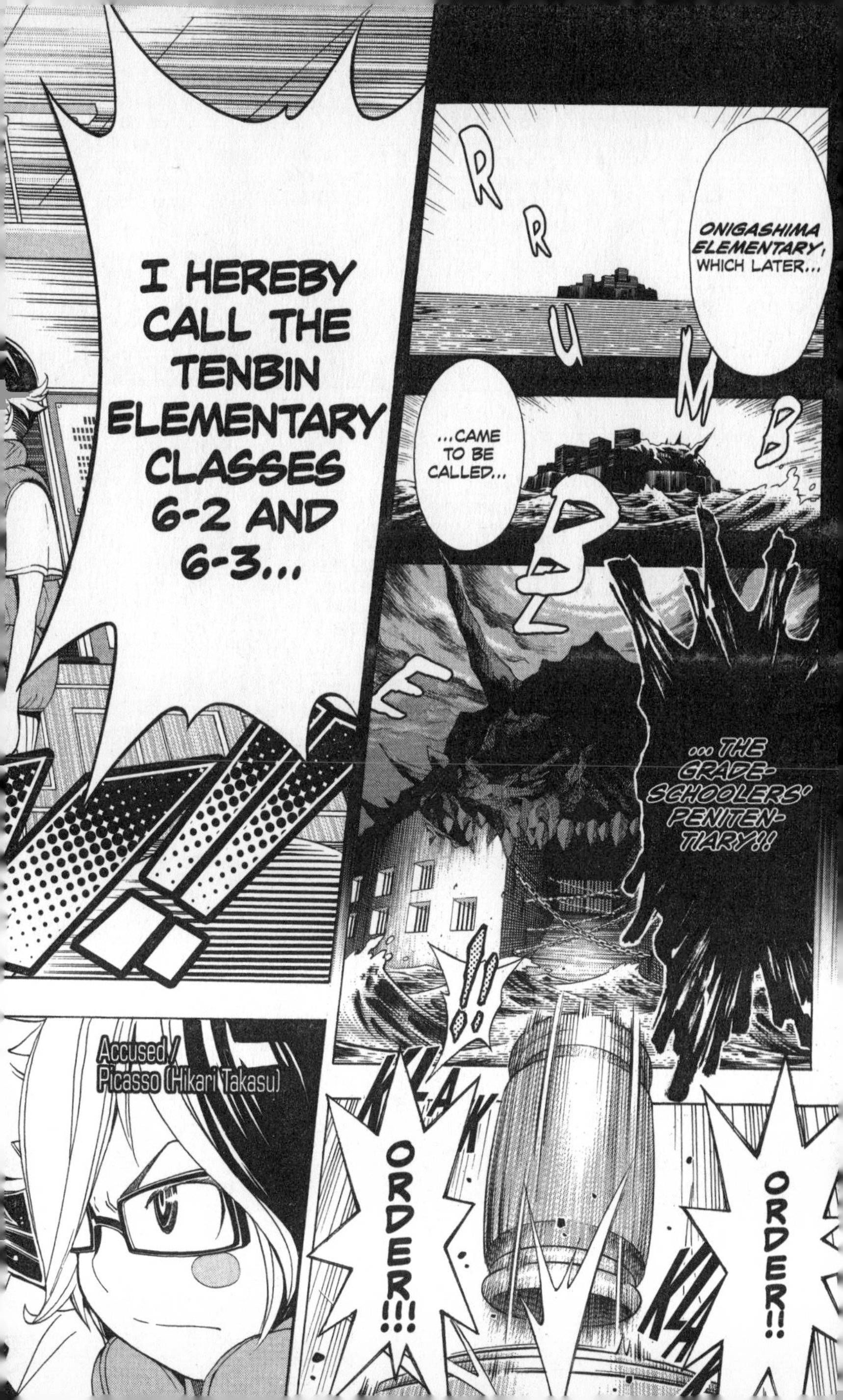
ONIGASHIMA ELEMENTARY, WHICH LATER...
RRUMBBLE
...CAME TO BE CALLED...
...THE GRADE-SCHOOLERS' PENITENTIARY!!
I HEREBY CALL THE TENBIN ELEMENTARY CLASSES 6-2 AND 6-3...
!!
KLAK
ORDER!!
ORDER!!!
KLA
Accused / Picasso (Hikari Takasu)

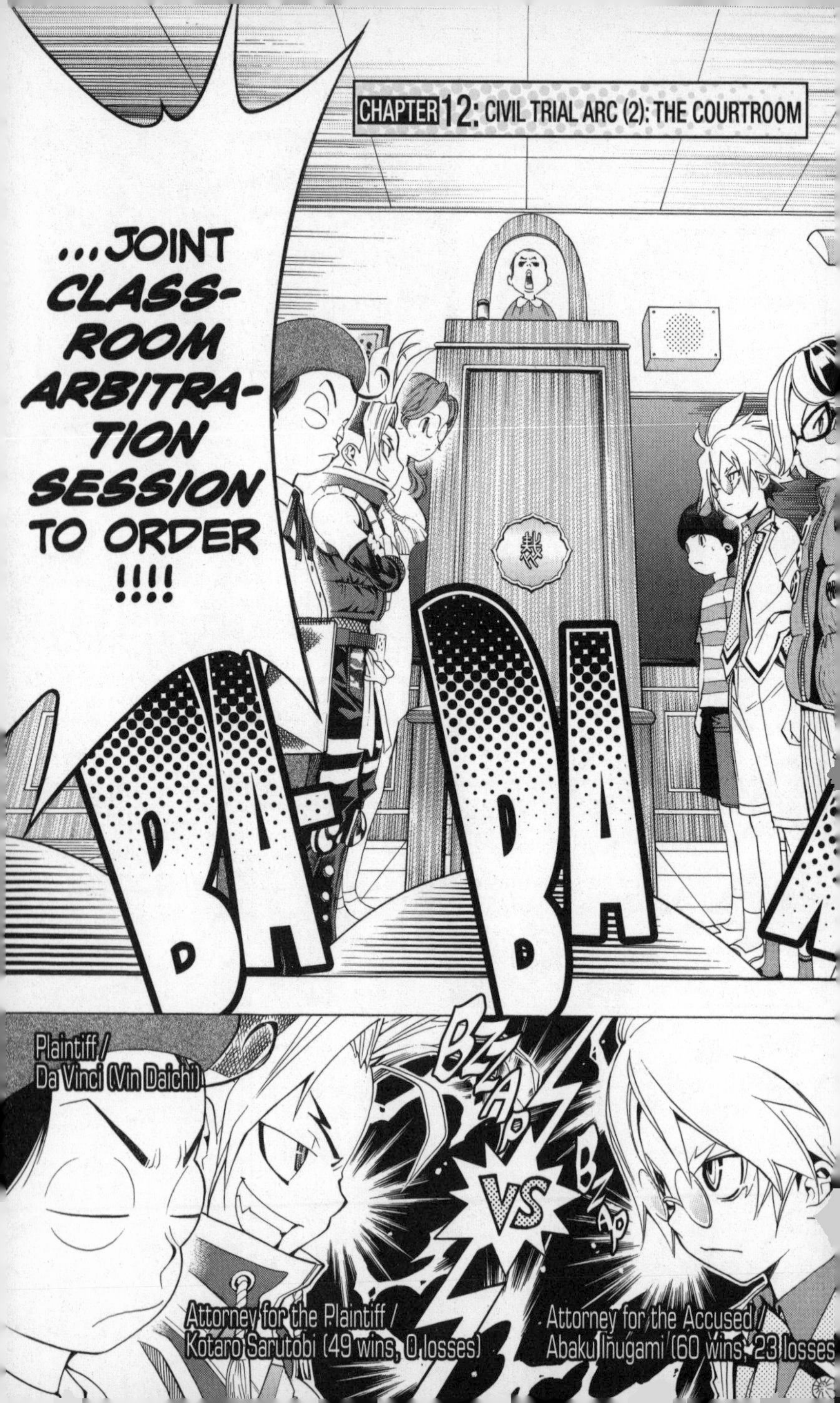
CHAPTER 12: CIVIL TRIAL ARC (2): THE COURTROOM
...JOINT CLASS-ROOM ARBITRA-TION SESSION TO ORDER!!!!
BA-BA
Attorney for the Accused / Abaku Inugami (60 wins, 23 losses)
BZAP
VS
BZZAP
Plaintiff / Da Vinci (Vin Daichi)
Attorney for the Plaintiff / Kotaro Sarutobi (49 wins, 0 losses)

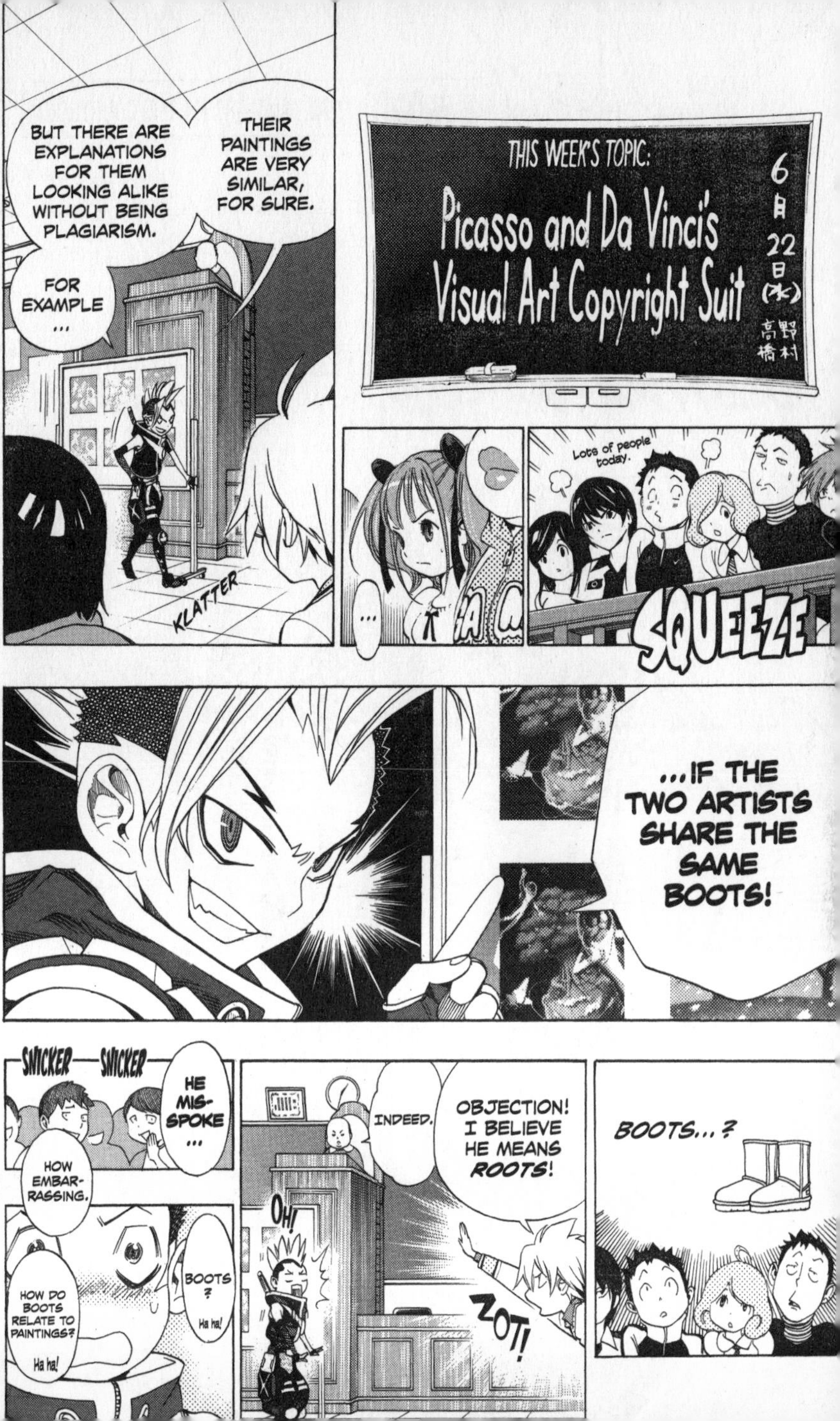

THIS WEEK'S TOPIC:
Picasso and Da Vinci's Visual Art Copyright Suit
6月22日(水)
野村
高橋
Lots of people today.
SQUEEZE
...
THEIR PAINTINGS ARE VERY SIMILAR, FOR SURE.
BUT THERE ARE EXPLANATIONS FOR THEM LOOKING ALIKE WITHOUT BEING PLAGIARISM.
FOR EXAMPLE...
KLATTER
...IF THE TWO ARTISTS SHARE THE SAME BOOTS!
BOOTS...?
OBJECTION! I BELIEVE HE MEANS ROOTS!
INDEED.
OH!
ZOT!
SNICKER
SNICKER
HE MIS-SPOKE...
HOW EMBAR-RASSING.
BOOTS?
Ha ha!
HOW DO BOOTS RELATE TO PAINTINGS?
Ha ha!

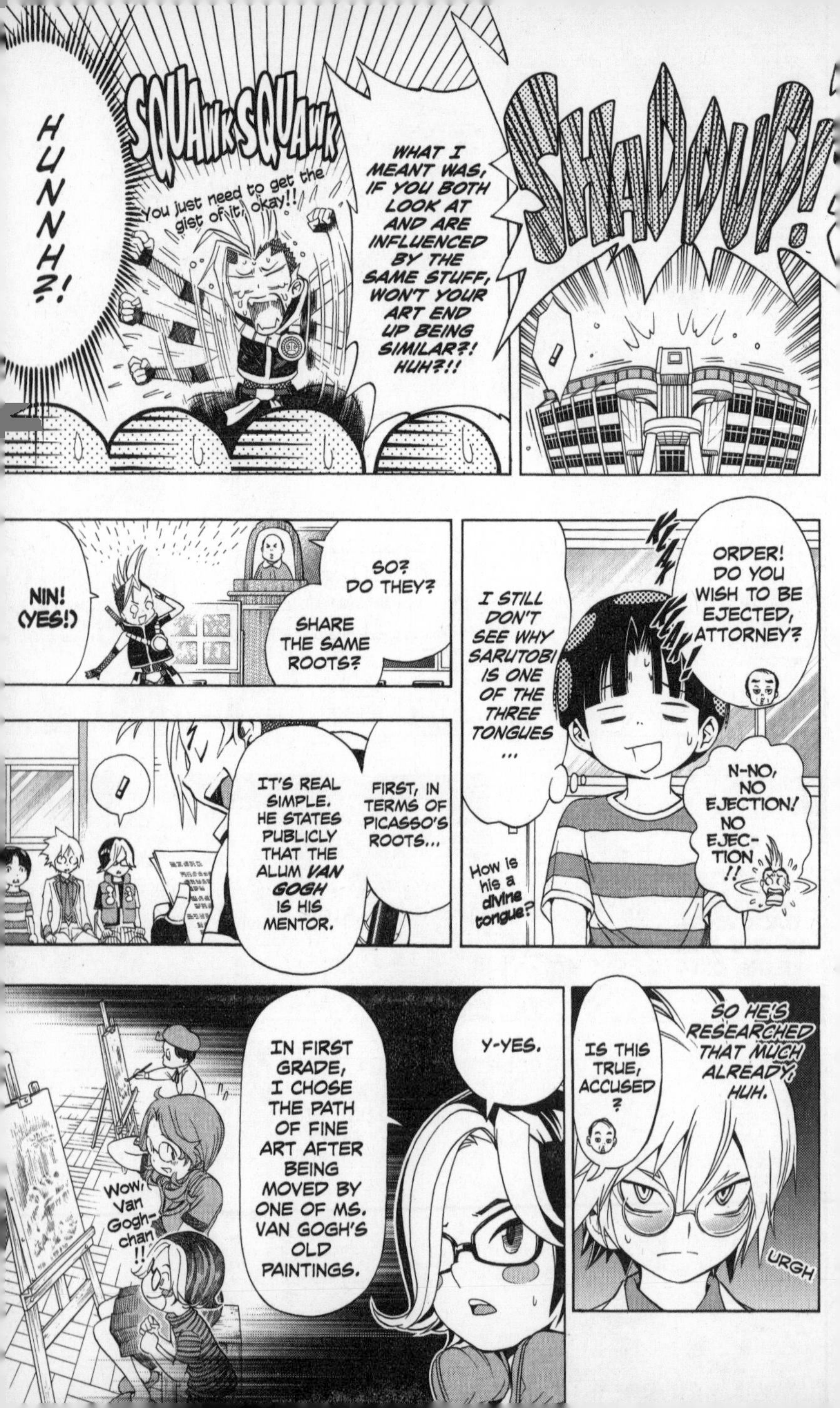
SHADDUP!!
WHAT I MEANT WAS, IF YOU BOTH LOOK AT AND ARE INFLUENCED BY THE SAME STUFF, WON'T YOUR ART END UP BEING SIMILAR?! HUH?!!
SQUAWK SQUAWK
You just need to get the gist of it, okay!!
HUNNNH?!
ORDER! DO YOU WISH TO BE EJECTED, ATTORNEY?
I STILL DON'T SEE WHY SARUTOBI IS ONE OF THE THREE TONGUES ...
N-NO, NO EJECTION! NO EJECTION!!
How is his a divine tongue?
SO? DO THEY?
SHARE THE SAME ROOTS?
NIN! (YES!)
FIRST, IN TERMS OF PICASSO'S ROOTS...
IT'S REAL SIMPLE. HE STATES PUBLICLY THAT THE ALUM VAN GOGH IS HIS MENTOR.
!
SO HE'S RESEARCHED THAT MUCH ALREADY, HUH.
IS THIS TRUE, ACCUSED?
URGH
Y-YES.
IN FIRST GRADE, I CHOSE THE PATH OF FINE ART AFTER BEING MOVED BY ONE OF MS. VAN GOGH'S OLD PAINTINGS.
Wow, Van Gogh-chan!!

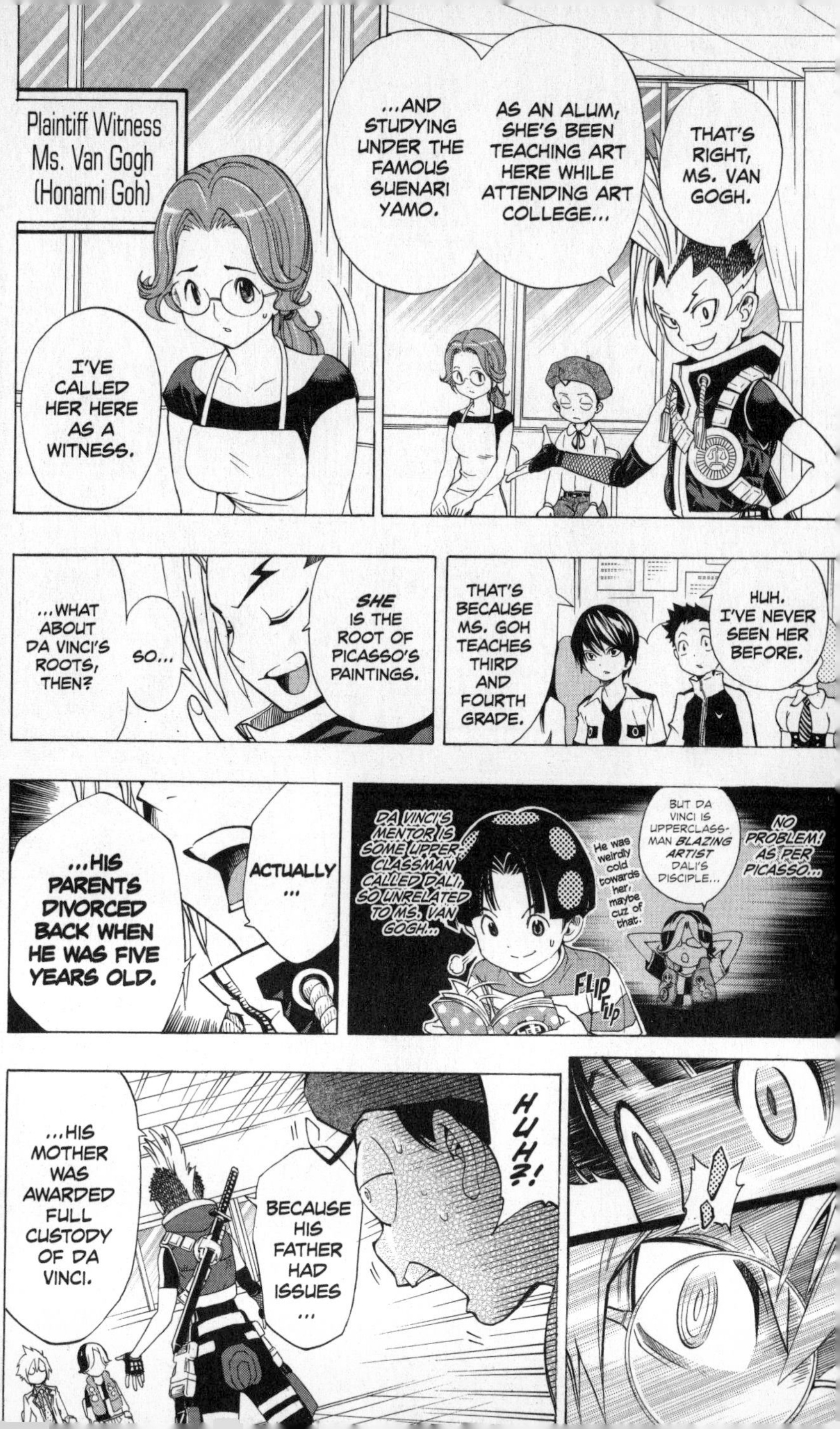
THAT'S RIGHT, MS. VAN GOGH.
AS AN ALUM, SHE'S BEEN TEACHING ART HERE WHILE ATTENDING ART COLLEGE...
...AND STUDYING UNDER THE FAMOUS SUENARI YAMO.
Plaintiff Witness Ms. Van Gogh (Honami Goh)
I'VE CALLED HER HERE AS A WITNESS.
HUH. I'VE NEVER SEEN HER BEFORE.
THAT'S BECAUSE MS. GOH TEACHES THIRD AND FOURTH GRADE.
SHE IS THE ROOT OF PICASSO'S PAINTINGS.
SO...
...WHAT ABOUT DA VINCI'S ROOTS, THEN?
NO PROBLEM! AS PER PICASSO...
BUT DA VINCI IS UPPERCLASSMAN *BLAZING ARTIST* DALI'S DISCIPLE...
He was weirdly cold towards her, maybe cuz of that.
DA VINCI'S MENTOR IS SOME UPPERCLASSMAN CALLED DALI, SO UNRELATED TO MS. VAN GOGH...
FLIP FLIP
ACTUALLY...
...HIS PARENTS DIVORCED BACK WHEN HE WAS FIVE YEARS OLD.
HUH?!
BECAUSE HIS FATHER HAD ISSUES...
...HIS MOTHER WAS AWARDED FULL CUSTODY OF DA VINCI.

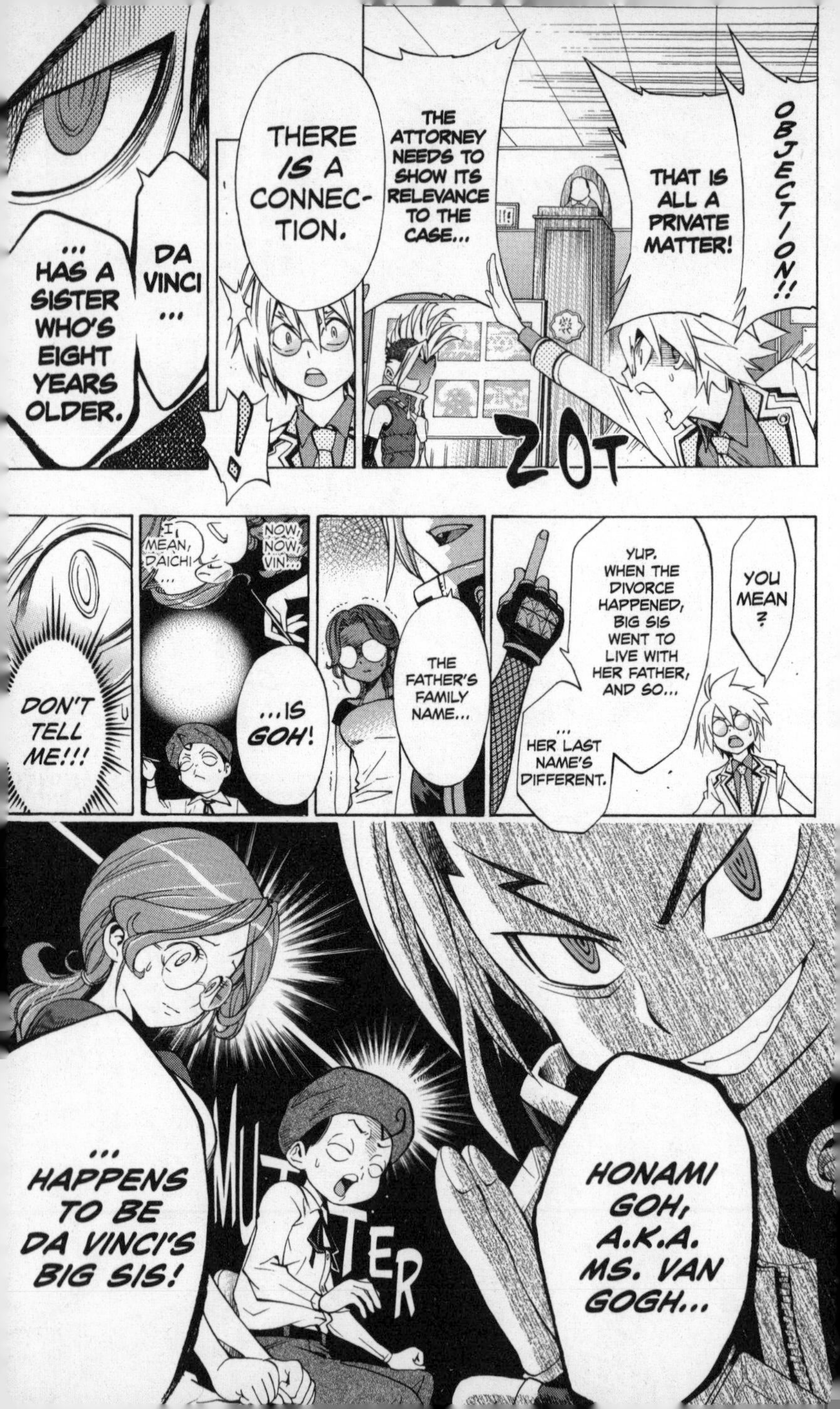
OBJECTION!!
THAT IS ALL A PRIVATE MATTER!
THE ATTORNEY NEEDS TO SHOW ITS RELEVANCE TO THE CASE...
ZOT
THERE IS A CONNECTION.
!
DA VINCI...
...HAS A SISTER WHO'S EIGHT YEARS OLDER.
YOU MEAN?
YUP. WHEN THE DIVORCE HAPPENED, BIG SIS WENT TO LIVE WITH HER FATHER, AND SO...
...HER LAST NAME'S DIFFERENT.
THE FATHER'S FAMILY NAME...
...IS GOH!
NOW, NOW, VIN...
I, MEAN, DAICHI...
DON'T TELL ME!!!
HONAMI GOH, A.K.A. MS. VAN GOGH...
...HAPPENS TO BE DA VINCI'S BIG SIS!
MUTTER

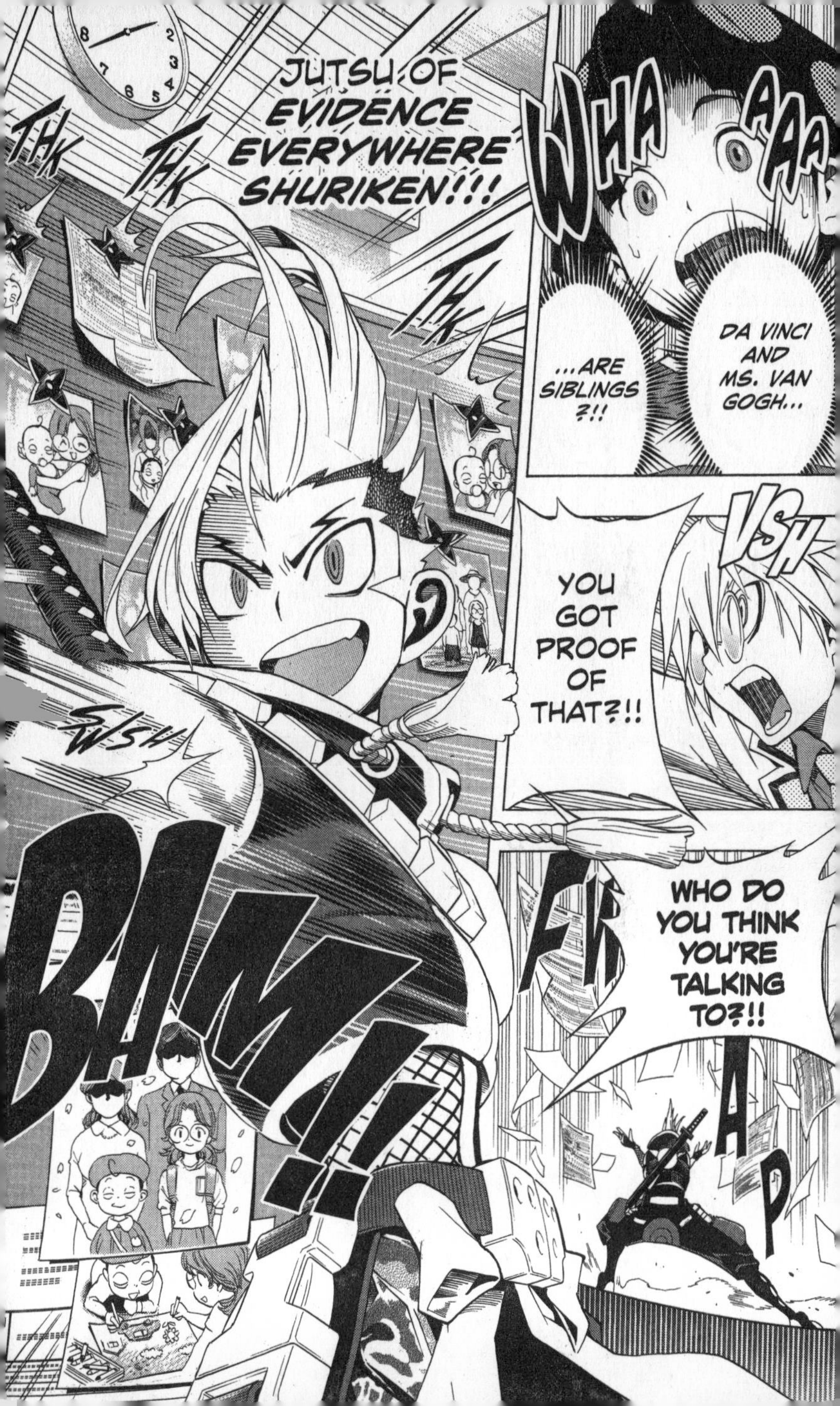
WHAAAA
DA VINCI AND MS. VAN GOGH...
...ARE SIBLINGS?!!
VSH
YOU GOT PROOF OF THAT?!!
FK
WHO DO YOU THINK YOU'RE TALKING TO?!!
AP
JUTSU OF EVIDENCE EVERYWHERE SHURIKEN!!!
THK
THK
THK
SWSH
BAM!!

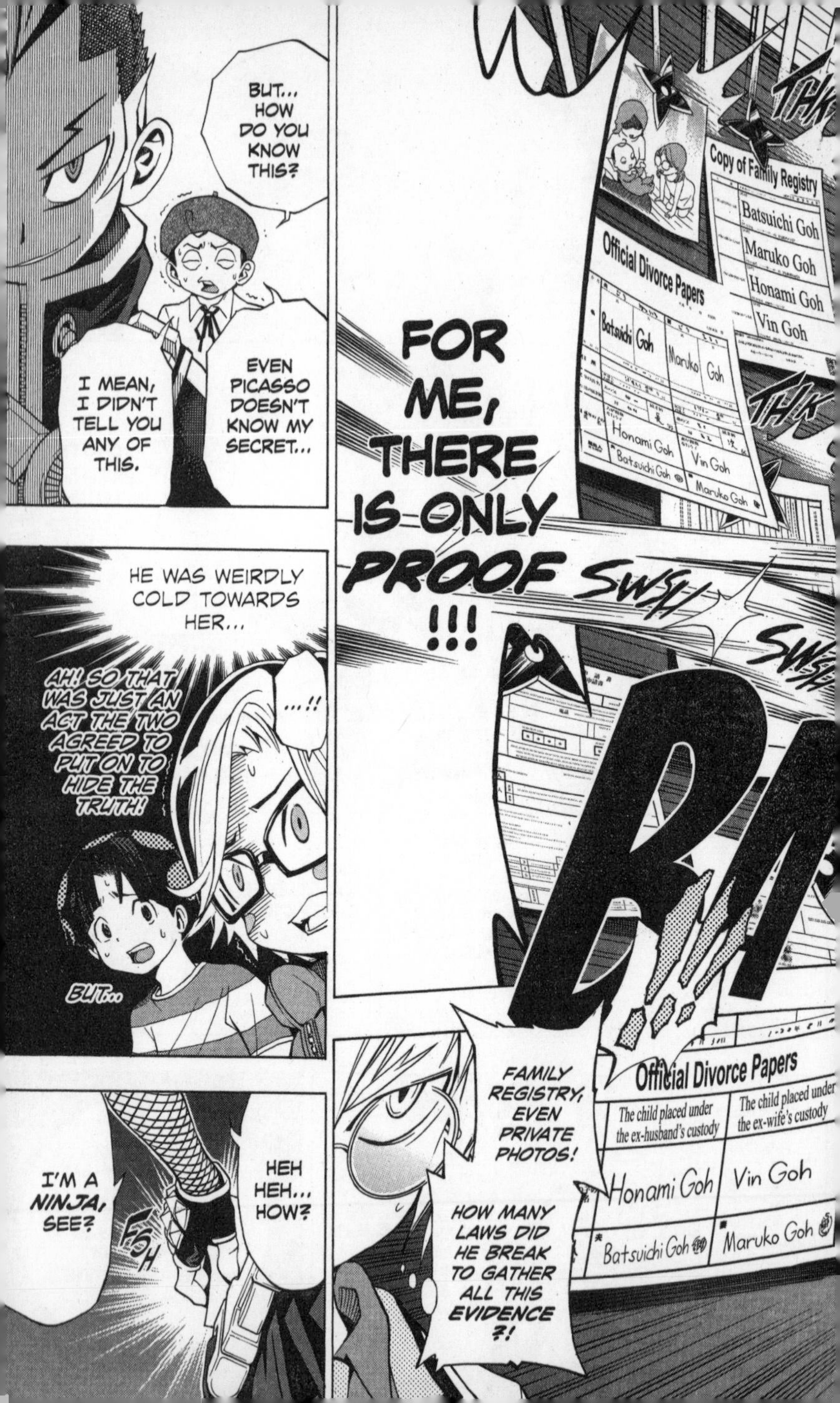
THK
Copy of Family Registry
Batsuichi Goh
Maruko Goh
Honami Goh
Vin Goh
Official Divorce Papers
Batsuichi Goh Maruko Goh
Honami Goh Vin Goh
Batsuichi Goh Maruko Goh
THK
FOR ME, THERE IS ONLY PROOF!!!
SWSH
SWSH
BUT... HOW DO YOU KNOW THIS?
EVEN PICASSO DOESN'T KNOW MY SECRET...
I MEAN, I DIDN'T TELL YOU ANY OF THIS.
HE WAS WEIRDLY COLD TOWARDS HER...
...!!
AH! SO THAT WAS JUST AN ACT THE TWO AGREED TO PUT ON TO HIDE THE TRUTH!
BUT...
Official Divorce Papers
The child placed under the ex-wife's custody
The child placed under the ex-husband's custody
Vin Goh
Honami Goh
Maruko Goh
Batsuichi Goh
FAMILY REGISTRY, EVEN PRIVATE PHOTOS!
HOW MANY LAWS DID HE BREAK TO GATHER ALL THIS EVIDENCE?!
HEH HEH... HOW?
I'M A NINJA, SEE?
FSH

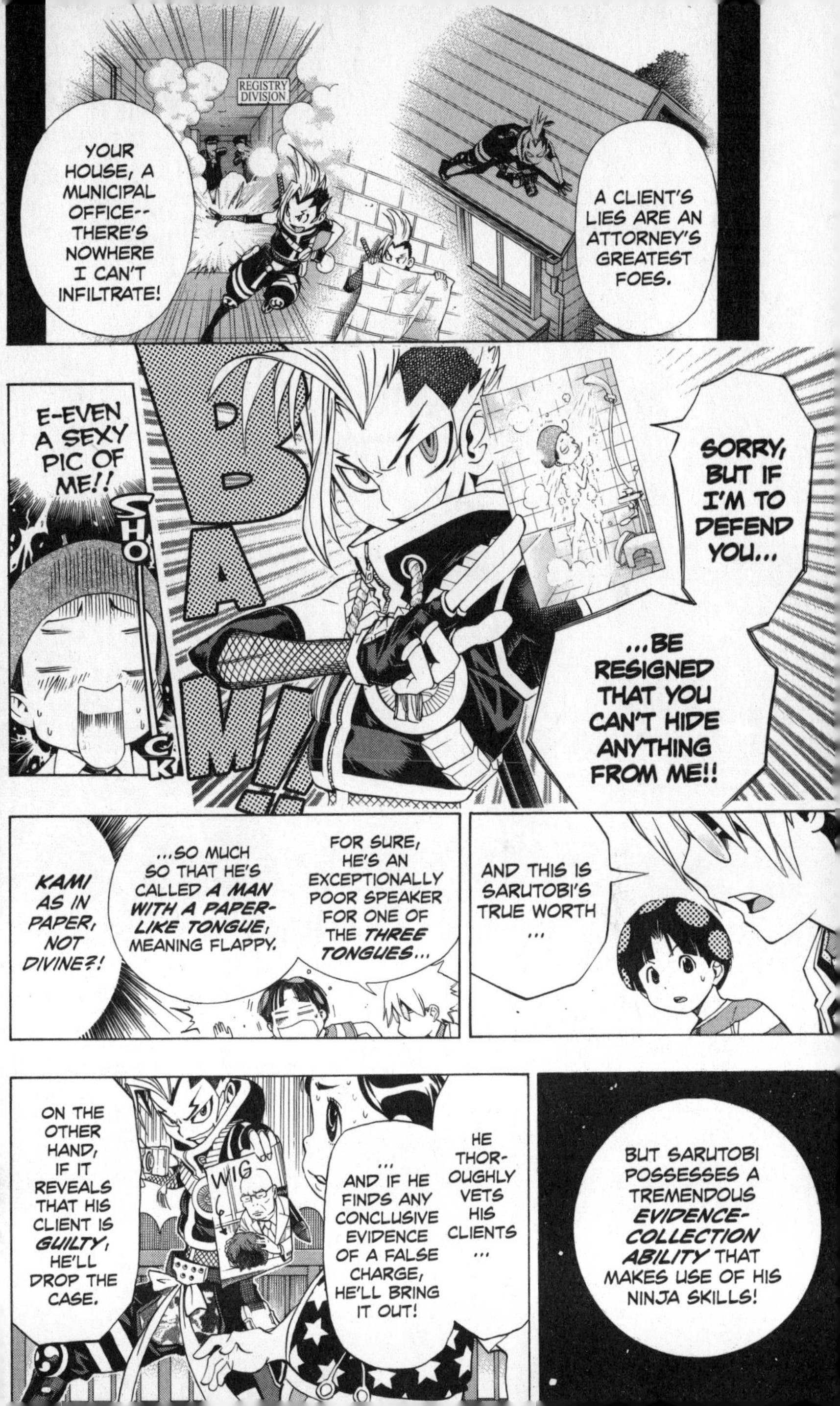
A CLIENT'S LIES ARE AN ATTORNEY'S GREATEST FOES.
REGISTRY DIVISION
YOUR HOUSE, A MUNICIPAL OFFICE-- THERE'S NOWHERE I CAN'T INFILTRATE!
SORRY, BUT IF I'M TO DEFEND YOU...
...BE RESIGNED THAT YOU CAN'T HIDE ANYTHING FROM ME!!
BAM!!
E-EVEN A SEXY PIC OF ME!!
SHOCK
AND THIS IS SARUTOBI'S TRUE WORTH ...
FOR SURE, HE'S AN EXCEPTIONALLY POOR SPEAKER FOR ONE OF THE *THREE TONGUES*...
...SO MUCH SO THAT HE'S CALLED *A MAN WITH A PAPER-LIKE TONGUE*, MEANING FLAPPY.
KAMI AS IN PAPER, NOT DIVINE?!
BUT SARUTOBI POSSESSES A TREMENDOUS *EVIDENCE-COLLECTION ABILITY* THAT MAKES USE OF HIS NINJA SKILLS!
HE THOROUGHLY VETS HIS CLIENTS ...
... AND IF HE FINDS ANY CONCLUSIVE EVIDENCE OF A FALSE CHARGE, HE'LL BRING IT OUT!
WIG
ON THE OTHER HAND, IF IT REVEALS THAT HIS CLIENT IS *GUILTY*, HE'LL DROP THE CASE.

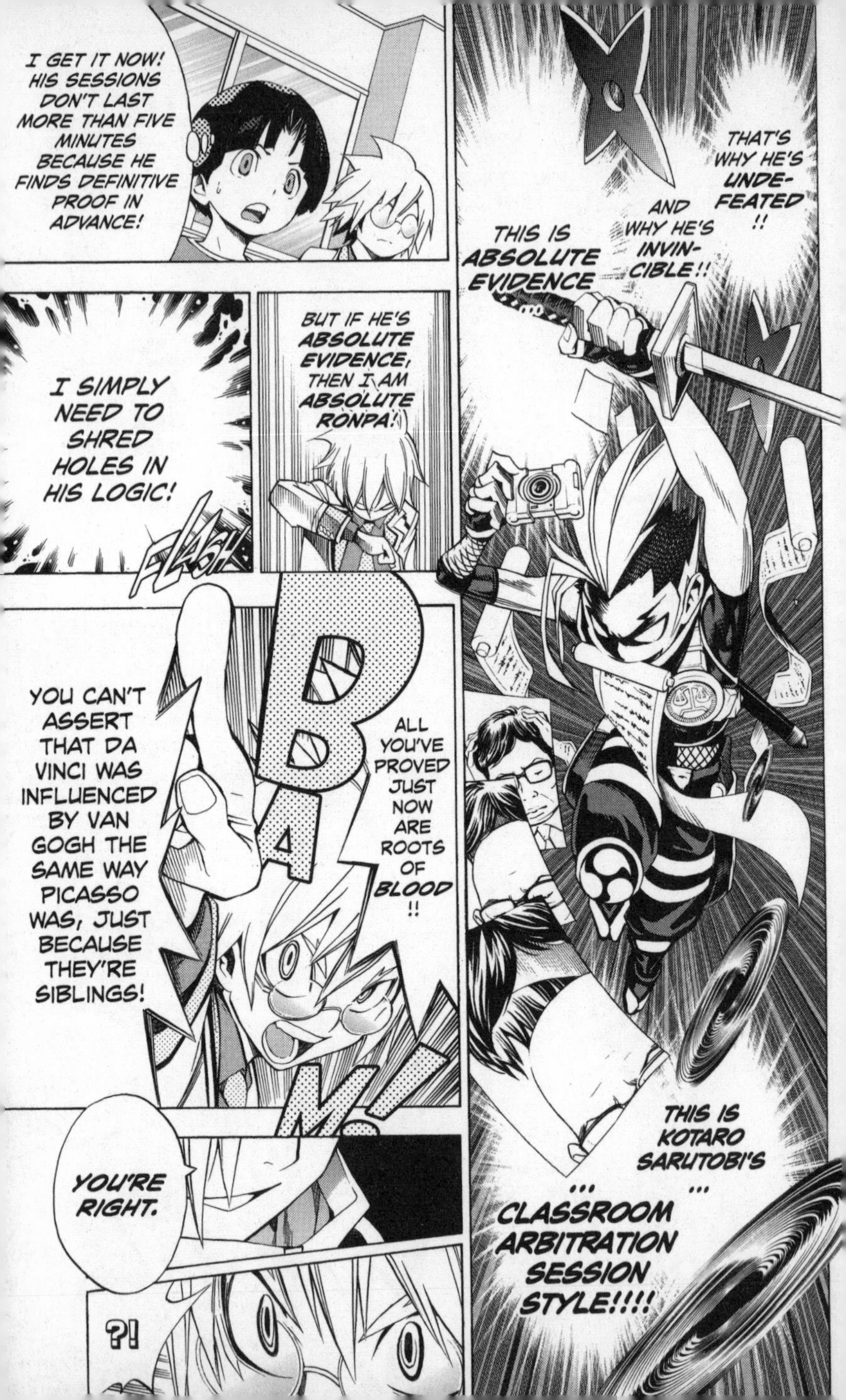

THAT'S WHY HE'S UNDEFEATED!!
AND WHY HE'S INVINCIBLE!!
THIS IS ABSOLUTE EVIDENCE
THIS IS KOTARO SARUTOBI'S ...
... CLASSROOM ARBITRATION SESSION STYLE!!!!
I GET IT NOW! HIS SESSIONS DON'T LAST MORE THAN FIVE MINUTES BECAUSE HE FINDS DEFINITIVE PROOF IN ADVANCE!
BUT IF HE'S ABSOLUTE EVIDENCE, THEN I AM ABSOLUTE RONPA!
I SIMPLY NEED TO SHRED HOLES IN HIS LOGIC!
FLASH!
BAM!
ALL YOU'VE PROVED JUST NOW ARE ROOTS OF BLOOD!!
YOU CAN'T ASSERT THAT DA VINCI WAS INFLUENCED BY VAN GOGH THE SAME WAY PICASSO WAS, JUST BECAUSE THEY'RE SIBLINGS!
YOU'RE RIGHT.
?!

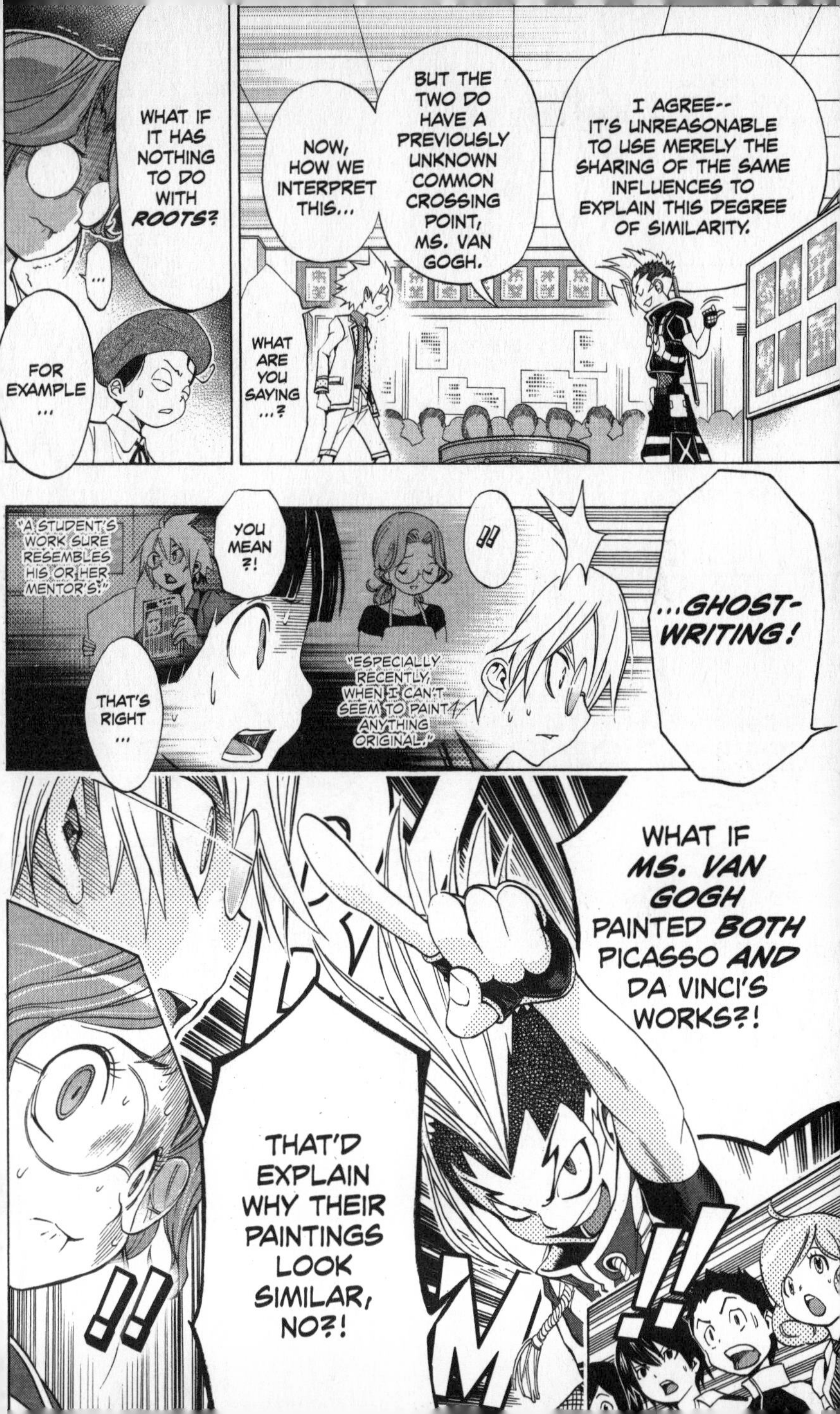
I AGREE-- IT'S UNREASONABLE TO USE MERELY THE SHARING OF THE SAME INFLUENCES TO EXPLAIN THIS DEGREE OF SIMILARITY.
BUT THE TWO DO HAVE A PREVIOUSLY UNKNOWN COMMON CROSSING POINT, MS. VAN GOGH.
NOW, HOW WE INTERPRET THIS...
WHAT ARE YOU SAYING...?
WHAT IF IT HAS NOTHING TO DO WITH ROOTS?
...
FOR EXAMPLE...
...GHOST-WRITING!
!!
YOU MEAN?!
"ESPECIALLY RECENTLY, WHEN I CAN'T SEEM TO PAINT ANYTHING ORIGINAL."
"A STUDENT'S WORK SURE RESEMBLES HIS OR HER MENTOR'S."
THAT'S RIGHT...
WHAT IF MS. VAN GOGH PAINTED BOTH PICASSO AND DA VINCI'S WORKS?!
THAT'D EXPLAIN WHY THEIR PAINTINGS LOOK SIMILAR, NO?!
!!
!!

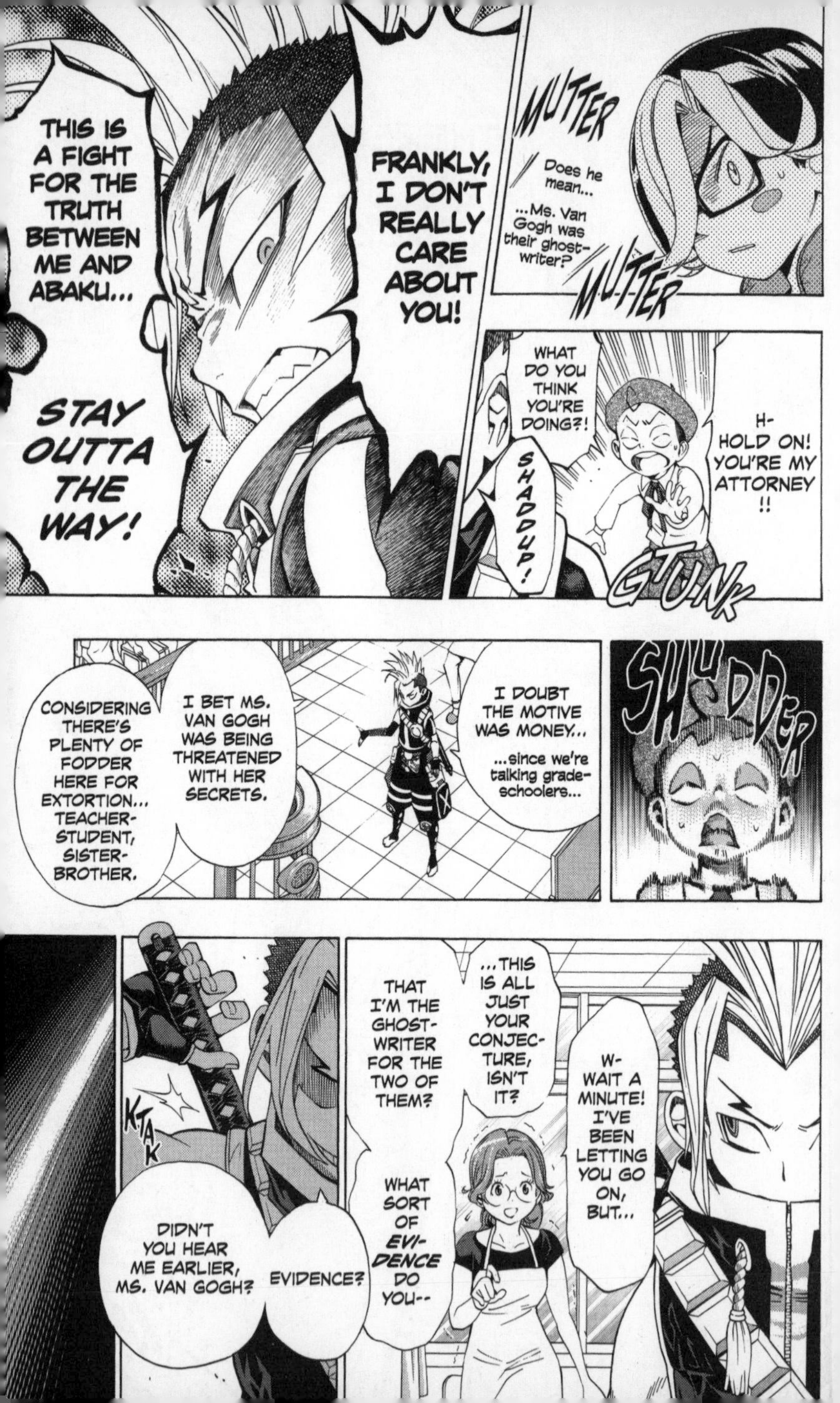
MUTTER
Does he mean...
...Ms. Van Gogh was their ghost-writer?
MUTTER
WHAT DO YOU THINK YOU'RE DOING?!
H- HOLD ON! YOU'RE MY ATTORNEY!!
SHADDUP!
GTUNK
FRANKLY, I DON'T REALLY CARE ABOUT YOU!
THIS IS A FIGHT FOR THE TRUTH BETWEEN ME AND ABAKU...
STAY OUTTA THE WAY!
SHUDDER
I DOUBT THE MOTIVE WAS MONEY...
...since we're talking grade-schoolers...
I BET MS. VAN GOGH WAS BEING THREATENED WITH HER SECRETS.
CONSIDERING THERE'S PLENTY OF FODDER HERE FOR EXTORTION... TEACHER-STUDENT, SISTER-BROTHER.
W- WAIT A MINUTE! I'VE BEEN LETTING YOU GO ON, BUT...
...THIS IS ALL JUST YOUR CONJECTURE, ISN'T IT?
THAT I'M THE GHOST-WRITER FOR THE TWO OF THEM?
WHAT SORT OF EVIDENCE DO YOU--
KTAK
EVIDENCE?
DIDN'T YOU HEAR ME EARLIER, MS. VAN GOGH?

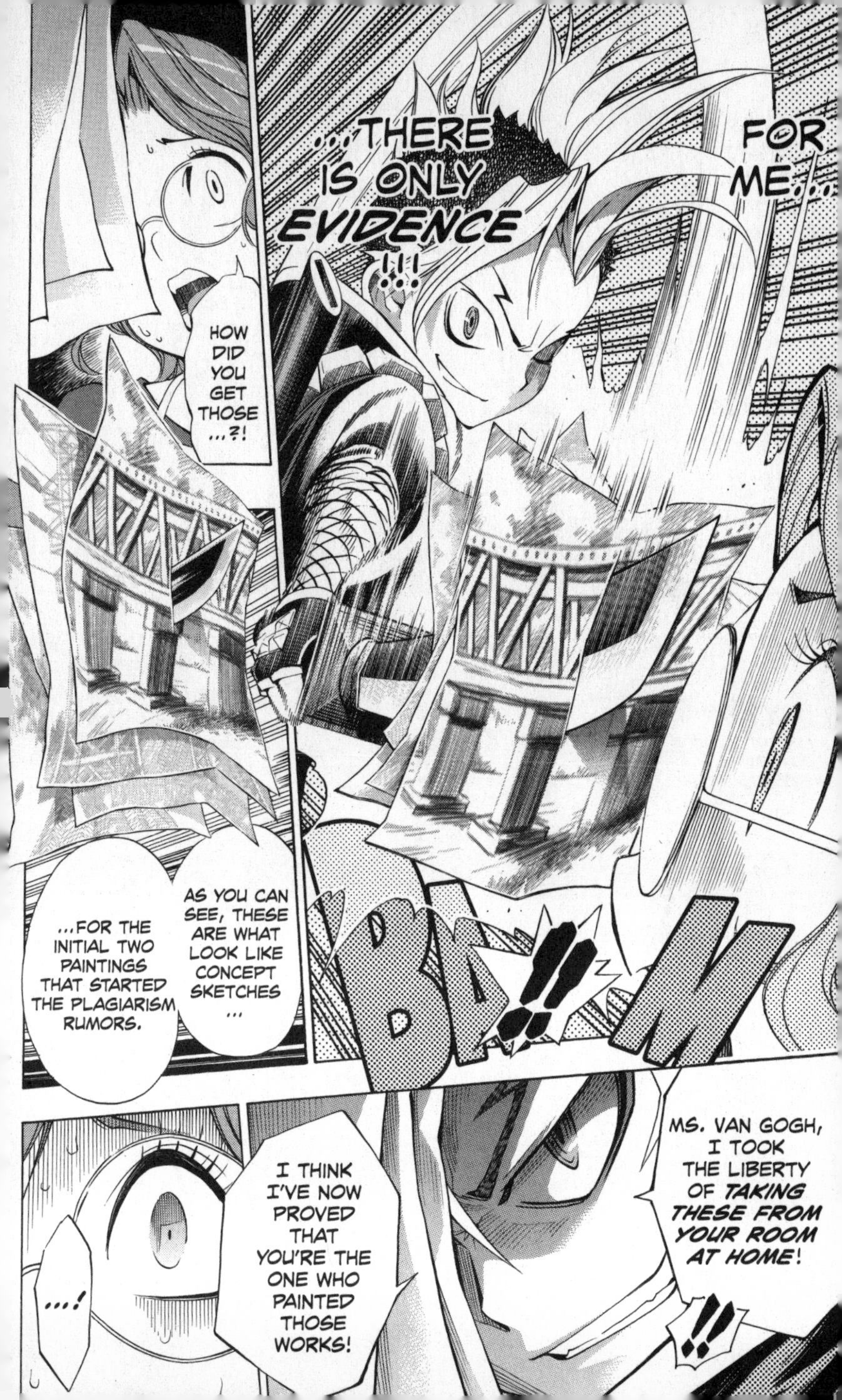
FOR ME...
...THERE IS ONLY EVIDENCE !!!
HOW DID YOU GET THOSE ...?!
BAM!!
AS YOU CAN SEE, THESE ARE WHAT LOOK LIKE CONCEPT SKETCHES ...
...FOR THE INITIAL TWO PAINTINGS THAT STARTED THE PLAGIARISM RUMORS.
MS. VAN GOGH, I TOOK THE LIBERTY OF *TAKING THESE FROM YOUR ROOM AT HOME*!
!!
I THINK I'VE NOW PROVED THAT YOU'RE THE ONE WHO PAINTED THOSE WORKS!
...!

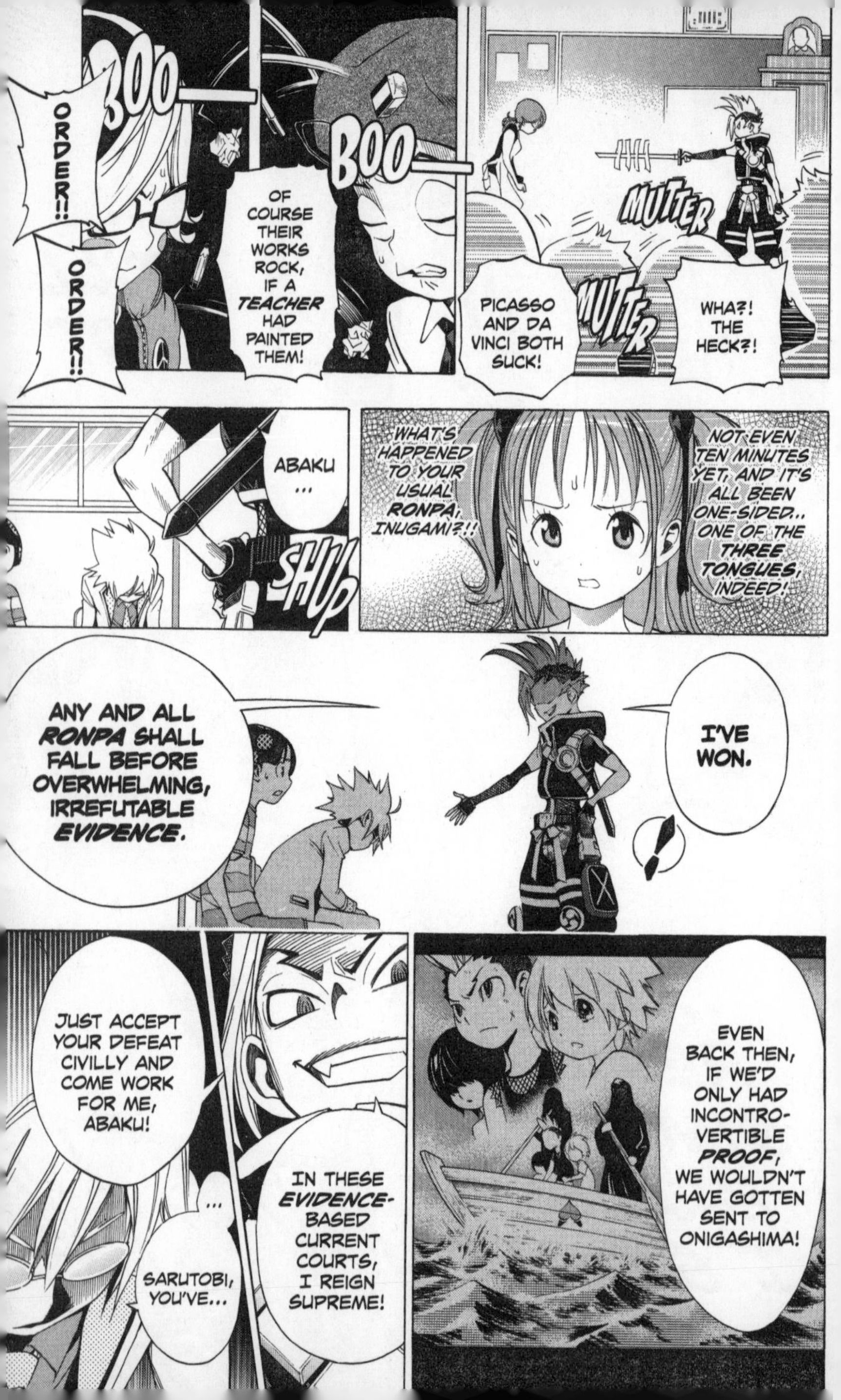
WHA?! THE HECK?!
MUTTER
MUTTER
PICASSO AND DA VINCI BOTH SUCK!
BOO
OF COURSE THEIR WORKS ROCK, IF A TEACHER HAD PAINTED THEM!
ORDER!!
ORDER!!
NOT EVEN TEN MINUTES YET, AND IT'S ALL BEEN ONE-SIDED.. ONE OF THE THREE TONGUES, INDEED!
WHAT'S HAPPENED TO YOUR USUAL RONPA, INUGAMI?!!
ABAKU ...
SHUP
I'VE WON.
!
ANY AND ALL RONPA SHALL FALL BEFORE OVERWHELMING, IRREFUTABLE EVIDENCE.
EVEN BACK THEN, IF WE'D ONLY HAD INCONTRO-VERTIBLE PROOF, WE WOULDN'T HAVE GOTTEN SENT TO ONIGASHIMA!
JUST ACCEPT YOUR DEFEAT CIVILLY AND COME WORK FOR ME, ABAKU!
IN THESE EVIDENCE-BASED CURRENT COURTS, I REIGN SUPREME!
...
SARUTOBI, YOU'VE...

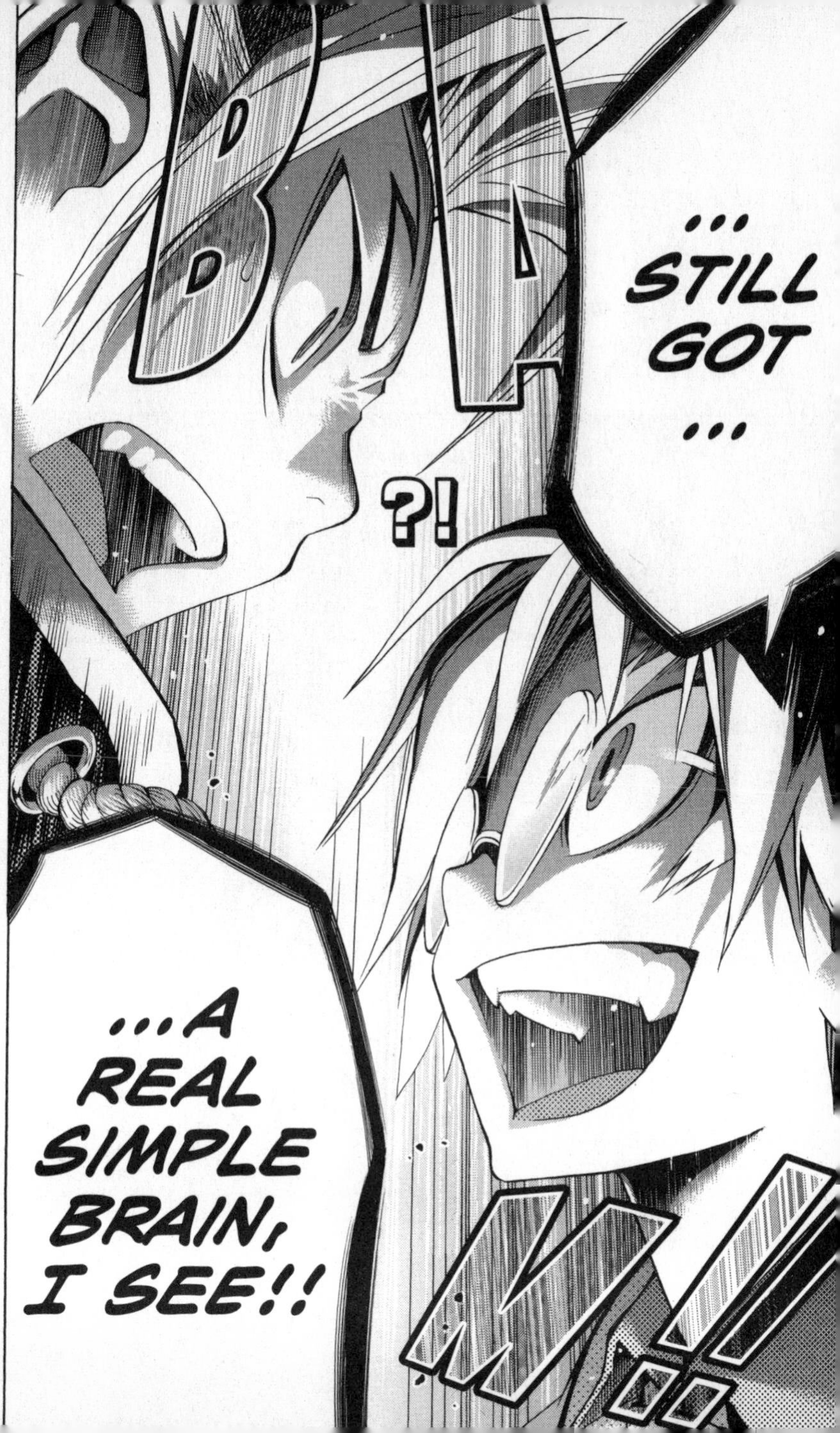

...STILL GOT...
BA
?!
...A REAL SIMPLE BRAIN, I SEE!!
M!!

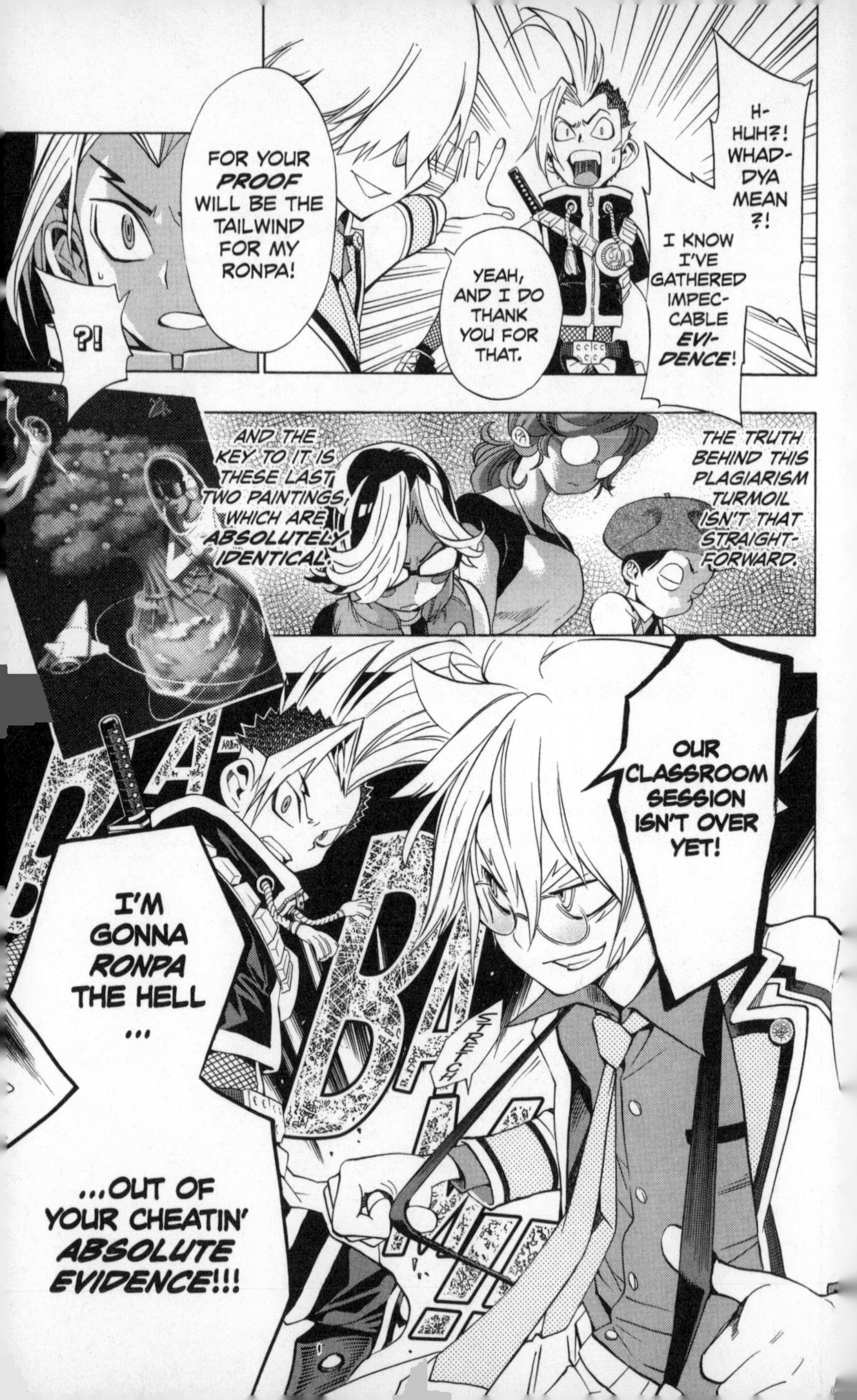
H-HUH?! WHADDYA MEAN?!
I KNOW I'VE GATHERED IMPECCABLE EVIDENCE!
YEAH, AND I DO THANK YOU FOR THAT.
FOR YOUR PROOF WILL BE THE TAILWIND FOR MY RONPA!
?!
THE TRUTH BEHIND THIS PLAGIARISM TURMOIL ISN'T THAT STRAIGHT-FORWARD.
AND THE KEY TO IT IS THESE LAST TWO PAINTINGS, WHICH ARE ABSOLUTELY IDENTICAL.
OUR CLASSROOM SESSION ISN'T OVER YET!
STRETCH
I'M GONNA RONPA THE HELL...
...OUT OF YOUR CHEATIN' ABSOLUTE EVIDENCE!!!

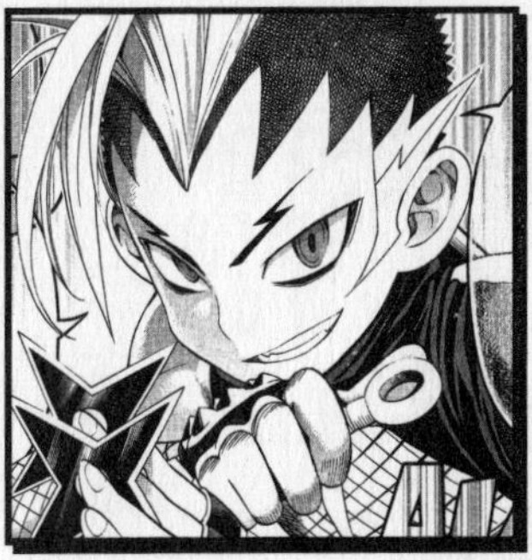
(Obata's final version)

Kotaro Sarutobi

Height: 5'
Dislikes: Language, math, studying in general...

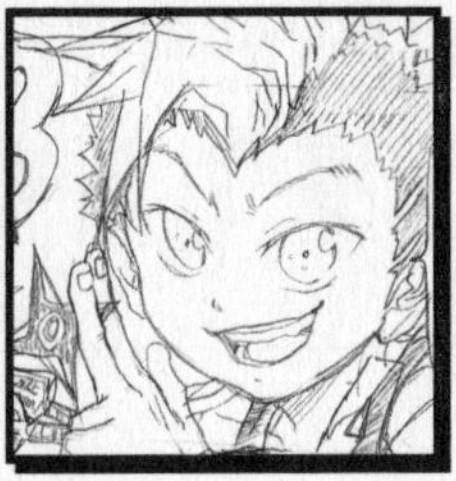
(Enoki's draft version)

A ninja and a defense attorney! He's a child who looks like he'd be the one getting put on trial since he does not shy away from breaking the rules to gather evidence.

A long-standing rival of Abaku's who knows his past... Their relationship may be commonplace, but I had difficulty writing their relationship. This character was pretty troublesome. When my editor first saw the rough draft, he said, "Sarutobi's love of Abaku is showing through too much." So ever since, I kept working on hiding Sarutobi's feelings for Abaku so it wouldn't be too obvious. I wanted to make it kind of like a first crush or puppy love. I have a feeling this kind of became more obvious in volume 3 (spoiler!).

By the way, the "Sharaaaa!" that Sarutobi says a lot in Japanese is derived from the English "Shaddup (Shut up!)," but at some point the author forgot he had such a catchphrase... So now I'm taking the opportunity here to apologize so it never happens again.

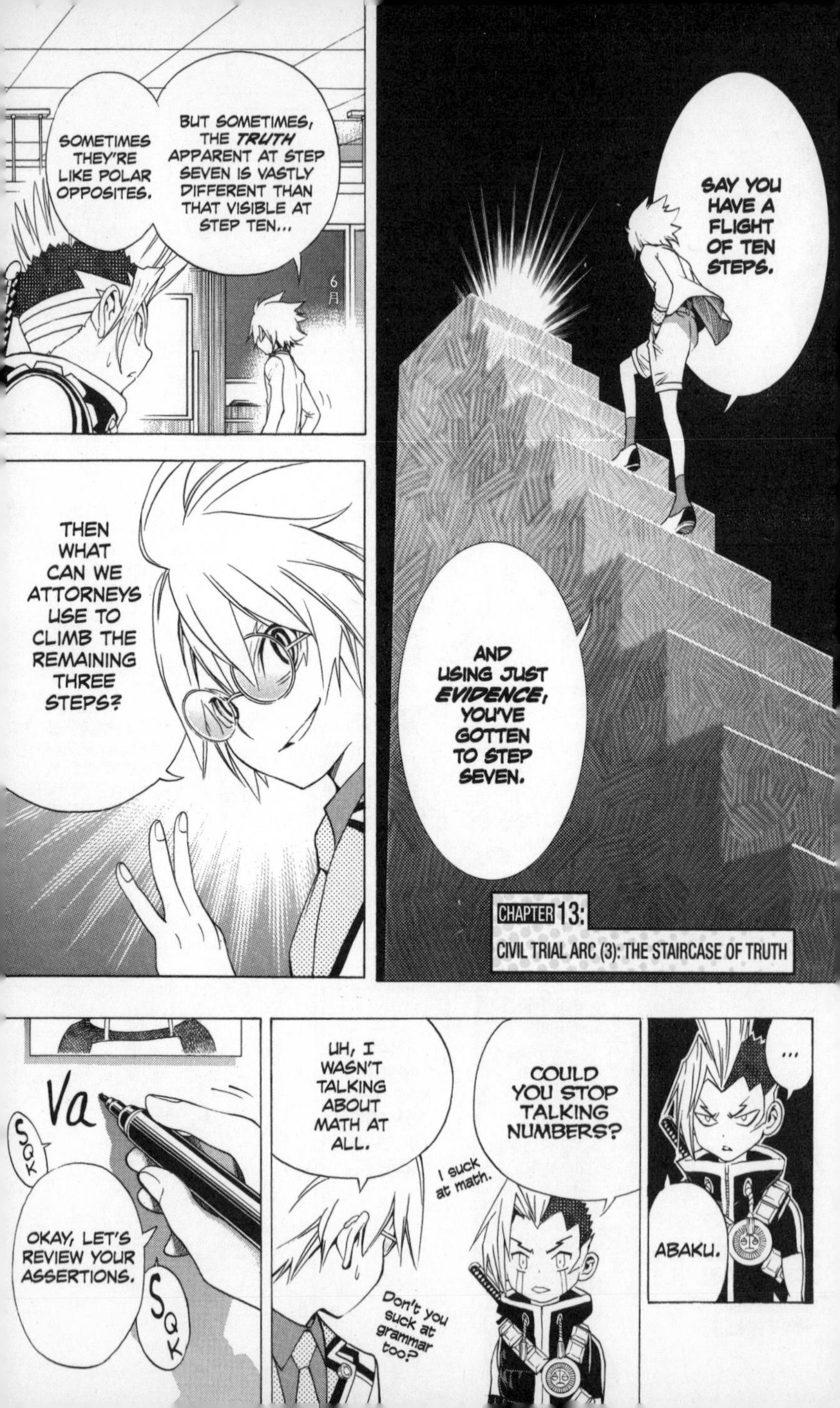
SAY YOU HAVE A FLIGHT OF TEN STEPS.
AND USING JUST EVIDENCE, YOU'VE GOTTEN TO STEP SEVEN.
CHAPTER 13:
CIVIL TRIAL ARC (3): THE STAIRCASE OF TRUTH
BUT SOMETIMES, THE TRUTH APPARENT AT STEP SEVEN IS VASTLY DIFFERENT THAN THAT VISIBLE AT STEP TEN...
SOMETIMES THEY'RE LIKE POLAR OPPOSITES.
6月
THEN WHAT CAN WE ATTORNEYS USE TO CLIMB THE REMAINING THREE STEPS?
...
ABAKU.
COULD YOU STOP TALKING NUMBERS?
I suck at math.
UH, I WASN'T TALKING ABOUT MATH AT ALL.
Don't you suck at grammar too?
Va
SQK
OKAY, LET'S REVIEW YOUR ASSERTIONS.
SQK

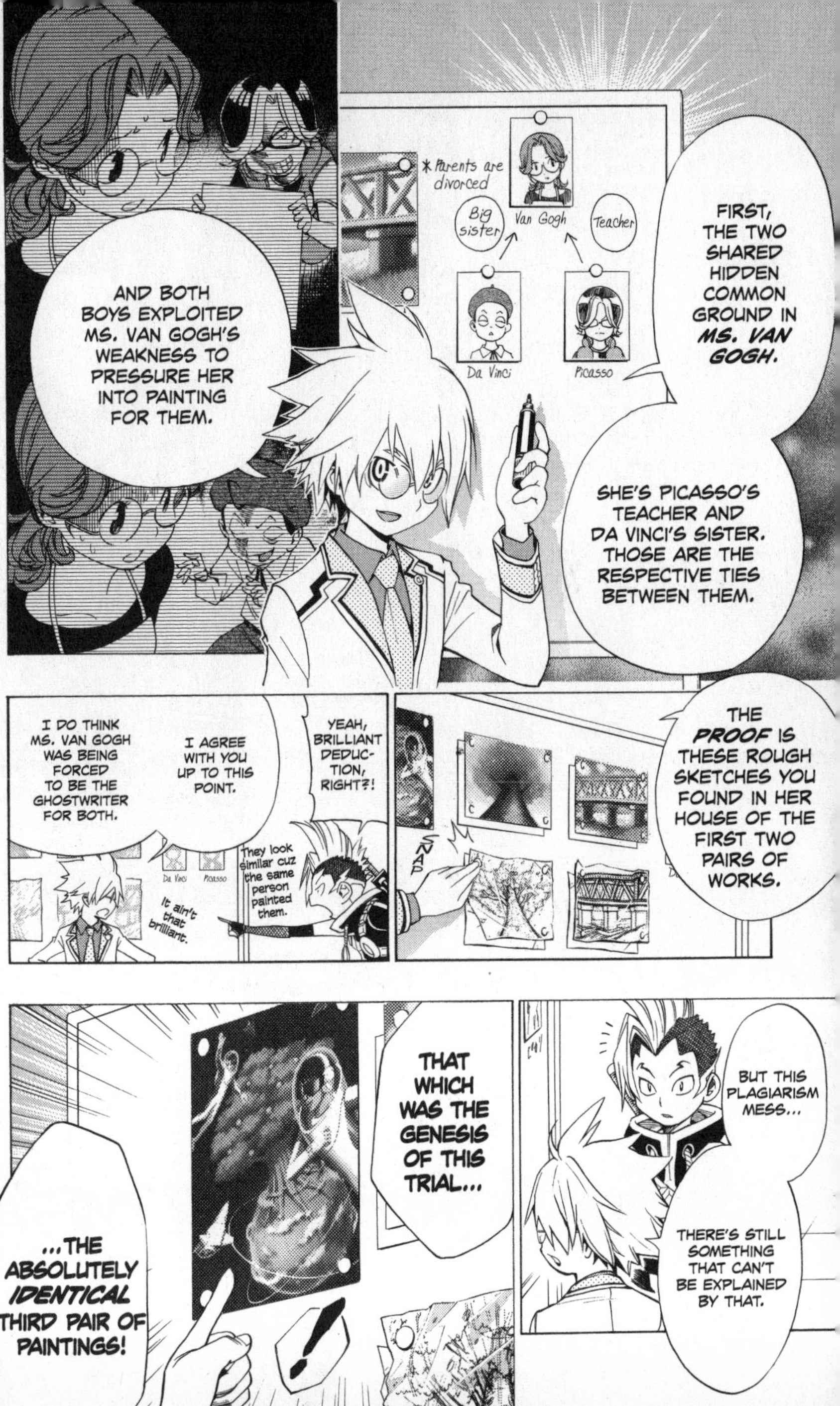
FIRST, THE TWO SHARED HIDDEN COMMON GROUND IN MS. VAN GOGH.
*Parents are divorced
Van Gogh
Big sister
Teacher
Da Vinci
Picasso
SHE'S PICASSO'S TEACHER AND DA VINCI'S SISTER. THOSE ARE THE RESPECTIVE TIES BETWEEN THEM.
AND BOTH BOYS EXPLOITED MS. VAN GOGH'S WEAKNESS TO PRESSURE HER INTO PAINTING FOR THEM.
THE PROOF IS THESE ROUGH SKETCHES YOU FOUND IN HER HOUSE OF THE FIRST TWO PAIRS OF WORKS.
SNAP
YEAH, BRILLIANT DEDUCTION, RIGHT?!
They look similar cuz the same person painted them.
I AGREE WITH YOU UP TO THIS POINT.
I DO THINK MS. VAN GOGH WAS BEING FORCED TO BE THE GHOSTWRITER FOR BOTH.
Da Vinci
Picasso
It ain't that brilliant.
BUT THIS PLAGIARISM MESS...
THERE'S STILL SOMETHING THAT CAN'T BE EXPLAINED BY THAT.
THAT WHICH WAS THE GENESIS OF THIS TRIAL...
...THE ABSOLUTELY IDENTICAL THIRD PAIR OF PAINTINGS!

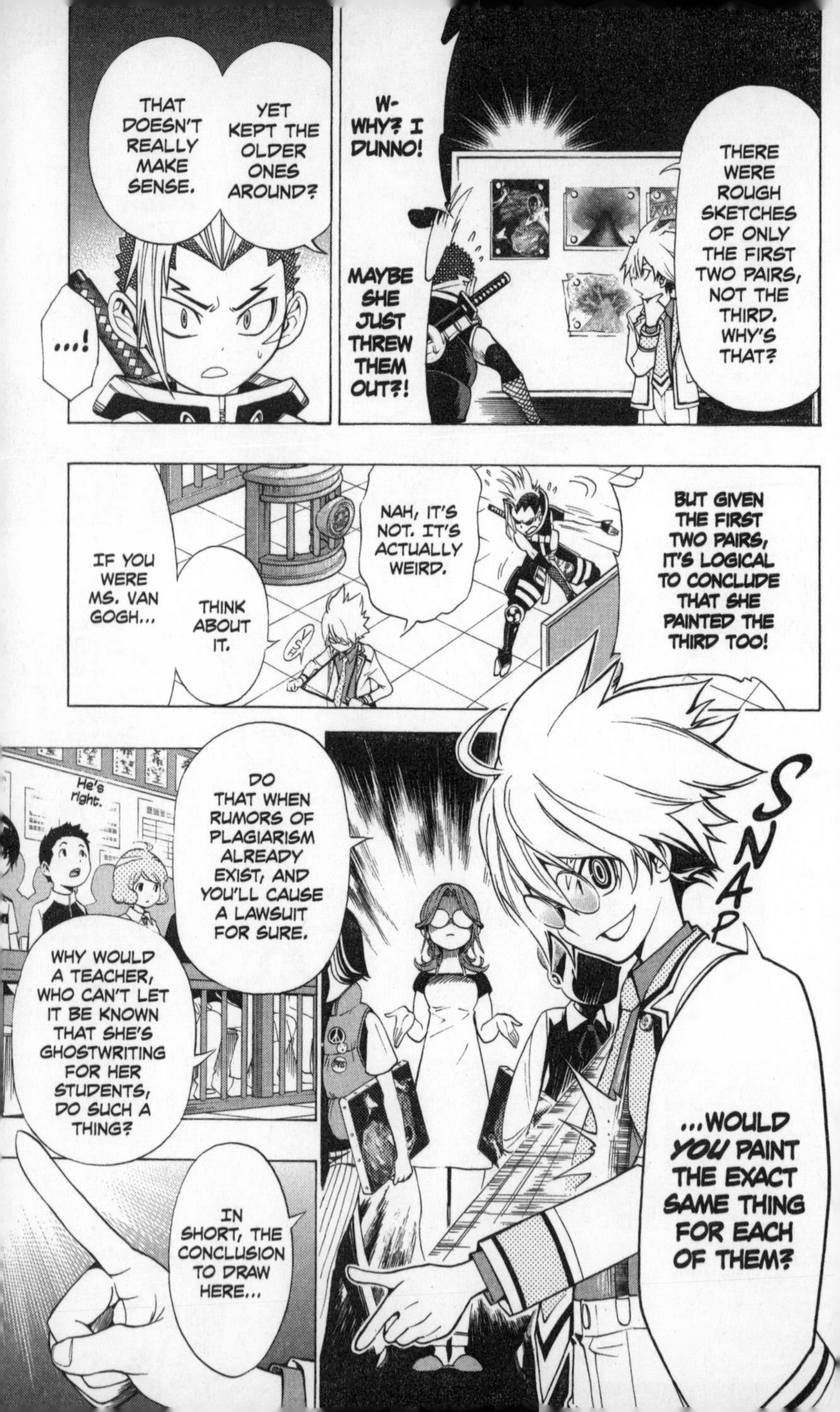
THERE WERE ROUGH SKETCHES OF ONLY THE FIRST TWO PAIRS, NOT THE THIRD. WHY'S THAT?
W-WHY? I DUNNO!
MAYBE SHE JUST THREW THEM OUT?!
YET KEPT THE OLDER ONES AROUND?
THAT DOESN'T REALLY MAKE SENSE.
...!
BUT GIVEN THE FIRST TWO PAIRS, IT'S LOGICAL TO CONCLUDE THAT SHE PAINTED THE THIRD TOO!
NAH, IT'S NOT. IT'S ACTUALLY WEIRD.
THINK ABOUT IT.
IF YOU WERE MS. VAN GOGH...
SNAP
...WOULD *YOU* PAINT THE EXACT SAME THING FOR EACH OF THEM?
DO THAT WHEN RUMORS OF PLAGIARISM ALREADY EXIST, AND YOU'LL CAUSE A LAWSUIT FOR SURE.
He's right.
WHY WOULD A TEACHER, WHO CAN'T LET IT BE KNOWN THAT SHE'S GHOSTWRITING FOR HER STUDENTS, DO SUCH A THING?
IN SHORT, THE CONCLUSION TO DRAW HERE...

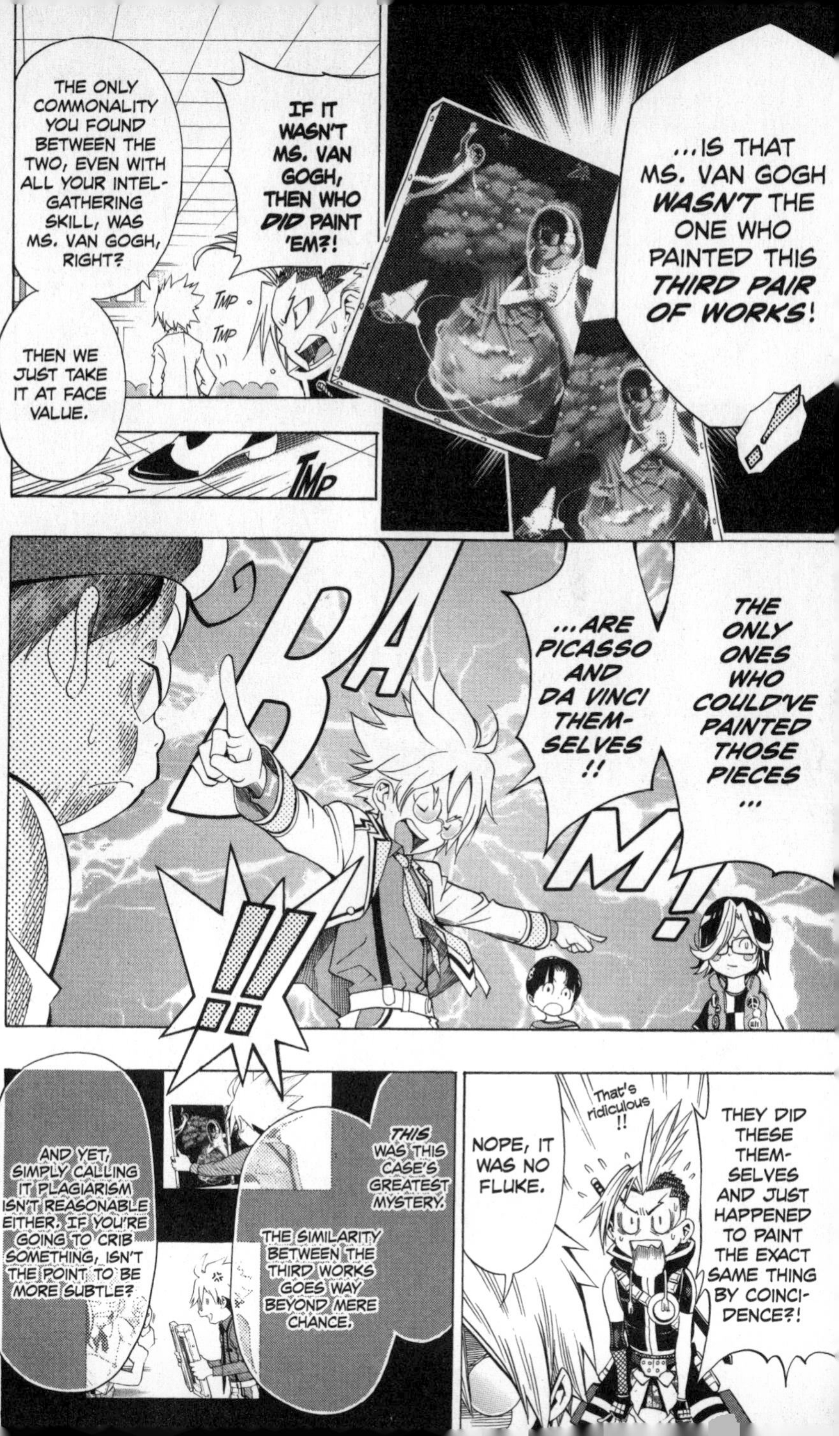
...IS THAT MS. VAN GOGH WASN'T THE ONE WHO PAINTED THIS THIRD PAIR OF WORKS!
IF IT WASN'T MS. VAN GOGH, THEN WHO DID PAINT 'EM?!
THE ONLY COMMONALITY YOU FOUND BETWEEN THE TWO, EVEN WITH ALL YOUR INTEL-GATHERING SKILL, WAS MS. VAN GOGH, RIGHT?
TMP
TMP
THEN WE JUST TAKE IT AT FACE VALUE.
TMP
BAM!
THE ONLY ONES WHO COULD'VE PAINTED THOSE PIECES ...
...ARE PICASSO AND DA VINCI THEMSELVES !!
!!
THEY DID THESE THEMSELVES AND JUST HAPPENED TO PAINT THE EXACT SAME THING BY COINCIDENCE?!
That's ridiculous !!
NOPE, IT WAS NO FLUKE.
THIS WAS THIS CASE'S GREATEST MYSTERY.
THE SIMILARITY BETWEEN THE THIRD WORKS GOES WAY BEYOND MERE CHANCE.
AND YET, SIMPLY CALLING IT PLAGIARISM ISN'T REASONABLE EITHER. IF YOU'RE GOING TO CRIB SOMETHING, ISN'T THE POINT TO BE MORE SUBTLE?

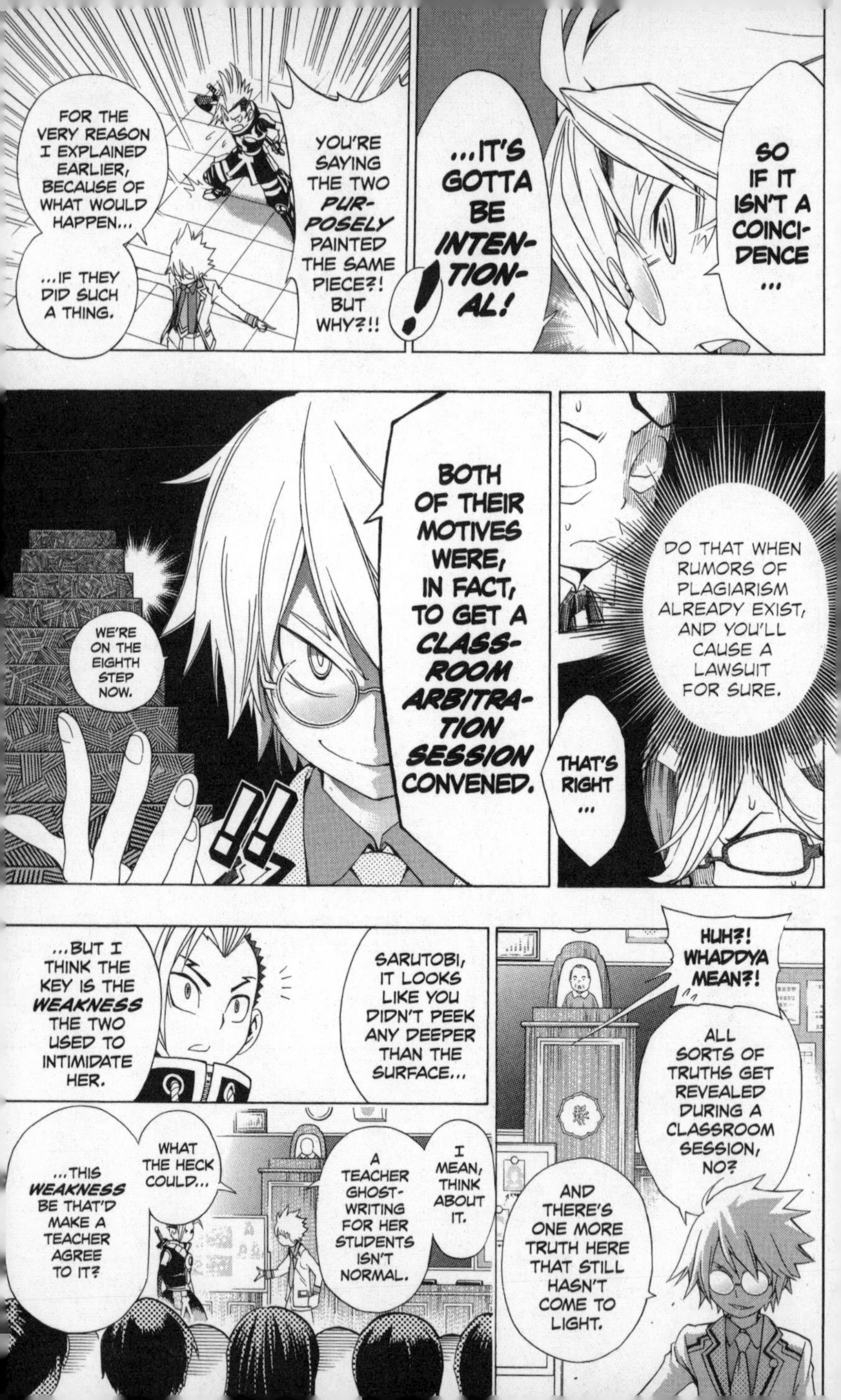
SO IF IT ISN'T A COINCIDENCE...
...IT'S GOTTA BE INTENTIONAL!
!
YOU'RE SAYING THE TWO PURPOSELY PAINTED THE SAME PIECE?! BUT WHY?!!
FOR THE VERY REASON I EXPLAINED EARLIER, BECAUSE OF WHAT WOULD HAPPEN...
...IF THEY DID SUCH A THING.
DO THAT WHEN RUMORS OF PLAGIARISM ALREADY EXIST, AND YOU'LL CAUSE A LAWSUIT FOR SURE.
THAT'S RIGHT...
BOTH OF THEIR MOTIVES WERE, IN FACT, TO GET A CLASSROOM ARBITRATION SESSION CONVENED.
!!
WE'RE ON THE EIGHTH STEP NOW.
HUH?! WHADDYA MEAN?!
ALL SORTS OF TRUTHS GET REVEALED DURING A CLASSROOM SESSION, NO?
AND THERE'S ONE MORE TRUTH HERE THAT STILL HASN'T COME TO LIGHT.
SARUTOBI, IT LOOKS LIKE YOU DIDN'T PEEK ANY DEEPER THAN THE SURFACE...
...BUT I THINK THE KEY IS THE WEAKNESS THE TWO USED TO INTIMIDATE HER.
I MEAN, THINK ABOUT IT.
A TEACHER GHOST-WRITING FOR HER STUDENTS ISN'T NORMAL.
WHAT THE HECK COULD...
...THIS WEAKNESS BE THAT'D MAKE A TEACHER AGREE TO IT?

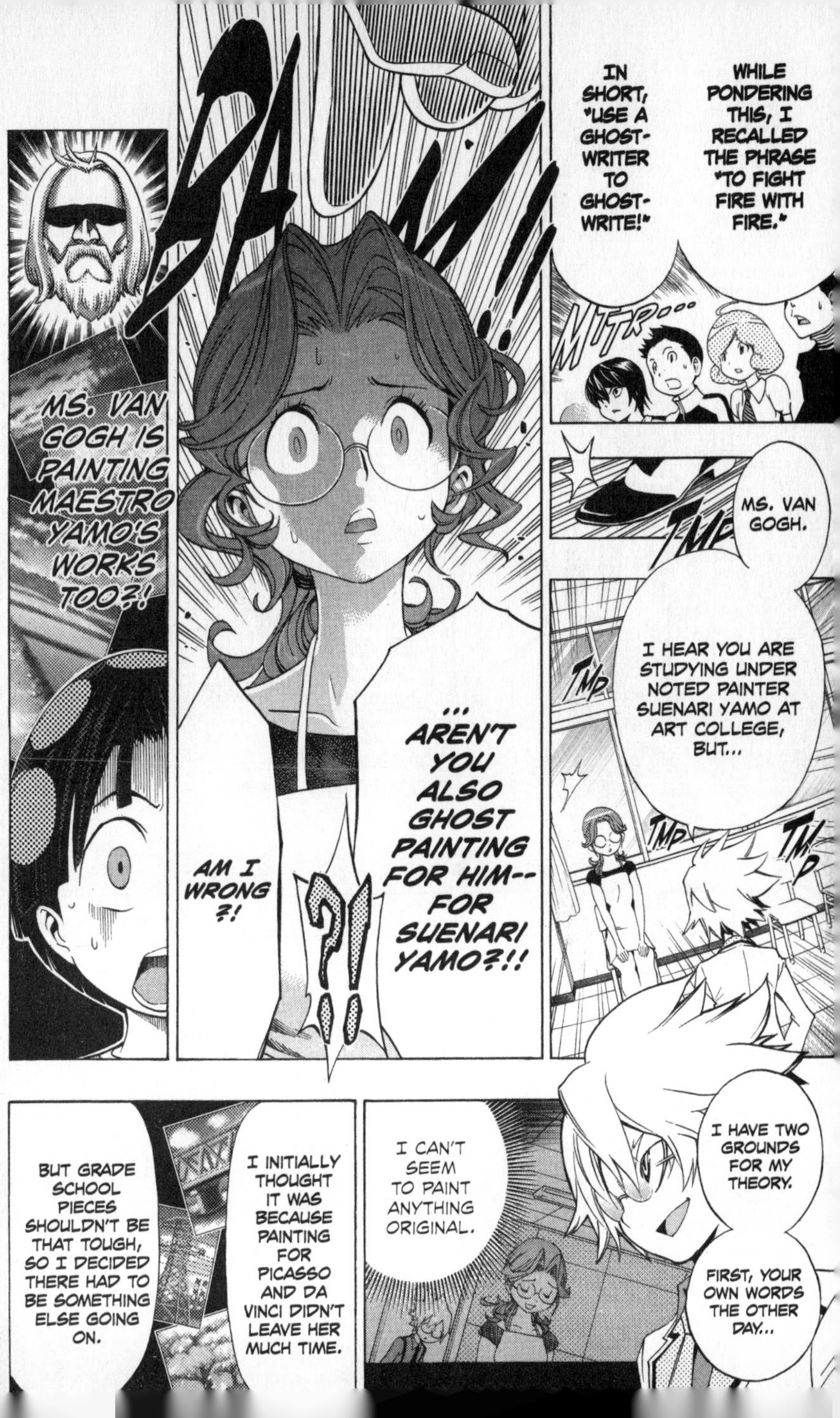
WHILE PONDERING THIS, I RECALLED THE PHRASE "TO FIGHT FIRE WITH FIRE."
IN SHORT, "USE A GHOST-WRITER TO GHOST-WRITE!"
MITR...
TMP
MS. VAN GOGH.
I HEAR YOU ARE STUDYING UNDER NOTED PAINTER SUENARI YAMO AT ART COLLEGE, BUT...
TMP
TMP
TMP
BAM!!
...AREN'T YOU ALSO GHOST PAINTING FOR HIM--FOR SUENARI YAMO?!!
AM I WRONG?!
?!!
MS. VAN GOGH IS PAINTING MAESTRO YAMO'S WORKS TOO?!
I HAVE TWO GROUNDS FOR MY THEORY.
FIRST, YOUR OWN WORDS THE OTHER DAY...
I CAN'T SEEM TO PAINT ANYTHING ORIGINAL.
I INITIALLY THOUGHT IT WAS BECAUSE PAINTING FOR PICASSO AND DA VINCI DIDN'T LEAVE HER MUCH TIME.
BUT GRADE SCHOOL PIECES SHOULDN'T BE THAT TOUGH, SO I DECIDED THERE HAD TO BE SOMETHING ELSE GOING ON.

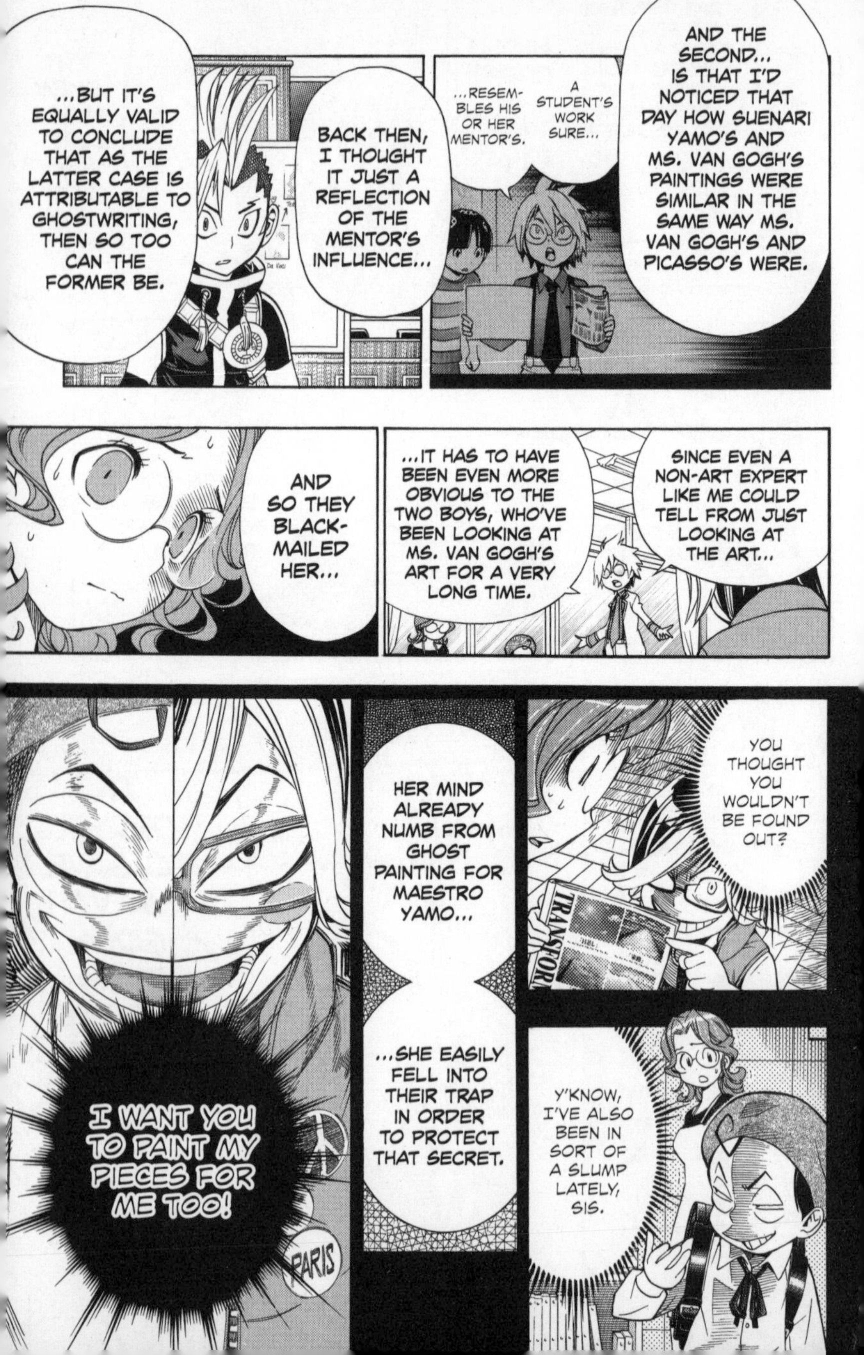
AND THE SECOND... IS THAT I'D NOTICED THAT DAY HOW SUENARI YAMO'S AND MS. VAN GOGH'S PAINTINGS WERE SIMILAR IN THE SAME WAY MS. VAN GOGH'S AND PICASSO'S WERE.
A STUDENT'S WORK SURE...
...RESEMBLES HIS OR HER MENTOR'S.
BACK THEN, I THOUGHT IT JUST A REFLECTION OF THE MENTOR'S INFLUENCE...
...BUT IT'S EQUALLY VALID TO CONCLUDE THAT AS THE LATTER CASE IS ATTRIBUTABLE TO GHOSTWRITING, THEN SO TOO CAN THE FORMER BE.
SINCE EVEN A NON-ART EXPERT LIKE ME COULD TELL FROM JUST LOOKING AT THE ART...
...IT HAS TO HAVE BEEN EVEN MORE OBVIOUS TO THE TWO BOYS, WHO'VE BEEN LOOKING AT MS. VAN GOGH'S ART FOR A VERY LONG TIME.
AND SO THEY BLACKMAILED HER...
YOU THOUGHT YOU WOULDN'T BE FOUND OUT?
Y'KNOW, I'VE ALSO BEEN IN SORT OF A SLUMP LATELY, SIS.
HER MIND ALREADY NUMB FROM GHOST PAINTING FOR MAESTRO YAMO...
...SHE EASILY FELL INTO THEIR TRAP IN ORDER TO PROTECT THAT SECRET.
I WANT YOU TO PAINT MY PIECES FOR ME TOO!
PARIS

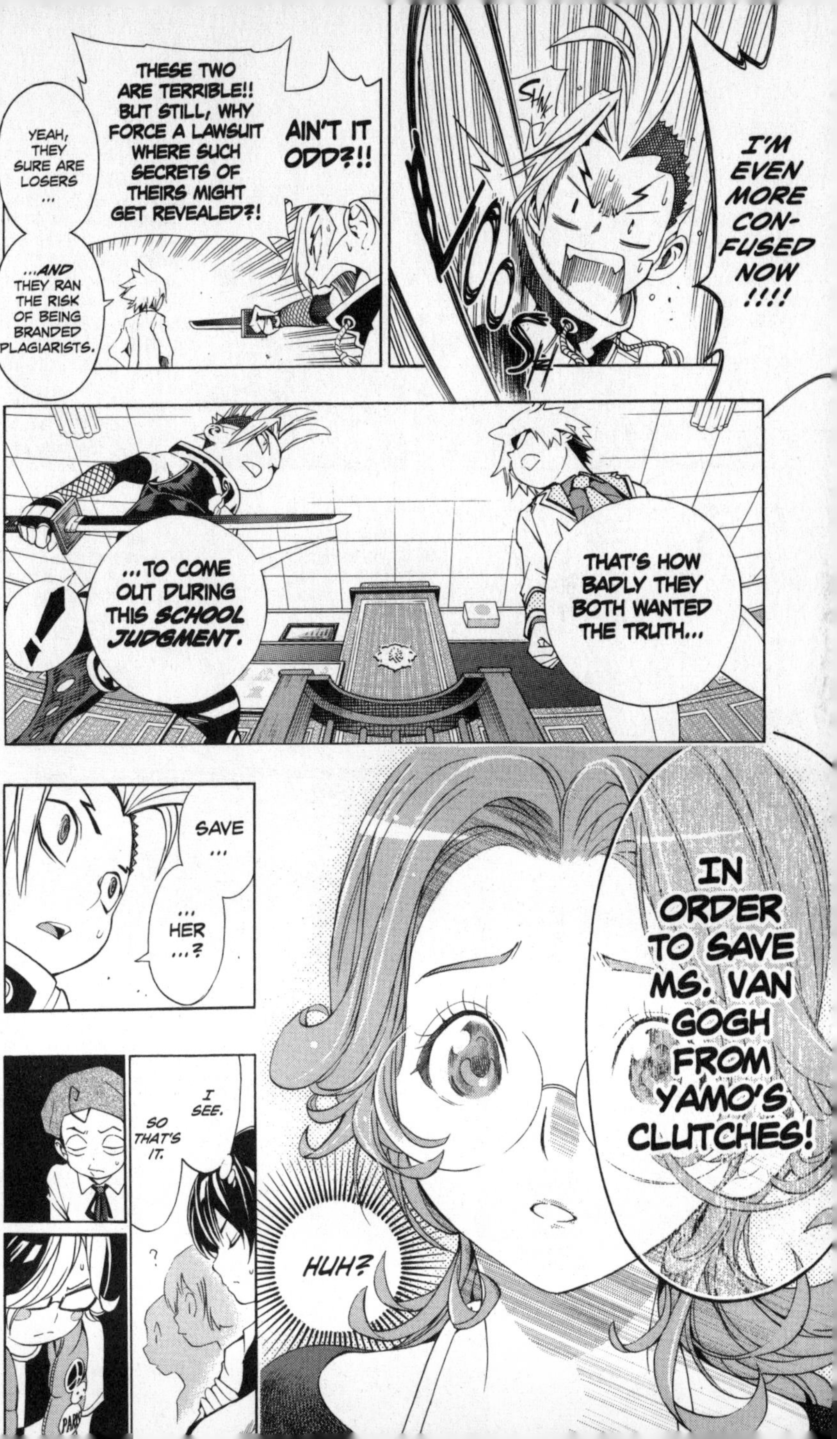
SHINK
I'M EVEN MORE CON-FUSED NOW!!!!
THESE TWO ARE TERRIBLE!! BUT STILL, WHY FORCE A LAWSUIT WHERE SUCH SECRETS OF THEIRS MIGHT GET REVEALED?!
AIN'T IT ODD?!!
YEAH, THEY SURE ARE LOSERS ...
...AND THEY RAN THE RISK OF BEING BRANDED PLAGIARISTS.
THAT'S HOW BADLY THEY BOTH WANTED THE TRUTH...
...TO COME OUT DURING THIS SCHOOL JUDGMENT.
!
IN ORDER TO SAVE MS. VAN GOGH FROM YAMO'S CLUTCHES!
HUH?
SAVE ...
... HER ...?
I SEE.
SO THAT'S IT.
?

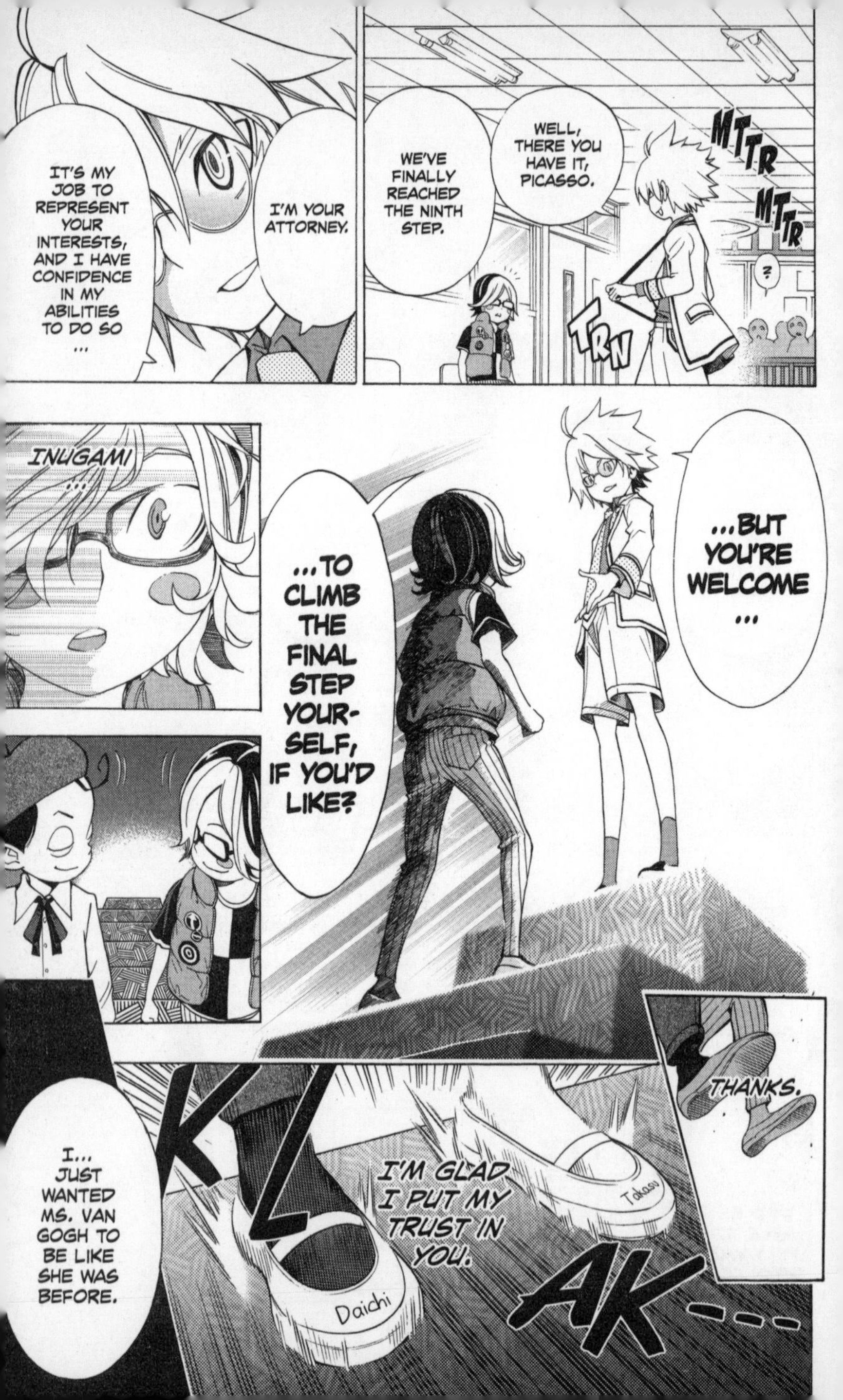

MTTR MTTR
WELL, THERE YOU HAVE IT, PICASSO.
WE'VE FINALLY REACHED THE NINTH STEP.
?
TRN
I'M YOUR ATTORNEY.
IT'S MY JOB TO REPRESENT YOUR INTERESTS, AND I HAVE CONFIDENCE IN MY ABILITIES TO DO SO ...
...BUT YOU'RE WELCOME ...
...TO CLIMB THE FINAL STEP YOURSELF, IF YOU'D LIKE?
INUGAMI ...
THANKS.
Takasu
I'M GLAD I PUT MY TRUST IN YOU.
I... JUST WANTED MS. VAN GOGH TO BE LIKE SHE WAS BEFORE.
KLAK---
Daichi

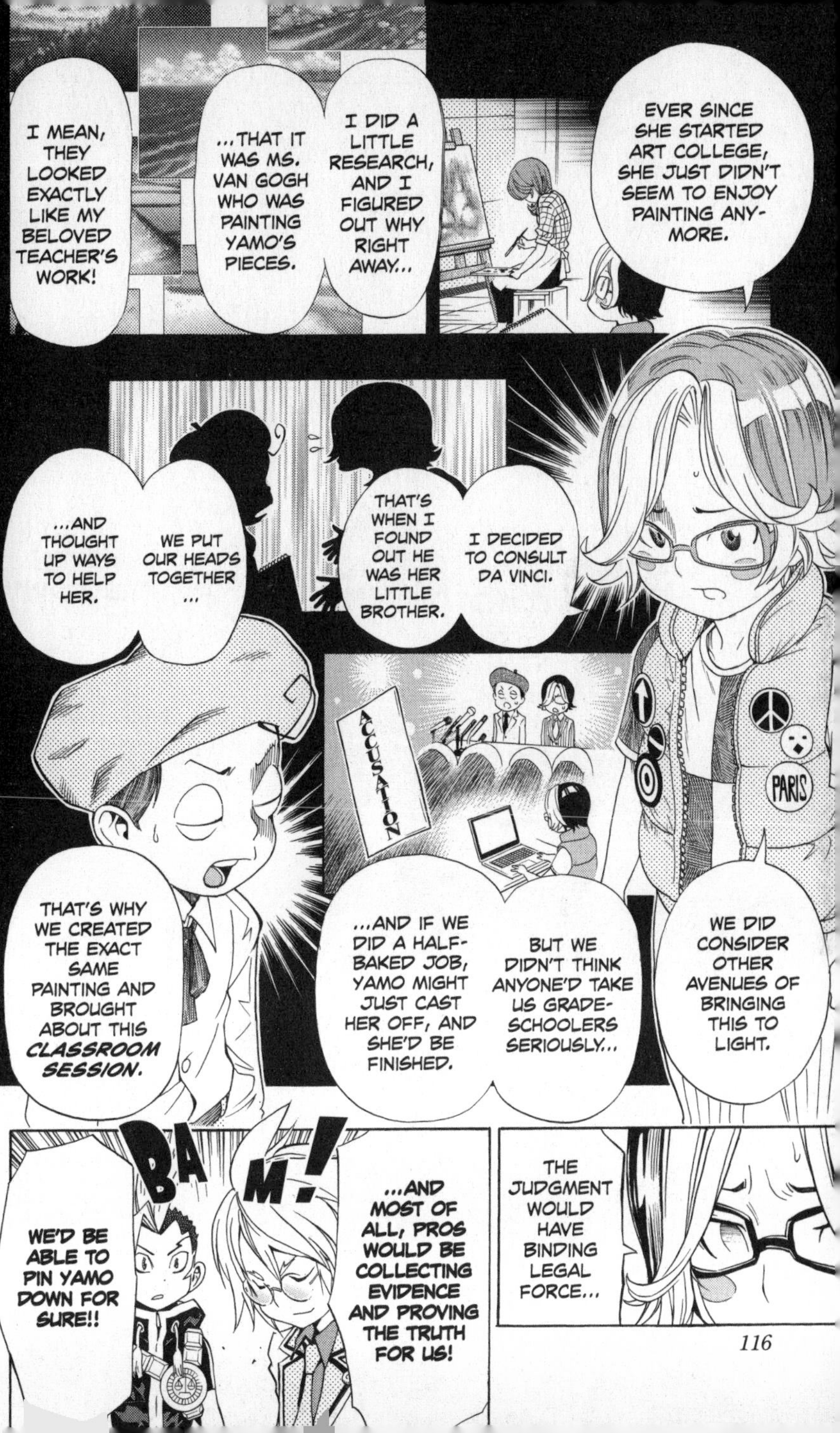
EVER SINCE SHE STARTED ART COLLEGE, SHE JUST DIDN'T SEEM TO ENJOY PAINTING ANY-MORE.
I DID A LITTLE RESEARCH, AND I FIGURED OUT WHY RIGHT AWAY...
...THAT IT WAS MS. VAN GOGH WHO WAS PAINTING YAMO'S PIECES.
I MEAN, THEY LOOKED EXACTLY LIKE MY BELOVED TEACHER'S WORK!
I DECIDED TO CONSULT DA VINCI.
THAT'S WHEN I FOUND OUT HE WAS HER LITTLE BROTHER.
WE PUT OUR HEADS TOGETHER ...
...AND THOUGHT UP WAYS TO HELP HER.
ACCUSATION
PARIS
WE DID CONSIDER OTHER AVENUES OF BRINGING THIS TO LIGHT.
BUT WE DIDN'T THINK ANYONE'D TAKE US GRADE-SCHOOLERS SERIOUSLY...
...AND IF WE DID A HALF-BAKED JOB, YAMO MIGHT JUST CAST HER OFF, AND SHE'D BE FINISHED.
THAT'S WHY WE CREATED THE EXACT SAME PAINTING AND BROUGHT ABOUT THIS *CLASSROOM SESSION*.
THE JUDGMENT WOULD HAVE BINDING LEGAL FORCE...
...AND MOST OF ALL, PROS WOULD BE COLLECTING EVIDENCE AND PROVING THE TRUTH FOR US!
BAM!
WE'D BE ABLE TO PIN YAMO DOWN FOR SURE!!

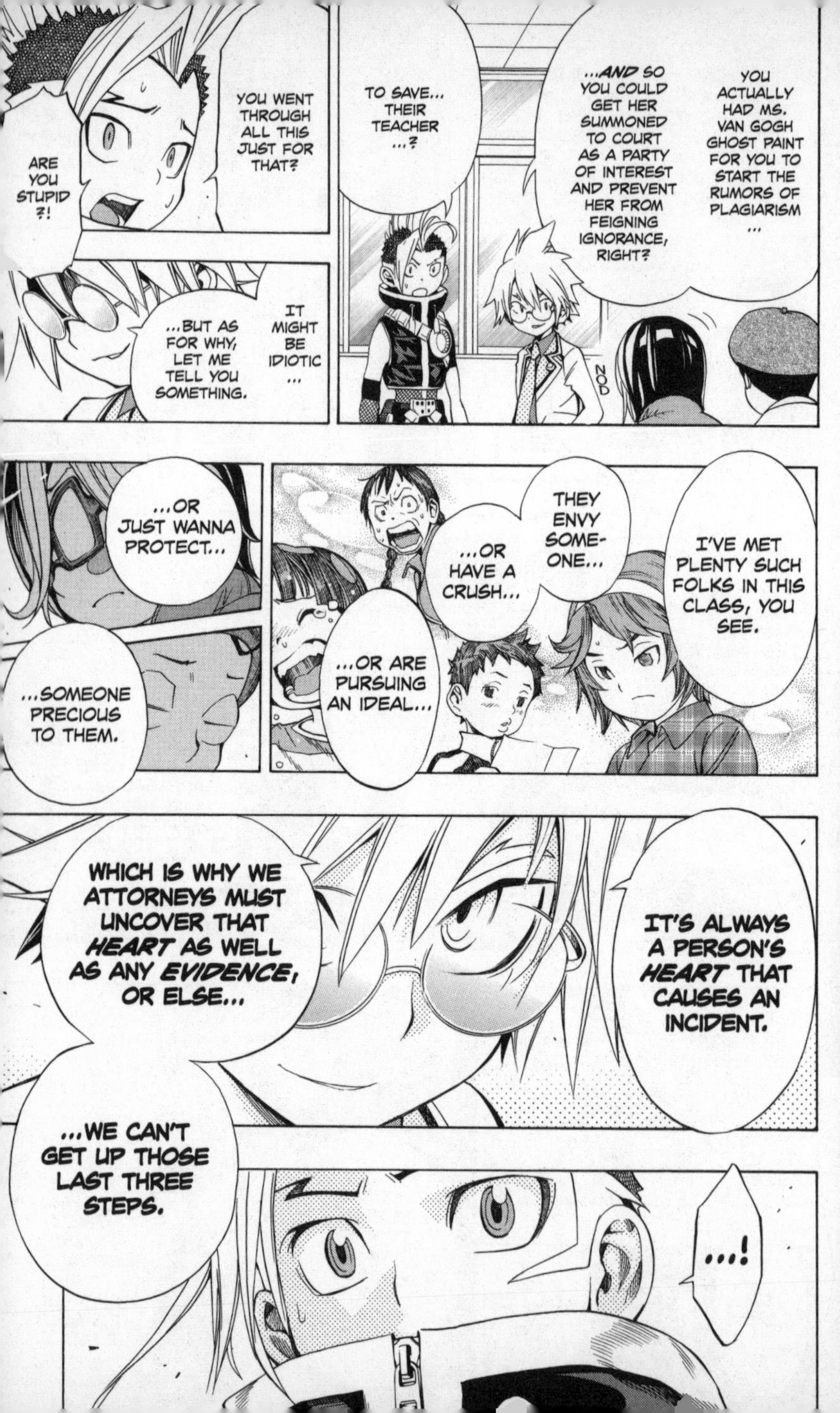
YOU ACTUALLY HAD MS. VAN GOGH GHOST PAINT FOR YOU TO START THE RUMORS OF PLAGIARISM ...
...AND SO YOU COULD GET HER SUMMONED TO COURT AS A PARTY OF INTEREST AND PREVENT HER FROM FEIGNING IGNORANCE, RIGHT?
NOD
TO SAVE... THEIR TEACHER ...?
YOU WENT THROUGH ALL THIS JUST FOR THAT?
ARE YOU STUPID ?!
IT MIGHT BE IDIOTIC ...
...BUT AS FOR WHY, LET ME TELL YOU SOMETHING.
I'VE MET PLENTY SUCH FOLKS IN THIS CLASS, YOU SEE.
THEY ENVY SOME-ONE...
...OR HAVE A CRUSH...
...OR ARE PURSUING AN IDEAL...
...OR JUST WANNA PROTECT...
...SOMEONE PRECIOUS TO THEM.
IT'S ALWAYS A PERSON'S HEART THAT CAUSES AN INCIDENT.
WHICH IS WHY WE ATTORNEYS MUST UNCOVER THAT HEART AS WELL AS ANY EVIDENCE, OR ELSE...
...WE CAN'T GET UP THOSE LAST THREE STEPS.
...!

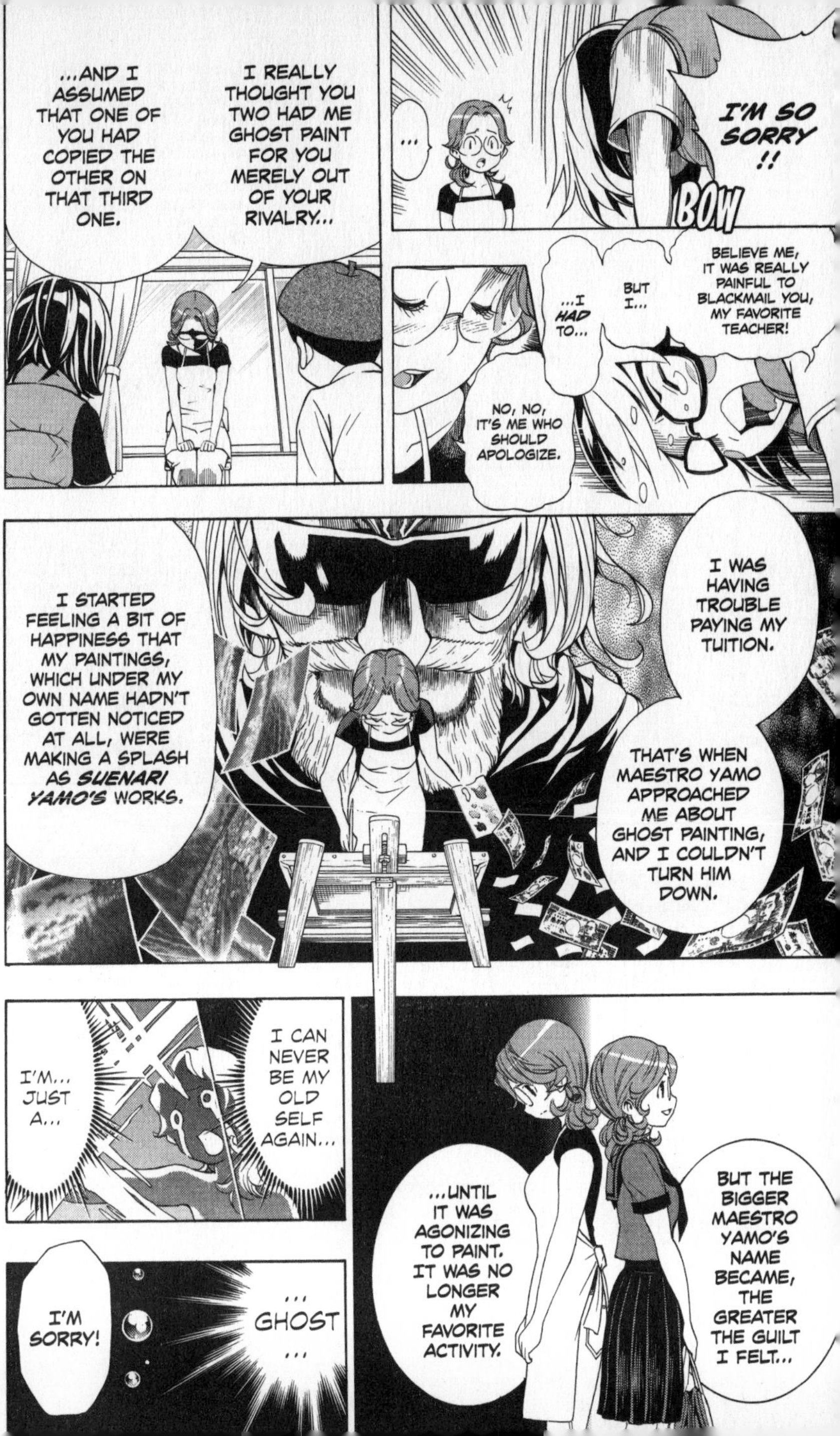
I'M SO SORRY!!
BOW
...
BELIEVE ME, IT WAS REALLY PAINFUL TO BLACKMAIL YOU, MY FAVORITE TEACHER!
BUT I...
...I HAD TO...
NO, NO, IT'S ME WHO SHOULD APOLOGIZE.
I REALLY THOUGHT YOU TWO HAD ME GHOST PAINT FOR YOU MERELY OUT OF YOUR RIVALRY...
...AND I ASSUMED THAT ONE OF YOU HAD COPIED THE OTHER ON THAT THIRD ONE.
I WAS HAVING TROUBLE PAYING MY TUITION.
THAT'S WHEN MAESTRO YAMO APPROACHED ME ABOUT GHOST PAINTING, AND I COULDN'T TURN HIM DOWN.
I STARTED FEELING A BIT OF HAPPINESS THAT MY PAINTINGS, WHICH UNDER MY OWN NAME HADN'T GOTTEN NOTICED AT ALL, WERE MAKING A SPLASH AS SUENARI YAMO'S WORKS.
BUT THE BIGGER MAESTRO YAMO'S NAME BECAME, THE GREATER THE GUILT I FELT...
...UNTIL IT WAS AGONIZING TO PAINT. IT WAS NO LONGER MY FAVORITE ACTIVITY.
I CAN NEVER BE MY OLD SELF AGAIN...
I'M... JUST A...
...GHOST...
I'M SORRY!

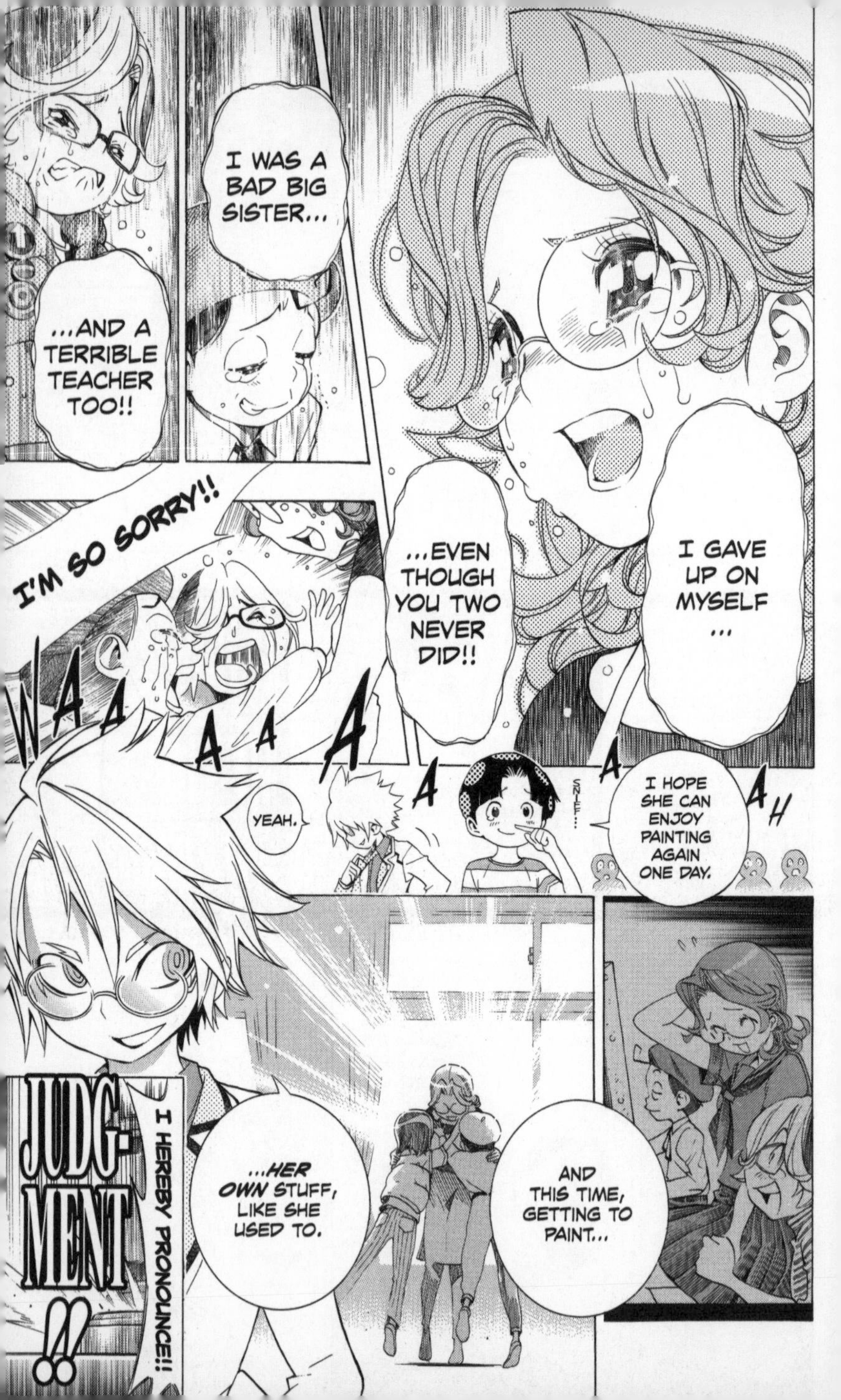
I GAVE UP ON MYSELF ...
...EVEN THOUGH YOU TWO NEVER DID!!
I WAS A BAD BIG SISTER...
...AND A TERRIBLE TEACHER TOO!!
I'M SO SORRY!!
WAAAAAAAAH
SNIFF...
I HOPE SHE CAN ENJOY PAINTING AGAIN ONE DAY.
YEAH.
AND THIS TIME, GETTING TO PAINT...
...*HER OWN* STUFF, LIKE SHE USED TO.
I HEREBY PRONOUNCE!!
JUDG-MENT!!

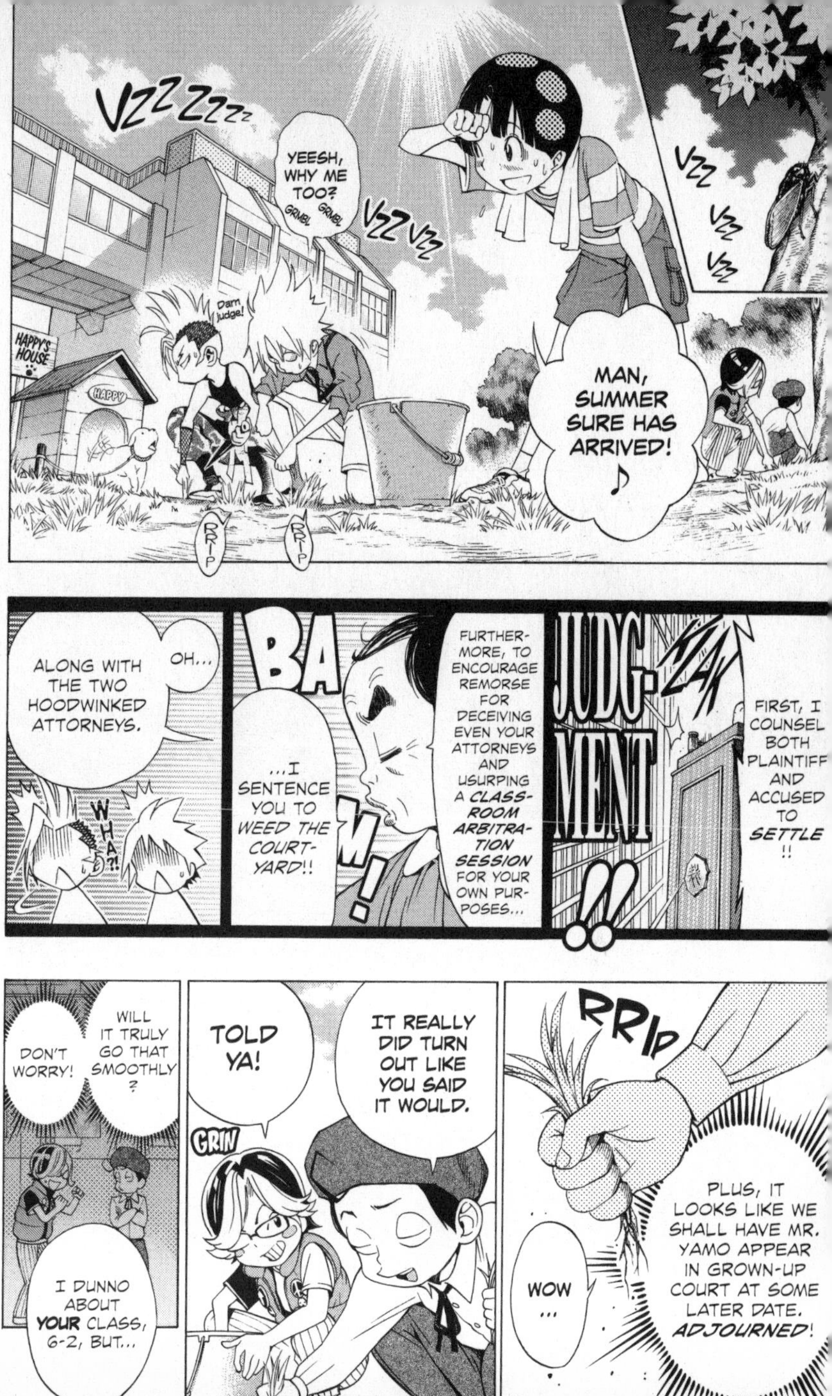
VZZ
VZZ
VZZ
MAN, SUMMER SURE HAS ARRIVED! ♪
VZZ VZZ
YEESH, WHY ME TOO?
GRMBL GRMBL
VZZ ZZZzz
Darn judge!
HAPPY'S HOUSE
HAPPY
RRIP
RRIP
JUDGMENT!!
KLAK
FIRST, I COUNSEL BOTH PLAINTIFF AND ACCUSED TO *SETTLE*!!
FURTHERMORE, TO ENCOURAGE REMORSE FOR DECEIVING EVEN YOUR ATTORNEYS AND USURPING A ***CLASSROOM ARBITRATION SESSION*** FOR YOUR OWN PURPOSES...
BAM!
...I SENTENCE YOU TO *WEED THE COURTYARD*!!
OH...
ALONG WITH THE TWO HOODWINKED ATTORNEYS.
WHA?!
RRIP
PLUS, IT LOOKS LIKE WE SHALL HAVE MR. YAMO APPEAR IN GROWN-UP COURT AT SOME LATER DATE. ***ADJOURNED***!
WOW...
IT REALLY DID TURN OUT LIKE YOU SAID IT WOULD.
TOLD YA!
GRIN
WILL IT TRULY GO THAT SMOOTHLY?
DON'T WORRY!
I DUNNO ABOUT **YOUR** CLASS, 6-2, BUT...

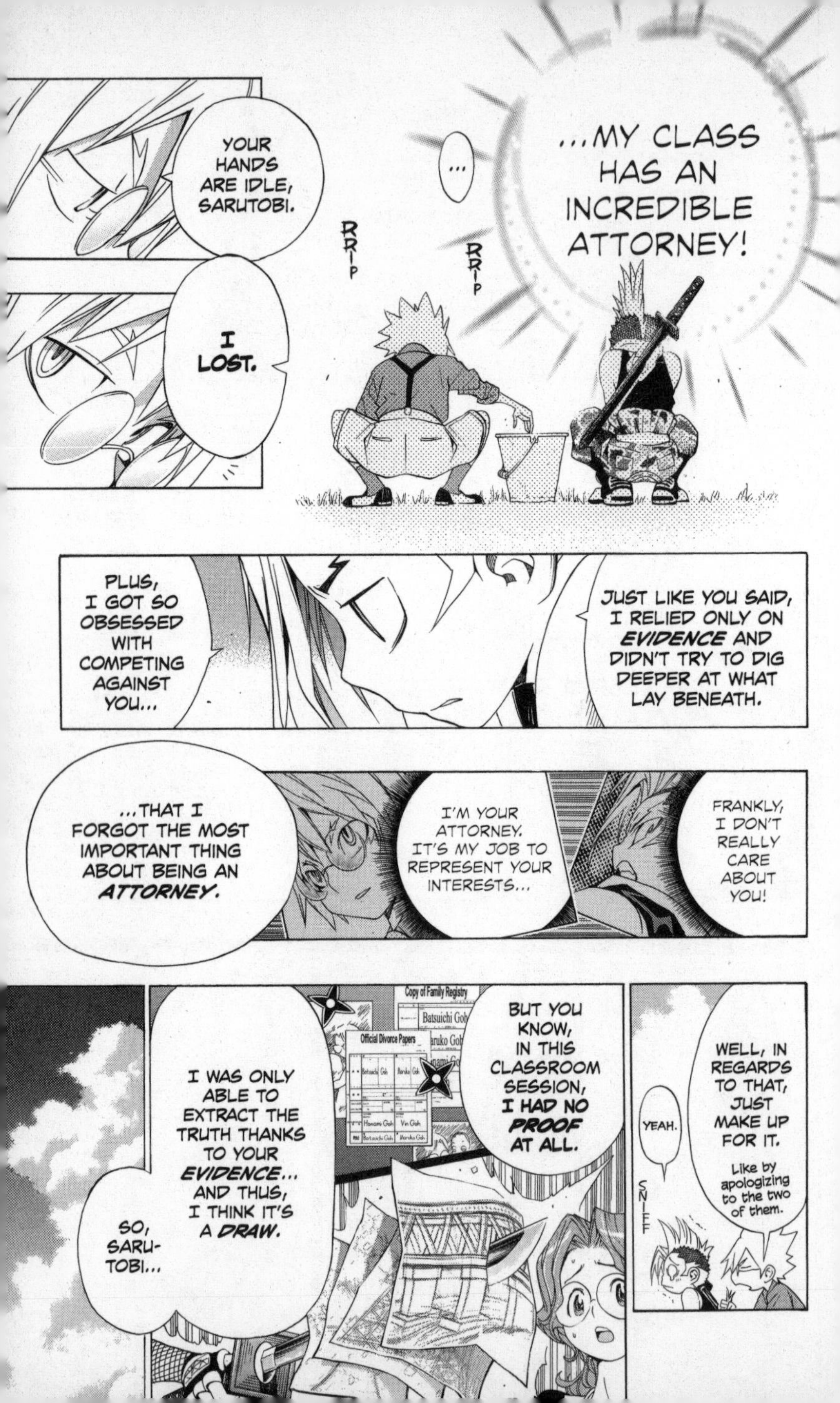
...MY CLASS HAS AN INCREDIBLE ATTORNEY!
...
DRIP
DRIP
YOUR HANDS ARE IDLE, SARUTOBI.
I LOST.
JUST LIKE YOU SAID, I RELIED ONLY ON *EVIDENCE* AND DIDN'T TRY TO DIG DEEPER AT WHAT LAY BENEATH.
PLUS, I GOT SO OBSESSED WITH COMPETING AGAINST YOU...
FRANKLY, I DON'T REALLY CARE ABOUT YOU!
I'M YOUR ATTORNEY. IT'S MY JOB TO REPRESENT YOUR INTERESTS...
...THAT I FORGOT THE MOST IMPORTANT THING ABOUT BEING AN *ATTORNEY*.
WELL, IN REGARDS TO THAT, JUST MAKE UP FOR IT.
Like by apologizing to the two of them.
YEAH.
SNIFF
Copy of Family Registry
Official Divorce Papers
BUT YOU KNOW, IN THIS CLASSROOM SESSION, **I HAD NO *PROOF* AT ALL.**
I WAS ONLY ABLE TO EXTRACT THE TRUTH THANKS TO YOUR *EVIDENCE*... AND THUS, I THINK IT'S A ***DRAW***.
SO, SARUTOBI...

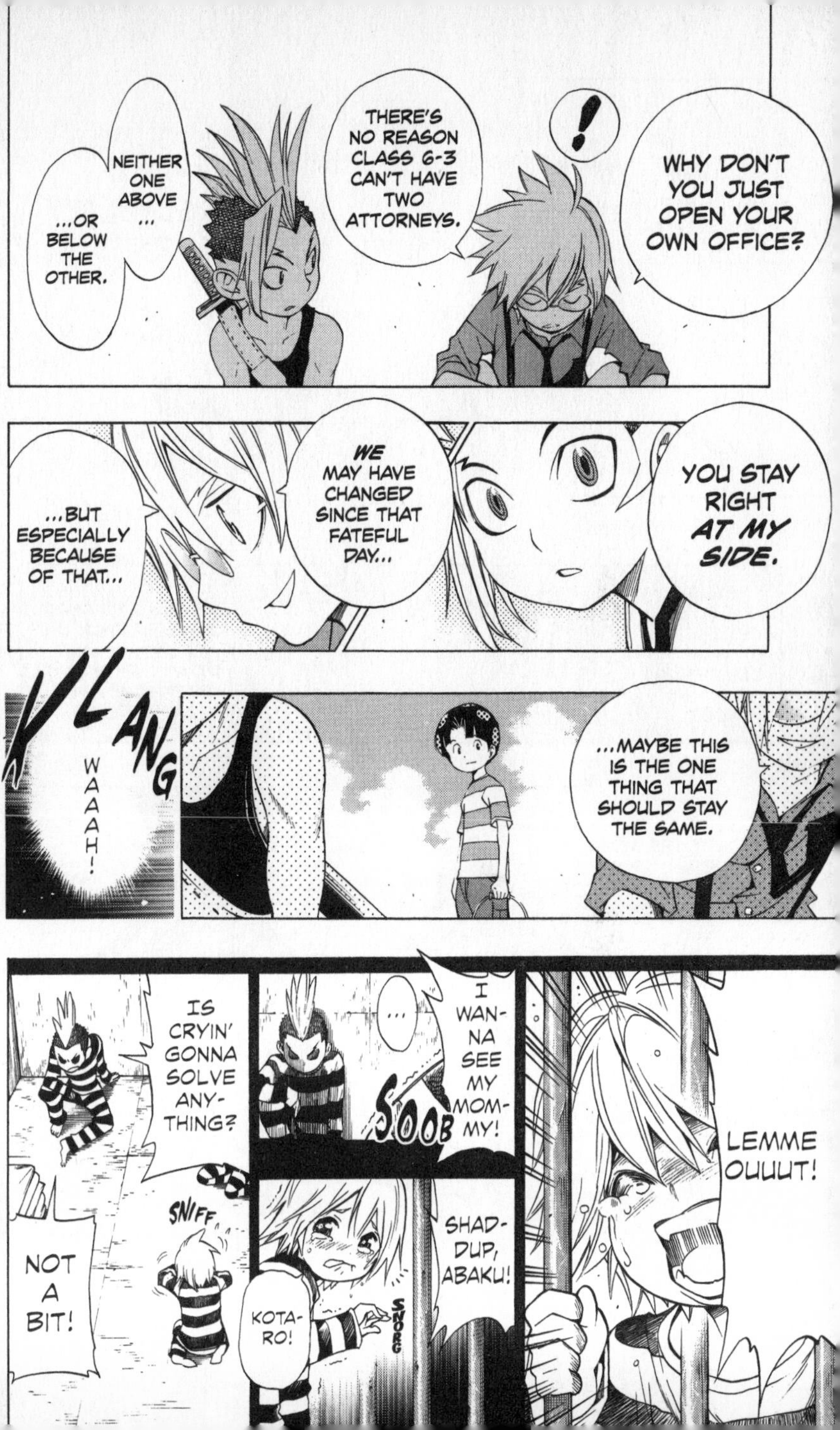
!
WHY DON'T YOU JUST OPEN YOUR OWN OFFICE?
THERE'S NO REASON CLASS 6-3 CAN'T HAVE TWO ATTORNEYS.
NEITHER ONE ABOVE ...
...OR BELOW THE OTHER.
YOU STAY RIGHT AT MY SIDE.
WE MAY HAVE CHANGED SINCE THAT FATEFUL DAY...
...BUT ESPECIALLY BECAUSE OF THAT...
...MAYBE THIS IS THE ONE THING THAT SHOULD STAY THE SAME.
KLANG
WAAAAH!
LEMME OUUUT!
I WAN-NA SEE MY MOM-MY!
...
SOOB
SHAD-DUP, ABAKU!
SNORG
KOTA-RO!
IS CRYIN' GONNA SOLVE ANY-THING?
SNIFF...
NOT A BIT!

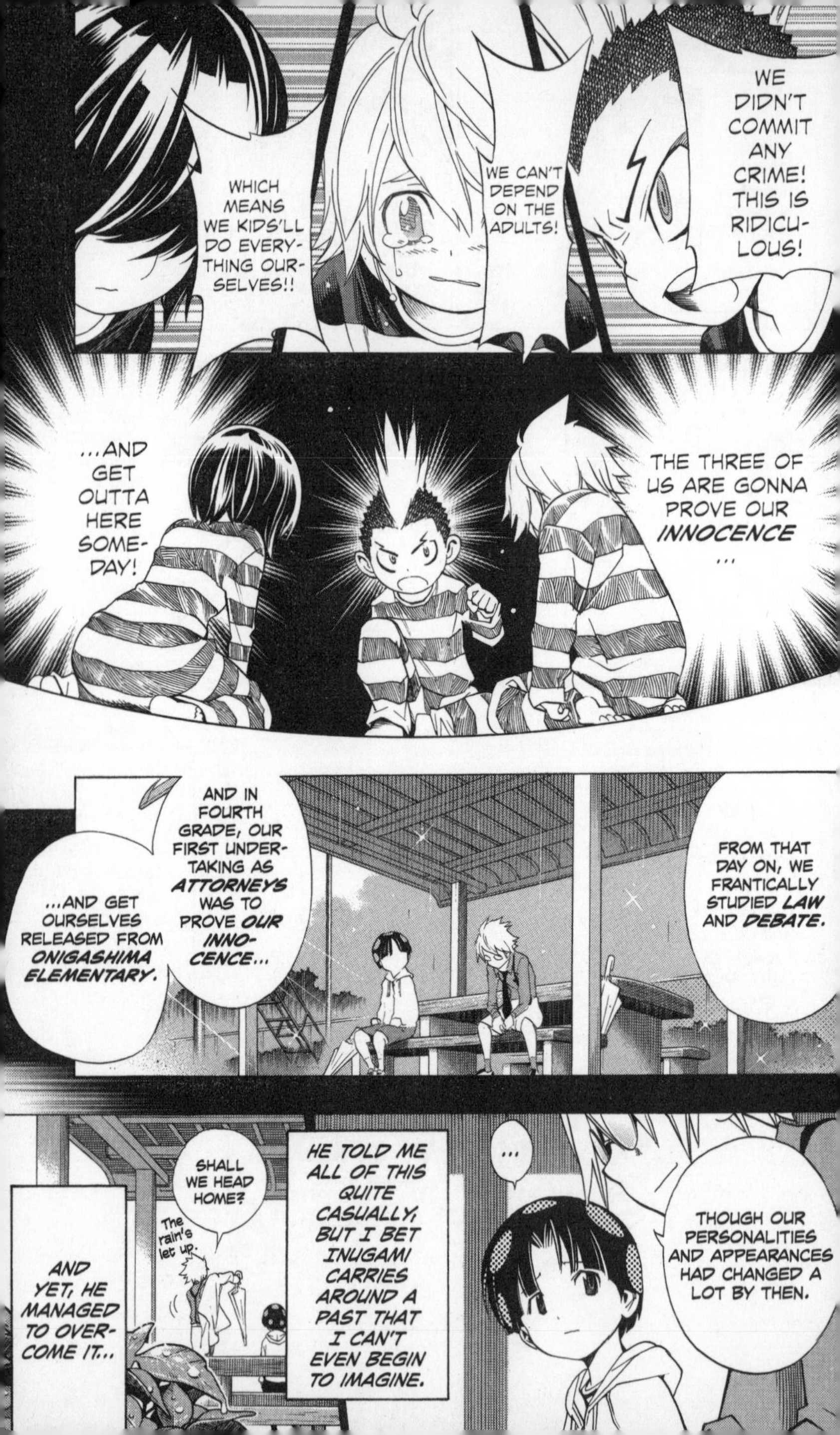
WE DIDN'T COMMIT ANY CRIME! THIS IS RIDICULOUS!
WE CAN'T DEPEND ON THE ADULTS!
WHICH MEANS WE KIDS'LL DO EVERYTHING OURSELVES!!
THE THREE OF US ARE GONNA PROVE OUR *INNOCENCE*...
...AND GET OUTTA HERE SOMEDAY!
FROM THAT DAY ON, WE FRANTICALLY STUDIED *LAW* AND *DEBATE*.
AND IN FOURTH GRADE, OUR FIRST UNDERTAKING AS *ATTORNEYS* WAS TO PROVE *OUR INNOCENCE*...
...AND GET OURSELVES RELEASED FROM *ONIGASHIMA ELEMENTARY*.
THOUGH OUR PERSONALITIES AND APPEARANCES HAD CHANGED A LOT BY THEN.
...
HE TOLD ME ALL OF THIS QUITE CASUALLY, BUT I BET INUGAMI CARRIES AROUND A PAST THAT I CAN'T EVEN BEGIN TO IMAGINE.
SHALL WE HEAD HOME?
The rain's let up.
AND YET, HE MANAGED TO OVERCOME IT...

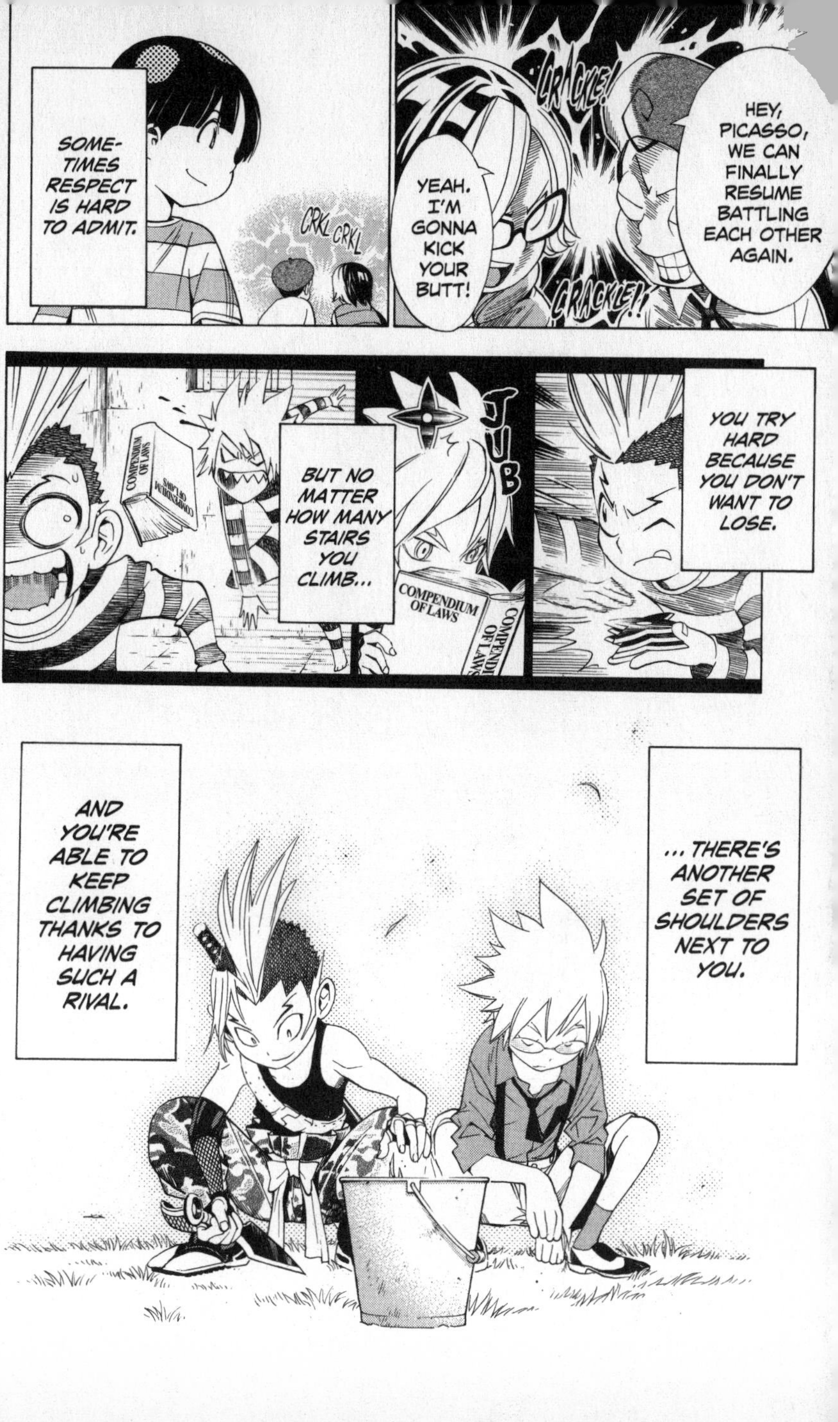

HEY, PICASSO, WE CAN FINALLY RESUME BATTLING EACH OTHER AGAIN.
CRACKLE!
YEAH. I'M GONNA KICK YOUR BUTT!
CRACKLE!!
SOME-TIMES RESPECT IS HARD TO ADMIT.
CRKL CRKL
YOU TRY HARD BECAUSE YOU DON'T WANT TO LOSE.
JUB
BUT NO MATTER HOW MANY STAIRS YOU CLIMB...
COMPENDIUM OF LAWS
COMPENDIUM OF LAWS
COMPENDIUM OF LAWS
...THERE'S ANOTHER SET OF SHOULDERS NEXT TO YOU.
AND YOU'RE ABLE TO KEEP CLIMBING THANKS TO HAVING SUCH A RIVAL.

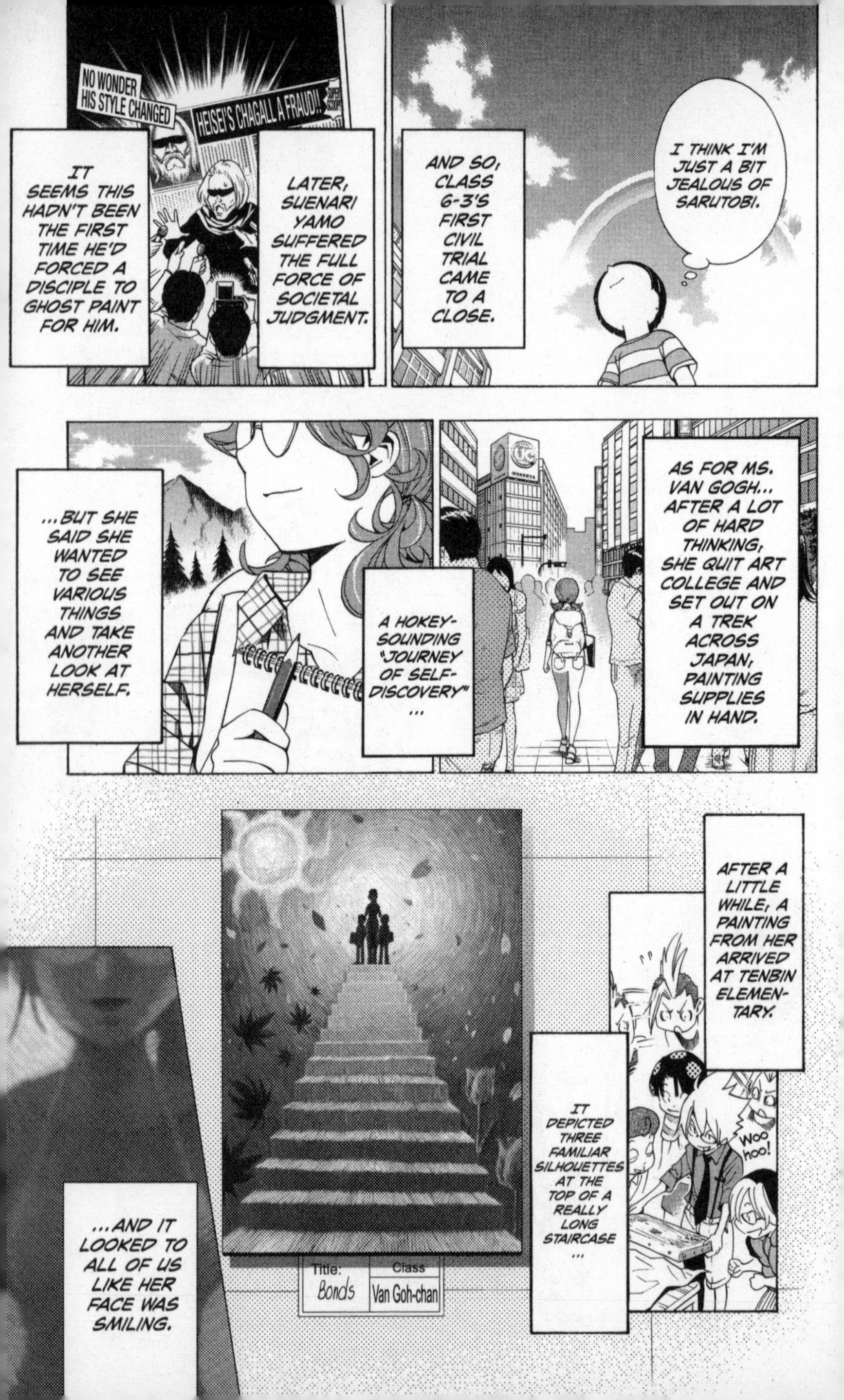
I THINK I'M JUST A BIT JEALOUS OF SARUTOBI.
AND SO, CLASS 6-3'S FIRST CIVIL TRIAL CAME TO A CLOSE.
SUPER SCOOP!
HEISEI'S CHAGALL A FRAUD!!
NO WONDER HIS STYLE CHANGED
LATER, SUENARI YAMO SUFFERED THE FULL FORCE OF SOCIETAL JUDGMENT.
IT SEEMS THIS HADN'T BEEN THE FIRST TIME HE'D FORCED A DISCIPLE TO GHOST PAINT FOR HIM.
AS FOR MS. VAN GOGH... AFTER A LOT OF HARD THINKING, SHE QUIT ART COLLEGE AND SET OUT ON A TREK ACROSS JAPAN, PAINTING SUPPLIES IN HAND.
A HOKEY-SOUNDING "JOURNEY OF SELF-DISCOVERY"...
...BUT SHE SAID SHE WANTED TO SEE VARIOUS THINGS AND TAKE ANOTHER LOOK AT HERSELF.
AFTER A LITTLE WHILE, A PAINTING FROM HER ARRIVED AT TENBIN ELEMENTARY.
Woo hoo!
IT DEPICTED THREE FAMILIAR SILHOUETTES AT THE TOP OF A REALLY LONG STAIRCASE...
Title: Bonds
Class Van Goh-chan
...AND IT LOOKED TO ALL OF US LIKE HER FACE WAS SMILING.

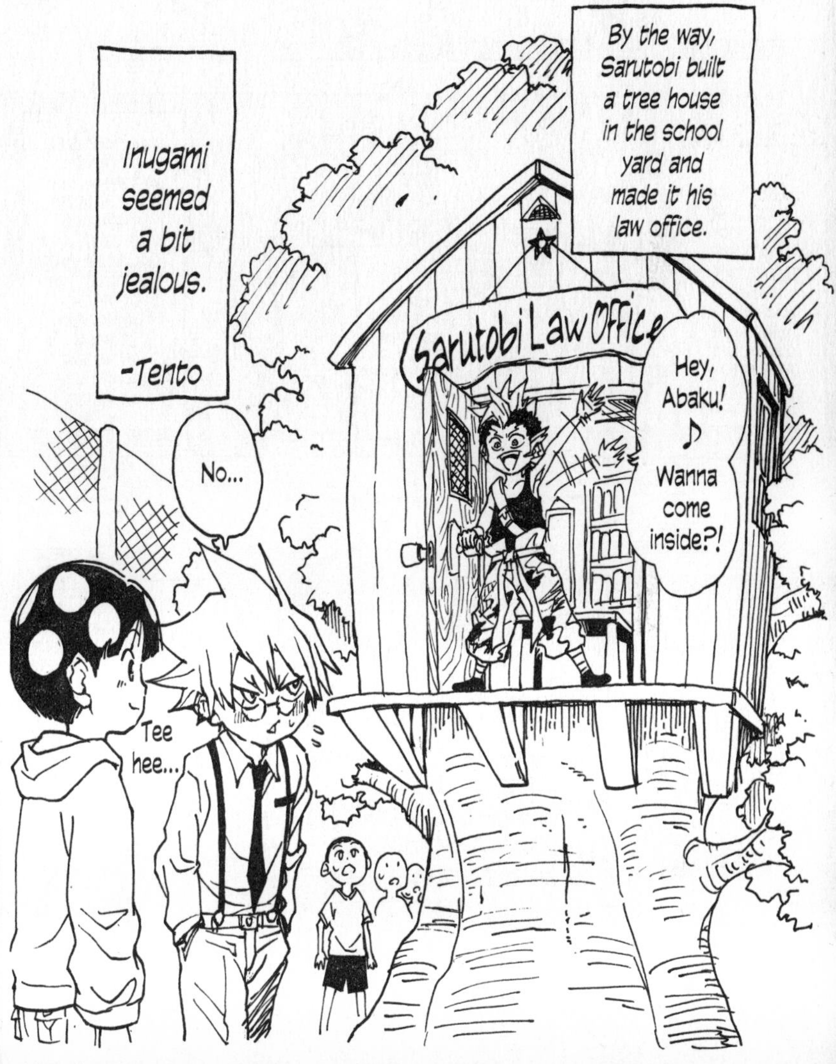
By the way, Sarutobi built a tree house in the school yard and made it his law office.
Sarutobi Law Office
Hey, Abaku! ♪ Wanna come inside?!
Inugami seemed a bit jealous.
-Tento
No...
Tee hee...

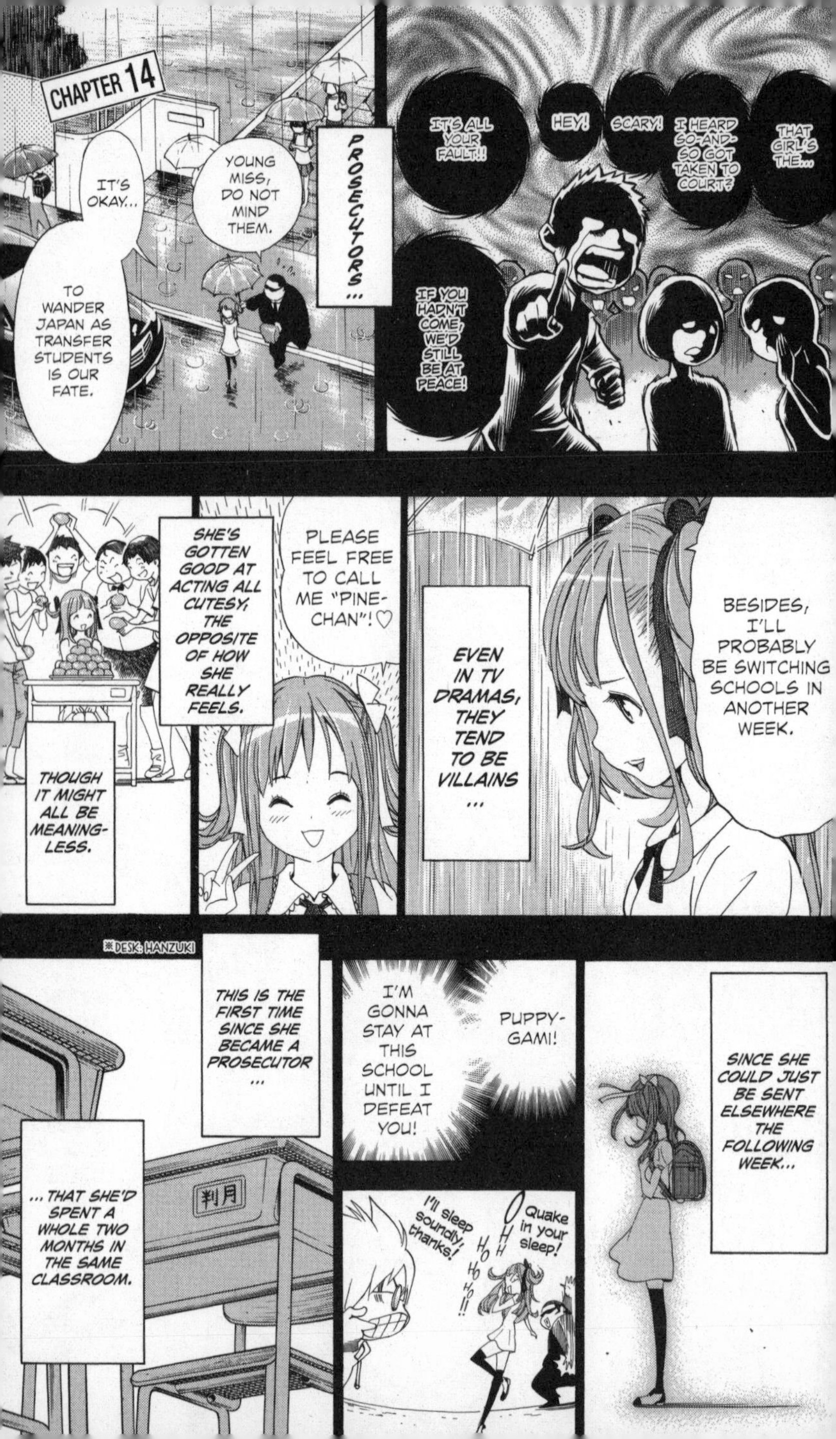
THAT GIRL'S THE...
I HEARD SO-AND-SO GOT TAKEN TO COURT?
SCARY!
HEY!
IT'S ALL YOUR FAULT!!
IF YOU HADN'T COME, WE'D STILL BE AT PEACE!
CHAPTER 14
PROSECUTORS...
YOUNG MISS, DO NOT MIND THEM.
IT'S OKAY...
TO WANDER JAPAN AS TRANSFER STUDENTS IS OUR FATE.
BESIDES, I'LL PROBABLY BE SWITCHING SCHOOLS IN ANOTHER WEEK.
EVEN IN TV DRAMAS, THEY TEND TO BE VILLAINS...
PLEASE FEEL FREE TO CALL ME "PINE-CHAN"!♡
SHE'S GOTTEN GOOD AT ACTING ALL CUTESY, THE OPPOSITE OF HOW SHE REALLY FEELS.
THOUGH IT MIGHT ALL BE MEANINGLESS.
SINCE SHE COULD JUST BE SENT ELSEWHERE THE FOLLOWING WEEK...
PUPPY-GAMI!
I'M GONNA STAY AT THIS SCHOOL UNTIL I DEFEAT YOU!
Quake in your sleep!
OHHH HO HO HO!!
I'll sleep soundly, thanks!
THIS IS THE FIRST TIME SINCE SHE BECAME A PROSECUTOR...
※DESK: HANZUKI
判月
...THAT SHE'D SPENT A WHOLE TWO MONTHS IN THE SAME CLASSROOM.

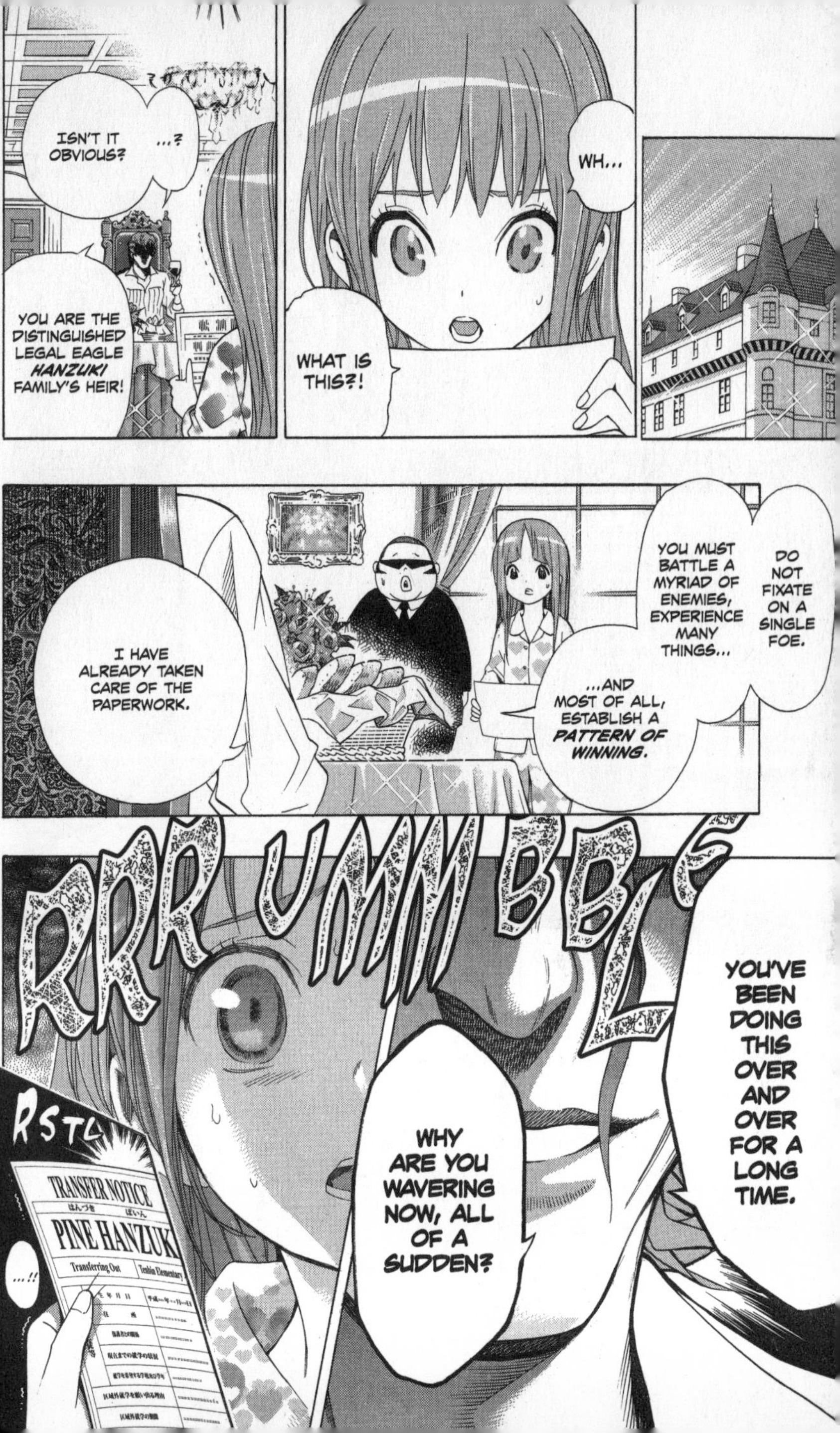
WH...
WHAT IS THIS?!
...?
ISN'T IT OBVIOUS?
YOU ARE THE DISTINGUISHED LEGAL EAGLE *HANZUKI* FAMILY'S HEIR!
DO NOT FIXATE ON A SINGLE FOE.
YOU MUST BATTLE A MYRIAD OF ENEMIES, EXPERIENCE MANY THINGS...
...AND MOST OF ALL, ESTABLISH A *PATTERN OF WINNING.*
I HAVE ALREADY TAKEN CARE OF THE PAPERWORK.
RRRUMMBBLE
YOU'VE BEEN DOING THIS OVER AND OVER FOR A LONG TIME.
WHY ARE YOU WAVERING NOW, ALL OF A SUDDEN?
RSTL
TRANSFER NOTICE
はんづき ぱいん
PINE HANZUKI
Transferring Out
Tenbin Elementary
...!!

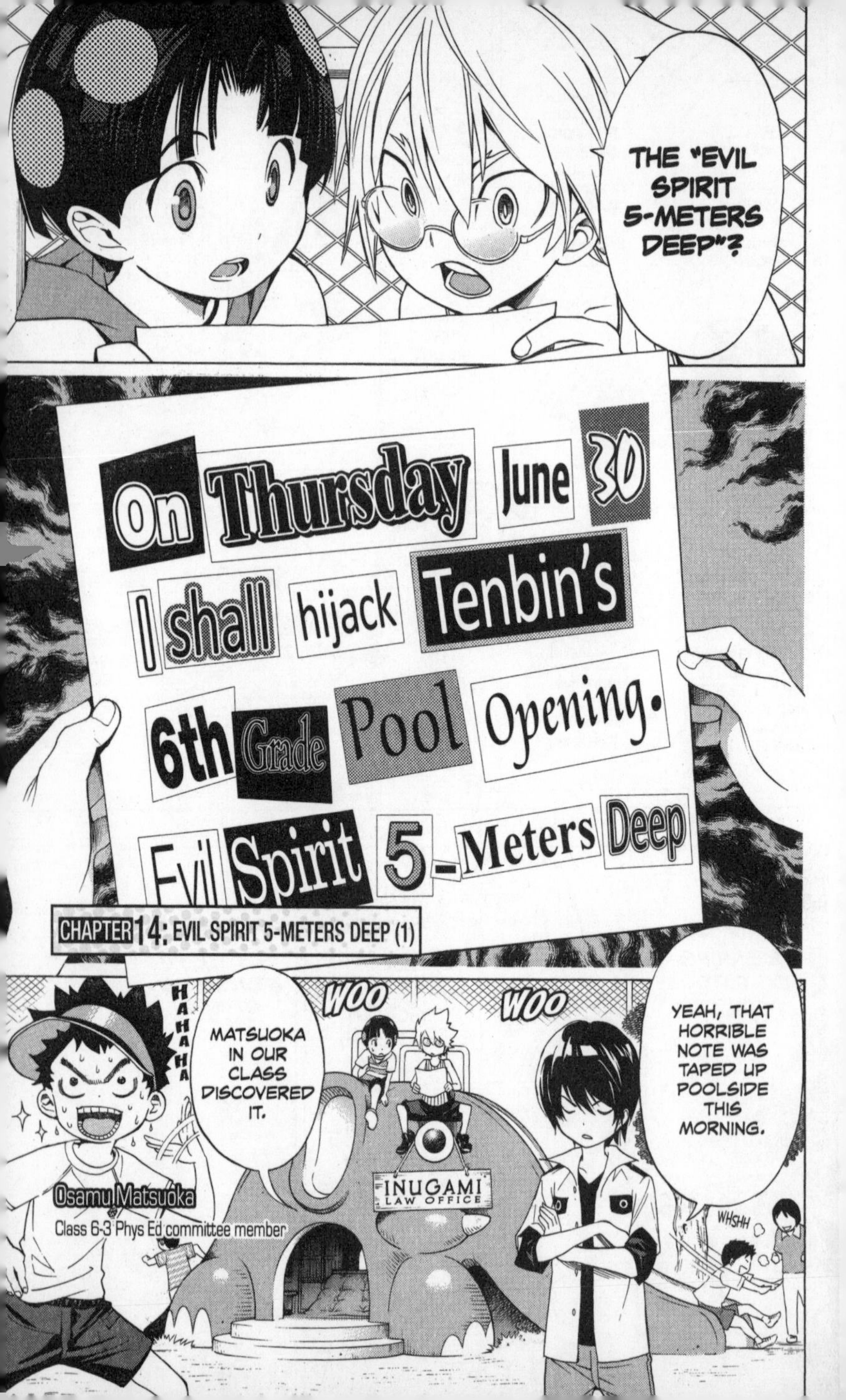
THE "EVIL SPIRIT 5-METERS DEEP"?
On Thursday June 30
I shall hijack Tenbin's
6th Grade Pool Opening.
Evil Spirit 5-Meters Deep
CHAPTER 14: EVIL SPIRIT 5-METERS DEEP (1)
WOO
YEAH, THAT HORRIBLE NOTE WAS TAPED UP POOLSIDE THIS MORNING.
WHSHH
INUGAMI LAW OFFICE
WOO
MATSUOKA IN OUR CLASS DISCOVERED IT.
HAHAHAHA
Osamu Matsuoka
Class 6-3 Phys Ed committee member

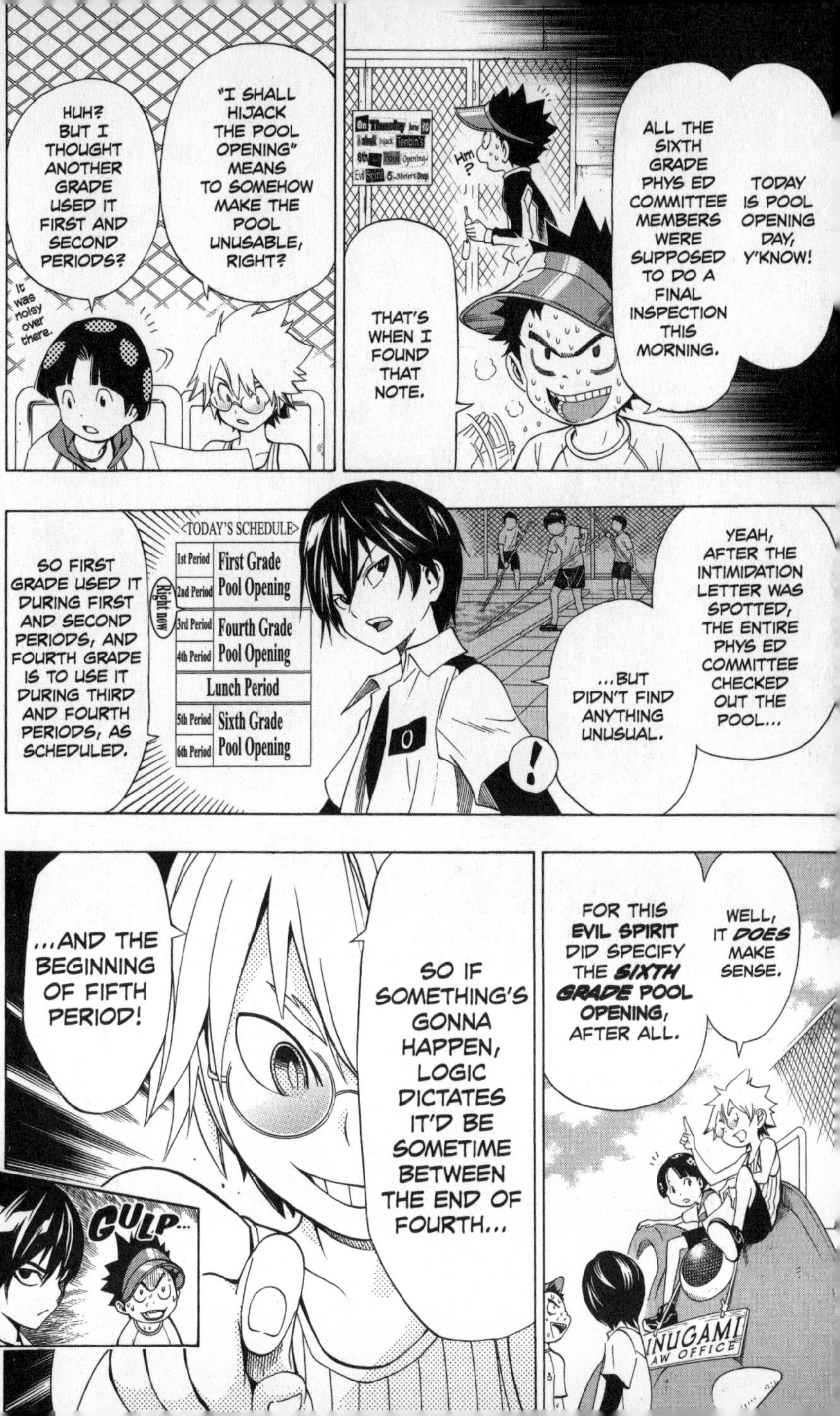
TODAY IS POOL OPENING DAY, Y'KNOW!
ALL THE SIXTH GRADE PHYS ED COMMITTEE MEMBERS WERE SUPPOSED TO DO A FINAL INSPECTION THIS MORNING.
Hm?
On Thursday June 30 I shall hijack Tenbin's 6th Pool Opening. Evil Spirit 5 Meters Deep
THAT'S WHEN I FOUND THAT NOTE.
"I SHALL HIJACK THE POOL OPENING" MEANS TO SOMEHOW MAKE THE POOL UNUSABLE, RIGHT?
HUH? BUT I THOUGHT ANOTHER GRADE USED IT FIRST AND SECOND PERIODS?
It was noisy over there.
YEAH, AFTER THE INTIMIDATION LETTER WAS SPOTTED, THE ENTIRE PHYS ED COMMITTEE CHECKED OUT THE POOL...
...BUT DIDN'T FIND ANYTHING UNUSUAL.
!
<TODAY'S SCHEDULE>
1st Period 2nd Period First Grade Pool Opening
Right now
3rd Period 4th Period Fourth Grade Pool Opening
Lunch Period
5th Period 6th Period Sixth Grade Pool Opening
SO FIRST GRADE USED IT DURING FIRST AND SECOND PERIODS, AND FOURTH GRADE IS TO USE IT DURING THIRD AND FOURTH PERIODS, AS SCHEDULED.
WELL, IT DOES MAKE SENSE.
FOR THIS EVIL SPIRIT DID SPECIFY THE SIXTH GRADE POOL OPENING, AFTER ALL.
INUGAMI LAW OFFICE
SO IF SOMETHING'S GONNA HAPPEN, LOGIC DICTATES IT'D BE SOMETIME BETWEEN THE END OF FOURTH...
...AND THE BEGINNING OF FIFTH PERIOD!
GULP...

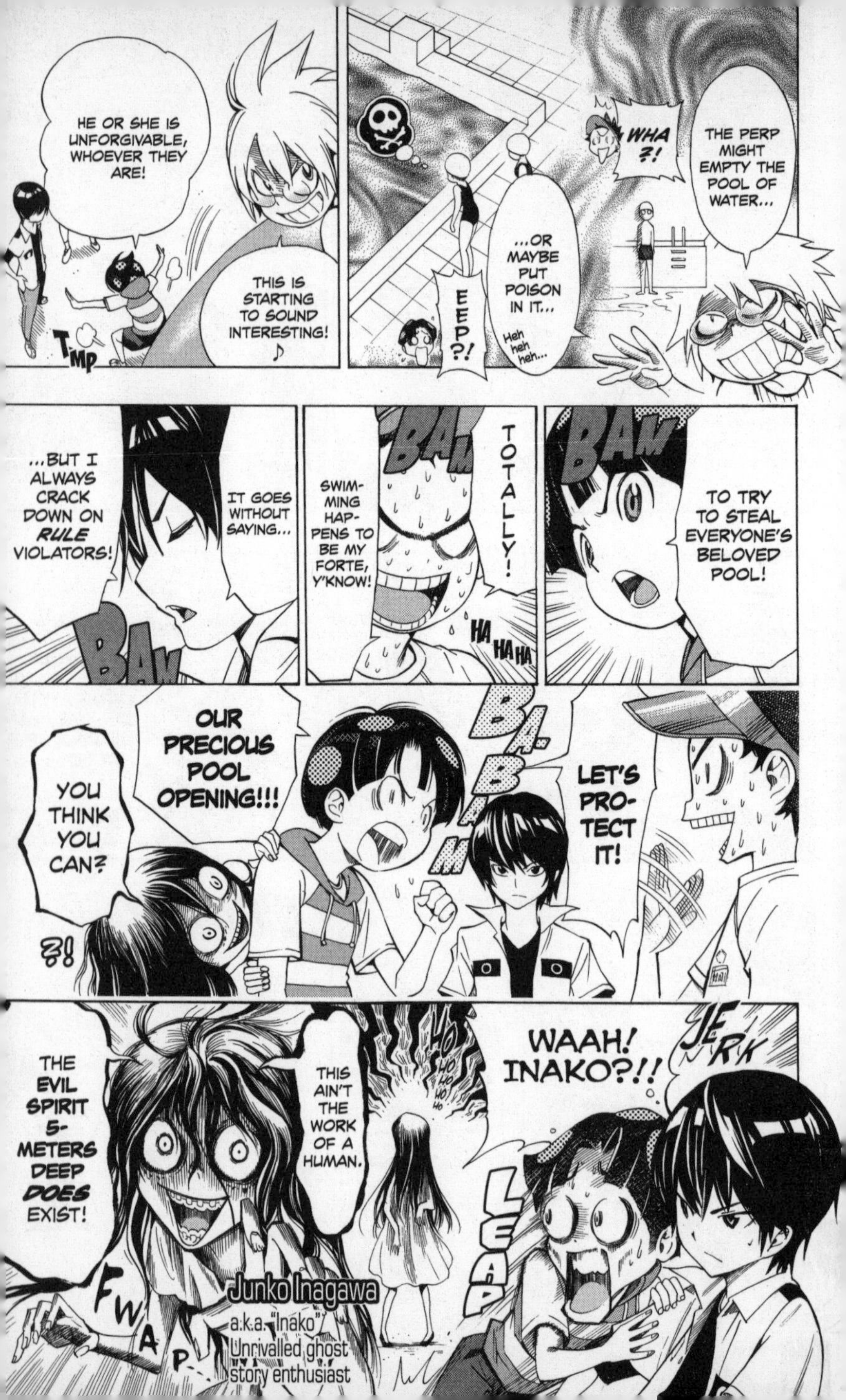
THE PERP MIGHT EMPTY THE POOL OF WATER...
WHA ?!
...OR MAYBE PUT POISON IN IT...
Heh heh heh...
EEP?!
THIS IS STARTING TO SOUND INTERESTING! ♪
HE OR SHE IS UNFORGIVABLE, WHOEVER THEY ARE!
TMP
BAM
TO TRY TO STEAL EVERYONE'S BELOVED POOL!
BAM
TOTALLY!
SWIMMING HAPPENS TO BE MY FORTE, Y'KNOW!
HA HA HA
IT GOES WITHOUT SAYING...
...BUT I ALWAYS CRACK DOWN ON RULE VIOLATORS!
BAM
LET'S PROTECT IT!
BA-BAAM
OUR PRECIOUS POOL OPENING!!!
YOU THINK YOU CAN?
?!
JERK
WAAH! INAKO?!!
LEAP
HO HO HO HO HO
THIS AIN'T THE WORK OF A HUMAN.
THE EVIL SPIRIT 5-METERS DEEP DOES EXIST!
FWAP
Junko Inagawa
a.k.a. "Inako"
Unrivalled ghost story enthusiast

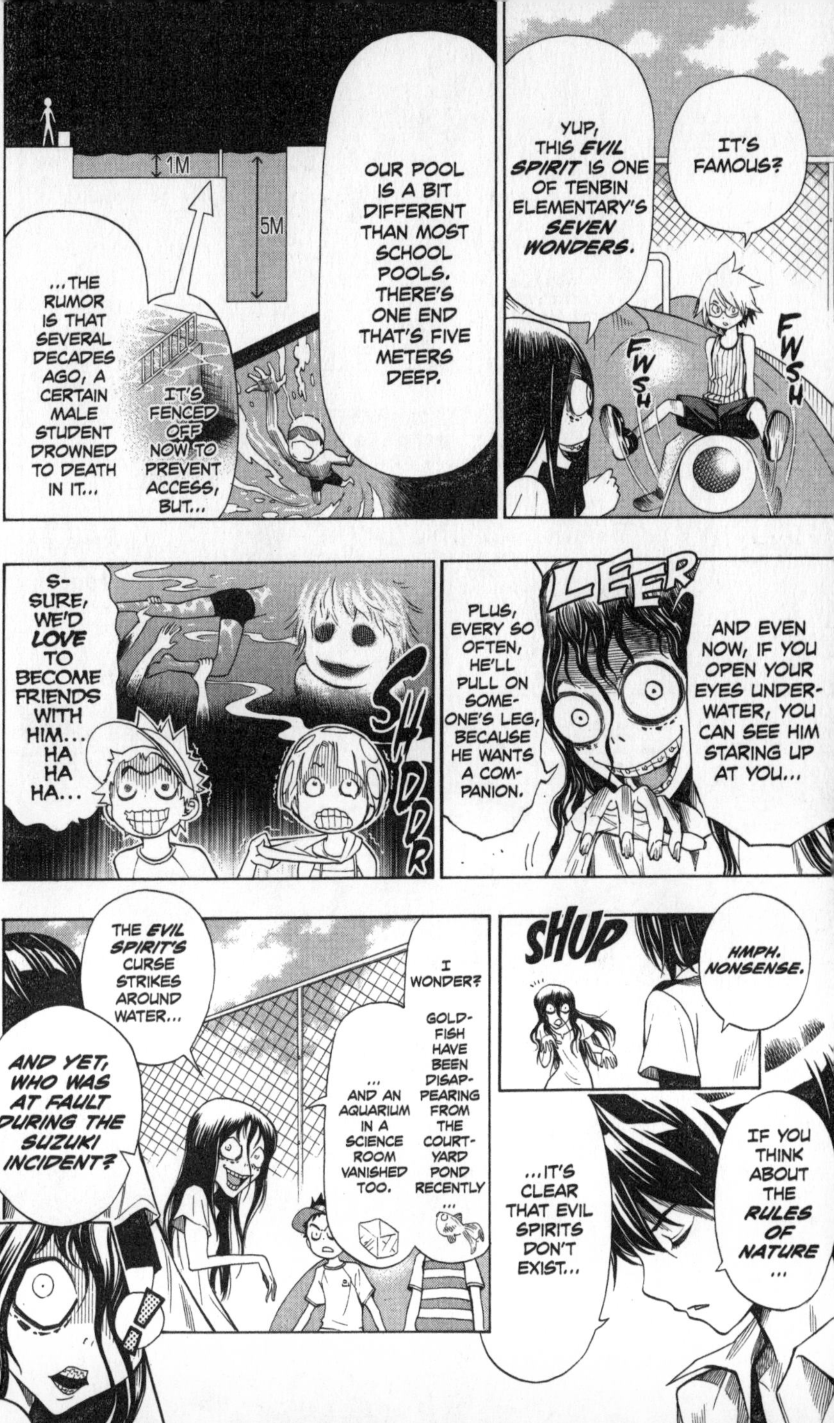
IT'S FAMOUS?
YUP, THIS EVIL SPIRIT IS ONE OF TENBIN ELEMENTARY'S SEVEN WONDERS.
FWSH
FWSH
OUR POOL IS A BIT DIFFERENT THAN MOST SCHOOL POOLS. THERE'S ONE END THAT'S FIVE METERS DEEP.
1M
5M
...THE RUMOR IS THAT SEVERAL DECADES AGO, A CERTAIN MALE STUDENT DROWNED TO DEATH IN IT...
IT'S FENCED OFF NOW TO PREVENT ACCESS, BUT...
LEER
AND EVEN NOW, IF YOU OPEN YOUR EYES UNDER-WATER, YOU CAN SEE HIM STARING UP AT YOU...
PLUS, EVERY SO OFTEN, HE'LL PULL ON SOME-ONE'S LEG, BECAUSE HE WANTS A COM-PANION.
SHUDDR
S-SURE, WE'D LOVE TO BECOME FRIENDS WITH HIM... HA HA HA...
SHUP
HMPH. NONSENSE.
IF YOU THINK ABOUT THE RULES OF NATURE...
...IT'S CLEAR THAT EVIL SPIRITS DON'T EXIST...
I WONDER?
GOLD-FISH HAVE BEEN DISAP-PEARING FROM THE COURT-YARD POND RECENTLY...
...AND AN AQUARIUM IN A SCIENCE ROOM VANISHED TOO.
THE EVIL SPIRIT'S CURSE STRIKES AROUND WATER...
AND YET, WHO WAS AT FAULT DURING THE SUZUKI INCIDENT?

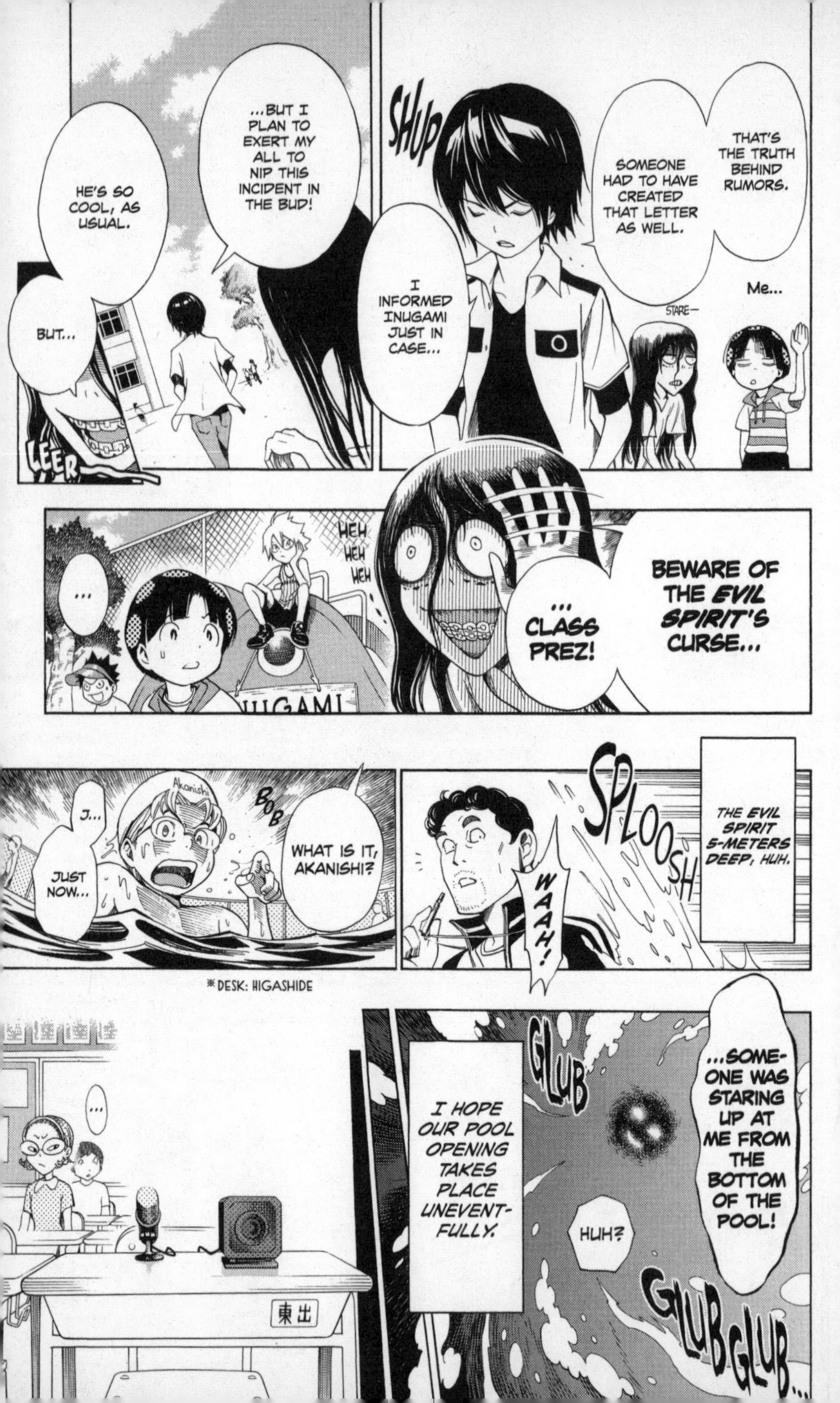
SHUP
THAT'S THE TRUTH BEHIND RUMORS.
SOMEONE HAD TO HAVE CREATED THAT LETTER AS WELL.
Me...
STARE—
I INFORMED INUGAMI JUST IN CASE...
...BUT I PLAN TO EXERT MY ALL TO NIP THIS INCIDENT IN THE BUD!
HE'S SO COOL, AS USUAL.
BUT...
LEER
BEWARE OF THE EVIL SPIRIT'S CURSE...
...CLASS PREZ!
HEH HEH HEH
...
THE EVIL SPIRIT 5-METERS DEEP, HUH.
SPLOOSH
WAAAH!
WHAT IS IT, AKANISHI?
BOB
Akanishi
J...
JUST NOW...
※DESK: HIGASHIDE
...SOME-ONE WAS STARING UP AT ME FROM THE BOTTOM OF THE POOL!
GLUB
HUH?
GLUB GLUB...
I HOPE OUR POOL OPENING TAKES PLACE UNEVENT-FULLY.
...
東出

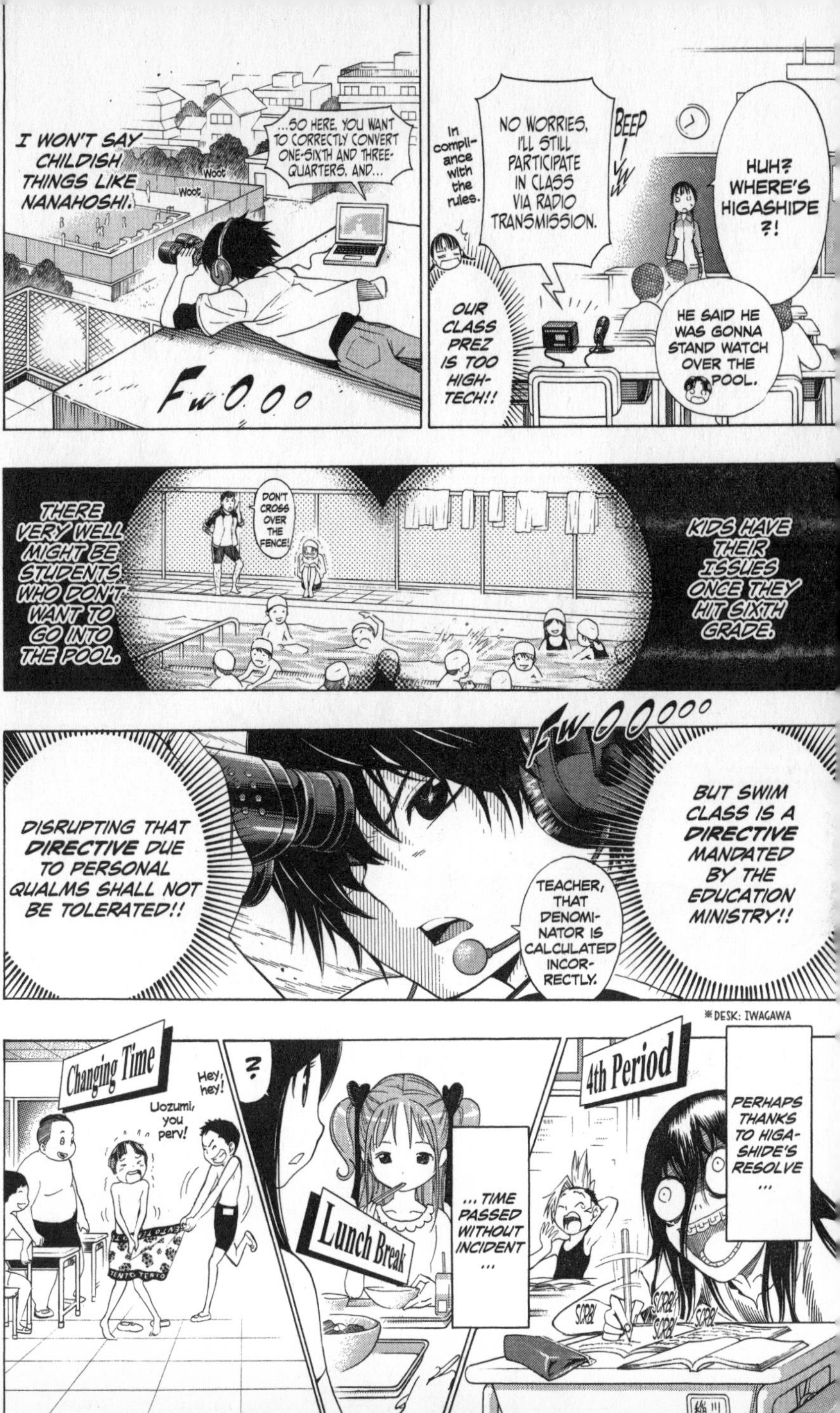
HUH? WHERE'S HIGASHIDE ?!
HE SAID HE WAS GONNA STAND WATCH OVER THE POOL.
BEEP
NO WORRIES, I'LL STILL PARTICIPATE IN CLASS VIA RADIO TRANSMISSION.
In compliance with the rules.
OUR CLASS PREZ IS TOO HIGH-TECH!!
...SO HERE, YOU WANT TO CORRECTLY CONVERT ONE-SIXTH AND THREE-QUARTERS, AND...
Woot
Woot
I WON'T SAY CHILDISH THINGS LIKE NANAHOSHI.
FWOOO
KIDS HAVE THEIR ISSUES ONCE THEY HIT SIXTH GRADE.
DON'T CROSS OVER THE FENCE!
THERE VERY WELL MIGHT BE STUDENTS WHO DON'T WANT TO GO INTO THE POOL.
FWOOOOO
BUT SWIM CLASS IS A DIRECTIVE MANDATED BY THE EDUCATION MINISTRY!!
TEACHER, THAT DENOMINATOR IS CALCULATED INCORRECTLY.
DISRUPTING THAT DIRECTIVE DUE TO PERSONAL QUALMS SHALL NOT BE TOLERATED!!
※DESK: IWAGAWA
4th Period
PERHAPS THANKS TO HIGASHIDE'S RESOLVE ...
SCRBL
SCRBL
SCRBL
SCRBL
?
Lunch Break
... TIME PASSED WITHOUT INCIDENT ...
Changing Time
Hey, hey!
Uozumi, you perv!

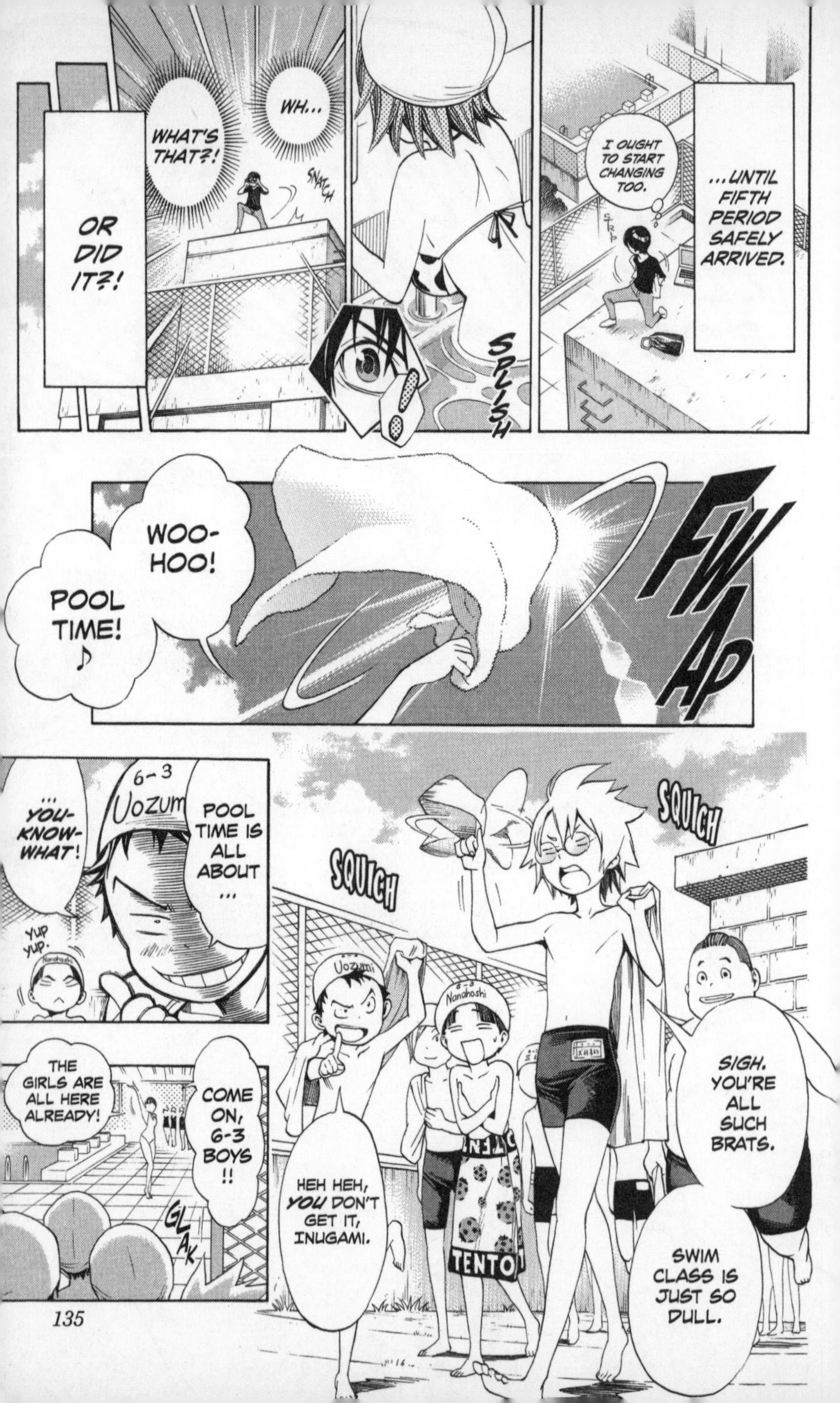
...UNTIL FIFTH PERIOD SAFELY ARRIVED.
I OUGHT TO START CHANGING TOO.
STRIP
WH...
SPLISH
WHAT'S THAT?!
SNATCH
OR DID IT?!
FWAP
WOO-HOO!
POOL TIME! ♪
SQUICH
SIGH. YOU'RE ALL SUCH BRATS.
SWIM CLASS IS JUST SO DULL.
SQUICH
HEH HEH, *YOU* DON'T GET IT, INUGAMI.
TENTO
6-3 Nanahoshi
Uozumi
6-3 Uozum
POOL TIME IS ALL ABOUT...
...*YOU-KNOW-WHAT*!
YUP YUP.
COME ON, 6-3 BOYS!!
THE GIRLS ARE ALL HERE ALREADY!
GLAK

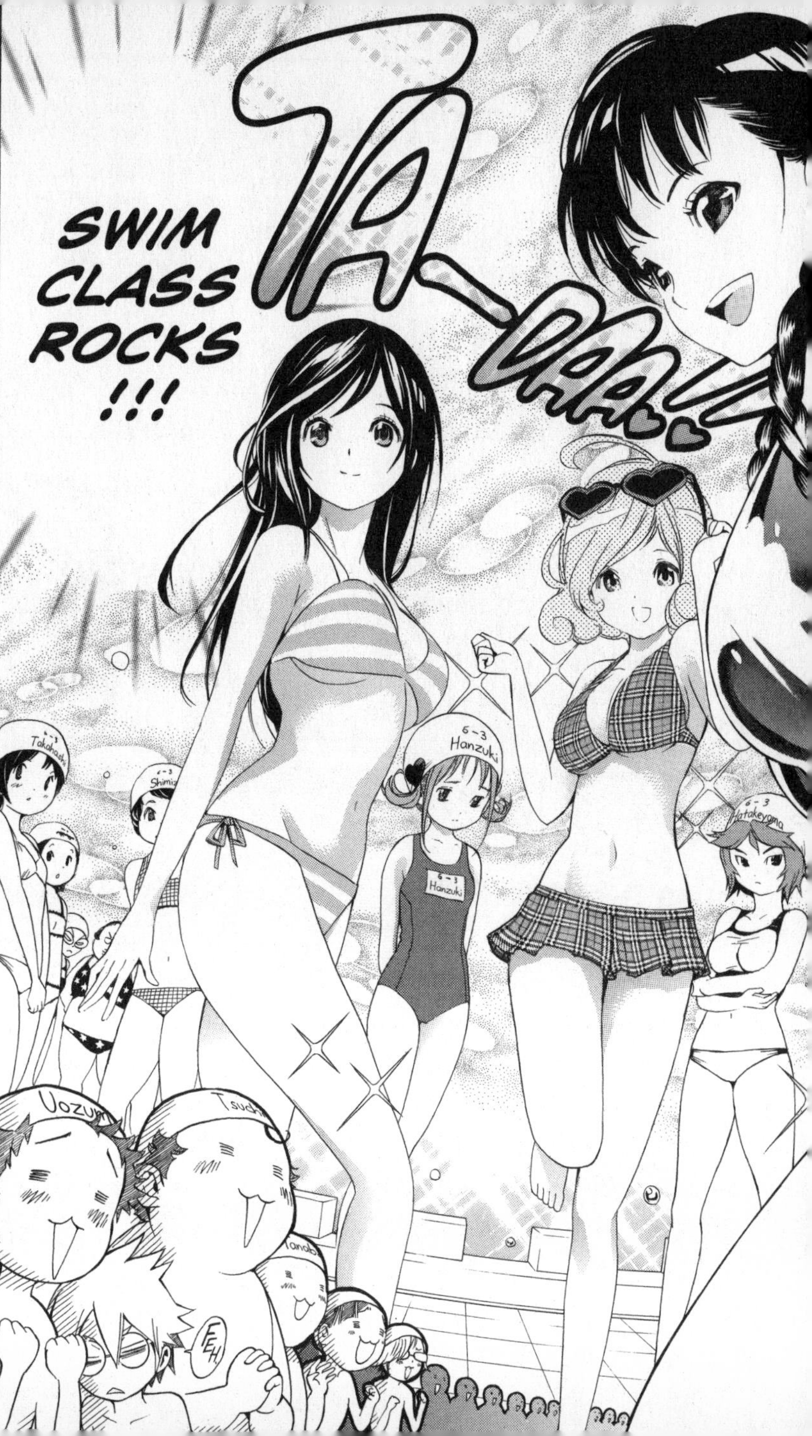
TA-MAA!!
SWIM CLASS ROCKS !!!
6-3 Hatakeyama
6-3 Hanzuki
6-3 Hanzuki
6-3 Takahashi
FEH

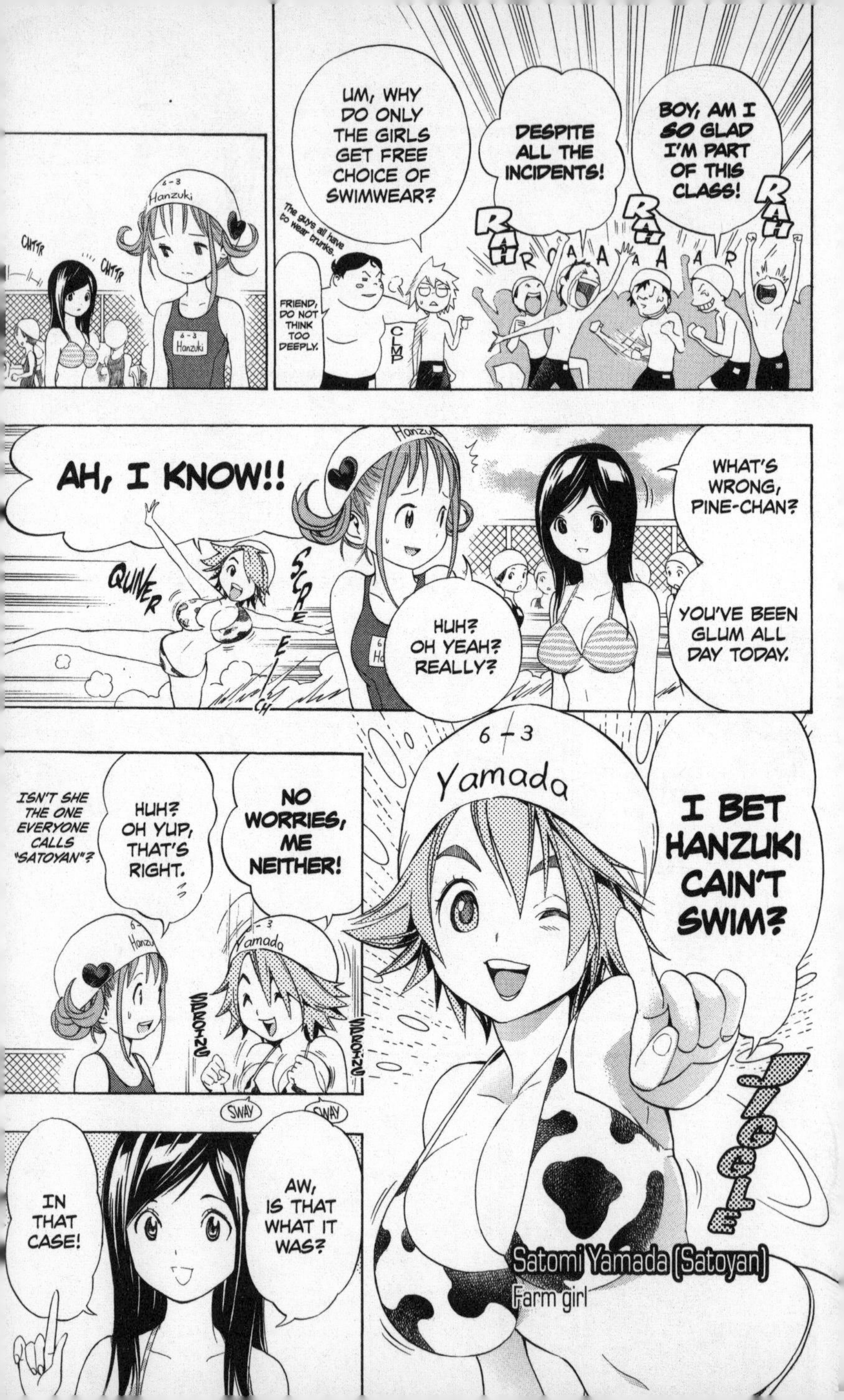

BOY, AM I SO GLAD I'M PART OF THIS CLASS!
DESPITE ALL THE INCIDENTS!
RAH RAH RAH
RAAAAAR
UM, WHY DO ONLY THE GIRLS GET FREE CHOICE OF SWIMWEAR?
The guys all have to wear trunks.
FRIEND, DO NOT THINK TOO DEEPLY.
CLMP
6-3 Hanzuki
CHTTR
CHTTR
WHAT'S WRONG, PINE-CHAN?
YOU'VE BEEN GLUM ALL DAY TODAY.
HUH? OH YEAH? REALLY?
AH, I KNOW!!
QUIVER
SCREEEATCH
6-3 Yamada
I BET HANZUKI CAIN'T SWIM?
JIGGLE
Satomi Yamada (Satoyan)
Farm girl
NO WORRIES, ME NEITHER!
HUH? OH YUP, THAT'S RIGHT.
ISN'T SHE THE ONE EVERYONE CALLS "SATOYAN"?
SPROING
SPROING
SWAY
SWAY
AW, IS THAT WHAT IT WAS?
IN THAT CASE!

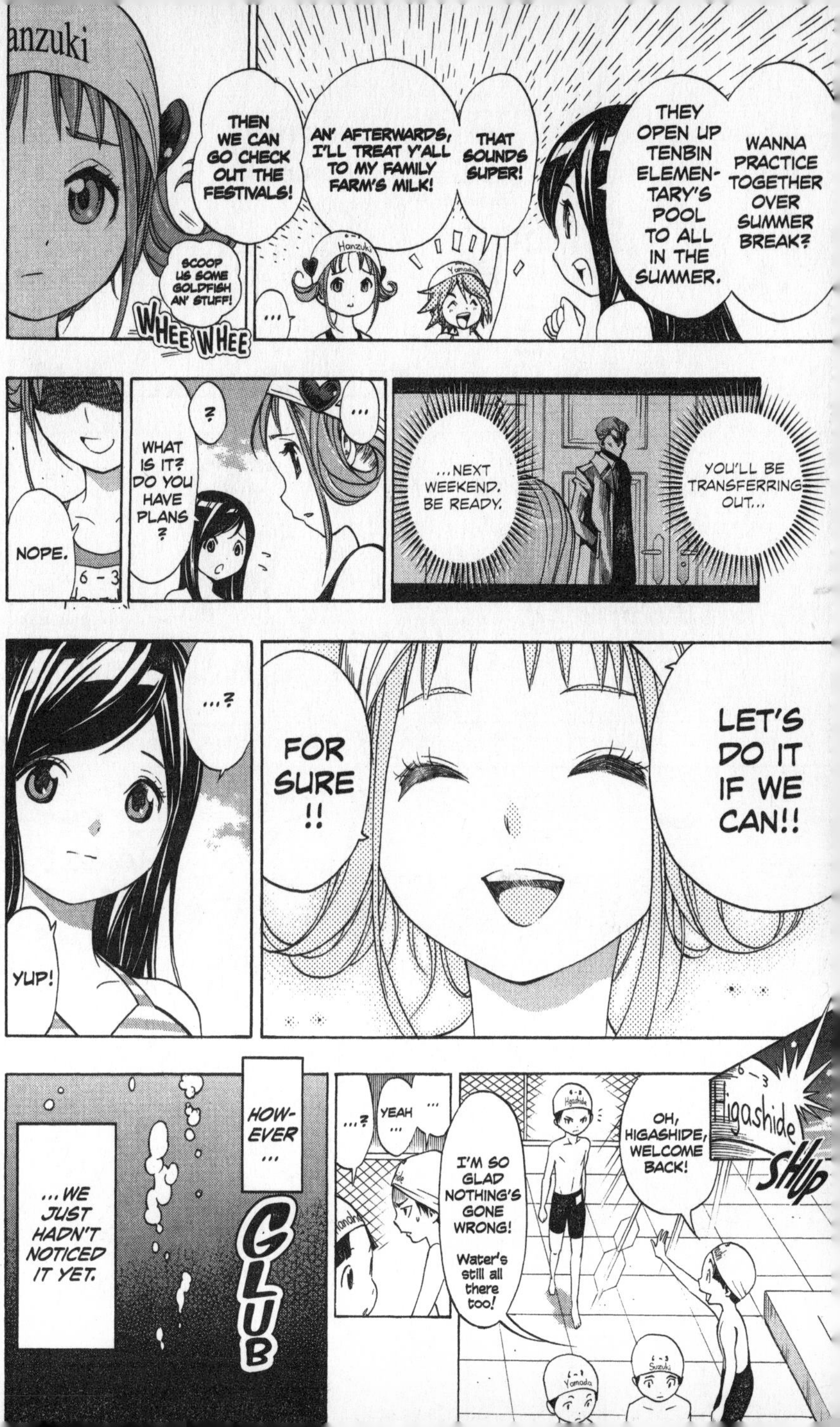
WANNA PRACTICE TOGETHER OVER SUMMER BREAK?
THEY OPEN UP TENBIN ELEMENTARY'S POOL TO ALL IN THE SUMMER.
THAT SOUNDS SUPER!
AN' AFTERWARDS, I'LL TREAT Y'ALL TO MY FAMILY FARM'S MILK!
THEN WE CAN GO CHECK OUT THE FESTIVALS!
SCOOP US SOME GOLDFISH AN' STUFF!
...
WHEE WHEE
anzuki
YOU'LL BE TRANSFERRING OUT...
...NEXT WEEKEND. BE READY.
...
?
WHAT IS IT? DO YOU HAVE PLANS?
NOPE.
LET'S DO IT IF WE CAN!!
FOR SURE!!
...?
YUP!
Higashide
SHIP
OH, HIGASHIDE, WELCOME BACK!
I'M SO GLAD NOTHING'S GONE WRONG!
Water's still all there too!
YEAH...
...?
HOW-EVER...
GLUB
...WE JUST HADN'T NOTICED IT YET.

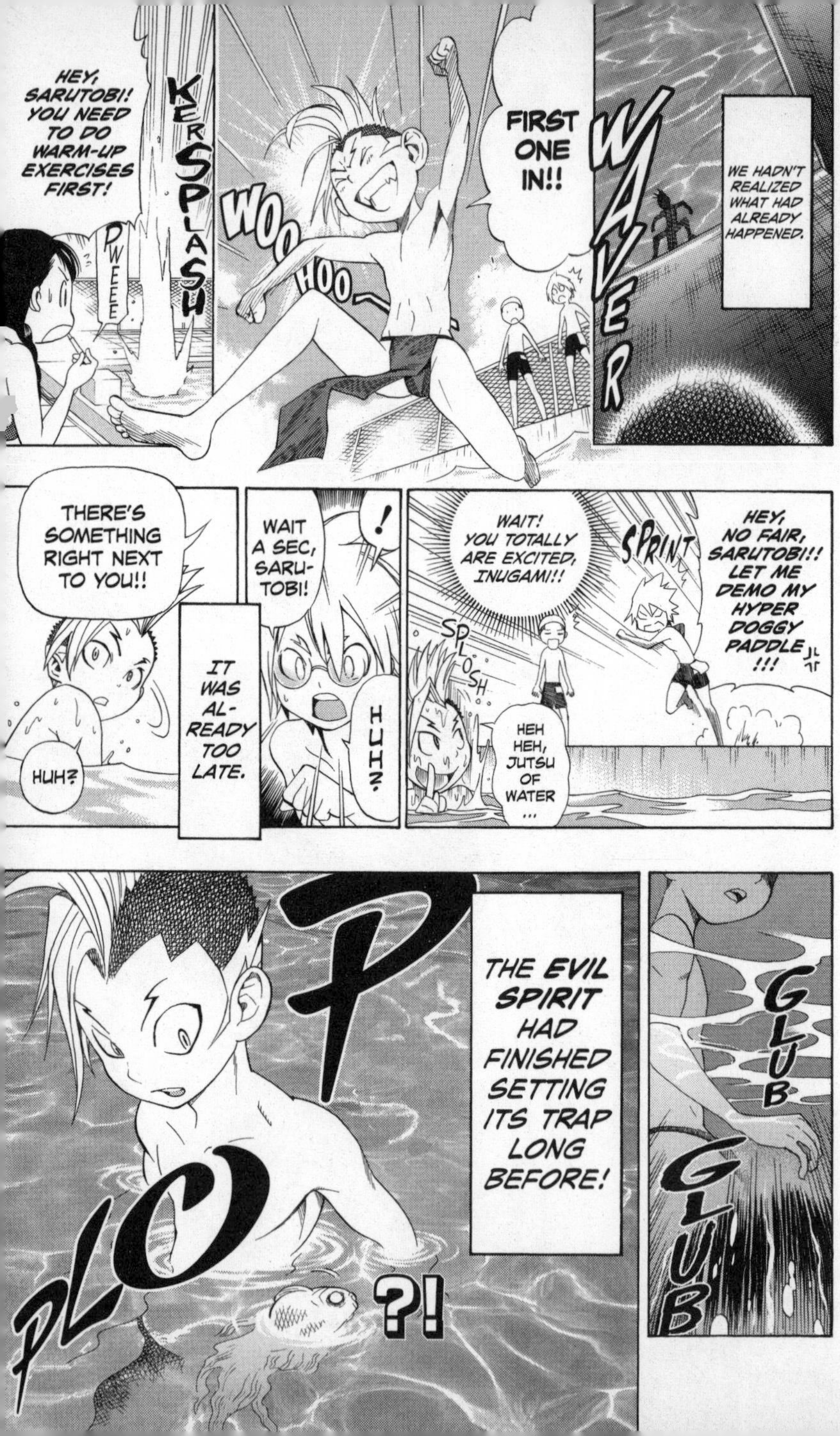
WE HADN'T REALIZED WHAT HAD ALREADY HAPPENED.
WAVER
FIRST ONE IN!!
WOO HOO—
KERSPLASH
HEY, SARUTOBI! YOU NEED TO DO WARM-UP EXERCISES FIRST!
PWEEE
HEY, NO FAIR, SARUTOBI!! LET ME DEMO MY HYPER DOGGY PADDLE!!!
SPRINT
WAIT! YOU TOTALLY ARE EXCITED, INUGAMI!!
SPLOSH
HEH HEH, JUTSU OF WATER ...
!
WAIT A SEC, SARU-TOBI!
HUH?
IT WAS AL-READY TOO LATE.
THERE'S SOMETHING RIGHT NEXT TO YOU!!
HUH?
GLUB
GLUB
THE EVIL SPIRIT HAD FINISHED SETTING ITS TRAP LONG BEFORE!
PLOP
?!

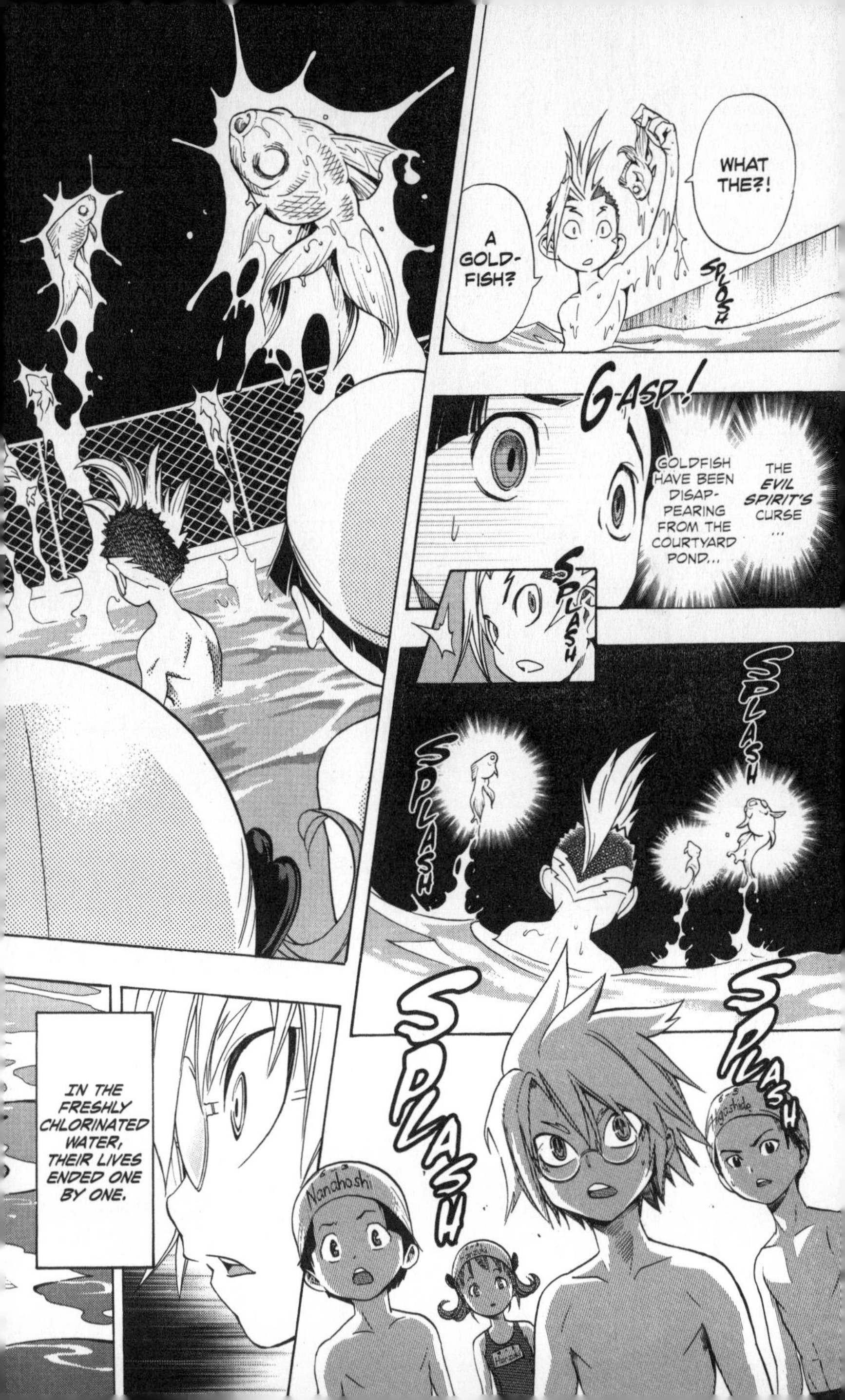
WHAT THE?!
A GOLD-FISH?
SPLOSH
GASP!
THE EVIL SPIRIT'S CURSE...
GOLDFISH HAVE BEEN DISAP-PEARING FROM THE COURTYARD POND...
SPLASH
SPLASH
SPLASH
SPLASH
SPLASH
Higashide
Nanchoshi
IN THE FRESHLY CHLORINATED WATER, THEIR LIVES ENDED ONE BY ONE.

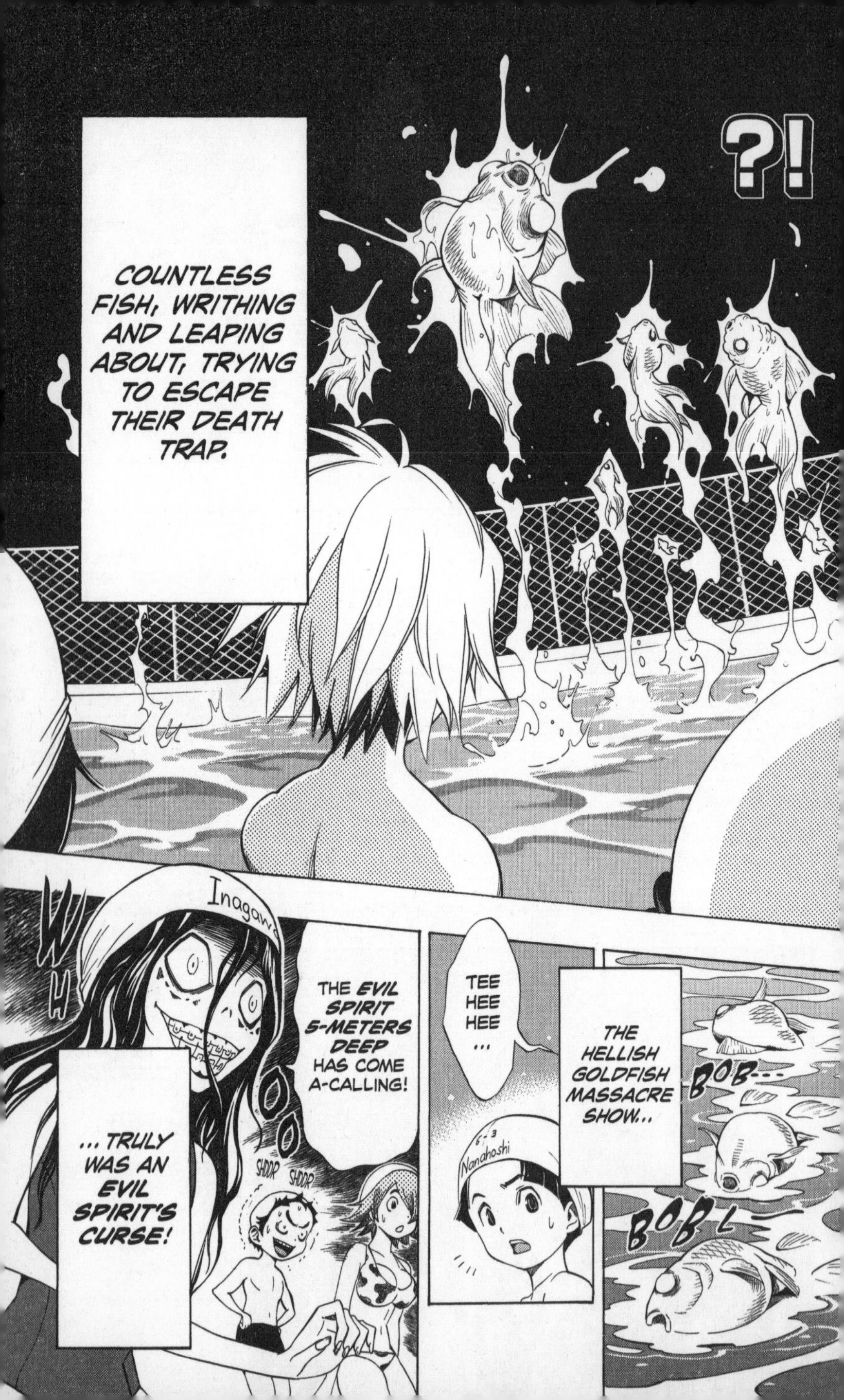
?!
COUNTLESS FISH, WRITHING AND LEAPING ABOUT, TRYING TO ESCAPE THEIR DEATH TRAP.
THE HELLISH GOLDFISH MASSACRE SHOW...
BOB...
BOBL
TEE HEE HEE ...
6-3 Nanahoshi
THE EVIL SPIRIT 5-METERS DEEP HAS COME A-CALLING!
WH
Inagawa
SHDDR SHDDR
...TRULY WAS AN EVIL SPIRIT'S CURSE!

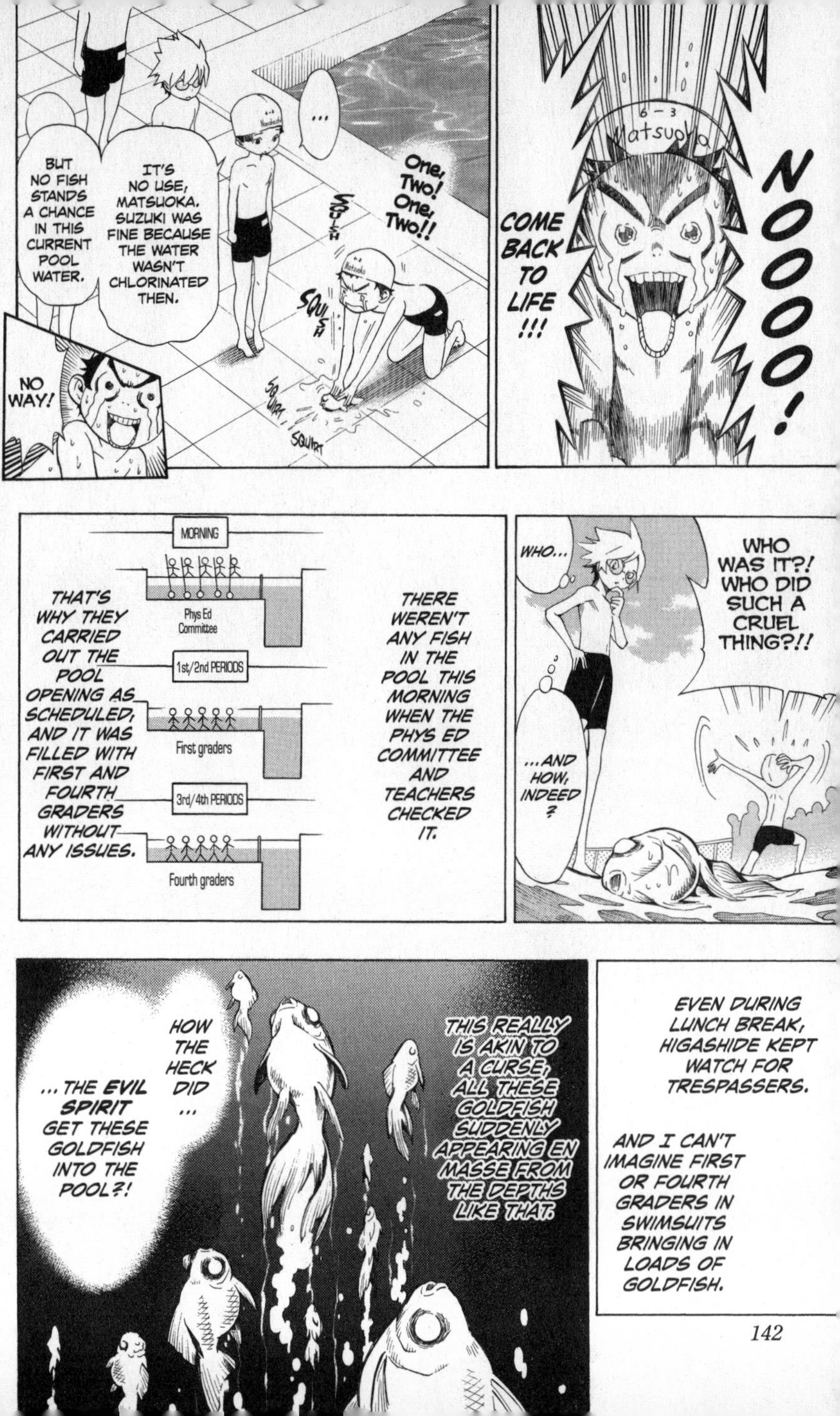

6-3
Matsuoka
NOOOOO!
COME BACK TO LIFE!!!
...
One, Two! One, Two!!
SQUISH
SQUISH
IT'S NO USE, MATSUOKA. SUZUKI WAS FINE BECAUSE THE WATER WASN'T CHLORINATED THEN.
BUT NO FISH STANDS A CHANCE IN THIS CURRENT POOL WATER.
SQUIRT
SQUIRT
NO WAY!
WHO WAS IT?! WHO DID SUCH A CRUEL THING?!!
WHO...
...AND HOW, INDEED?
THERE WEREN'T ANY FISH IN THE POOL THIS MORNING WHEN THE PHYS ED COMMITTEE AND TEACHERS CHECKED IT.
MORNING
Phys Ed Committee
1st/2nd PERIODS
First graders
3rd/4th PERIODS
Fourth graders
THAT'S WHY THEY CARRIED OUT THE POOL OPENING AS SCHEDULED, AND IT WAS FILLED WITH FIRST AND FOURTH GRADERS WITHOUT ANY ISSUES.
EVEN DURING LUNCH BREAK, HIGASHIDE KEPT WATCH FOR TRESPASSERS.
AND I CAN'T IMAGINE FIRST OR FOURTH GRADERS IN SWIMSUITS BRINGING IN LOADS OF GOLDFISH.
THIS REALLY IS AKIN TO A CURSE, ALL THESE GOLDFISH SUDDENLY APPEARING EN MASSE FROM THE DEPTHS LIKE THAT.
HOW THE HECK DID...
...THE EVIL SPIRIT GET THESE GOLDFISH INTO THE POOL?!

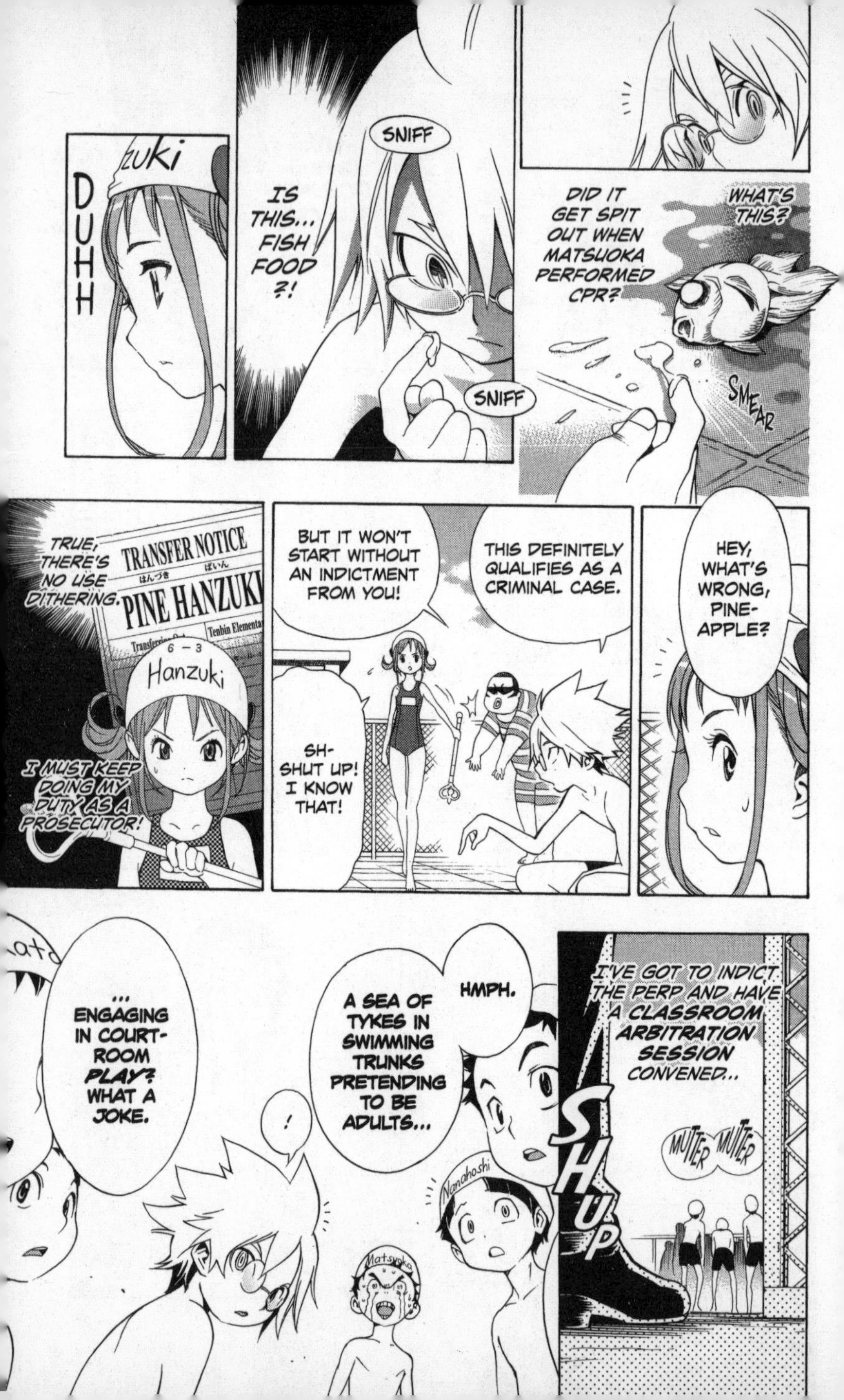
WHAT'S THIS?
DID IT GET SPIT OUT WHEN MATSUOKA PERFORMED CPR?
SMEAR
SNIFF
IS THIS... FISH FOOD?!
SNIFF
zuki
DUHH
HEY, WHAT'S WRONG, PINE-APPLE?
THIS DEFINITELY QUALIFIES AS A CRIMINAL CASE.
BUT IT WON'T START WITHOUT AN INDICTMENT FROM YOU!
SH-SHUT UP! I KNOW THAT!
TRUE, THERE'S NO USE DITHERING.
TRANSFER NOTICE
PINE HANZUKI
6-3
Hanzuki
I MUST KEEP DOING MY DUTY AS A PROSECUTOR!
I'VE GOT TO INDICT THE PERP AND HAVE A CLASSROOM ARBITRATION SESSION CONVENED...
SHUP
MUTTER MUTTER
HMPH.
A SEA OF TYKES IN SWIMMING TRUNKS PRETENDING TO BE ADULTS...
!
...ENGAGING IN COURTROOM PLAY? WHAT A JOKE.
Nanahoshi
Matsuoka

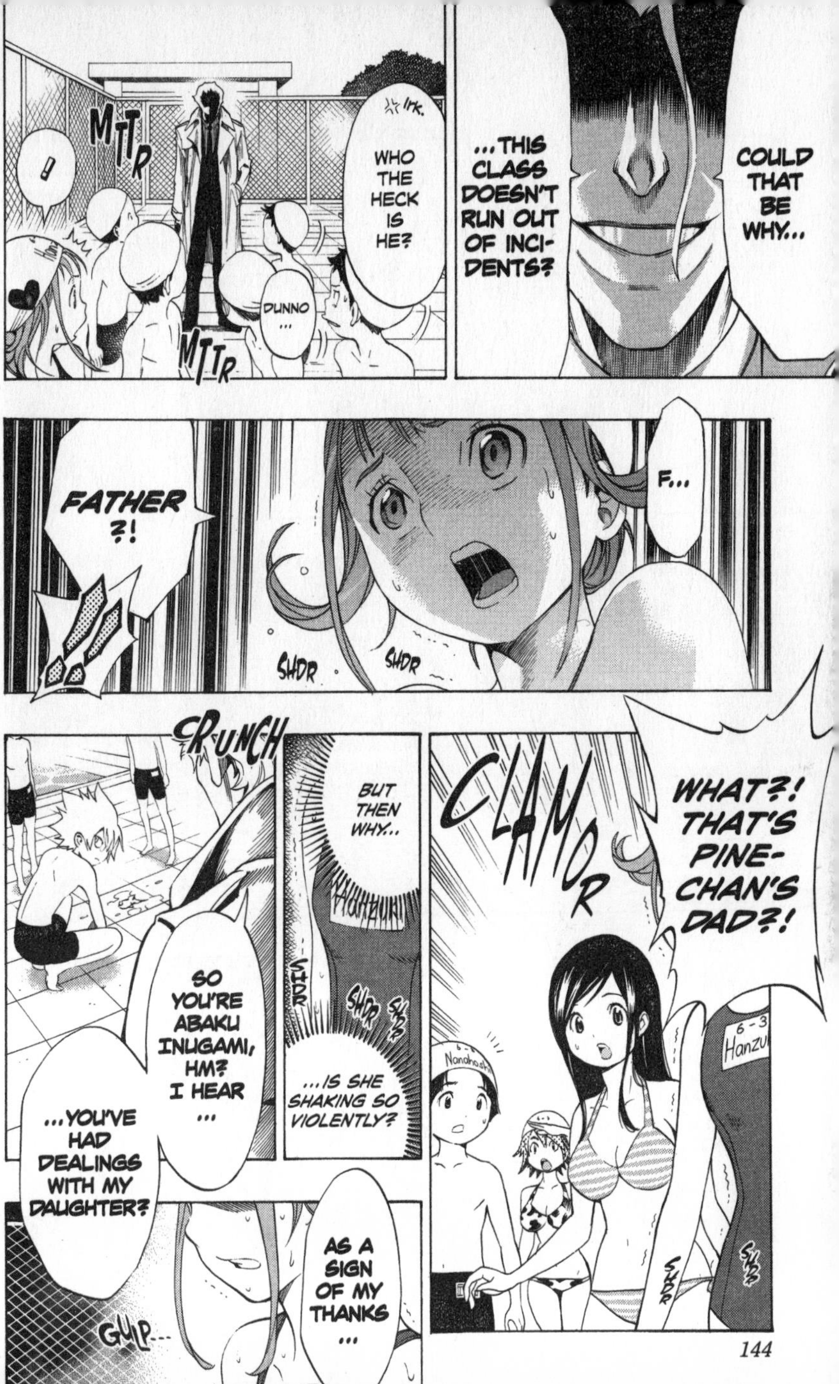
COULD THAT BE WHY...
...THIS CLASS DOESN'T RUN OUT OF INCIDENTS?
Irk.
WHO THE HECK IS HE?
MTTR
!
DUNNO...
MTTR
F...
FATHER?!
SHDR
SHDR
WHAT?! THAT'S PINE-CHAN'S DAD?!
CLAMOR
6-3 Hanzu
Nanahoshi
SHDR
SHDR
BUT THEN WHY...
SHDR
SHDR
SHDR
...IS SHE SHAKING SO VIOLENTLY?
CRUNCH
SO YOU'RE ABAKU INUGAMI, HM? I HEAR...
...YOU'VE HAD DEALINGS WITH MY DAUGHTER?
AS A SIGN OF MY THANKS...
GULP...

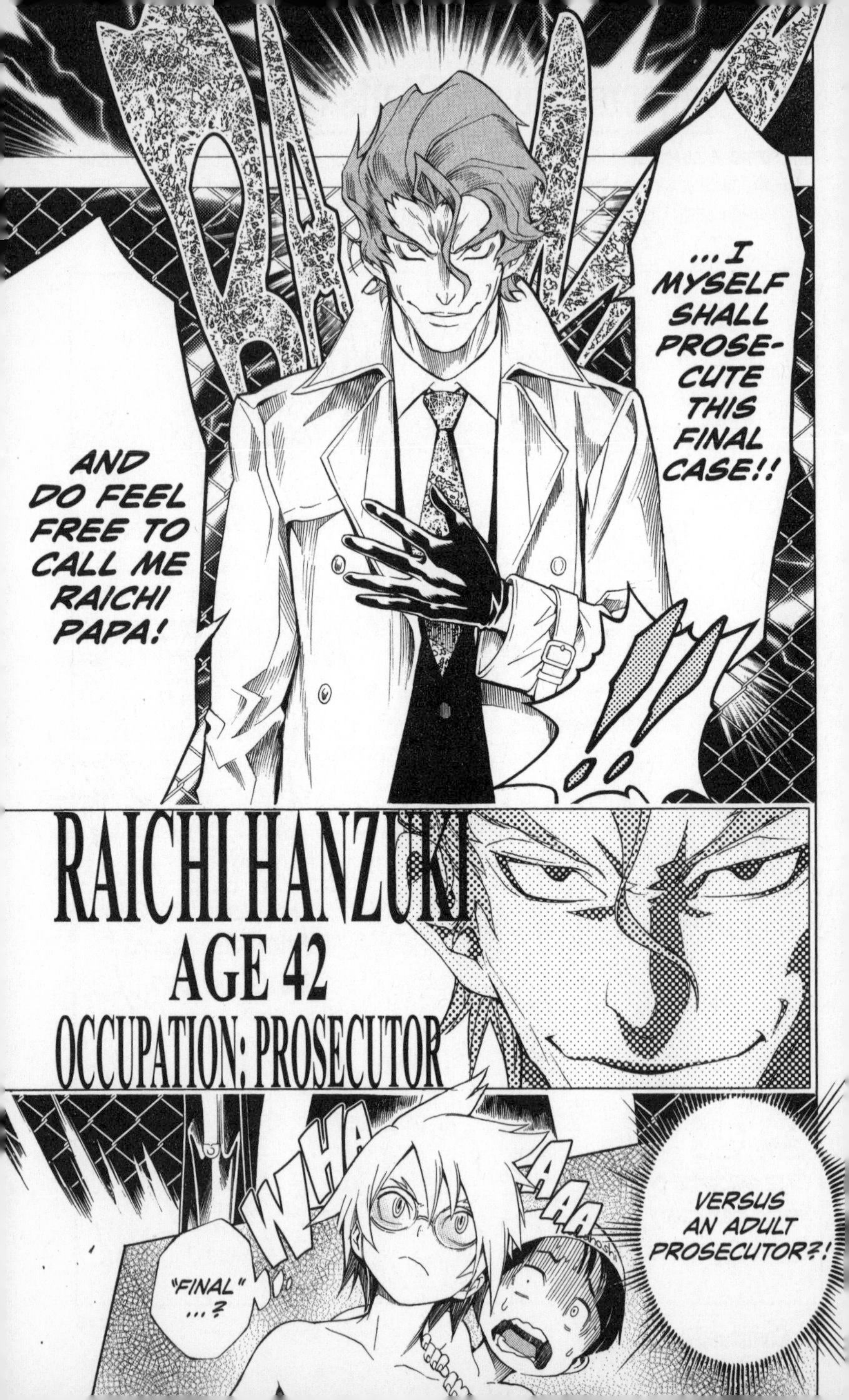
...I MYSELF SHALL PROSE-CUTE THIS FINAL CASE!!
AND DO FEEL FREE TO CALL ME RAICHI PAPA!
RAICHI HANZUKI
AGE 42
OCCUPATION: PROSECUTOR
VERSUS AN ADULT PROSECUTOR?!
"FINAL" ...?

Rejected Rough Drafts Gallery (1)

The spread of the female students' swimsuits was about three pages long at first. But due to overall length and other various circumstances, quite a bit got cut until it ended up shortened to just one page. Since I now have the opportunity, I thought I'd present the original version here! (Think of this as coming after p. 136's "Swim class rocks!!!" line.)

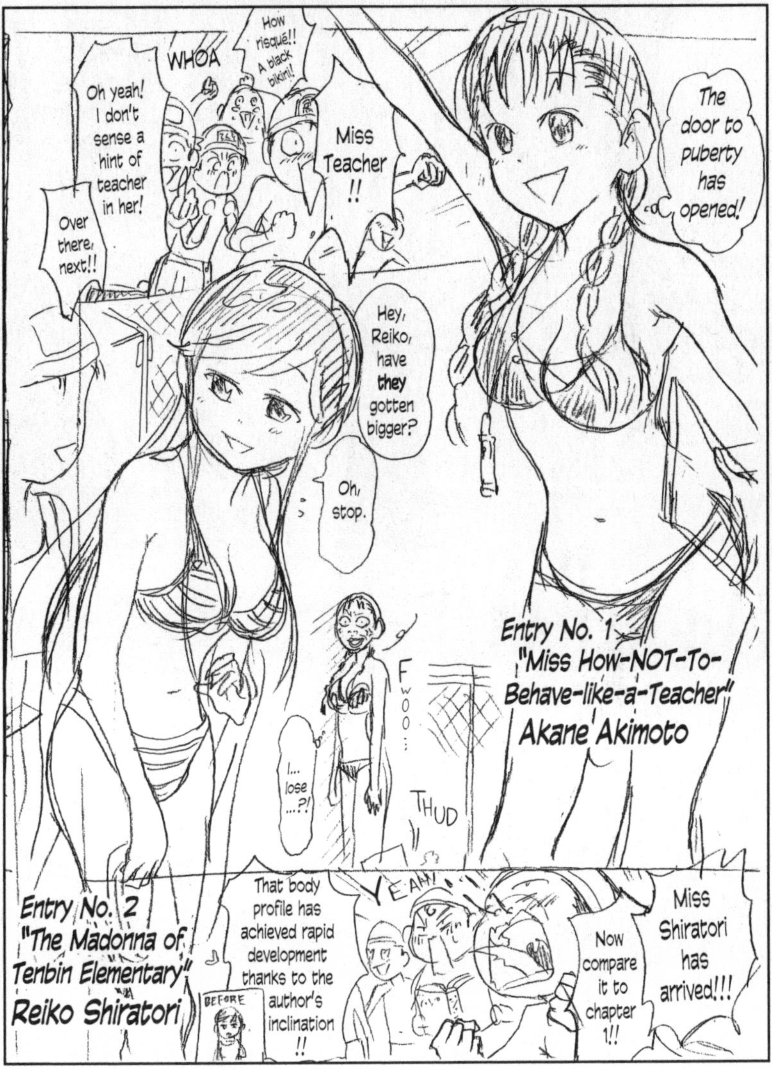
The door to puberty has opened!
Miss Teacher!!
How risqué!! A black bikini!!
WHOA
Oh yeah! I don't sense a hint of teacher in her!
Over there, next!!
Hey, Reiko, have they gotten bigger?
Oh, stop.
Entry No. 1 "Miss How-NOT-To-Behave-like-a-Teacher" Akane Akimoto
FWOO...
I... lose...?!
THUD
Miss Shiratori has arrived!!!
Now compare it to chapter 1!!
YEAH!
That body profile has achieved rapid development thanks to the author's inclination!!
BEFORE
Entry No. 2 "The Madonna of Tenbin Elementary" Reiko Shiratori

⇦ Continued on p. 166

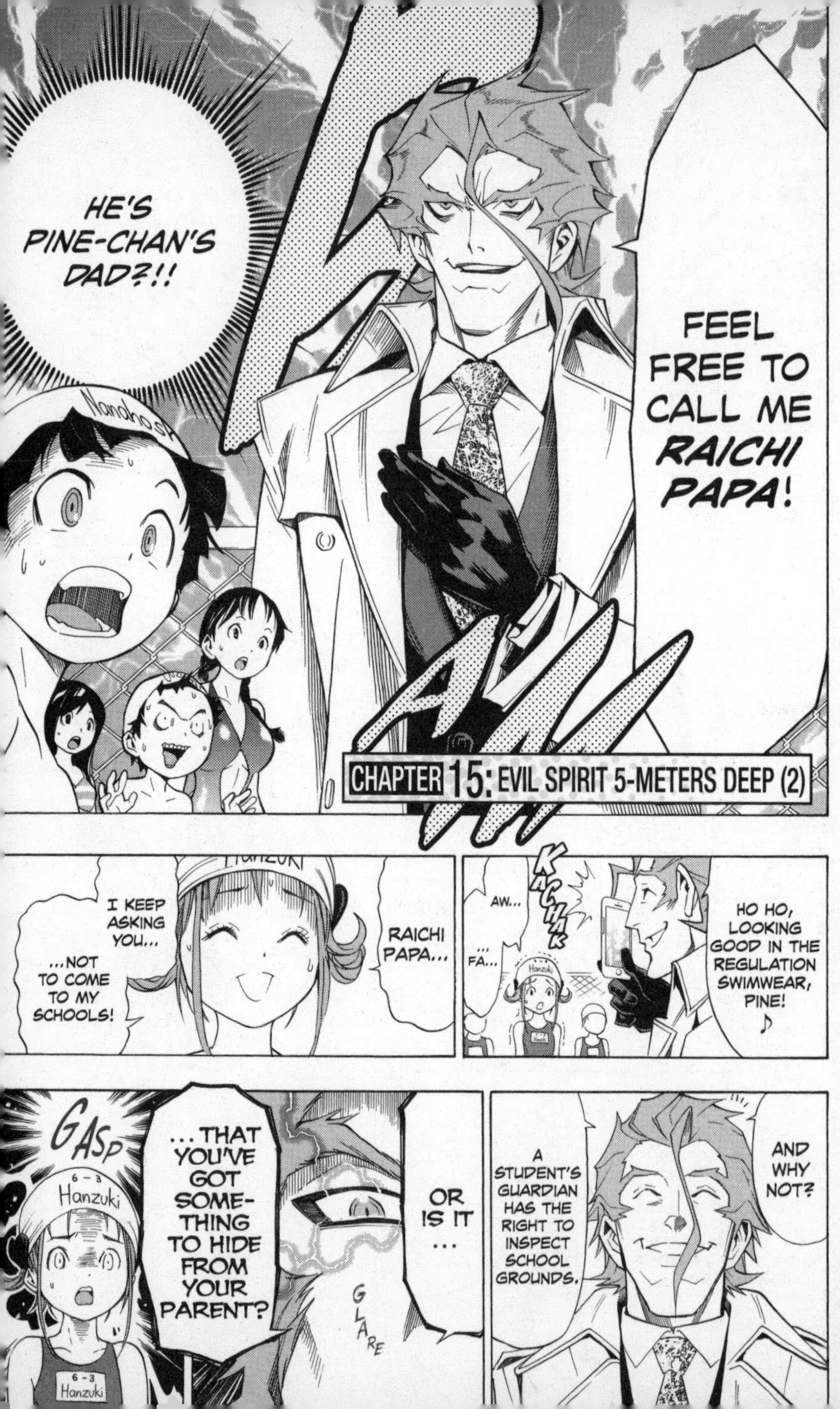
FEEL FREE TO CALL ME RAICHI PAPA!
HE'S PINE-CHAN'S DAD?!!
CHAPTER 15: EVIL SPIRIT 5-METERS DEEP (2)
HO HO, LOOKING GOOD IN THE REGULATION SWIMWEAR, PINE! ♪
KACHAK
AW...
... FA...
Hanzuki
RAICHI PAPA...
I KEEP ASKING YOU...
...NOT TO COME TO MY SCHOOLS!
AND WHY NOT?
A STUDENT'S GUARDIAN HAS THE RIGHT TO INSPECT SCHOOL GROUNDS.
OR IS IT ...
GLARE
...THAT YOU'VE GOT SOME-THING TO HIDE FROM YOUR PARENT?
GASP
6-3
Hanzuki
6-3
Hanzuki

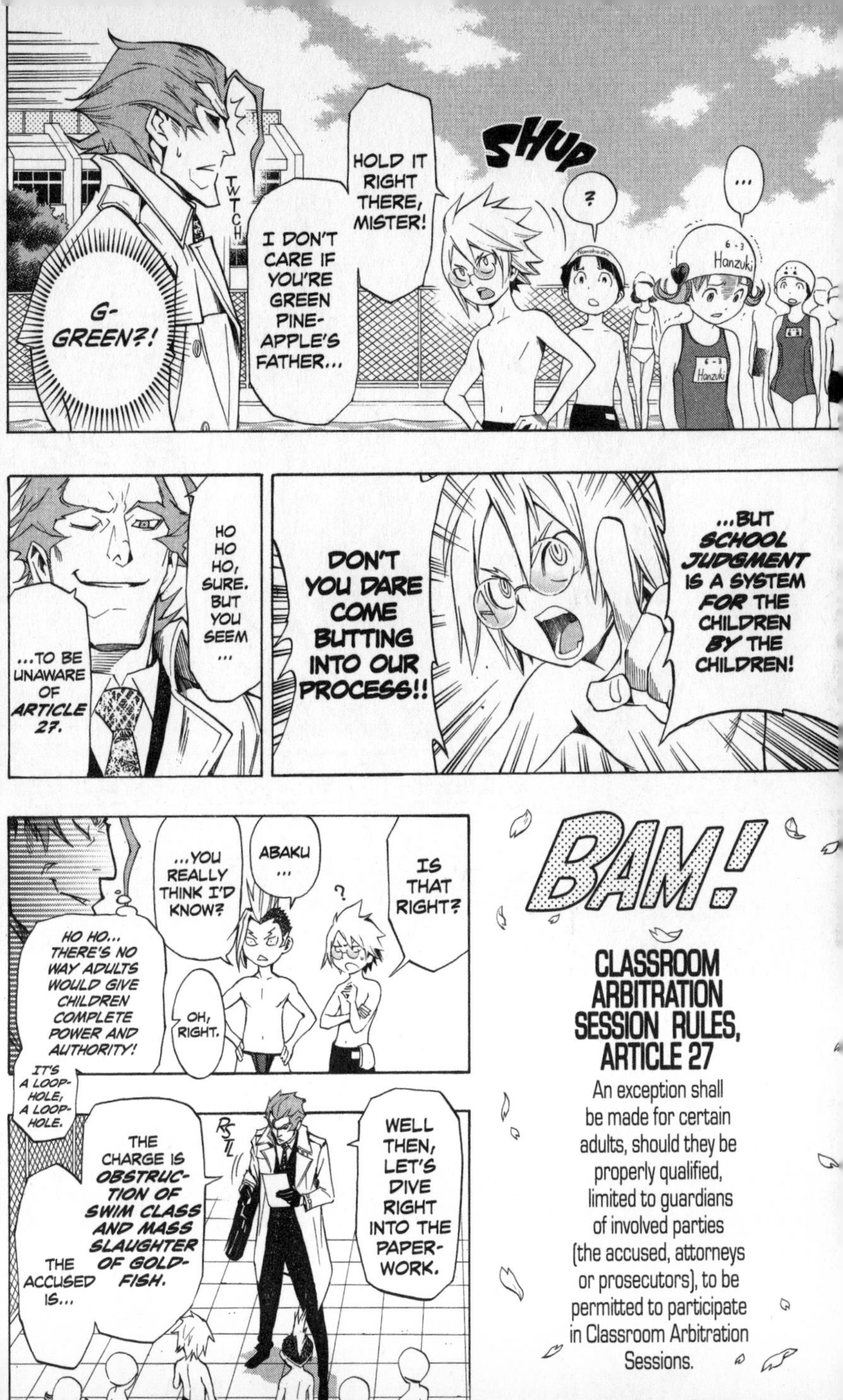
...
?
SHUP
HOLD IT RIGHT THERE, MISTER!
I DON'T CARE IF YOU'RE GREEN PINE-APPLE'S FATHER...
TWITCH
G-GREEN?!
...BUT SCHOOL JUDGMENT IS A SYSTEM FOR THE CHILDREN BY THE CHILDREN!
DON'T YOU DARE COME BUTTING INTO OUR PROCESS!!
HO HO HO, SURE. BUT YOU SEEM ...
...TO BE UNAWARE OF ARTICLE 27.
BAM!
CLASSROOM ARBITRATION SESSION RULES, ARTICLE 27
An exception shall be made for certain adults, should they be properly qualified, limited to guardians of involved parties (the accused, attorneys or prosecutors), to be permitted to participate in Classroom Arbitration Sessions.
IS THAT RIGHT?
ABAKU...
?
...YOU REALLY THINK I'D KNOW?
HO HO... THERE'S NO WAY ADULTS WOULD GIVE CHILDREN COMPLETE POWER AND AUTHORITY!
OH, RIGHT.
IT'S A LOOP-HOLE, A LOOP-HOLE.
WELL THEN, LET'S DIVE RIGHT INTO THE PAPER-WORK.
RSTL
THE CHARGE IS OBSTRUC-TION OF SWIM CLASS AND MASS SLAUGHTER OF GOLD-FISH.
THE ACCUSED IS...

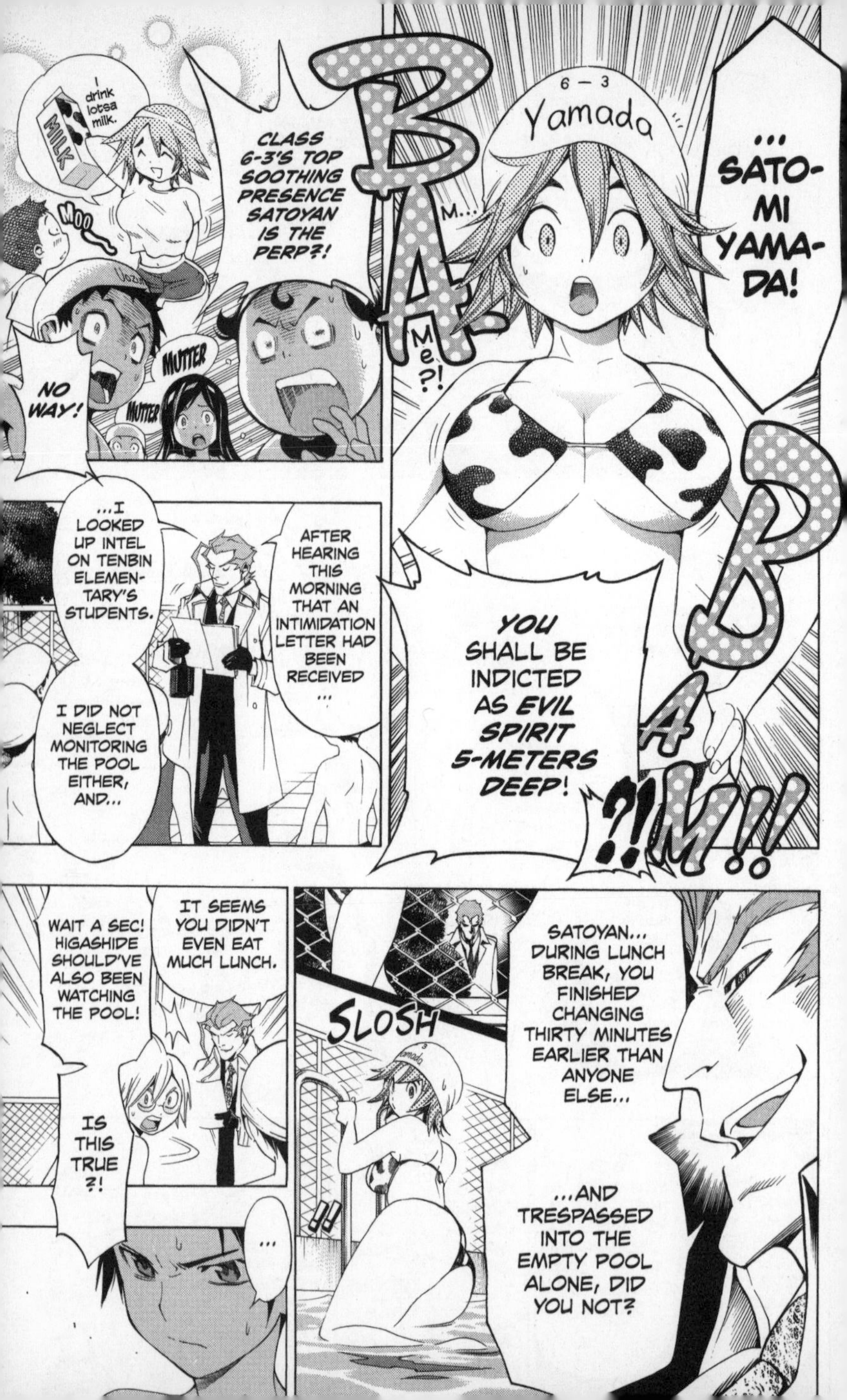
...SATOMI YAMADA!
6-3
Yamada
M...
Me?!
BAM
YOU SHALL BE INDICTED AS EVIL SPIRIT 5-METERS DEEP!
?!M!!
CLASS 6-3'S TOP SOOTHING PRESENCE SATOYAN IS THE PERP?!
I drink lotsa milk.
MILK
MOO
MUTTER
MUTTER
NO WAY!
AFTER HEARING THIS MORNING THAT AN INTIMIDATION LETTER HAD BEEN RECEIVED ...
...I LOOKED UP INTEL ON TENBIN ELEMENTARY'S STUDENTS.
I DID NOT NEGLECT MONITORING THE POOL EITHER, AND...
SATOYAN... DURING LUNCH BREAK, YOU FINISHED CHANGING THIRTY MINUTES EARLIER THAN ANYONE ELSE...
SLOSH
!!
...AND TRESPASSED INTO THE EMPTY POOL ALONE, DID YOU NOT?
IT SEEMS YOU DIDN'T EVEN EAT MUCH LUNCH.
WAIT A SEC! HIGASHIDE SHOULD'VE ALSO BEEN WATCHING THE POOL!
IS THIS TRUE?!
...

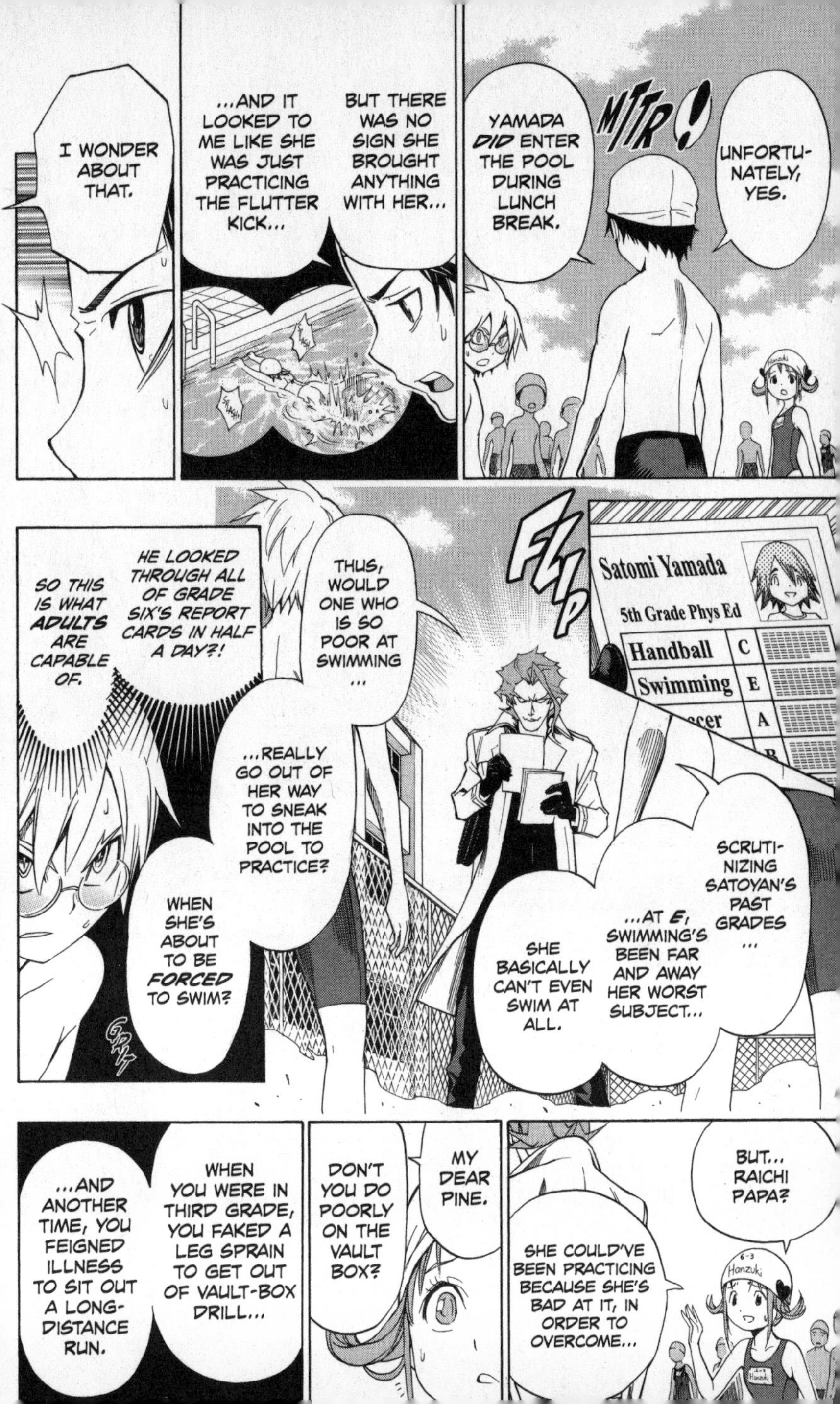
UNFORTUNATELY, YES.
MTTR!
YAMADA DID ENTER THE POOL DURING LUNCH BREAK.
BUT THERE WAS NO SIGN SHE BROUGHT ANYTHING WITH HER...
...AND IT LOOKED TO ME LIKE SHE WAS JUST PRACTICING THE FLUTTER KICK...
I WONDER ABOUT THAT.
Satomi Yamada
5th Grade Phys Ed
Handball C
Swimming E
FLIP
SCRUTINIZING SATOYAN'S PAST GRADES...
...AT E, SWIMMING'S BEEN FAR AND AWAY HER WORST SUBJECT...
SHE BASICALLY CAN'T EVEN SWIM AT ALL.
THUS, WOULD ONE WHO IS SO POOR AT SWIMMING...
...REALLY GO OUT OF HER WAY TO SNEAK INTO THE POOL TO PRACTICE?
WHEN SHE'S ABOUT TO BE FORCED TO SWIM?
HE LOOKED THROUGH ALL OF GRADE SIX'S REPORT CARDS IN HALF A DAY?!
SO THIS IS WHAT ADULTS ARE CAPABLE OF.
BUT... RAICHI PAPA?
SHE COULD'VE BEEN PRACTICING BECAUSE SHE'S BAD AT IT, IN ORDER TO OVERCOME...
MY DEAR PINE.
DON'T YOU DO POORLY ON THE VAULT BOX?
WHEN YOU WERE IN THIRD GRADE, YOU FAKED A LEG SPRAIN TO GET OUT OF VAULT-BOX DRILL...
...AND ANOTHER TIME, YOU FEIGNED ILLNESS TO SIT OUT A LONG-DISTANCE RUN.

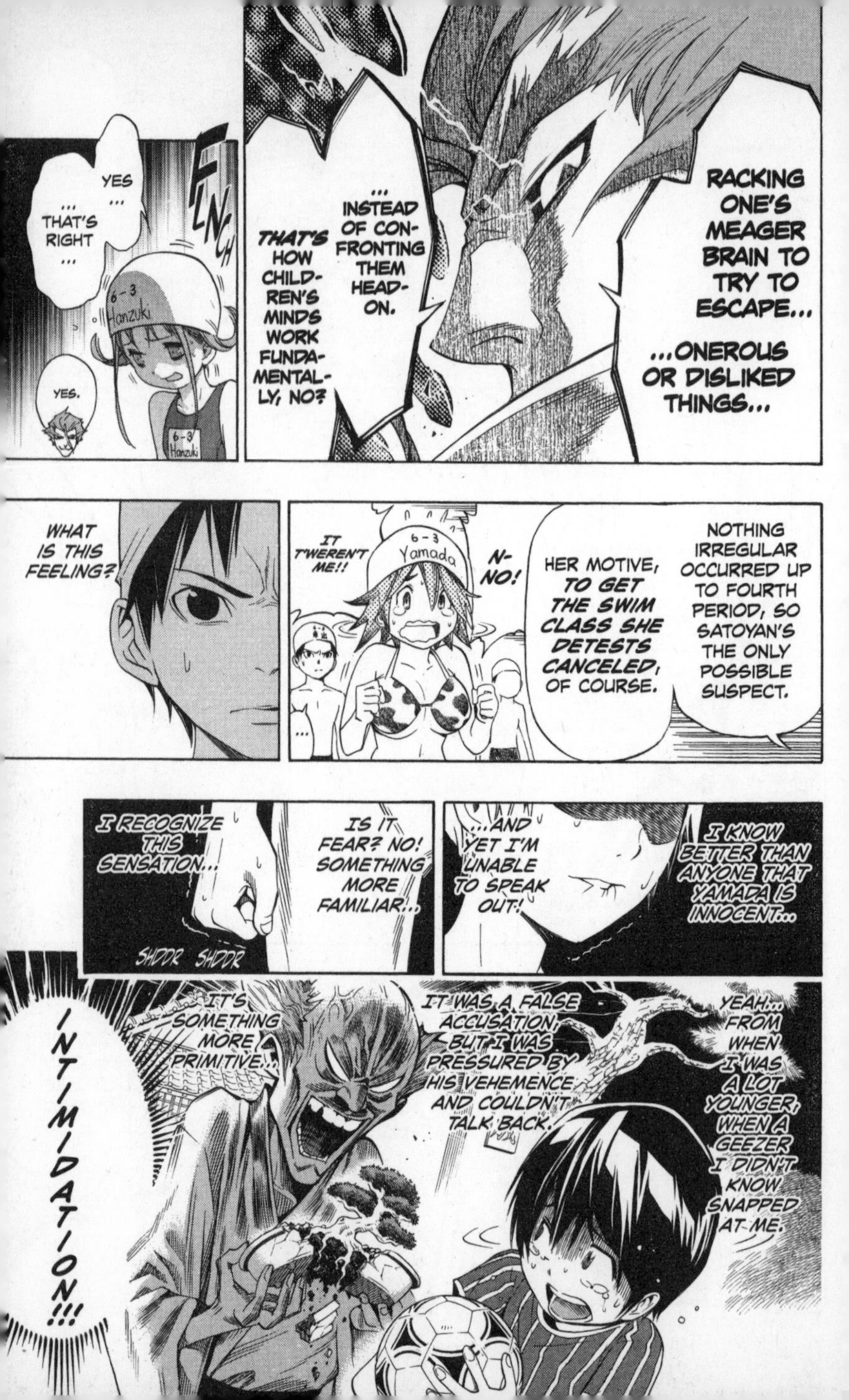
RACKING ONE'S MEAGER BRAIN TO TRY TO ESCAPE...
...ONEROUS OR DISLIKED THINGS...
...INSTEAD OF CONFRONTING THEM HEAD-ON.
THAT'S HOW CHILDREN'S MINDS WORK FUNDAMENTALLY, NO?
FLINCH
YES... ...THAT'S RIGHT...
YES.
NOTHING IRREGULAR OCCURRED UP TO FOURTH PERIOD, SO SATOYAN'S THE ONLY POSSIBLE SUSPECT.
HER MOTIVE, TO GET THE SWIM CLASS SHE DETESTS CANCELED, OF COURSE.
N-NO!
IT T'WERENT ME!!
...
WHAT IS THIS FEELING?
I KNOW BETTER THAN ANYONE THAT YAMADA IS INNOCENT...
...AND YET I'M UNABLE TO SPEAK OUT!
IS IT FEAR? NO! SOMETHING MORE FAMILIAR...
I RECOGNIZE THIS SENSATION...
SHDDR SHDDR
YEAH... FROM WHEN I WAS A LOT YOUNGER, WHEN A GEEZER I DIDN'T KNOW SNAPPED AT ME.
IT WAS A FALSE ACCUSATION, BUT I WAS PRESSURED BY HIS VEHEMENCE AND COULDN'T TALK BACK.
IT'S SOMETHING MORE PRIMITIVE...
INTIMIDATION!!!

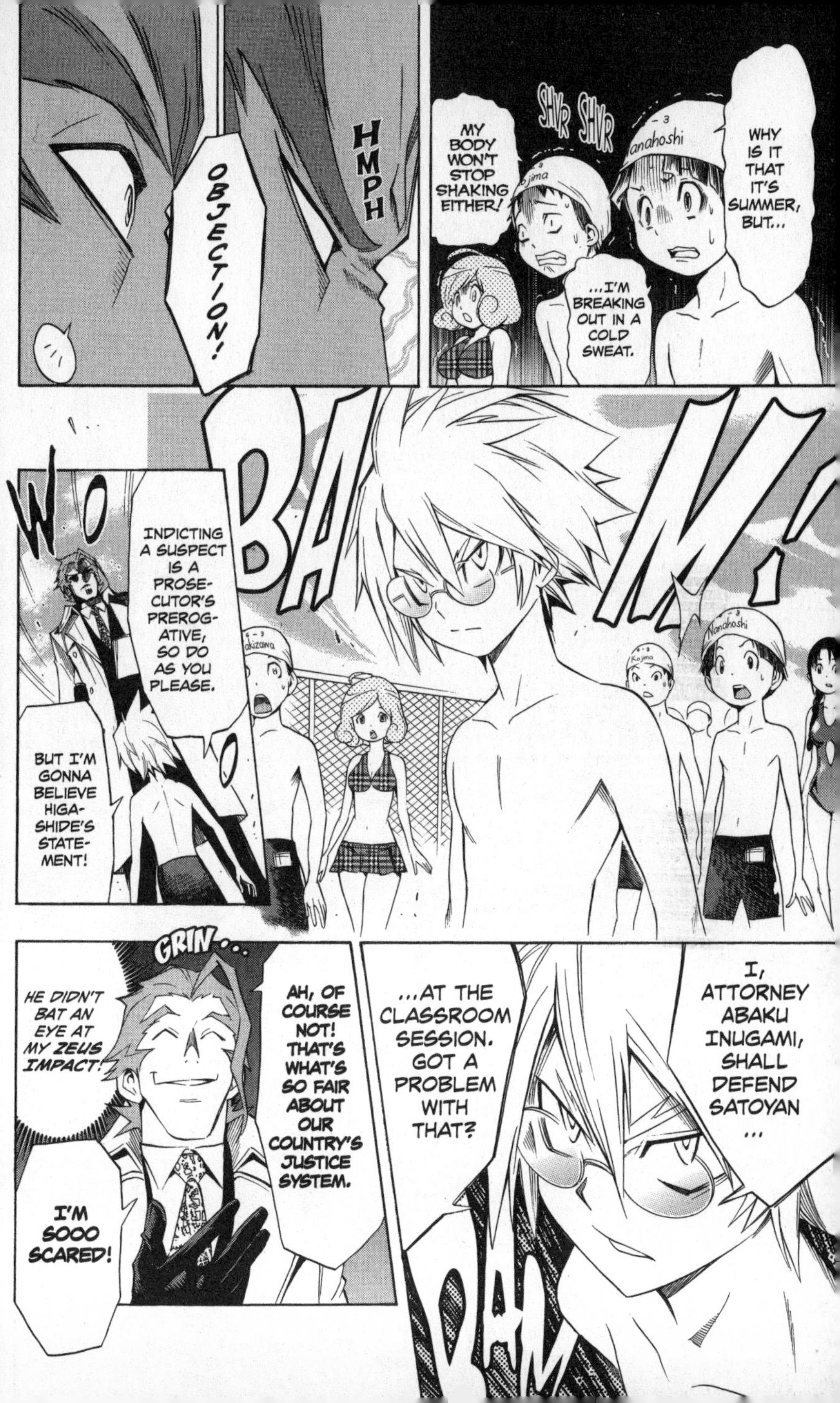
WHY IS IT THAT IT'S SUMMER, BUT...
SHVR SHVR
MY BODY WON'T STOP SHAKING EITHER!
...I'M BREAKING OUT IN A COLD SWEAT.
HMPH
OBJECTION!
...
BAM!
WOO
INDICTING A SUSPECT IS A PROSE-CUTOR'S PREROG-ATIVE, SO DO AS YOU PLEASE.
BUT I'M GONNA BELIEVE HIGA-SHIDE'S STATE-MENT!
I, ATTORNEY ABAKU INUGAMI, SHALL DEFEND SATOYAN ...
...AT THE CLASSROOM SESSION. GOT A PROBLEM WITH THAT?
GRIN...
AH, OF COURSE NOT! THAT'S WHAT'S SO FAIR ABOUT OUR COUNTRY'S JUSTICE SYSTEM.
HE DIDN'T BAT AN EYE AT MY ZEUS IMPACT!
I'M SOOO SCARED!

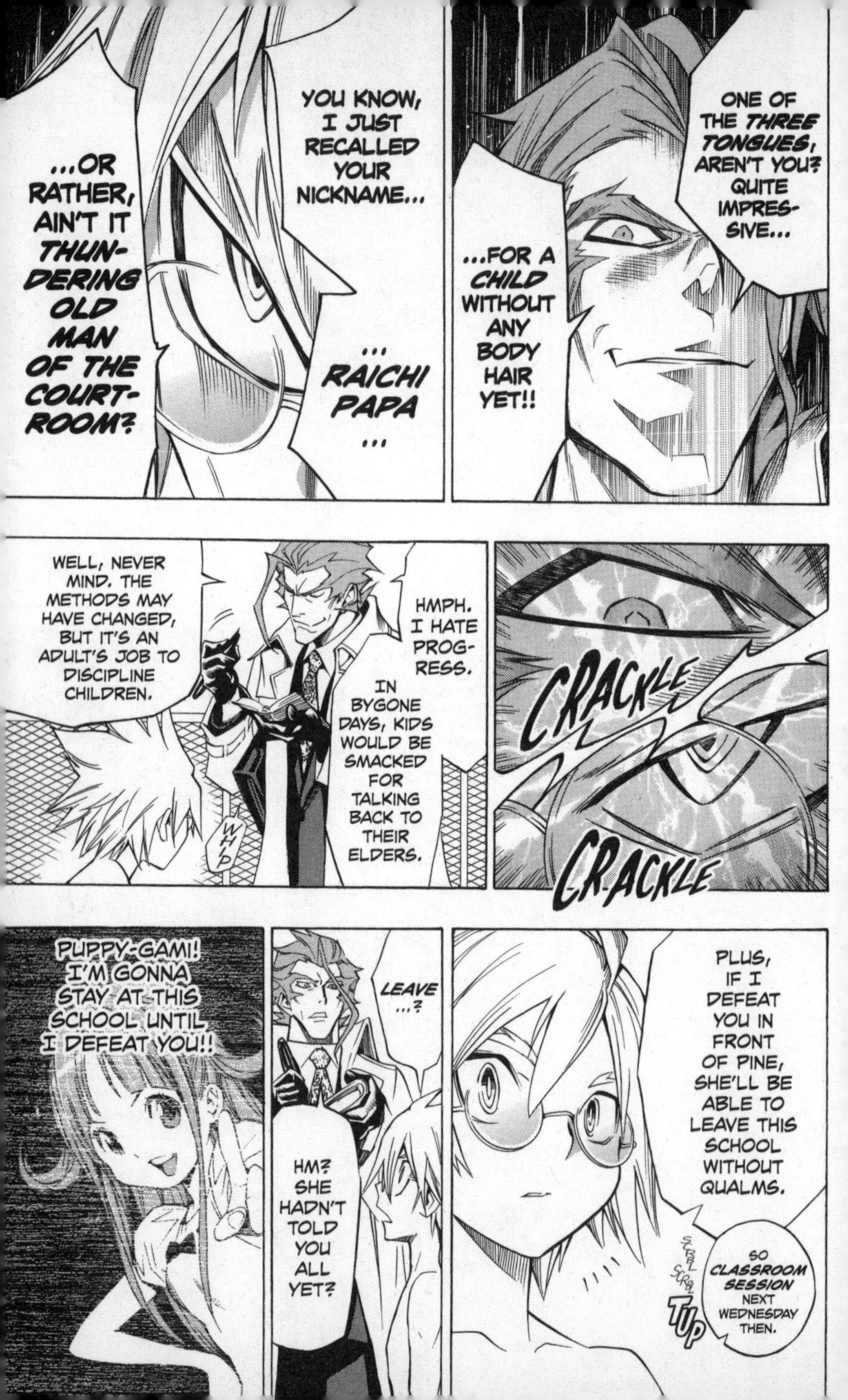
ONE OF THE THREE TONGUES, AREN'T YOU? QUITE IMPRESSIVE...
...FOR A CHILD WITHOUT ANY BODY HAIR YET!!
YOU KNOW, I JUST RECALLED YOUR NICKNAME...
...RAICHI PAPA...
...OR RATHER, AIN'T IT THUNDERING OLD MAN OF THE COURTROOM?
CRACKLE
CRACKLE
HMPH. I HATE PROGRESS.
IN BYGONE DAYS, KIDS WOULD BE SMACKED FOR TALKING BACK TO THEIR ELDERS.
WELL, NEVER MIND. THE METHODS MAY HAVE CHANGED, BUT IT'S AN ADULT'S JOB TO DISCIPLINE CHILDREN.
WHIP
PLUS, IF I DEFEAT YOU IN FRONT OF PINE, SHE'LL BE ABLE TO LEAVE THIS SCHOOL WITHOUT QUALMS.
SCRBL SCRBL
TUP
SO CLASSROOM SESSION NEXT WEDNESDAY THEN.
LEAVE...?
HM? SHE HADN'T TOLD YOU ALL YET?
PUPPY-GAMI! I'M GONNA STAY AT THIS SCHOOL UNTIL I DEFEAT YOU!!

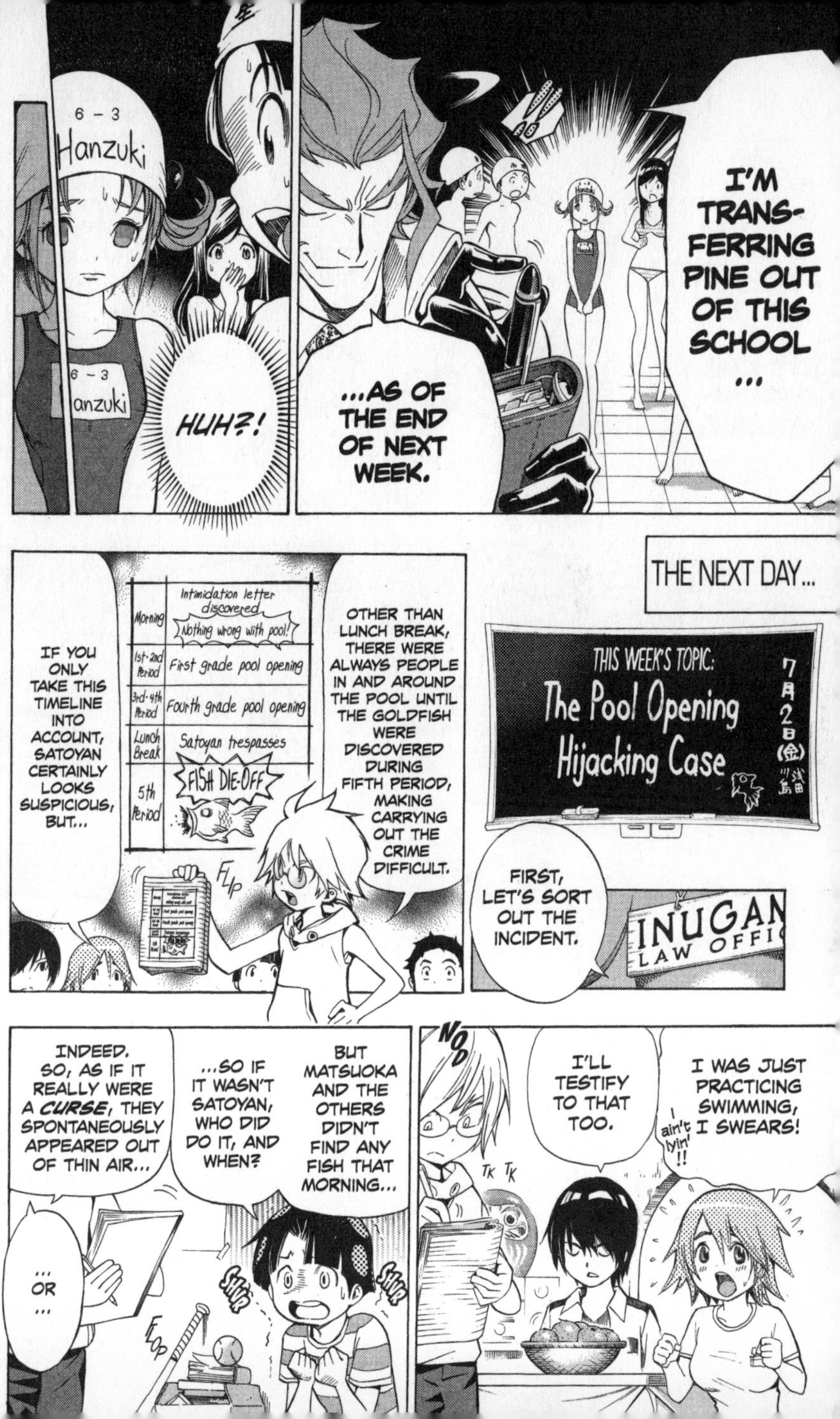
I'M TRANSFERRING PINE OUT OF THIS SCHOOL...
...AS OF THE END OF NEXT WEEK.
6 – 3 Hanzuki
HUH?!
6 – 3 Hanzuki
THE NEXT DAY...
THIS WEEK'S TOPIC: The Pool Opening Hijacking Case
7月2日(金)
浅田 川島
INUGAN LAW OFFI
FIRST, LET'S SORT OUT THE INCIDENT.
OTHER THAN LUNCH BREAK, THERE WERE ALWAYS PEOPLE IN AND AROUND THE POOL UNTIL THE GOLDFISH WERE DISCOVERED DURING FIFTH PERIOD, MAKING CARRYING OUT THE CRIME DIFFICULT.
Morning: Intimidation letter discovered / Nothing wrong with pool!
1st-2nd Period: First grade pool opening
3rd-4th Period: Fourth grade pool opening
Lunch Break: Satoyan trespasses
5th Period: FISH DIE-OFF
FLIP
IF YOU ONLY TAKE THIS TIMELINE INTO ACCOUNT, SATOYAN CERTAINLY LOOKS SUSPICIOUS, BUT...
I WAS JUST PRACTICING SWIMMING, I SWEARS!
I ain't lyin'!!
I'LL TESTIFY TO THAT TOO.
NOD
TK TK
BUT MATSUOKA AND THE OTHERS DIDN'T FIND ANY FISH THAT MORNING...
...SO IF IT WASN'T SATOYAN, WHO DID DO IT, AND WHEN?
SHVR SHVR
INDEED. SO, AS IF IT REALLY WERE A CURSE, THEY SPONTANEOUSLY APPEARED OUT OF THIN AIR...
... OR ...
FLOP

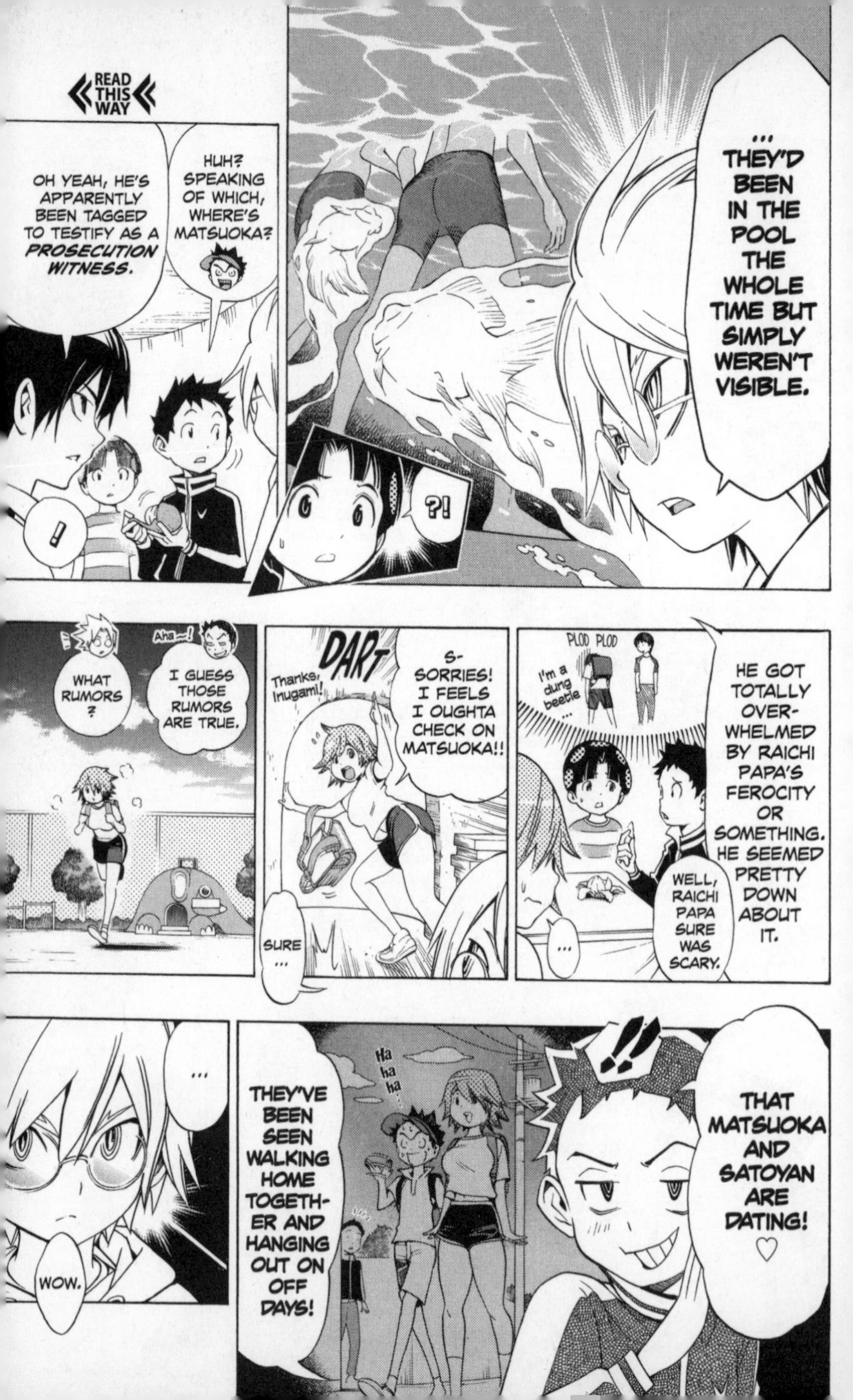
READ THIS WAY
... THEY'D BEEN IN THE POOL THE WHOLE TIME BUT SIMPLY WEREN'T VISIBLE.
?!
HUH? SPEAKING OF WHICH, WHERE'S MATSUOKA?
OH YEAH, HE'S APPARENTLY BEEN TAGGED TO TESTIFY AS A *PROSECUTION WITNESS.*
!
HE GOT TOTALLY OVER-WHELMED BY RAICHI PAPA'S FEROCITY OR SOMETHING. HE SEEMED PRETTY DOWN ABOUT IT.
PLOD PLOD
I'm a dung beetle ...
WELL, RAICHI PAPA SURE WAS SCARY.
...
S-SORRIES! I FEELS I OUGHTA CHECK ON MATSUOKA!!
DART
Thanks, Inugami!
SURE ...
Aha~!
I GUESS THOSE RUMORS ARE TRUE.
!
WHAT RUMORS?
THAT MATSUOKA AND SATOYAN ARE DATING! ♡
THEY'VE BEEN SEEN WALKING HOME TOGETH-ER AND HANGING OUT ON OFF DAYS!
Ha ha ha...
...
WOW.

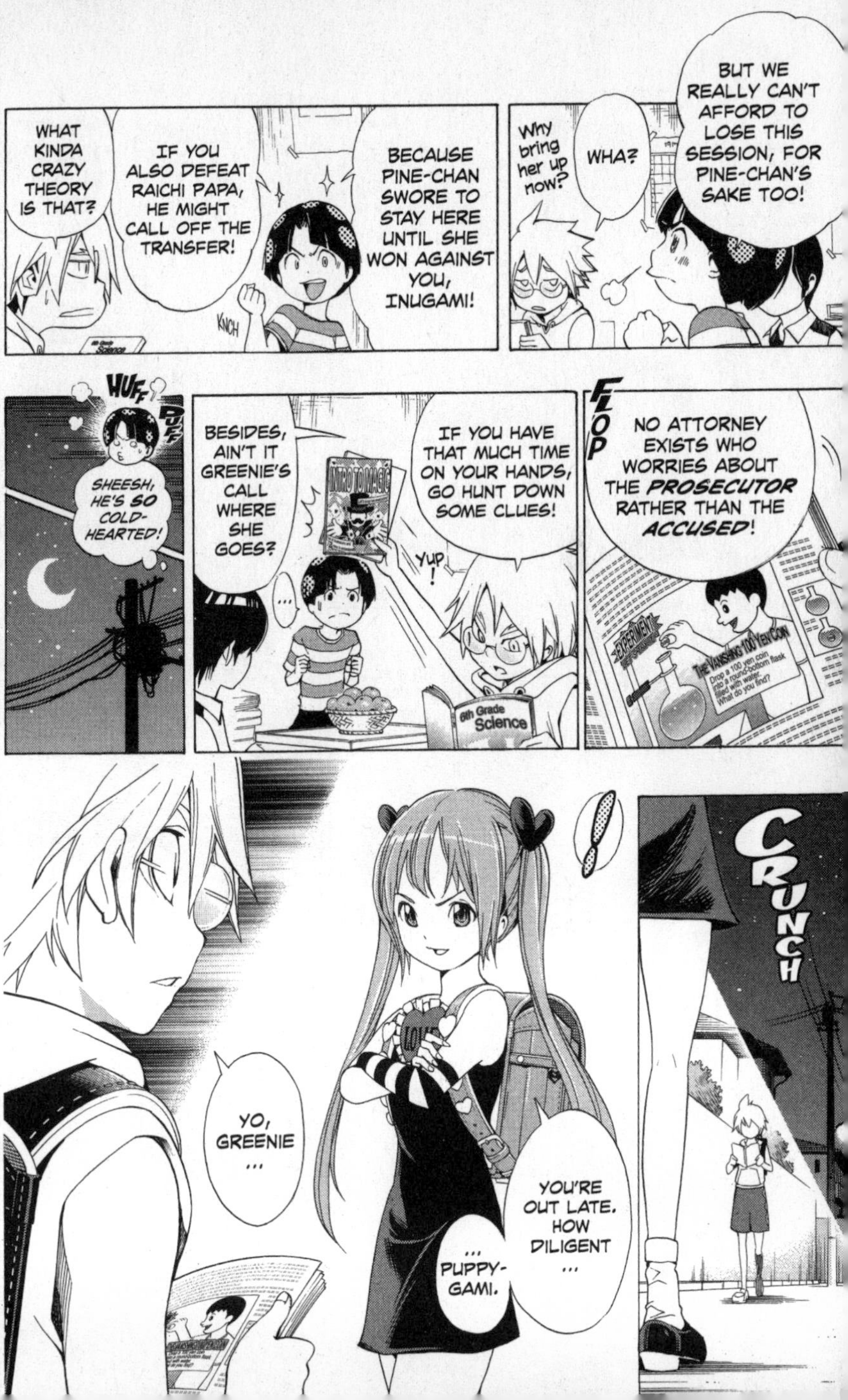
BUT WE REALLY CAN'T AFFORD TO LOSE THIS SESSION, FOR PINE-CHAN'S SAKE TOO!
WHA?
Why bring her up now?
BECAUSE PINE-CHAN SWORE TO STAY HERE UNTIL SHE WON AGAINST YOU, INUGAMI!
IF YOU ALSO DEFEAT RAICHI PAPA, HE MIGHT CALL OFF THE TRANSFER!
KNCH
WHAT KINDA CRAZY THEORY IS THAT?
FLOP
NO ATTORNEY EXISTS WHO WORRIES ABOUT THE PROSECUTOR RATHER THAN THE ACCUSED!
EXPERIMENT
THE VANISHING 100 YEN COIN
Drop a 100 yen coin into a round-bottom flask filled with water. What do you find?
IF YOU HAVE THAT MUCH TIME ON YOUR HANDS, GO HUNT DOWN SOME CLUES!
YUP!
6th Grade Science
INTRO TO MAGIC
BESIDES, AIN'T IT GREENIE'S CALL WHERE SHE GOES?
...
HUFF
PUFF
SHEESH, HE'S SO COLD-HEARTED!
CRUNCH
!
YOU'RE OUT LATE. HOW DILIGENT ...
... PUPPY-GAMI.
YO, GREENIE ...

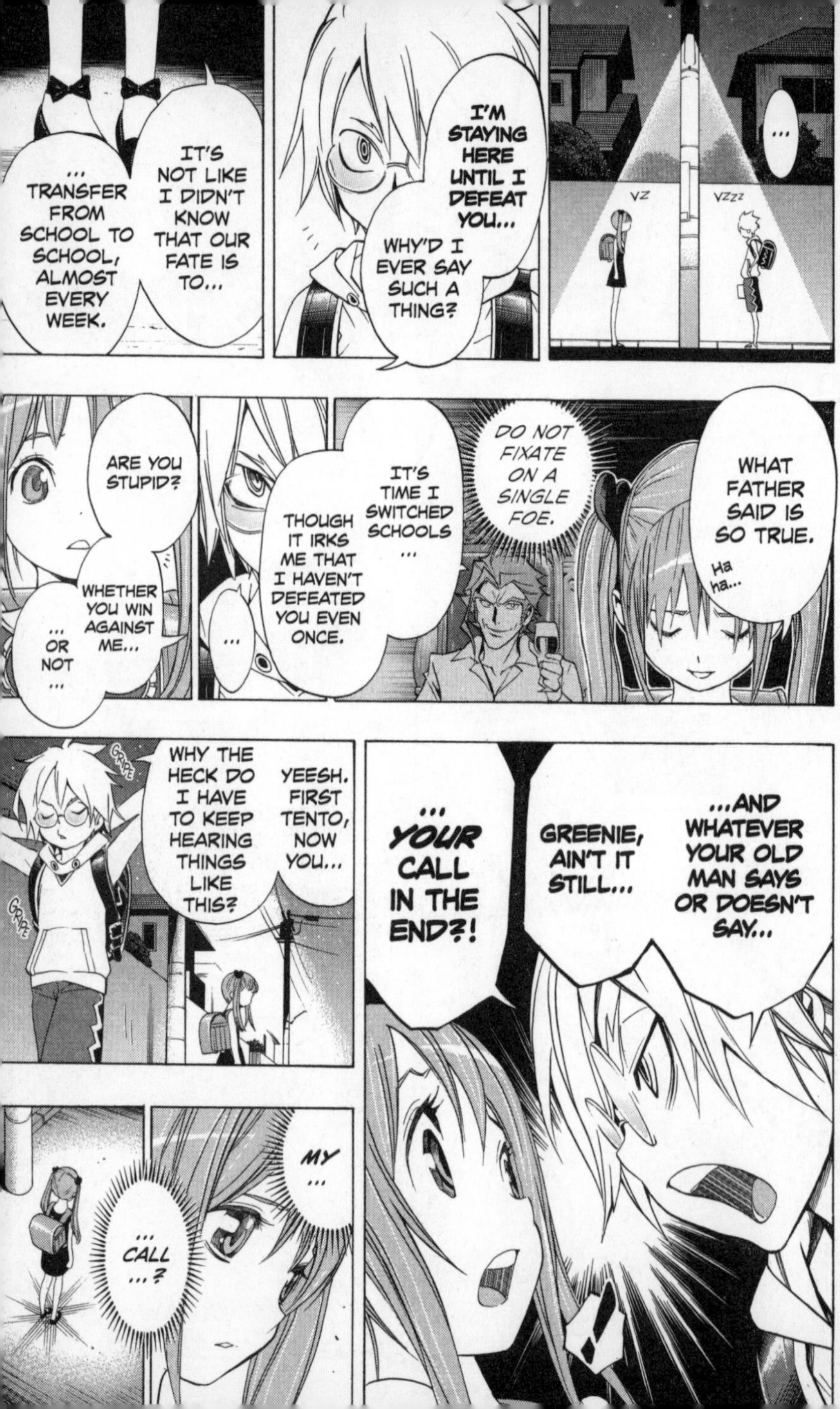
...
VZ
VZZZ
I'M STAYING HERE UNTIL I DEFEAT YOU...
WHY'D I EVER SAY SUCH A THING?
IT'S NOT LIKE I DIDN'T KNOW THAT OUR FATE IS TO...
...TRANSFER FROM SCHOOL TO SCHOOL, ALMOST EVERY WEEK.
WHAT FATHER SAID IS SO TRUE.
Ha ha...
DO NOT FIXATE ON A SINGLE FOE.
IT'S TIME I SWITCHED SCHOOLS...
THOUGH IT IRKS ME THAT I HAVEN'T DEFEATED YOU EVEN ONCE.
...
ARE YOU STUPID?
WHETHER YOU WIN AGAINST ME...
...OR NOT...
...AND WHATEVER YOUR OLD MAN SAYS OR DOESN'T SAY...
GREENIE, AIN'T IT STILL...
...YOUR CALL IN THE END?!
YEESH. FIRST TENTO, NOW YOU...
WHY THE HECK DO I HAVE TO KEEP HEARING THINGS LIKE THIS?
GRIPE
GRIPE
MY...
...CALL...?

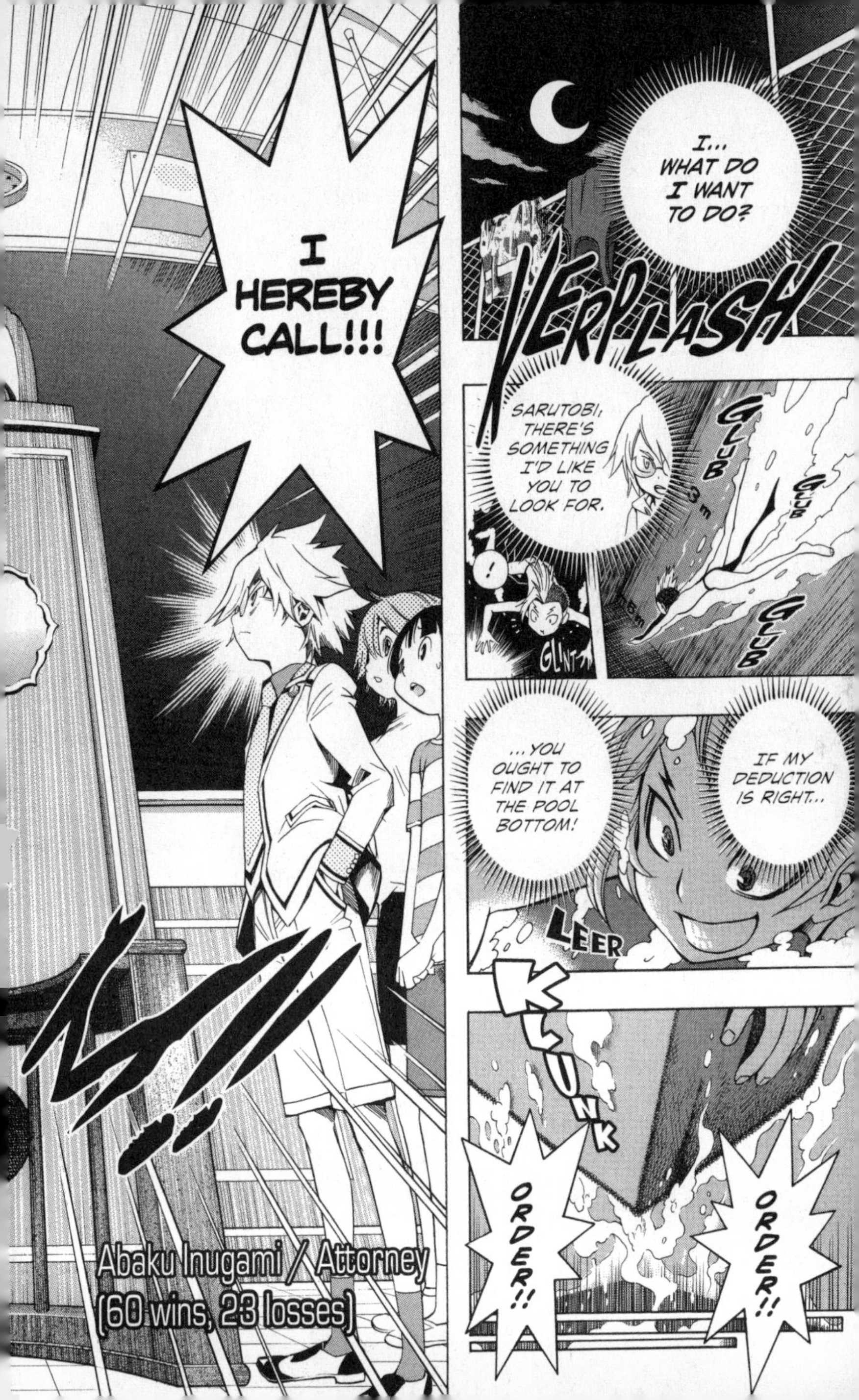
I... WHAT DO I WANT TO DO?
VERPLASH
GLUB
GLUB
GLUB
SARUTOBI, THERE'S SOMETHING I'D LIKE YOU TO LOOK FOR.
!
GLINT
IF MY DEDUCTION IS RIGHT...
...YOU OUGHT TO FIND IT AT THE POOL BOTTOM!
LEER
KLUNK
ORDER!!
ORDER!!
I HEREBY CALL!!!
Abaku Inugami / Attorney
(60 wins, 23 losses)

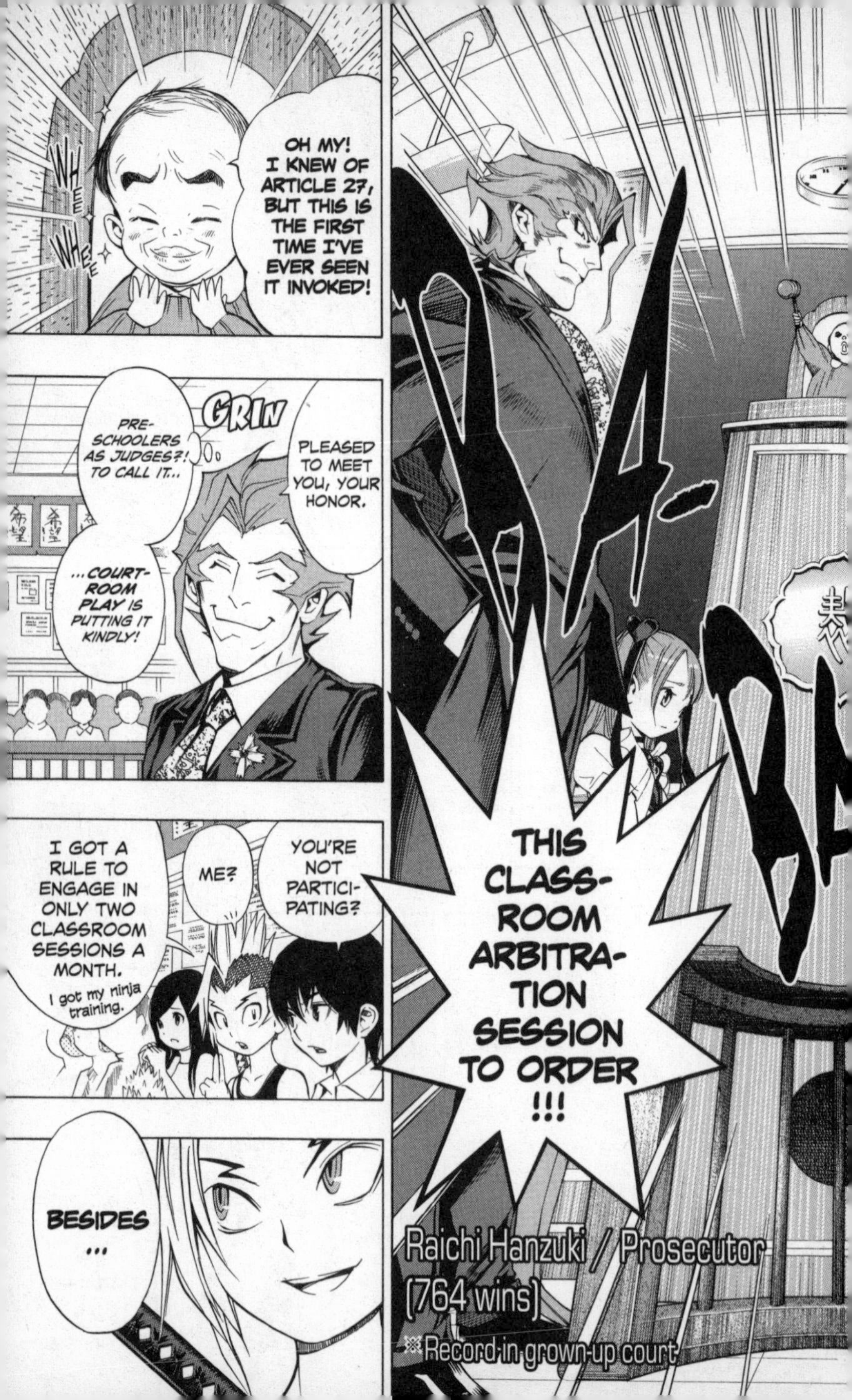
BA-BA
THIS CLASSROOM ARBITRATION SESSION TO ORDER !!!
Raichi Hanzuki / Prosecutor (764 wins)
※Record in grown-up court
WHEE WHEE
OH MY! I KNEW OF ARTICLE 27, BUT THIS IS THE FIRST TIME I'VE EVER SEEN IT INVOKED!
GRIN
PLEASED TO MEET YOU, YOUR HONOR.
PRE-SCHOOLERS AS JUDGES?! TO CALL IT...
...COURTROOM PLAY IS PUTTING IT KINDLY!
YOU'RE NOT PARTICIPATING?
ME?
I GOT A RULE TO ENGAGE IN ONLY TWO CLASSROOM SESSIONS A MONTH.
I got my ninja training.
BESIDES ...

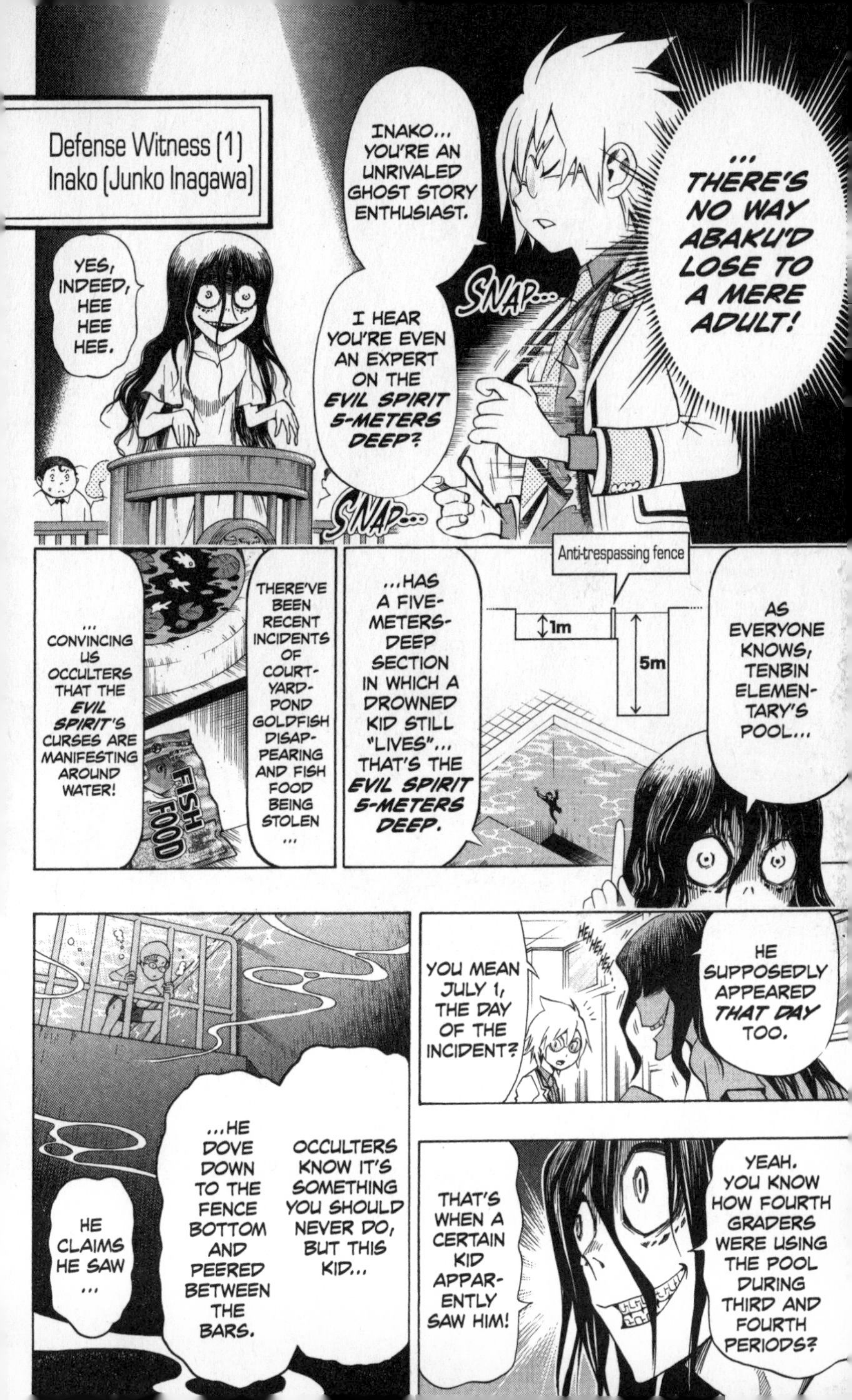
...THERE'S NO WAY ABAKU'D LOSE TO A MERE ADULT!
INAKO... YOU'RE AN UNRIVALED GHOST STORY ENTHUSIAST.
SNAP...
I HEAR YOU'RE EVEN AN EXPERT ON THE EVIL SPIRIT 5-METERS DEEP?
SNAP...
Defense Witness (1) Inako (Junko Inagawa)
YES, INDEED, HEE HEE HEE.
AS EVERYONE KNOWS, TENBIN ELEMENTARY'S POOL...
Anti-trespassing fence
1m
5m
...HAS A FIVE-METERS-DEEP SECTION IN WHICH A DROWNED KID STILL "LIVES"... THAT'S THE EVIL SPIRIT 5-METERS DEEP.
THERE'VE BEEN RECENT INCIDENTS OF COURT-YARD-POND GOLDFISH DISAP-PEARING AND FISH FOOD BEING STOLEN...
... CONVINCING US OCCULTERS THAT THE EVIL SPIRIT'S CURSES ARE MANIFESTING AROUND WATER!
FISH FOOD
HE SUPPOSEDLY APPEARED THAT DAY TOO.
HEH HEH HEH
YOU MEAN JULY 1, THE DAY OF THE INCIDENT?
YEAH. YOU KNOW HOW FOURTH GRADERS WERE USING THE POOL DURING THIRD AND FOURTH PERIODS?
THAT'S WHEN A CERTAIN KID APPAR-ENTLY SAW HIM!
OCCULTERS KNOW IT'S SOMETHING YOU SHOULD NEVER DO, BUT THIS KID...
...HE DOVE DOWN TO THE FENCE BOTTOM AND PEERED BETWEEN THE BARS.
HE CLAIMS HE SAW...

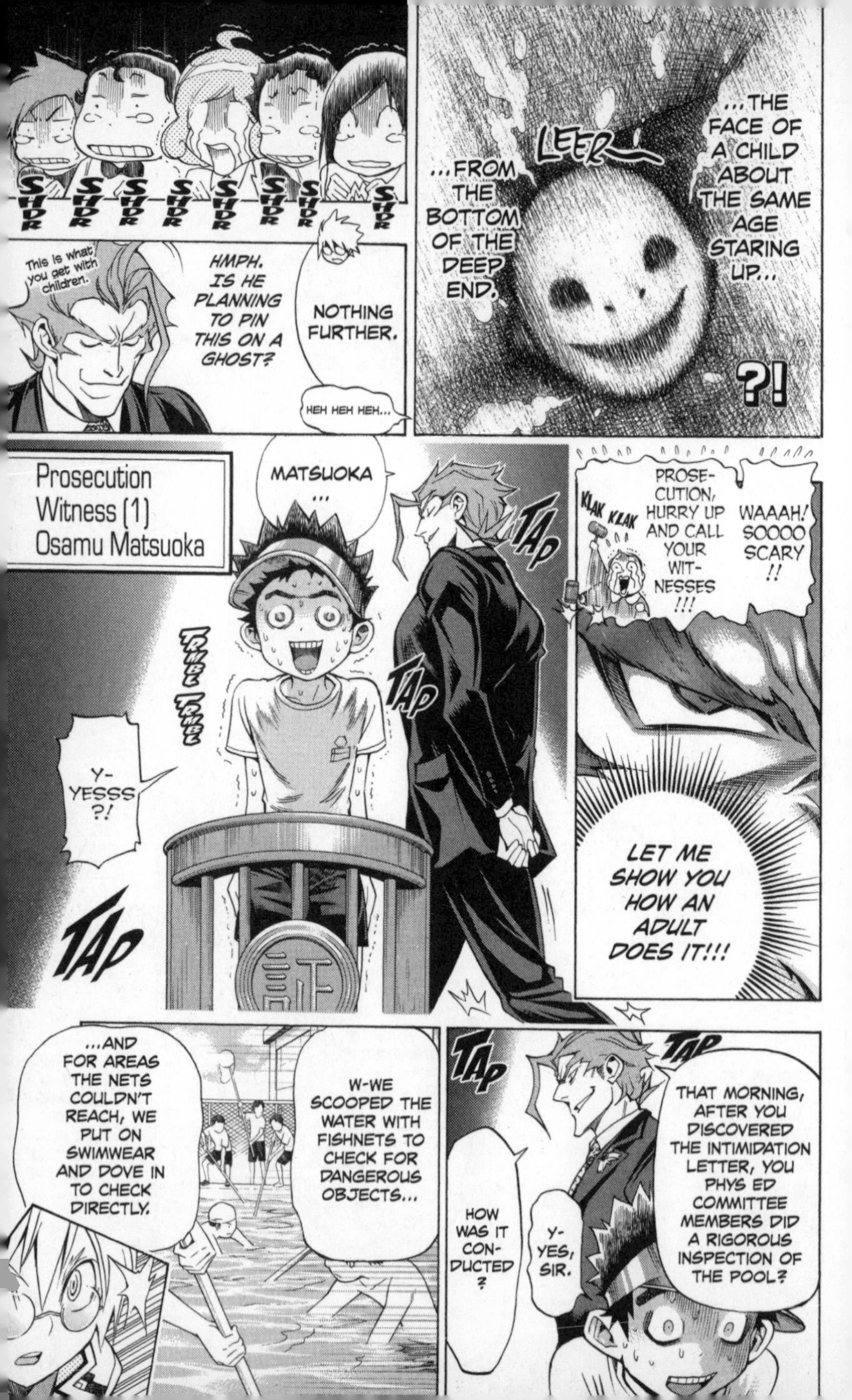

...THE FACE OF A CHILD ABOUT THE SAME AGE STARING UP...
LEER
...FROM THE BOTTOM OF THE DEEP END.
?!
SHDR SHDR SHDR SHDR SHDR SHDR SHDR SHDR
NOTHING FURTHER.
HMPH. IS HE PLANNING TO PIN THIS ON A GHOST?
This is what you get with children.
HEH HEH HEH...
WAAAH! SOOOO SCARY!!
PROSECUTION, HURRY UP AND CALL YOUR WITNESSES!!!
KLAK KLAK
LET ME SHOW YOU HOW AN ADULT DOES IT!!!
TAP
MATSUOKA...
Prosecution Witness (1) Osamu Matsuoka
TAP
TRMBL TRMBL
Y-YESSS?!
TAP
TAP
TAP
THAT MORNING, AFTER YOU DISCOVERED THE INTIMIDATION LETTER, YOU PHYS ED COMMITTEE MEMBERS DID A RIGOROUS INSPECTION OF THE POOL?
Y-YES, SIR.
HOW WAS IT CONDUCTED?
W-WE SCOOPED THE WATER WITH FISHNETS TO CHECK FOR DANGEROUS OBJECTS...
...AND FOR AREAS THE NETS COULDN'T REACH, WE PUT ON SWIMWEAR AND DOVE IN TO CHECK DIRECTLY.

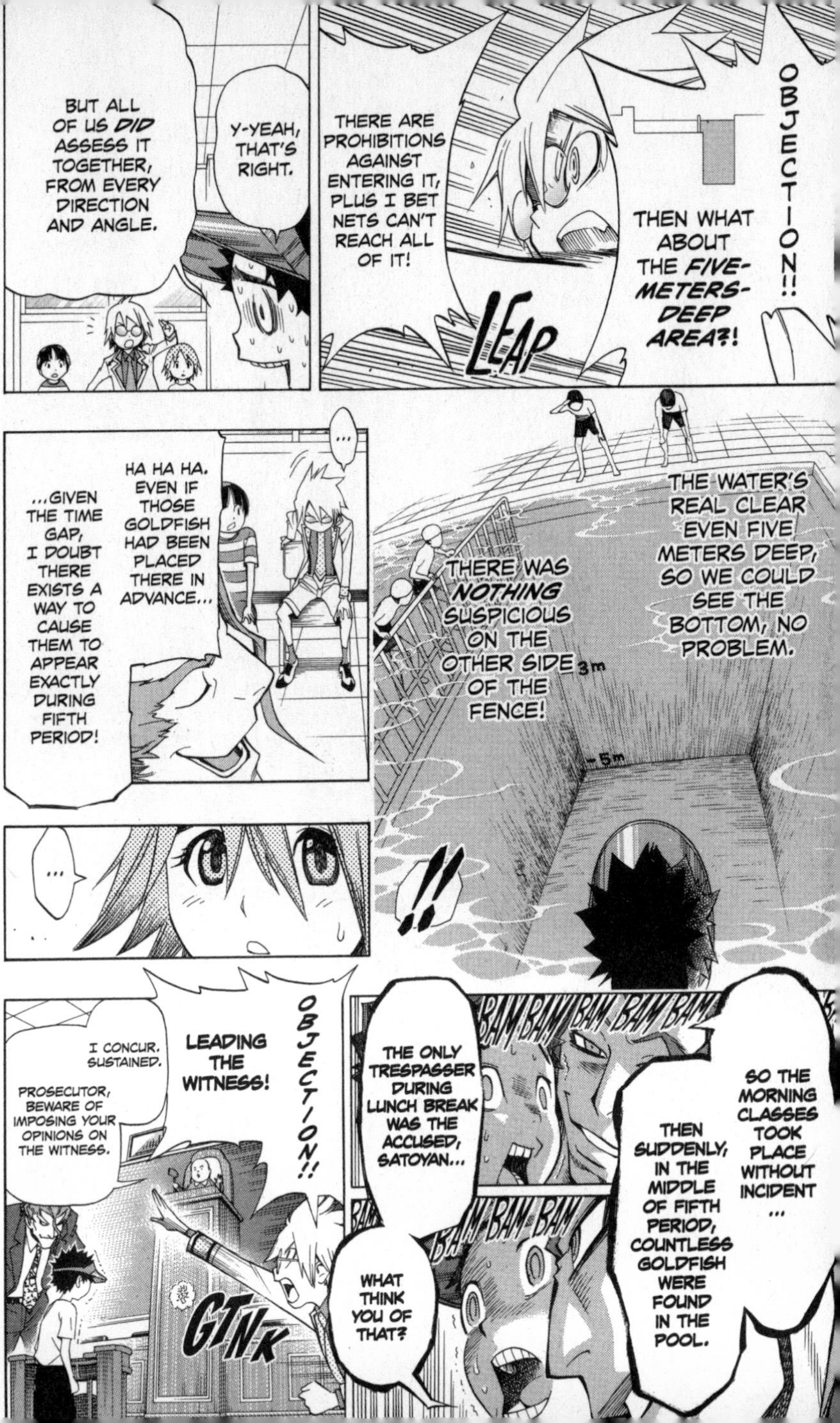
OBJECTION!!
THEN WHAT ABOUT THE FIVE-METERS-DEEP AREA?!
THERE ARE PROHIBITIONS AGAINST ENTERING IT, PLUS I BET NETS CAN'T REACH ALL OF IT!
LEAP
Y-YEAH, THAT'S RIGHT.
BUT ALL OF US DID ASSESS IT TOGETHER, FROM EVERY DIRECTION AND ANGLE.
THE WATER'S REAL CLEAR EVEN FIVE METERS DEEP, SO WE COULD SEE THE BOTTOM, NO PROBLEM.
THERE WAS NOTHING SUSPICIOUS ON THE OTHER SIDE OF THE FENCE!
3m
5m
!!
...
HA HA HA. EVEN IF THOSE GOLDFISH HAD BEEN PLACED THERE IN ADVANCE...
...GIVEN THE TIME GAP, I DOUBT THERE EXISTS A WAY TO CAUSE THEM TO APPEAR EXACTLY DURING FIFTH PERIOD!
...
SO THE MORNING CLASSES TOOK PLACE WITHOUT INCIDENT...
THEN SUDDENLY, IN THE MIDDLE OF FIFTH PERIOD, COUNTLESS GOLDFISH WERE FOUND IN THE POOL.
BAM BAM BAM BAM BAM
THE ONLY TRESPASSER DURING LUNCH BREAK WAS THE ACCUSED, SATOYAN...
BAM BAM BAM BAM
WHAT THINK YOU OF THAT?
OBJECTION!!
LEADING THE WITNESS!
I CONCUR. SUSTAINED.
PROSECUTOR, BEWARE OF IMPOSING YOUR OPINIONS ON THE WITNESS.
GTNK

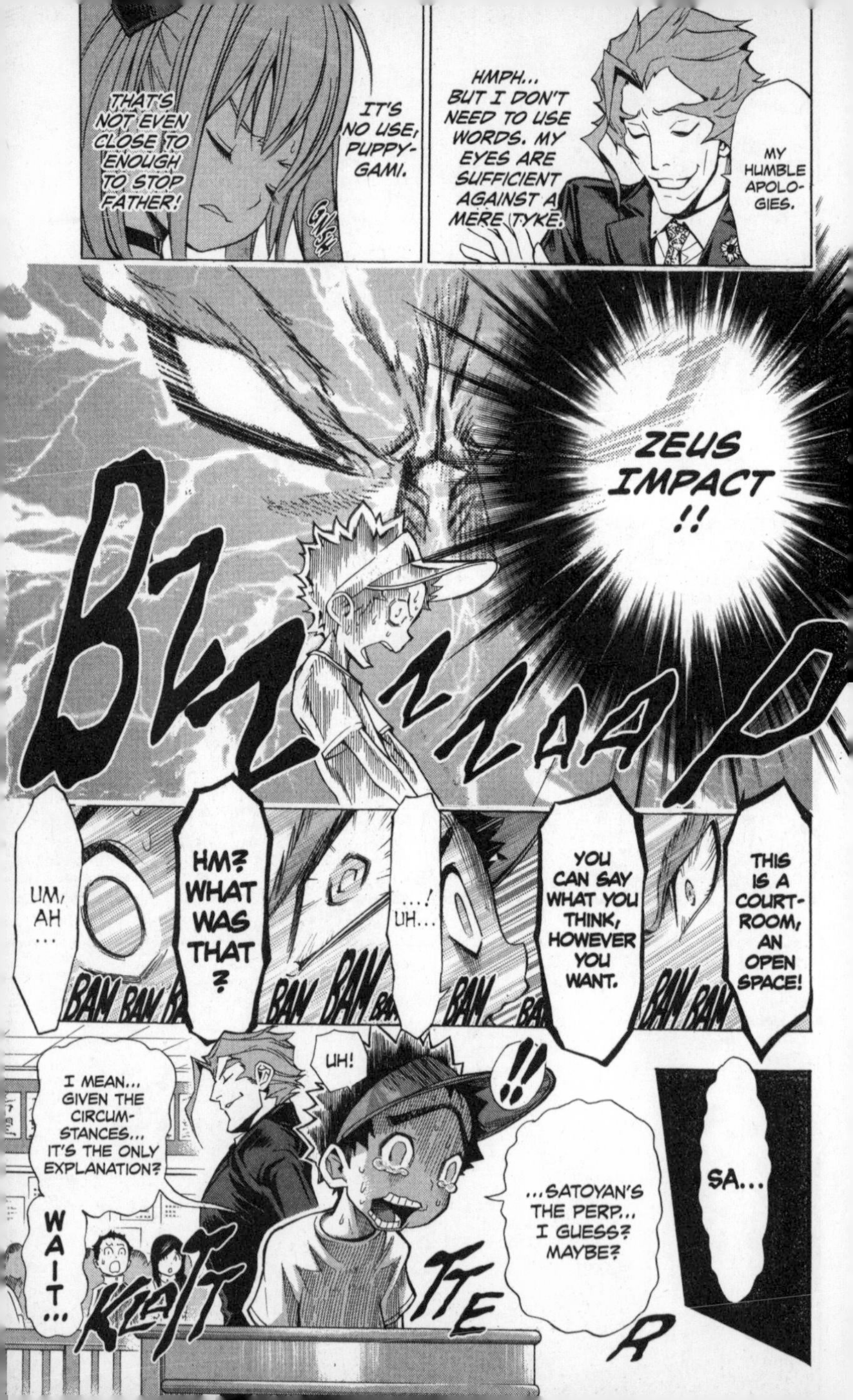
MY HUMBLE APOLOGIES.
HMPH... BUT I DON'T NEED TO USE WORDS. MY EYES ARE SUFFICIENT AGAINST A MERE TYKE.
IT'S NO USE, PUPPY-GAMI.
THAT'S NOT EVEN CLOSE TO ENOUGH TO STOP FATHER!
ZEUS IMPACT!!
BZZZAAP
THIS IS A COURTROOM, AN OPEN SPACE!
YOU CAN SAY WHAT YOU THINK, HOWEVER YOU WANT.
...! UH...
HM? WHAT WAS THAT?
UM, AH...
BAM BAM BAM BAM BAM BAM BAM BAM BAM BAM BAM
SA...
!!
UH!
...SATOYAN'S THE PERP... I GUESS? MAYBE?
I MEAN... GIVEN THE CIRCUMSTANCES... IT'S THE ONLY EXPLANATION?
WAIT...
KLATTTER

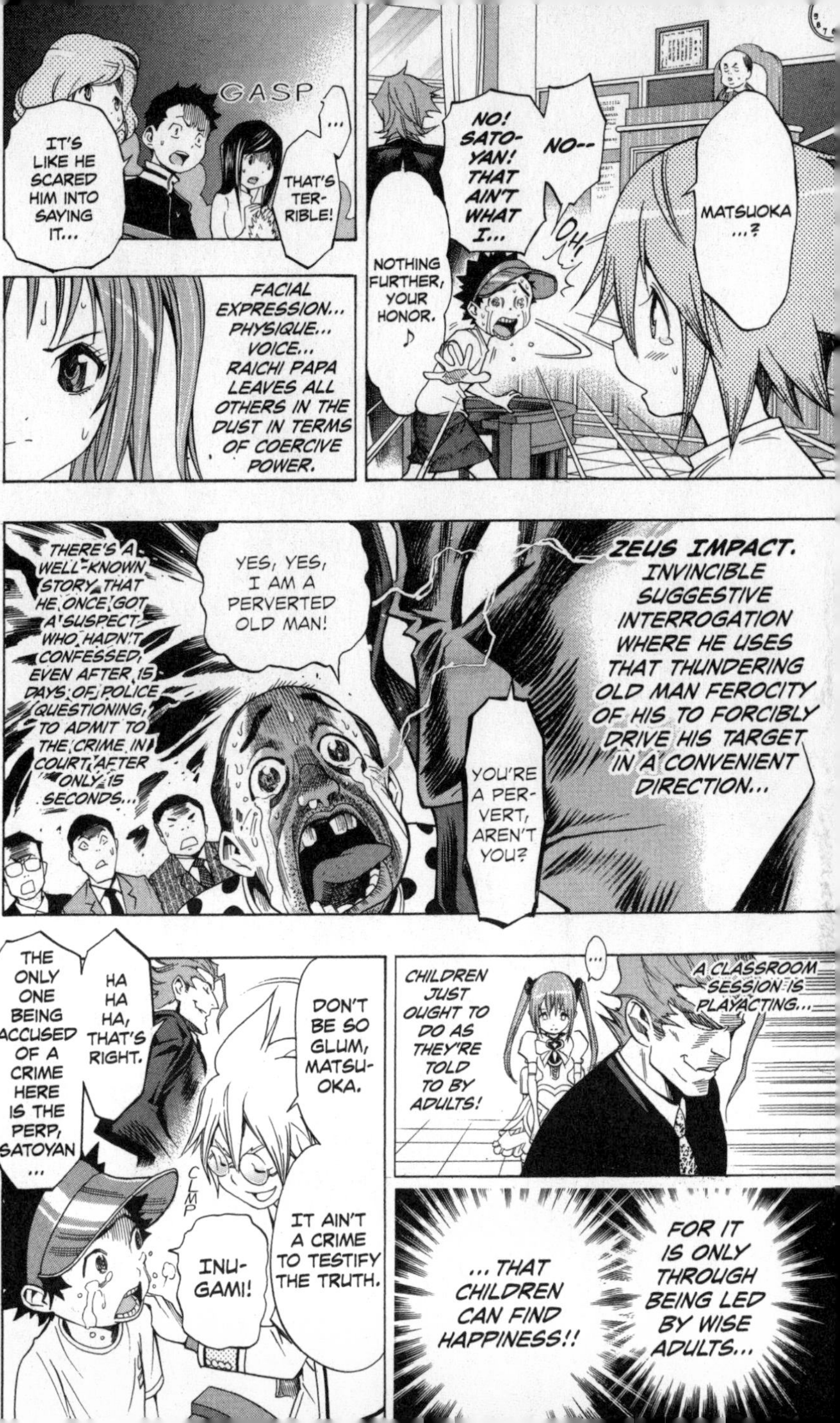
MATSUOKA ...?
NO--
NO! SATO-YAN! THAT AIN'T WHAT I...
OH!
NOTHING FURTHER, YOUR HONOR. ♪
GASP
...
THAT'S TERRIBLE!
IT'S LIKE HE SCARED HIM INTO SAYING IT...
FACIAL EXPRESSION... PHYSIQUE... VOICE... RAICHI PAPA LEAVES ALL OTHERS IN THE DUST IN TERMS OF COERCIVE POWER.
ZEUS IMPACT. INVINCIBLE SUGGESTIVE INTERROGATION WHERE HE USES THAT THUNDERING OLD MAN FEROCITY OF HIS TO FORCIBLY DRIVE HIS TARGET IN A CONVENIENT DIRECTION...
YOU'RE A PERVERT, AREN'T YOU?
YES, YES, I AM A PERVERTED OLD MAN!
THERE'S A WELL-KNOWN STORY THAT HE ONCE GOT A SUSPECT WHO HADN'T CONFESSED, EVEN AFTER 15 DAYS OF POLICE QUESTIONING, TO ADMIT TO THE CRIME IN COURT AFTER ONLY 15 SECONDS...
A CLASSROOM SESSION IS PLAYACTING...
...
CHILDREN JUST OUGHT TO DO AS THEY'RE TOLD TO BY ADULTS!
FOR IT IS ONLY THROUGH BEING LED BY WISE ADULTS...
...THAT CHILDREN CAN FIND HAPPINESS!!
DON'T BE SO GLUM, MATSUOKA.
HA HA HA, THAT'S RIGHT.
THE ONLY ONE BEING ACCUSED OF A CRIME HERE IS THE PERP, SATOYAN...
CLMP
IT AIN'T A CRIME TO TESTIFY THE TRUTH.
INUGAMI!

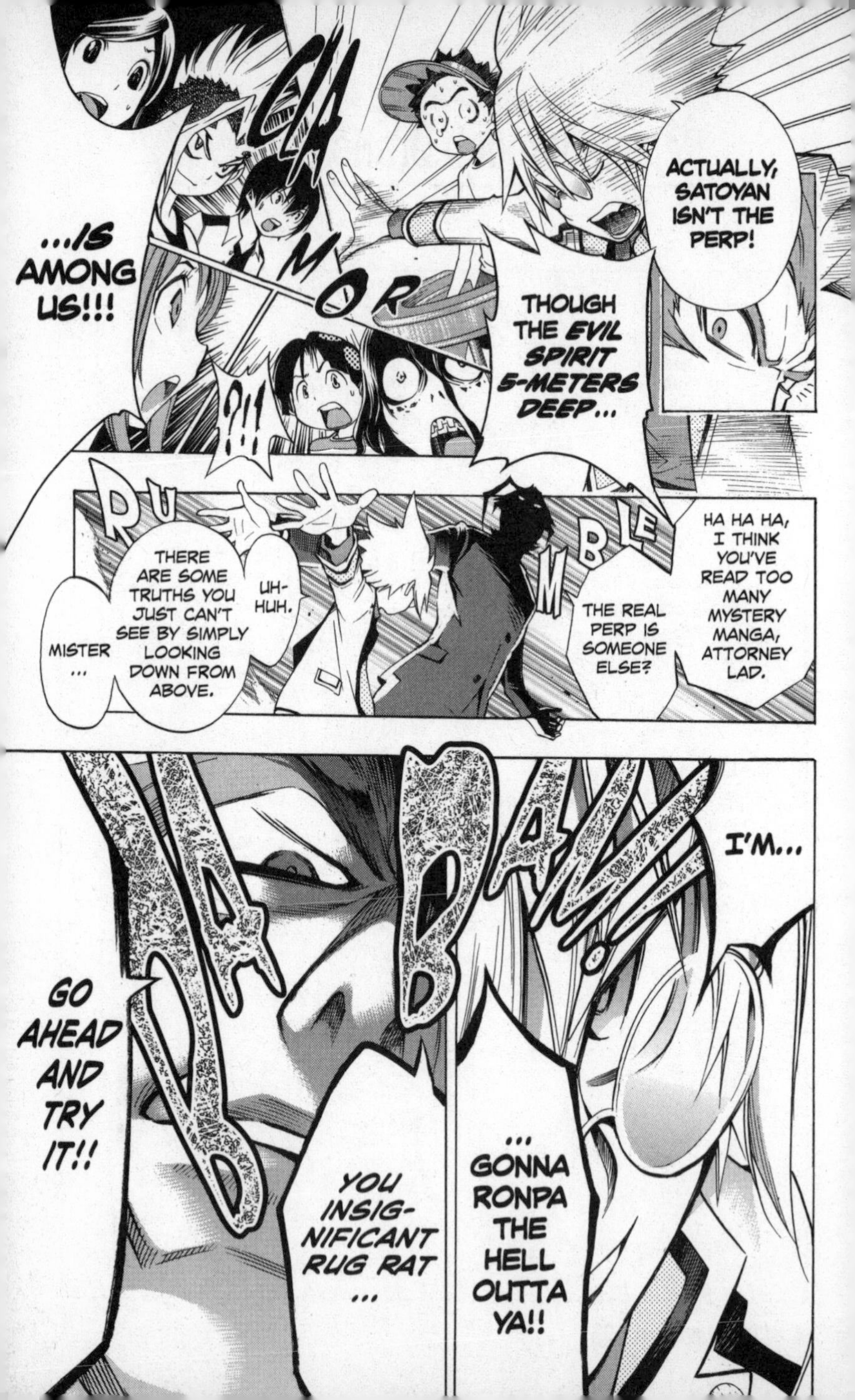
ACTUALLY, SATOYAN ISN'T THE PERP!
THOUGH THE EVIL SPIRIT 5-METERS DEEP...
...IS AMONG US!!!
CLAMOR
?!!
RUMBLE
HA HA HA, I THINK YOU'VE READ TOO MANY MYSTERY MANGA, ATTORNEY LAD.
THE REAL PERP IS SOMEONE ELSE?
UH-HUH.
THERE ARE SOME TRUTHS YOU JUST CAN'T SEE BY SIMPLY LOOKING DOWN FROM ABOVE.
MISTER...
BADAM!
I'M...
...GONNA RONPA THE HELL OUTTA YA!!
YOU INSIGNIFICANT RUG RAT...
GO AHEAD AND TRY IT!!

Rejected Rough Drafts Gallery (2)

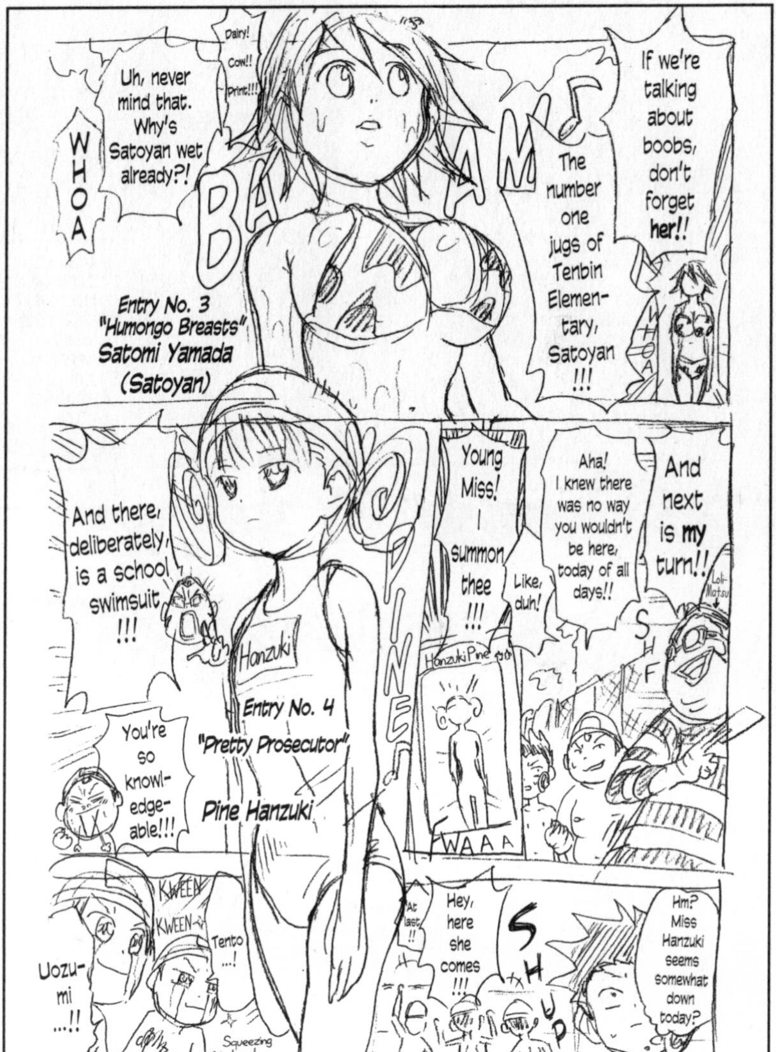
If we're talking about boobs, don't forget her!!
The number one jugs of Tenbin Elementary, Satoyan!!!
WHOA
Dairy! Cow!! Print!!!
Uh, never mind that. Why's Satoyan wet already?!
WHOA
Entry No. 3 "Humongo Breasts" Satomi Yamada (Satoyan)
And next is my turn!!
Loli-Matsu
SHF
Aha! I knew there was no way you wouldn't be here, today of all days!!
Like, duh!
Young Miss! I summon thee!!!
Hanzuki Pine
WAAA
PINE!
And there, deliberately, is a school swimsuit!!!
Hanzuki
Entry No. 4 "Pretty Prosecutor" Pine Hanzuki
You're so knowl-edge-able!!!
Hm? Miss Hanzuki seems somewhat down today?
SHUP
Hey, here she comes!!!
At last!!
Tento ...!
KWEEN KWEEN
Uozumi ...!!
Squeezing hand

⇦ Continued on p. 186

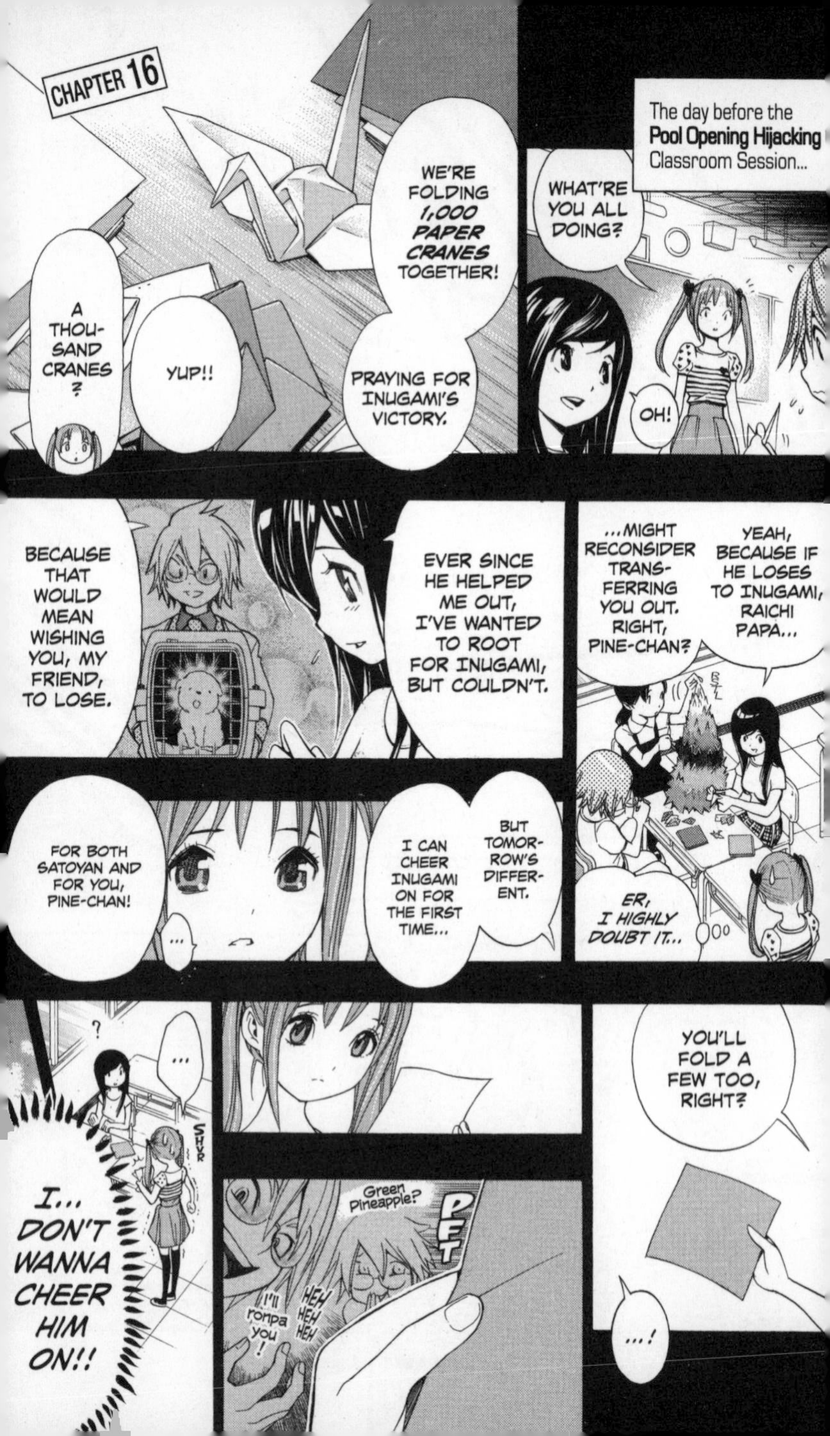
CHAPTER 16
The day before the Pool Opening Hijacking Classroom Session...
WHAT'RE YOU ALL DOING?
OH!
WE'RE FOLDING 1,000 PAPER CRANES TOGETHER!
A THOUSAND CRANES?
YUP!!
PRAYING FOR INUGAMI'S VICTORY.
YEAH, BECAUSE IF HE LOSES TO INUGAMI, RAICHI PAPA...
...MIGHT RECONSIDER TRANSFERRING YOU OUT. RIGHT, PINE-CHAN?
ER, I HIGHLY DOUBT IT...
EVER SINCE HE HELPED ME OUT, I'VE WANTED TO ROOT FOR INUGAMI, BUT COULDN'T.
BECAUSE THAT WOULD MEAN WISHING YOU, MY FRIEND, TO LOSE.
BUT TOMORROW'S DIFFERENT.
I CAN CHEER INUGAMI ON FOR THE FIRST TIME...
FOR BOTH SATOYAN AND FOR YOU, PINE-CHAN!
...
YOU'LL FOLD A FEW TOO, RIGHT?
...!
Green Pineapple?
PFT
HEH HEH HEH
I'll rompa you!
?
...
SHVR
I... DON'T WANNA CHEER HIM ON!!

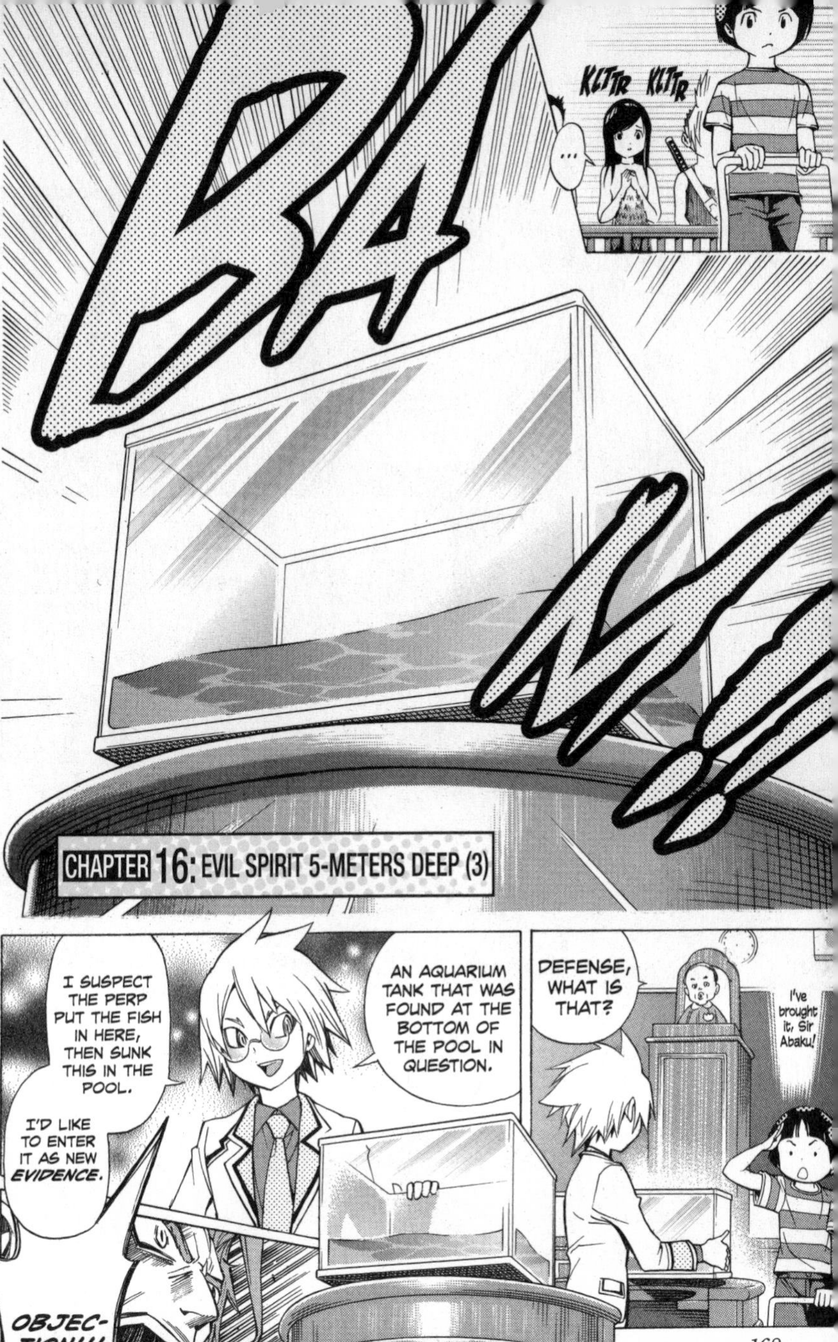
KLTTR KLTTR
...
BAM!!
CHAPTER 16: EVIL SPIRIT 5-METERS DEEP (3)
DEFENSE, WHAT IS THAT?
I've brought it, Sir Abaku!
AN AQUARIUM TANK THAT WAS FOUND AT THE BOTTOM OF THE POOL IN QUESTION.
I SUSPECT THE PERP PUT THE FISH IN HERE, THEN SUNK THIS IN THE POOL.
I'D LIKE TO ENTER IT AS NEW *EVIDENCE*.
OBJECTION!!!

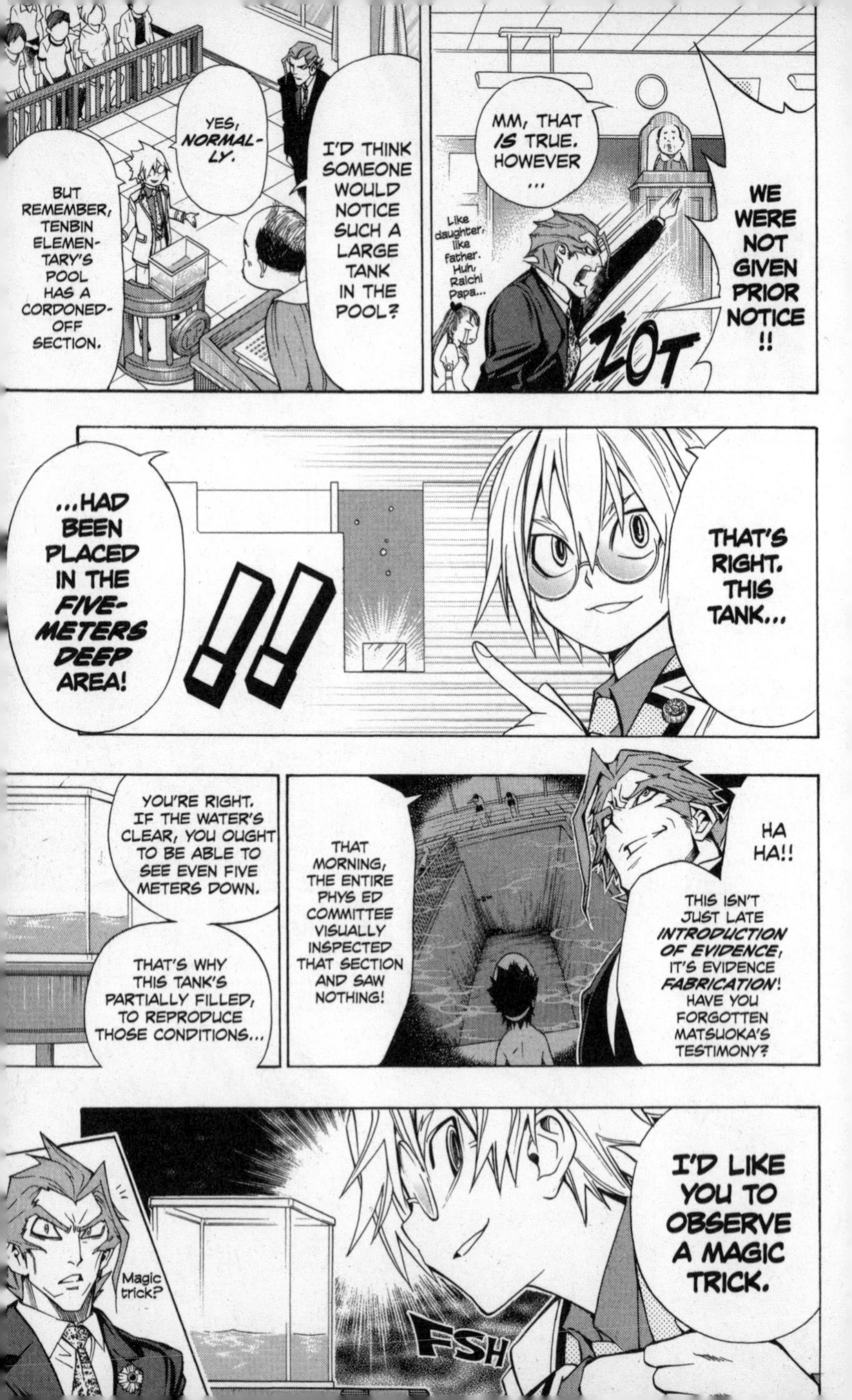
MM, THAT *IS* TRUE. HOWEVER ...
Like daughter, like father. Huh, Raichi Papa...
WE WERE NOT GIVEN PRIOR NOTICE !!
ZOT
I'D THINK SOMEONE WOULD NOTICE SUCH A LARGE TANK IN THE POOL?
YES, *NORMAL-LY.*
BUT REMEMBER, TENBIN ELEMEN-TARY'S POOL HAS A CORDONED-OFF SECTION.
THAT'S RIGHT. THIS TANK...
...HAD BEEN PLACED IN THE *FIVE-METERS DEEP* AREA!
!!
HA HA!!
THIS ISN'T JUST LATE *INTRODUCTION OF EVIDENCE*, IT'S EVIDENCE *FABRICATION*! HAVE YOU FORGOTTEN MATSUOKA'S TESTIMONY?
THAT MORNING, THE ENTIRE PHYS ED COMMITTEE VISUALLY INSPECTED THAT SECTION AND SAW NOTHING!
YOU'RE RIGHT. IF THE WATER'S CLEAR, YOU OUGHT TO BE ABLE TO SEE EVEN FIVE METERS DOWN.
THAT'S WHY THIS TANK'S PARTIALLY FILLED, TO REPRODUCE THOSE CONDITIONS...
I'D LIKE YOU TO OBSERVE A MAGIC TRICK.
FSH
Magic trick?

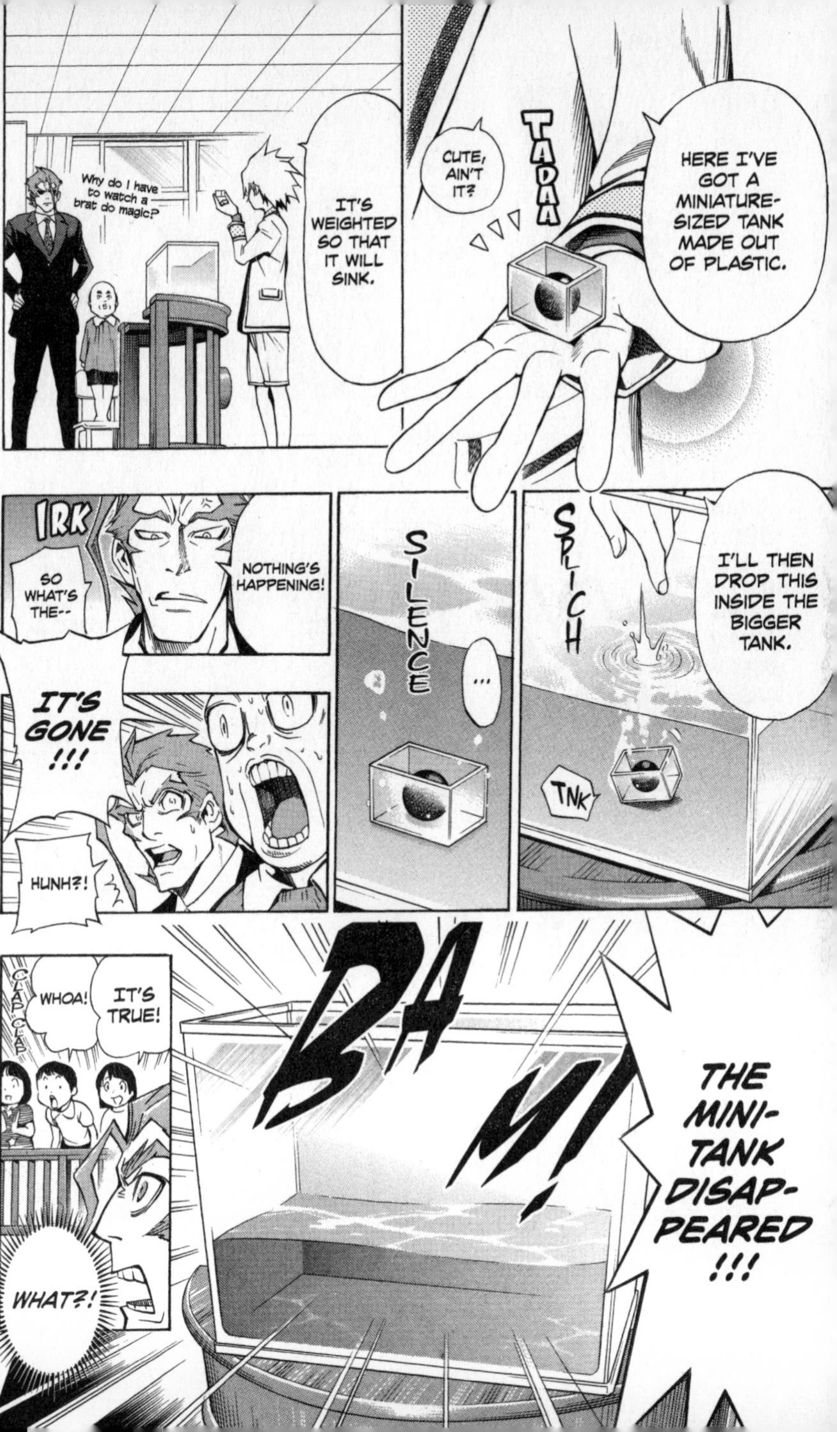
HERE I'VE GOT A MINIATURE-SIZED TANK MADE OUT OF PLASTIC.
TADAA
CUTE, AIN'T IT?
IT'S WEIGHTED SO THAT IT WILL SINK.
Why do I have to watch a brat do magic?
I'LL THEN DROP THIS INSIDE THE BIGGER TANK.
SPLICH
TNK
SILENCE
...
NOTHING'S HAPPENING!
IRK
SO WHAT'S THE--
IT'S GONE!!!
HUNH?!
BAM!
THE MINI-TANK DISAP-PEARED!!!
IT'S TRUE!
WHOA!
CLAP CLAP
WHAT?!

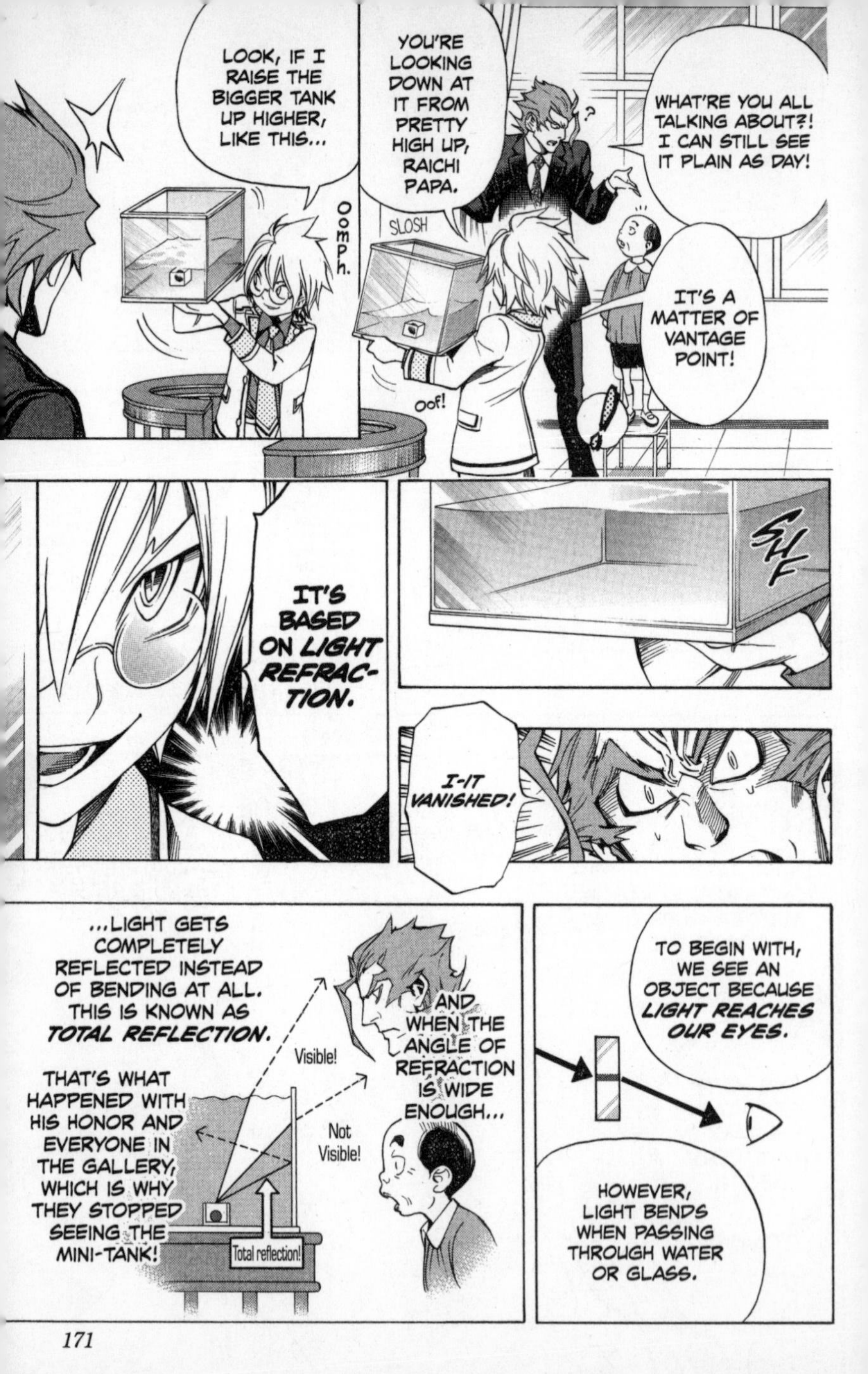
WHAT'RE YOU ALL TALKING ABOUT?! I CAN STILL SEE IT PLAIN AS DAY!
YOU'RE LOOKING DOWN AT IT FROM PRETTY HIGH UP, RAICHI PAPA.
?
IT'S A MATTER OF VANTAGE POINT!
SLOSH
Oof!
LOOK, IF I RAISE THE BIGGER TANK UP HIGHER, LIKE THIS...
Oomph.
SHF
I-IT VANISHED!
IT'S BASED ON *LIGHT REFRACTION*.
TO BEGIN WITH, WE SEE AN OBJECT BECAUSE *LIGHT REACHES OUR EYES*.
HOWEVER, LIGHT BENDS WHEN PASSING THROUGH WATER OR GLASS.
AND WHEN THE ANGLE OF REFRACTION IS WIDE ENOUGH...
...LIGHT GETS COMPLETELY REFLECTED INSTEAD OF BENDING AT ALL. THIS IS KNOWN AS *TOTAL REFLECTION*.
Visible!
Not Visible!
Total reflection!
THAT'S WHAT HAPPENED WITH HIS HONOR AND EVERYONE IN THE GALLERY, WHICH IS WHY THEY STOPPED SEEING THE MINI-TANK!

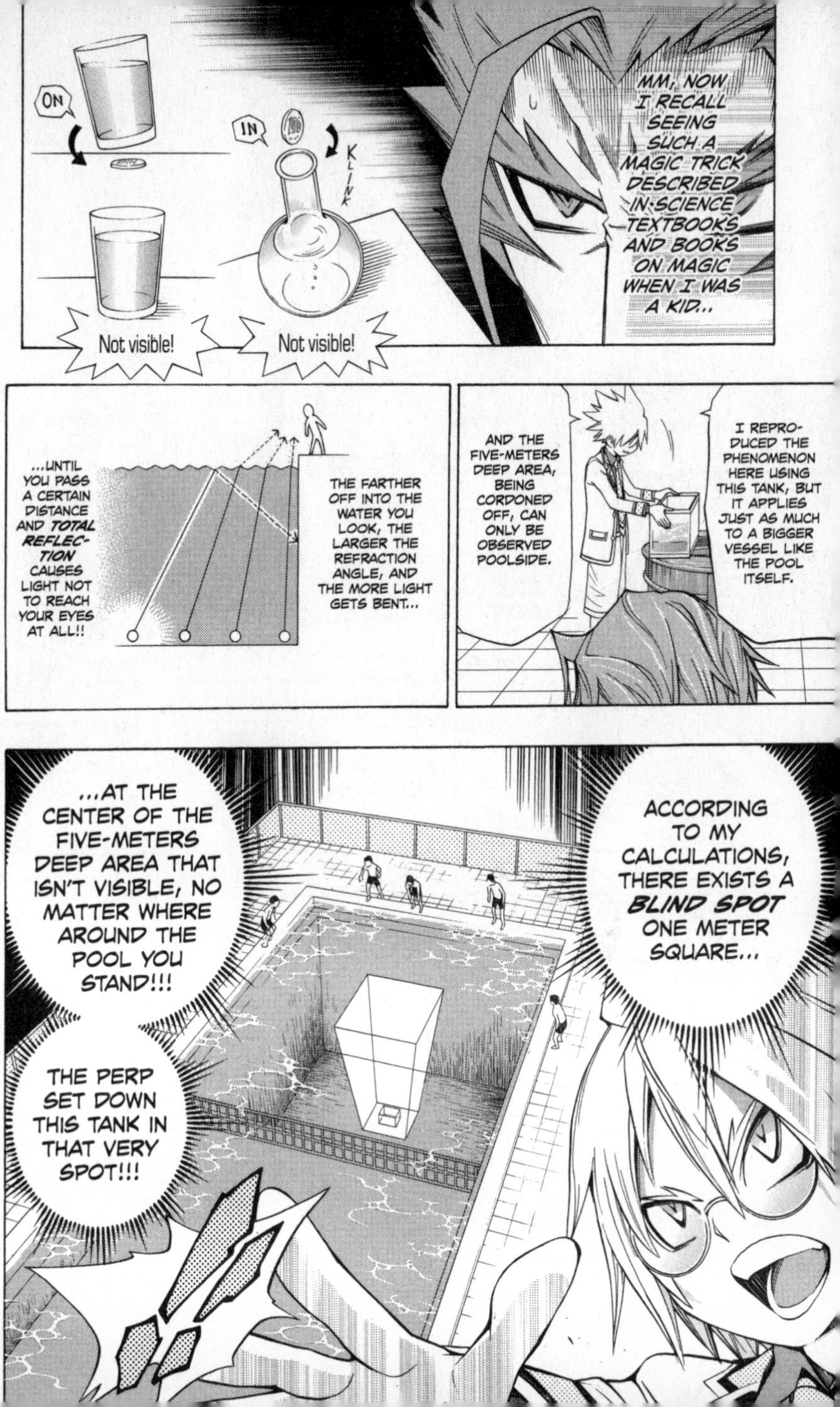
MM, NOW I RECALL SEEING SUCH A MAGIC TRICK DESCRIBED IN SCIENCE TEXTBOOKS AND BOOKS ON MAGIC WHEN I WAS A KID...
KLINK
IN
ON
Not visible!
Not visible!
I REPRODUCED THE PHENOMENON HERE USING THIS TANK, BUT IT APPLIES JUST AS MUCH TO A BIGGER VESSEL LIKE THE POOL ITSELF.
AND THE FIVE-METERS DEEP AREA, BEING CORDONED OFF, CAN ONLY BE OBSERVED POOLSIDE.
THE FARTHER OFF INTO THE WATER YOU LOOK, THE LARGER THE REFRACTION ANGLE, AND THE MORE LIGHT GETS BENT...
...UNTIL YOU PASS A CERTAIN DISTANCE AND TOTAL REFLECTION CAUSES LIGHT NOT TO REACH YOUR EYES AT ALL!!
ACCORDING TO MY CALCULATIONS, THERE EXISTS A BLIND SPOT ONE METER SQUARE...
...AT THE CENTER OF THE FIVE-METERS DEEP AREA THAT ISN'T VISIBLE, NO MATTER WHERE AROUND THE POOL YOU STAND!!!
THE PERP SET DOWN THIS TANK IN THAT VERY SPOT!!!

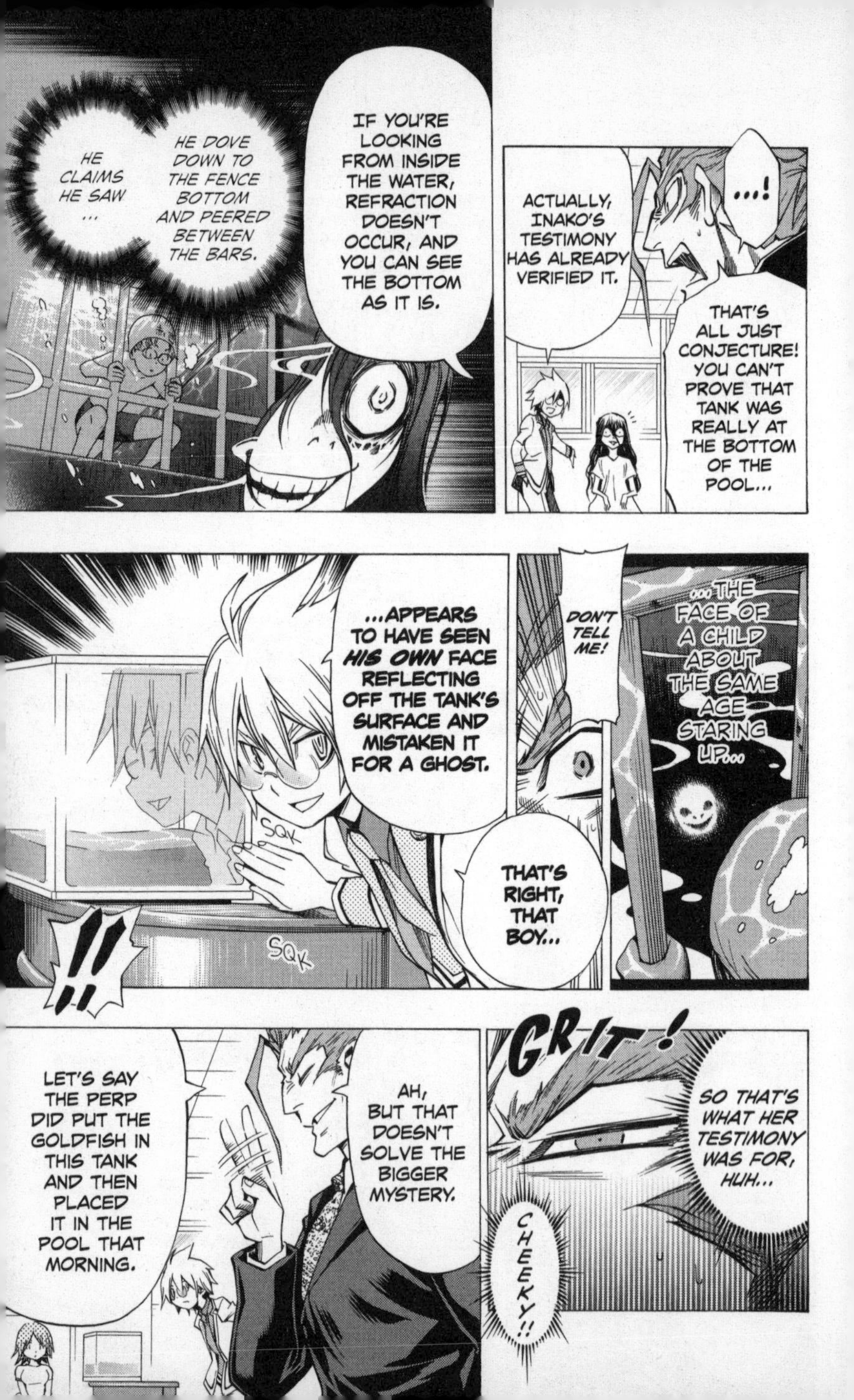
...!
THAT'S ALL JUST CONJECTURE! YOU CAN'T PROVE THAT TANK WAS REALLY AT THE BOTTOM OF THE POOL...
ACTUALLY, INAKO'S TESTIMONY HAS ALREADY VERIFIED IT.
IF YOU'RE LOOKING FROM INSIDE THE WATER, REFRACTION DOESN'T OCCUR, AND YOU CAN SEE THE BOTTOM AS IT IS.
HE DOVE DOWN TO THE FENCE BOTTOM AND PEERED BETWEEN THE BARS.
HE CLAIMS HE SAW ...
DON'T TELL ME!
...THE FACE OF A CHILD ABOUT THE SAME AGE STARING UP...
THAT'S RIGHT, THAT BOY...
...APPEARS TO HAVE SEEN *HIS OWN* FACE REFLECTING OFF THE TANK'S SURFACE AND MISTAKEN IT FOR A GHOST.
SQK
SQK
!!
GRIT!
SO THAT'S WHAT HER TESTIMONY WAS FOR, HUH...
CHEEKY!!
AH, BUT THAT DOESN'T SOLVE THE BIGGER MYSTERY.
LET'S SAY THE PERP DID PUT THE GOLDFISH IN THIS TANK AND THEN PLACED IT IN THE POOL THAT MORNING.

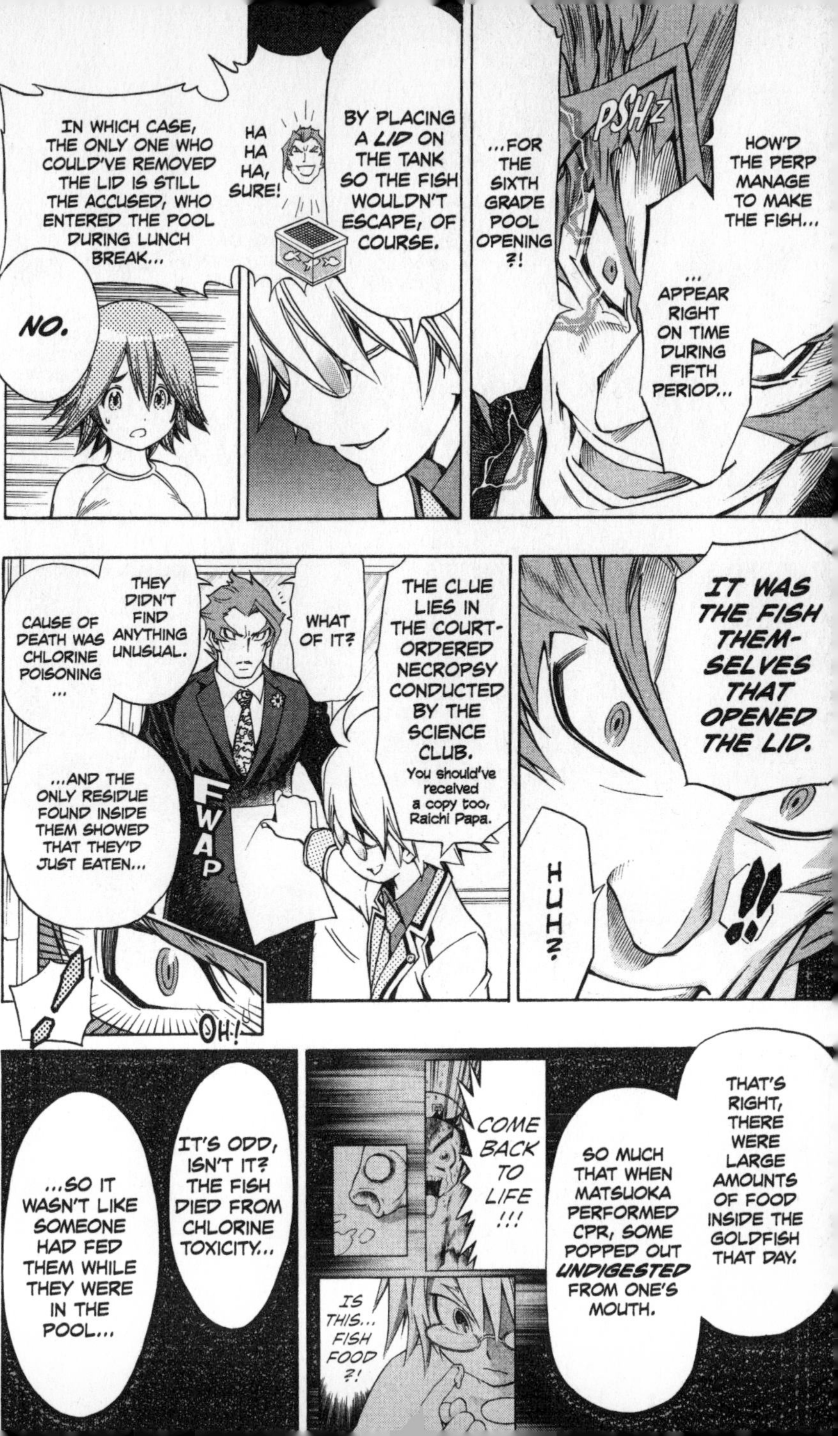

HOW'D THE PERP MANAGE TO MAKE THE FISH...
PSHZ
...APPEAR RIGHT ON TIME DURING FIFTH PERIOD...
...FOR THE SIXTH GRADE POOL OPENING?!
BY PLACING A *LID* ON THE TANK SO THE FISH WOULDN'T ESCAPE, OF COURSE.
HA HA HA, SURE!
IN WHICH CASE, THE ONLY ONE WHO COULD'VE REMOVED THE LID IS STILL THE ACCUSED, WHO ENTERED THE POOL DURING LUNCH BREAK...
NO.
IT WAS THE FISH THEMSELVES THAT OPENED THE LID.
HUH?
!!
THE CLUE LIES IN THE COURT-ORDERED NECROPSY CONDUCTED BY THE SCIENCE CLUB.
You should've received a copy too, Raichi Papa.
WHAT OF IT?
THEY DIDN'T FIND ANYTHING UNUSUAL.
CAUSE OF DEATH WAS CHLORINE POISONING...
FWAP
...AND THE ONLY RESIDUE FOUND INSIDE THEM SHOWED THAT THEY'D JUST EATEN...
OH!
THAT'S RIGHT, THERE WERE LARGE AMOUNTS OF FOOD INSIDE THE GOLDFISH THAT DAY.
SO MUCH THAT WHEN MATSUOKA PERFORMED CPR, SOME POPPED OUT *UNDIGESTED* FROM ONE'S MOUTH.
COME BACK TO LIFE!!!
IS THIS... FISH FOOD?!
IT'S ODD, ISN'T IT? THE FISH DIED FROM CHLORINE TOXICITY...
...SO IT WASN'T LIKE SOMEONE HAD FED THEM WHILE THEY WERE IN THE POOL...

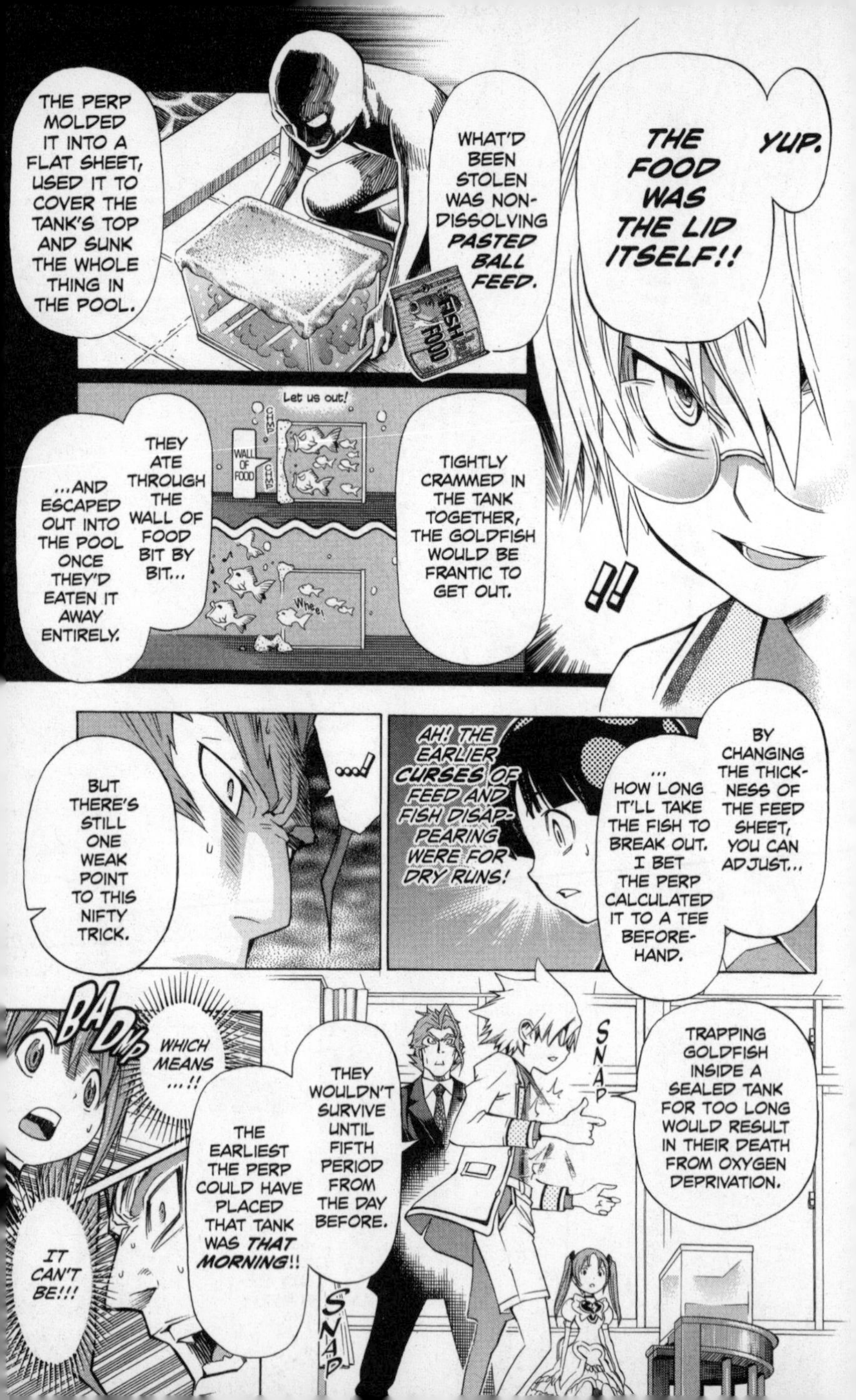
YUP.
THE FOOD WAS THE LID ITSELF!!
!!
WHAT'D BEEN STOLEN WAS NON-DISSOLVING PASTED BALL FEED.
FISH FOOD
THE PERP MOLDED IT INTO A FLAT SHEET, USED IT TO COVER THE TANK'S TOP AND SUNK THE WHOLE THING IN THE POOL.
Let us out!
CHMP
WALL OF FOOD
CHMP
TIGHTLY CRAMMED IN THE TANK TOGETHER, THE GOLDFISH WOULD BE FRANTIC TO GET OUT.
THEY ATE THROUGH THE WALL OF FOOD BIT BY BIT...
Whee!
...AND ESCAPED OUT INTO THE POOL ONCE THEY'D EATEN IT AWAY ENTIRELY.
BY CHANGING THE THICKNESS OF THE FEED SHEET, YOU CAN ADJUST...
...HOW LONG IT'LL TAKE THE FISH TO BREAK OUT. I BET THE PERP CALCULATED IT TO A TEE BEFOREHAND.
AH! THE EARLIER CURSES OF FEED AND FISH DISAPPEARING WERE FOR DRY RUNS!
...!
BUT THERE'S STILL ONE WEAK POINT TO THIS NIFTY TRICK.
TRAPPING GOLDFISH INSIDE A SEALED TANK FOR TOO LONG WOULD RESULT IN THEIR DEATH FROM OXYGEN DEPRIVATION.
SNAP
THEY WOULDN'T SURVIVE UNTIL FIFTH PERIOD FROM THE DAY BEFORE.
THE EARLIEST THE PERP COULD HAVE PLACED THAT TANK WAS THAT MORNING!!
SNAP
WHICH MEANS...!!
BADMP
IT CAN'T BE!!!

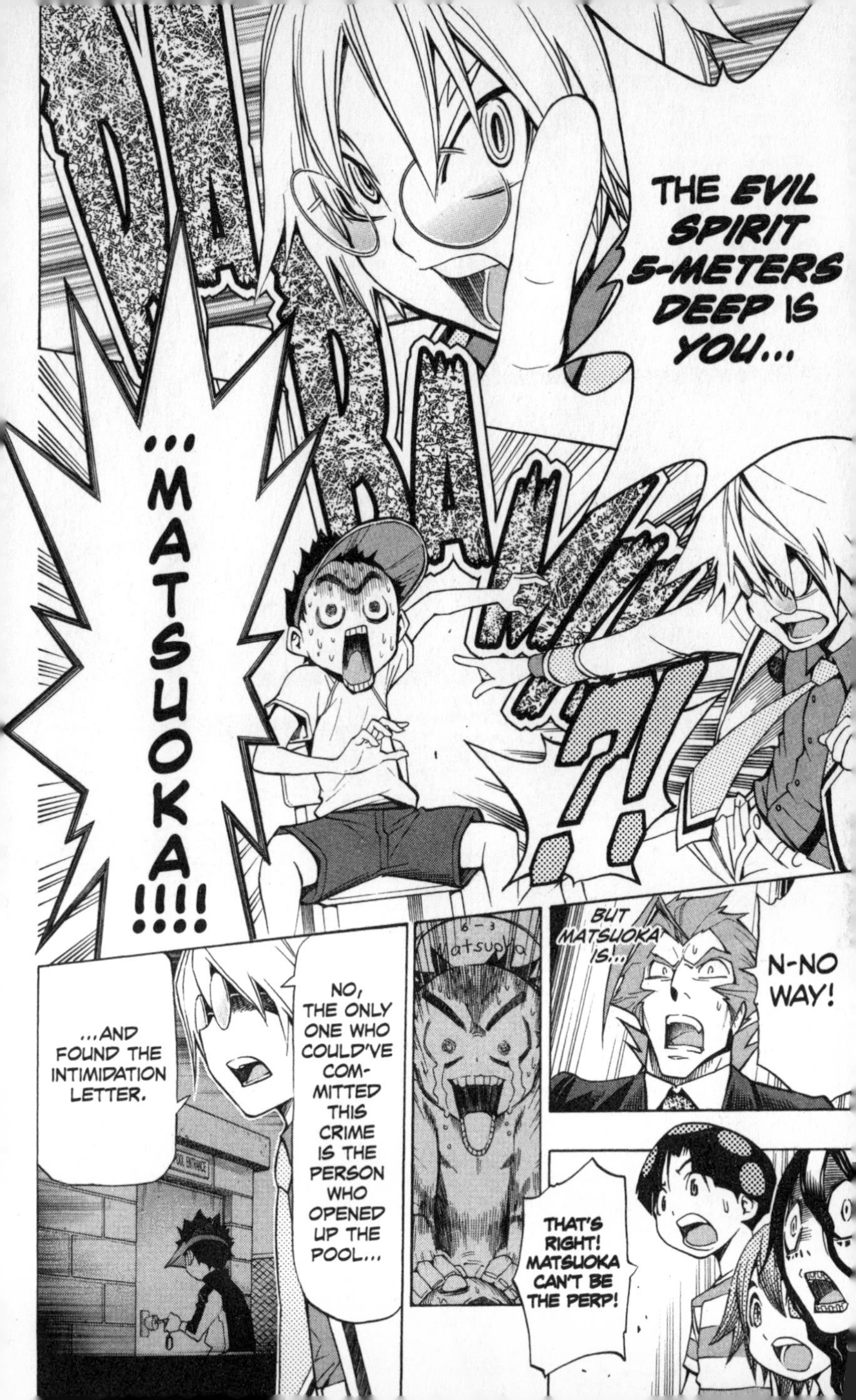
THE EVIL SPIRIT 5-METERS DEEP IS YOU...
...MATSUOKA!!!!
?!
N-NO WAY!
BUT MATSUOKA IS...
THAT'S RIGHT! MATSUOKA CAN'T BE THE PERP!
6-3 Matsuoka
NO, THE ONLY ONE WHO COULD'VE COM-MITTED THIS CRIME IS THE PERSON WHO OPENED UP THE POOL...
...AND FOUND THE INTIMIDATION LETTER.

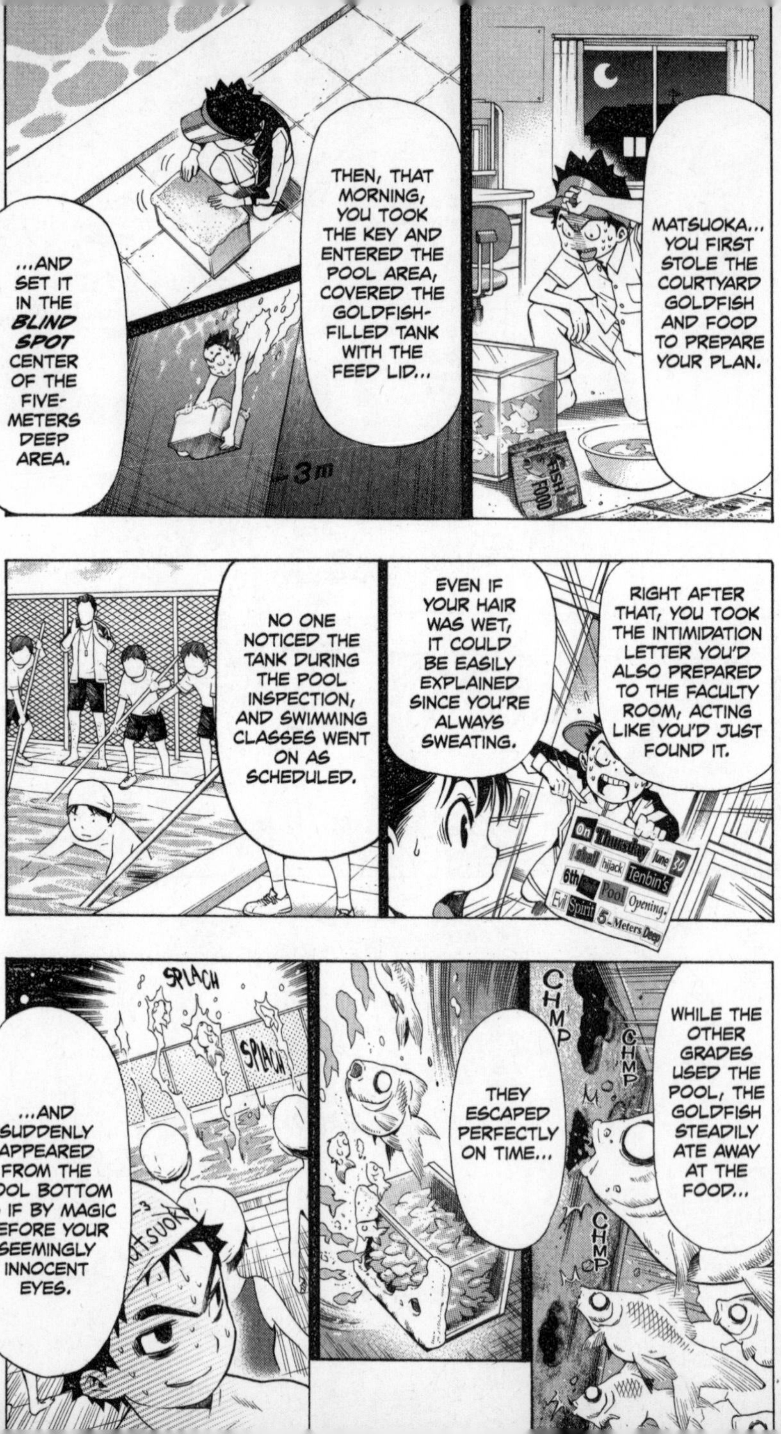
MATSUOKA... YOU FIRST STOLE THE COURTYARD GOLDFISH AND FOOD TO PREPARE YOUR PLAN.
FISH FOOD
THEN, THAT MORNING, YOU TOOK THE KEY AND ENTERED THE POOL AREA, COVERED THE GOLDFISH-FILLED TANK WITH THE FEED LID...
...AND SET IT IN THE *BLIND SPOT* CENTER OF THE FIVE-METERS DEEP AREA.
3m
RIGHT AFTER THAT, YOU TOOK THE INTIMIDATION LETTER YOU'D ALSO PREPARED TO THE FACULTY ROOM, ACTING LIKE YOU'D JUST FOUND IT.
EVEN IF YOUR HAIR WAS WET, IT COULD BE EASILY EXPLAINED SINCE YOU'RE ALWAYS SWEATING.
On Thursday June 30 I shall hijack Tenbin's 6th Pool Opening. Evil Spirit 5 Meters Deep
NO ONE NOTICED THE TANK DURING THE POOL INSPECTION, AND SWIMMING CLASSES WENT ON AS SCHEDULED.
WHILE THE OTHER GRADES USED THE POOL, THE GOLDFISH STEADILY ATE AWAY AT THE FOOD...
CHMP
CHMP
CHMP
THEY ESCAPED PERFECTLY ON TIME...
SPLACH
SPLACH
...AND SUDDENLY APPEARED FROM THE POOL BOTTOM AS IF BY MAGIC BEFORE YOUR SEEMINGLY INNOCENT EYES.

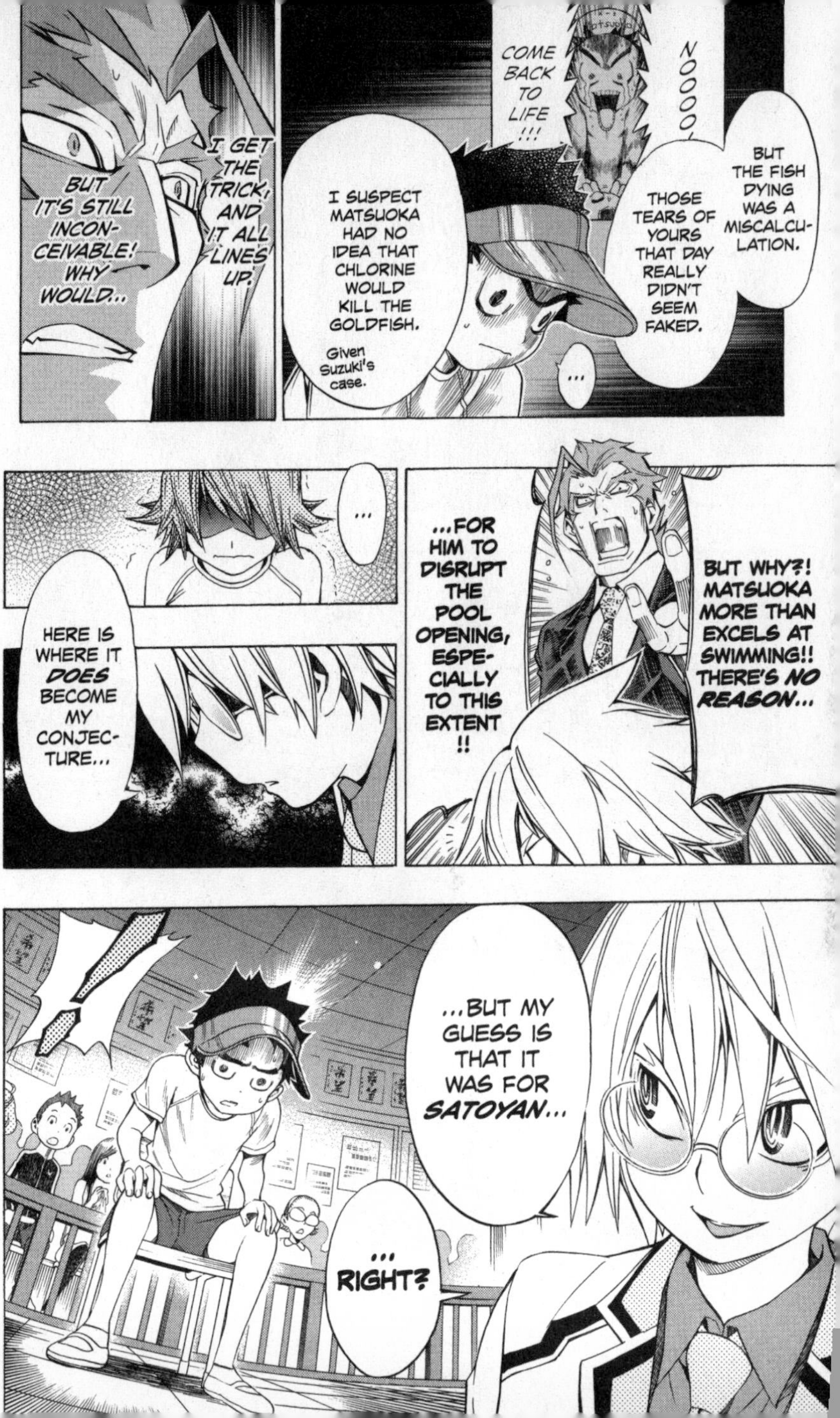
NOOOO!
COME BACK TO LIFE!!!
BUT THE FISH DYING WAS A MISCALCULATION.
THOSE TEARS OF YOURS THAT DAY REALLY DIDN'T SEEM FAKED.
...
I SUSPECT MATSUOKA HAD NO IDEA THAT CHLORINE WOULD KILL THE GOLDFISH.
Given Suzuki's case.
I GET THE TRICK, AND IT ALL LINES UP.
BUT IT'S STILL INCONCEIVABLE! WHY WOULD...
BUT WHY?! MATSUOKA MORE THAN EXCELS AT SWIMMING!! THERE'S *NO REASON*...
...FOR HIM TO DISRUPT THE POOL OPENING, ESPECIALLY TO THIS EXTENT!!
...
HERE IS WHERE IT *DOES* BECOME MY CONJECTURE...
...BUT MY GUESS IS THAT IT WAS FOR *SATOYAN*...
...RIGHT?

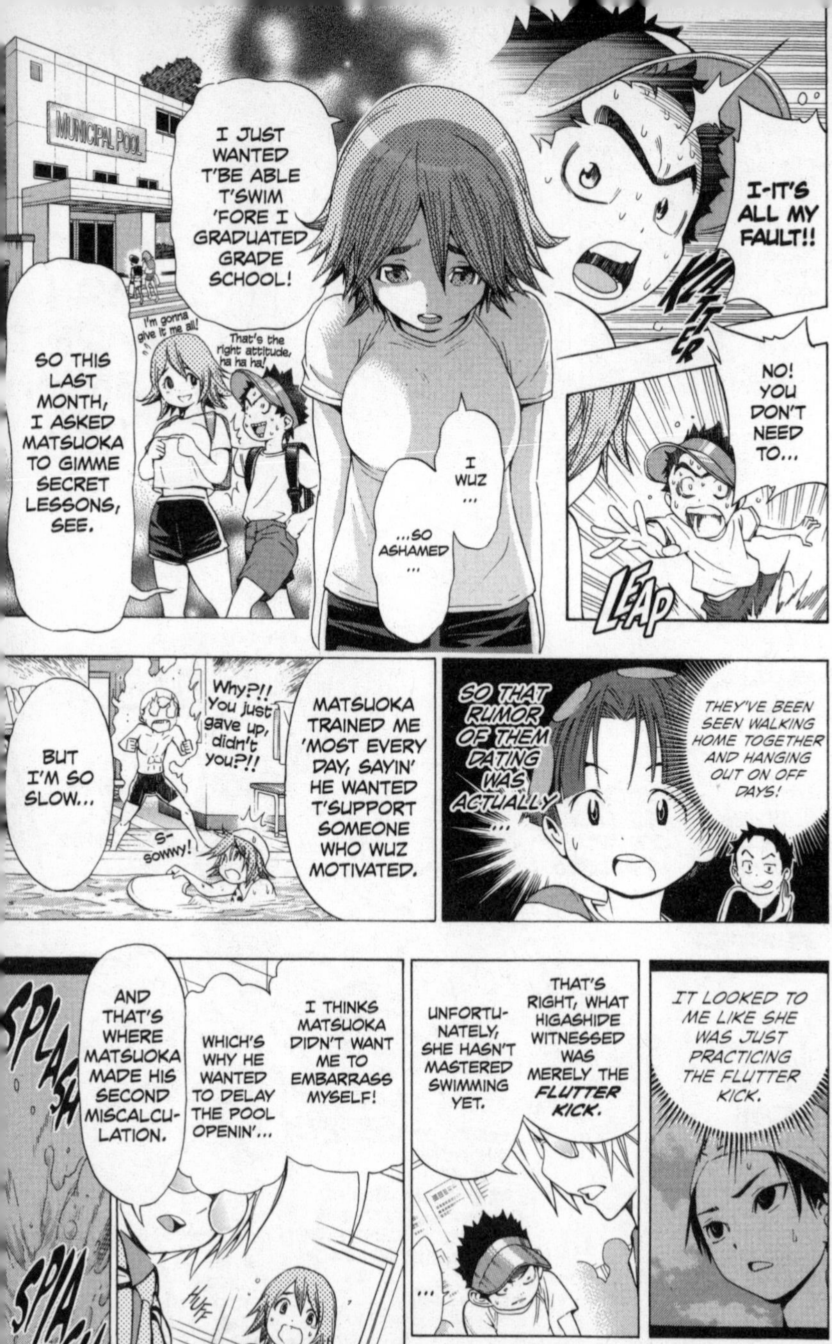
I-IT'S ALL MY FAULT!!
VATTER
NO! YOU DON'T NEED TO...
LEAP
I WUZ...
...SO ASHAMED...
I JUST WANTED T'BE ABLE T'SWIM 'FORE I GRADUATED GRADE SCHOOL!
MUNICIPAL POOL
SO THIS LAST MONTH, I ASKED MATSUOKA TO GIMME SECRET LESSONS, SEE.
That's the right attitude, ha ha ha!
I'm gonna give it me all!
THEY'VE BEEN SEEN WALKING HOME TOGETHER AND HANGING OUT ON OFF DAYS!
SO THAT RUMOR OF THEM DATING WAS ACTUALLY...
MATSUOKA TRAINED ME 'MOST EVERY DAY, SAYIN' HE WANTED T'SUPPORT SOMEONE WHO WUZ MOTIVATED.
Why?!! You just gave up, didn't you?!!
BUT I'M SO SLOW...
S-sowwy!
IT LOOKED TO ME LIKE SHE WAS JUST PRACTICING THE FLUTTER KICK.
THAT'S RIGHT, WHAT HIGASHIDE WITNESSED WAS MERELY THE FLUTTER KICK.
UNFORTUNATELY, SHE HASN'T MASTERED SWIMMING YET.
...
I THINKS MATSUOKA DIDN'T WANT ME TO EMBARRASS MYSELF!
WHICH'S WHY HE WANTED TO DELAY THE POOL OPENIN'...
AND THAT'S WHERE MATSUOKA MADE HIS SECOND MISCALCULATION.
HUFF
SPLASH
SPLASH

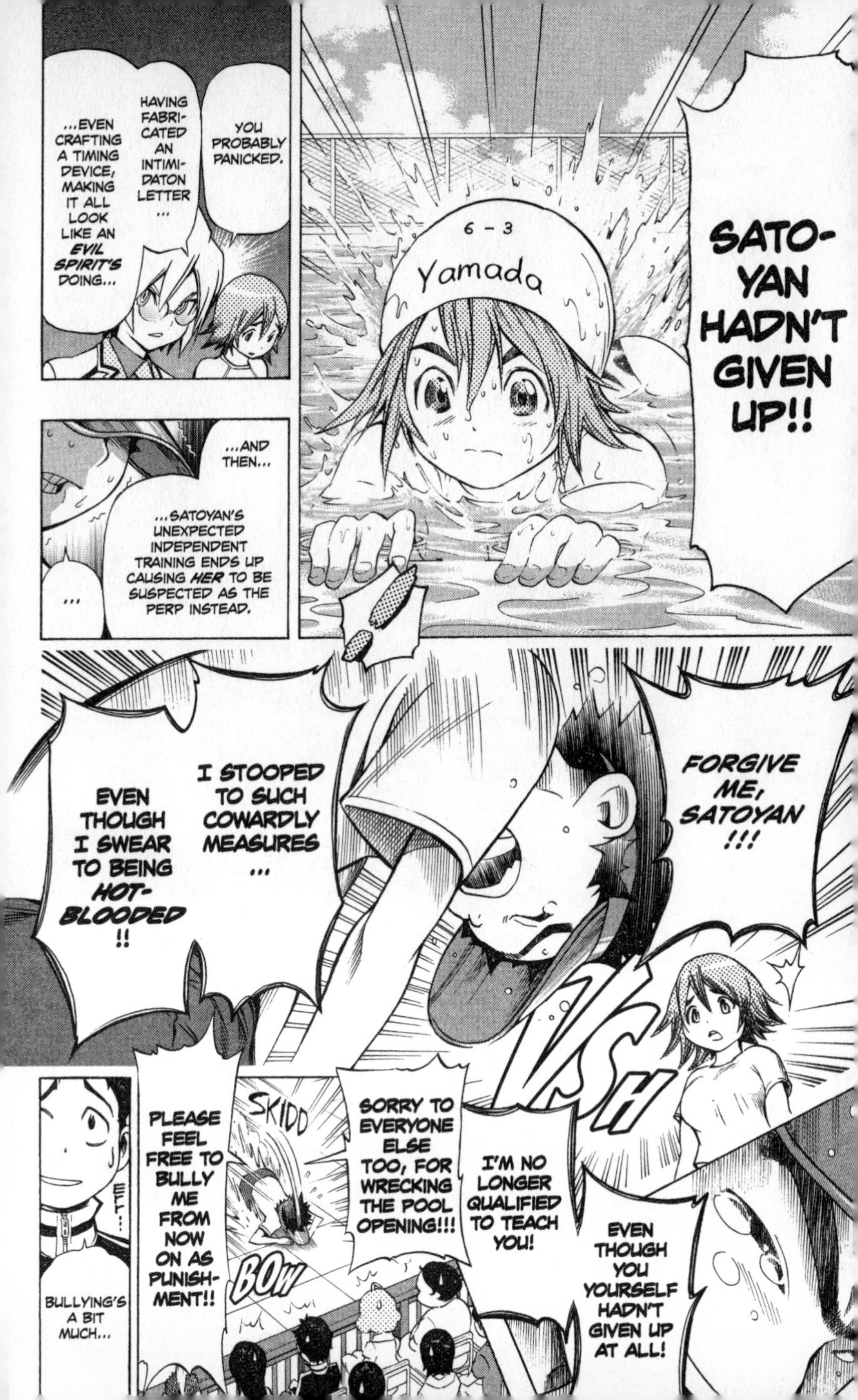
SATO-YAN HADN'T GIVEN UP!!
YOU PROBABLY PANICKED.
HAVING FABRICATED AN INTIMIDATON LETTER...
...EVEN CRAFTING A TIMING DEVICE, MAKING IT ALL LOOK LIKE AN *EVIL SPIRIT'S* DOING...
...AND THEN...
...SATOYAN'S UNEXPECTED INDEPENDENT TRAINING ENDS UP CAUSING *HER* TO BE SUSPECTED AS THE PERP INSTEAD.
...
6 - 3
Yamada
FORGIVE ME, SATOYAN!!!
I STOOPED TO SUCH COWARDLY MEASURES...
EVEN THOUGH I SWEAR TO BEING *HOT-BLOODED*!!
VSH
EVEN THOUGH YOU YOURSELF HADN'T GIVEN UP AT ALL!
I'M NO LONGER QUALIFIED TO TEACH YOU!
SORRY TO EVERYONE ELSE TOO, FOR WRECKING THE POOL OPENING!!!
SKIDD
PLEASE FEEL FREE TO BULLY ME FROM NOW ON AS PUNISHMENT!!
BOW
BULLYING'S A BIT MUCH...

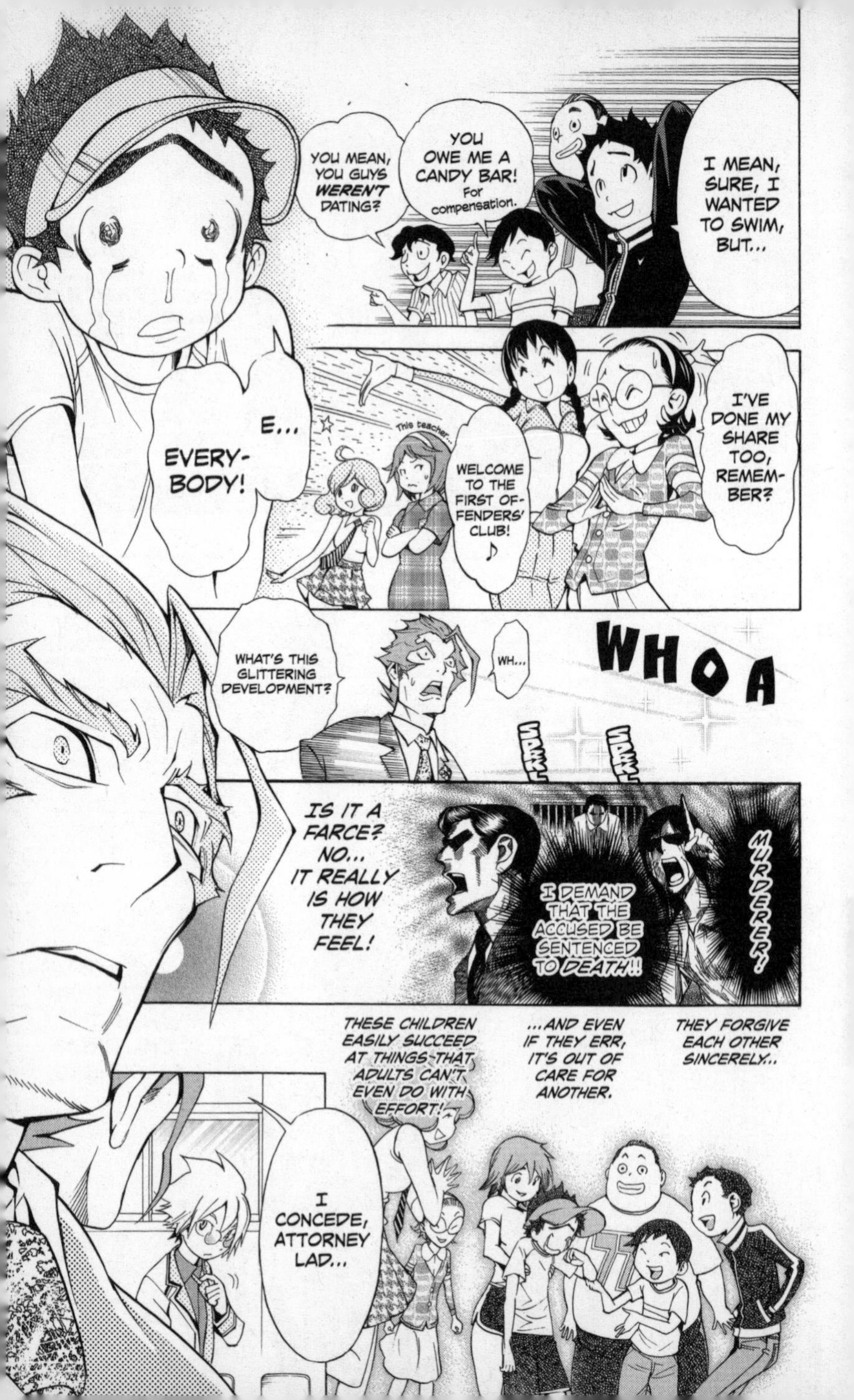
I MEAN, SURE, I WANTED TO SWIM, BUT...
YOU OWE ME A CANDY BAR! For compensation.
YOU MEAN, YOU GUYS *WEREN'T* DATING?
I'VE DONE MY SHARE TOO, REMEMBER?
WELCOME TO THE FIRST OFFENDERS' CLUB! ♪
This teacher...
E... EVERYBODY!
WHOA
WH...
WHAT'S THIS GLITTERING DEVELOPMENT?
MURDERER!
I DEMAND THAT THE ACCUSED BE SENTENCED TO DEATH!!
IS IT A FARCE? NO... IT REALLY IS HOW THEY FEEL!
THEY FORGIVE EACH OTHER SINCERELY...
...AND EVEN IF THEY ERR, IT'S OUT OF CARE FOR ANOTHER.
THESE CHILDREN EASILY SUCCEED AT THINGS THAT ADULTS CAN'T EVEN DO WITH EFFORT!
I CONCEDE, ATTORNEY LAD...

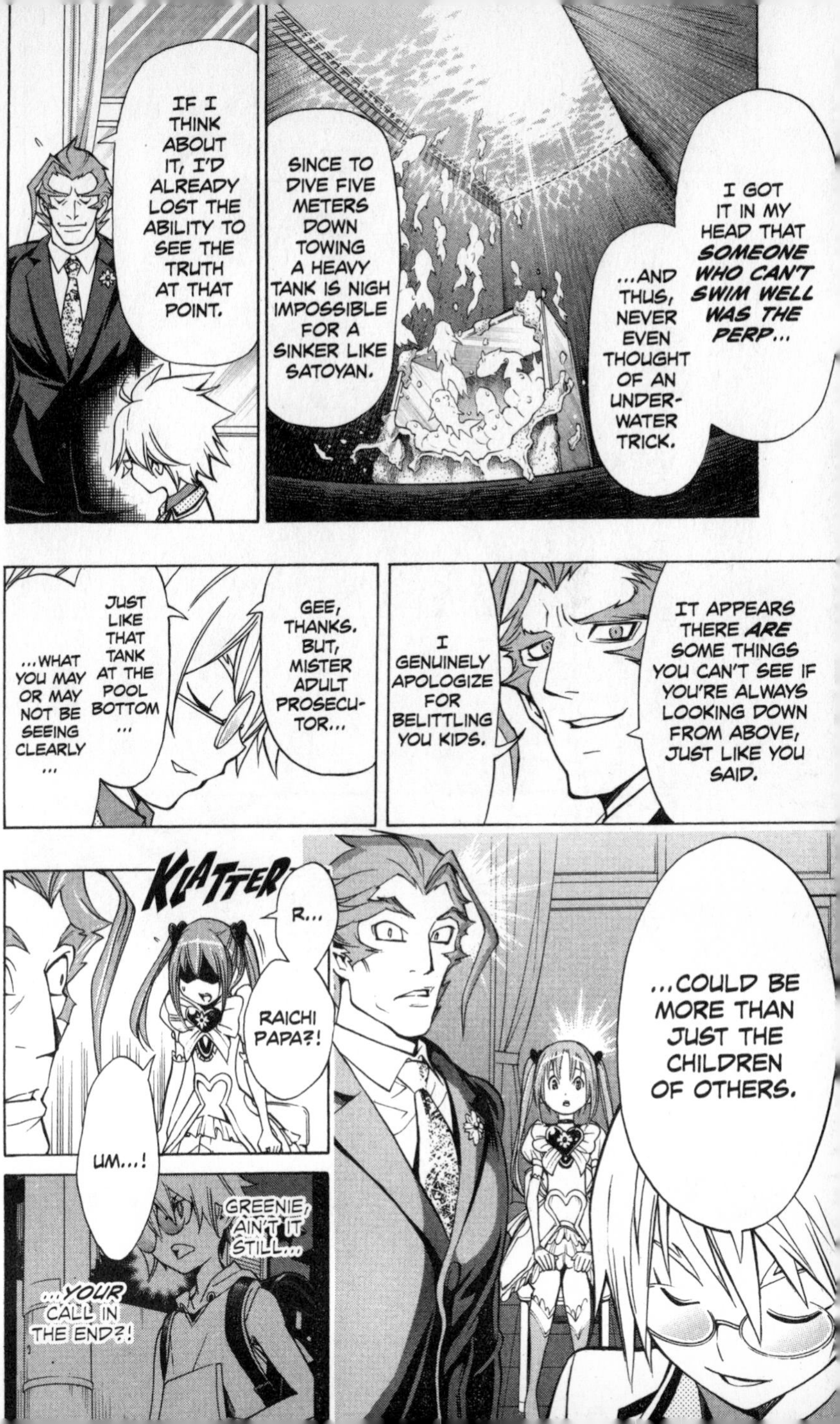
I GOT IT IN MY HEAD THAT *SOMEONE WHO CAN'T SWIM WELL WAS THE PERP*...
...AND THUS, NEVER EVEN THOUGHT OF AN UNDER-WATER TRICK.
SINCE TO DIVE FIVE METERS DOWN TOWING A HEAVY TANK IS NIGH IMPOSSIBLE FOR A SINKER LIKE SATOYAN.
IF I THINK ABOUT IT, I'D ALREADY LOST THE ABILITY TO SEE THE TRUTH AT THAT POINT.
IT APPEARS THERE *ARE* SOME THINGS YOU CAN'T SEE IF YOU'RE ALWAYS LOOKING DOWN FROM ABOVE, JUST LIKE YOU SAID.
I GENUINELY APOLOGIZE FOR BELITTLING YOU KIDS.
GEE, THANKS. BUT, MISTER ADULT PROSECU-TOR...
JUST LIKE THAT TANK AT THE POOL BOTTOM...
...WHAT YOU MAY OR MAY NOT BE SEEING CLEARLY...
...COULD BE MORE THAN JUST THE CHILDREN OF OTHERS.
R...
KLATTER
RAICHI PAPA?!
UM...!
GREENIE, AIN'T IT STILL...
...YOUR CALL IN THE END?!

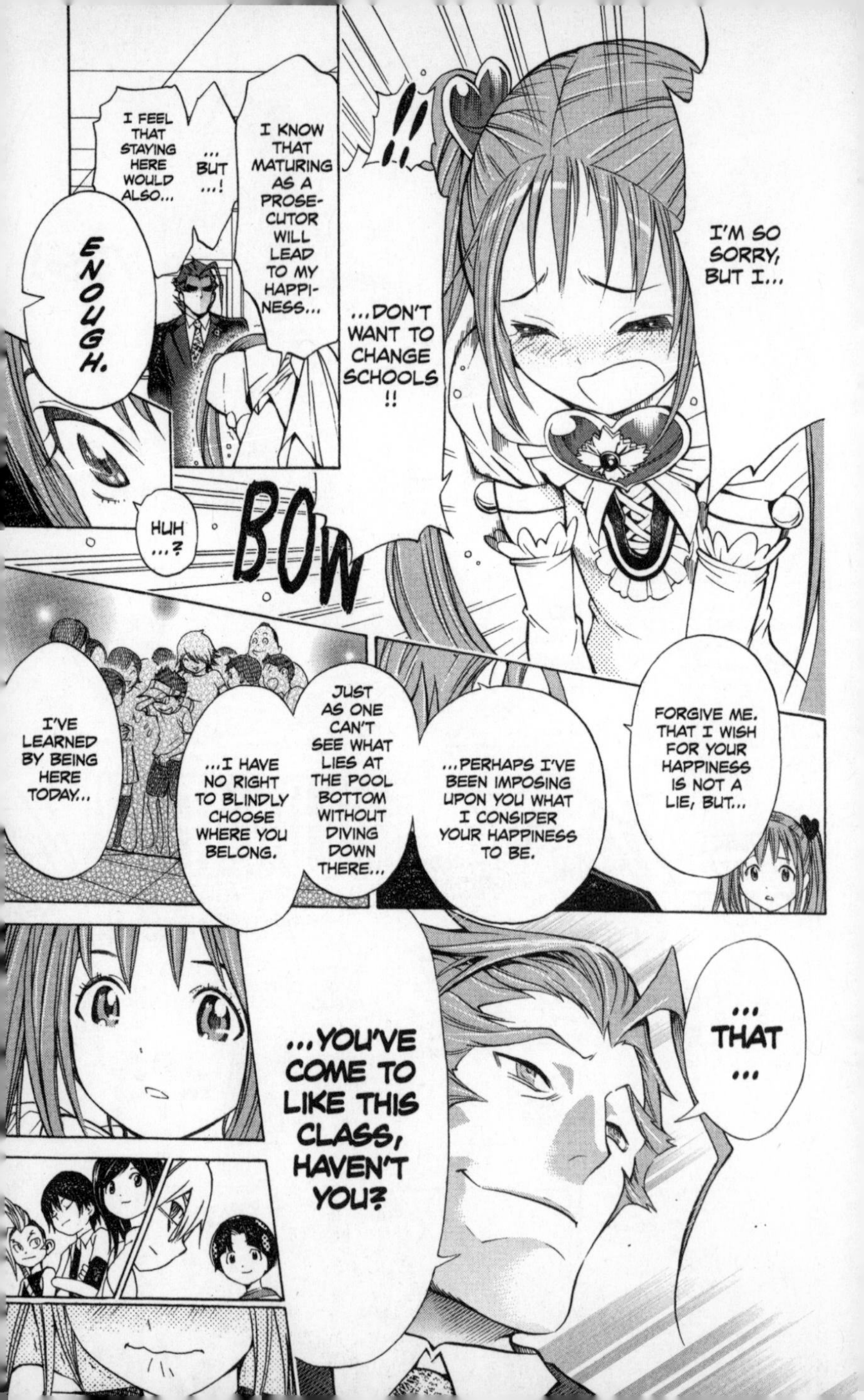
!!
I'M SO SORRY, BUT I...
...DON'T WANT TO CHANGE SCHOOLS !!
I KNOW THAT MATURING AS A PROSECUTOR WILL LEAD TO MY HAPPINESS...
...BUT ...!
I FEEL THAT STAYING HERE WOULD ALSO...
ENOUGH.
BOW
HUH ...?
FORGIVE ME. THAT I WISH FOR YOUR HAPPINESS IS NOT A LIE, BUT...
...PERHAPS I'VE BEEN IMPOSING UPON YOU WHAT I CONSIDER YOUR HAPPINESS TO BE.
JUST AS ONE CAN'T SEE WHAT LIES AT THE POOL BOTTOM WITHOUT DIVING DOWN THERE...
...I HAVE NO RIGHT TO BLINDLY CHOOSE WHERE YOU BELONG.
I'VE LEARNED BY BEING HERE TODAY...
...THAT...
...YOU'VE COME TO LIKE THIS CLASS, HAVEN'T YOU?

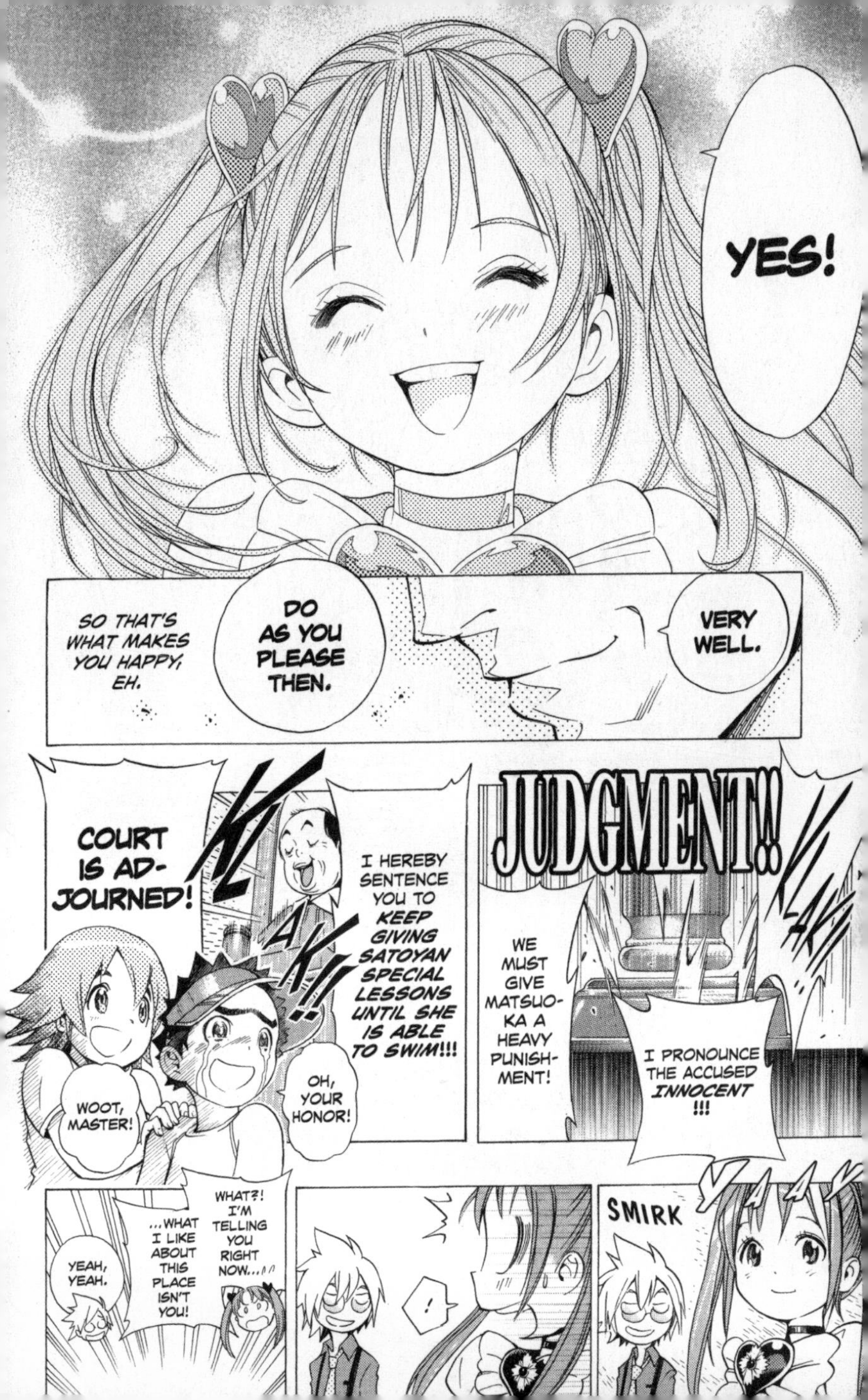
YES!
VERY WELL.
DO AS YOU PLEASE THEN.
SO THAT'S WHAT MAKES YOU HAPPY, EH.
JUDGMENT!!
KLAK!
I PRONOUNCE THE ACCUSED INNOCENT!!!
WE MUST GIVE MATSUO-KA A HEAVY PUNISH-MENT!
I HEREBY SENTENCE YOU TO KEEP GIVING SATOYAN SPECIAL LESSONS UNTIL SHE IS ABLE TO SWIM!!!
KLAK!!
COURT IS AD-JOURNED!
OH, YOUR HONOR!
WOOT, MASTER!
SMIRK
!
WHAT?! I'M TELLING YOU RIGHT NOW...
...WHAT I LIKE ABOUT THIS PLACE ISN'T YOU!
YEAH, YEAH.

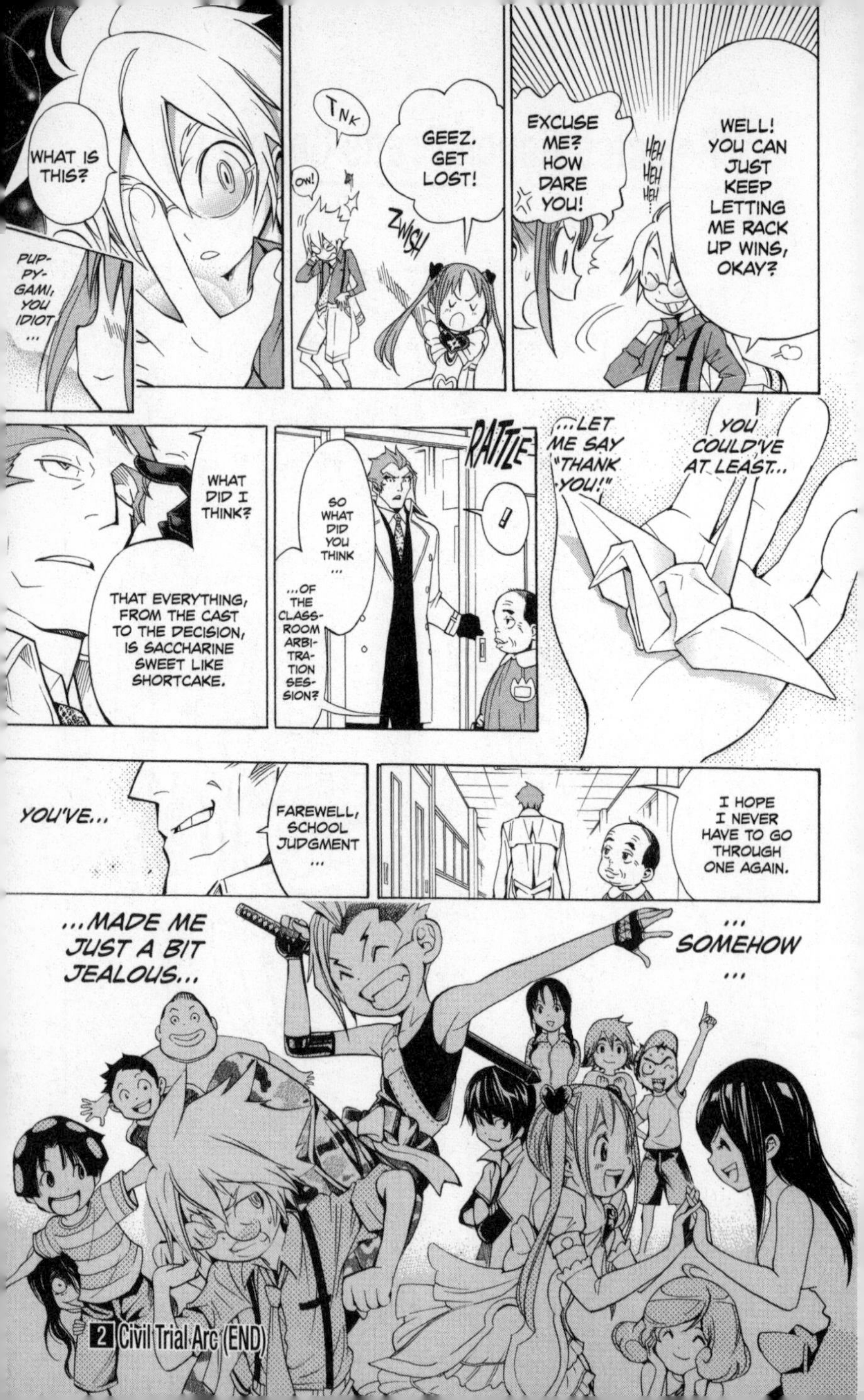
WELL! YOU CAN JUST KEEP LETTING ME RACK UP WINS, OKAY?
HEH HEH HEH
EXCUSE ME? HOW DARE YOU!
TNK
GEEZ. GET LOST!
OW!
ZWISH
WHAT IS THIS?
PUP-PY-GAMI, YOU IDIOT...
YOU COULD'VE AT LEAST...
...LET ME SAY "THANK YOU!"
RATTLE
!
SO WHAT DID YOU THINK...
...OF THE CLASS-ROOM ARBI-TRA-TION SES-SION?
WHAT DID I THINK?
THAT EVERYTHING, FROM THE CAST TO THE DECISION, IS SACCHARINE SWEET LIKE SHORTCAKE.
I HOPE I NEVER HAVE TO GO THROUGH ONE AGAIN.
FAREWELL, SCHOOL JUDGMENT...
YOU'VE...
...SOMEHOW...
...MADE ME JUST A BIT JEALOUS...

2 Civil Trial Arc (END)

Rejected Rough Drafts Gallery (3)

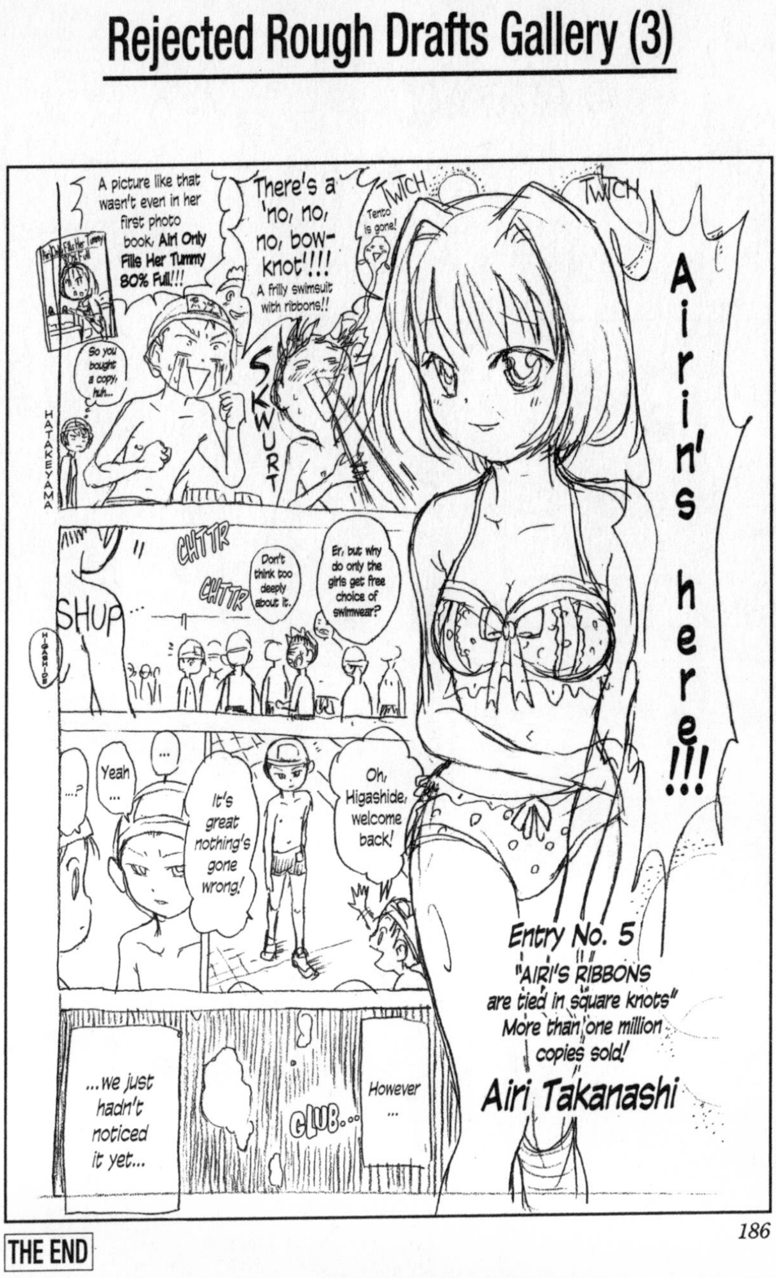
TWITCH
Airin' here!!!
Entry No. 5
"AIRI'S RIBBONS are tied in square knots"
More than one million copies sold!
Airi Takanashi
TWITCH
Tento is gone!
There's a 'no, no, no, bow-knot'!!!!
A frilly swimsuit with ribbons!!
A picture like that wasn't even in her first photo book, **Airi Only Fills Her Tummy 80% Full!!!**
Airi Only Fills Her Tummy 80% Full
SKWURT
So you bought a copy, huh...
HATAKEYAMA
Er, but why do only the girls get free choice of swimwear?
Don't think too deeply about it.
CHTTR
CHTTR
SHUP...
HIGASHIDE
Oh, Higashide, welcome back!
It's great nothing's gone wrong!
...
Yeah ...
...?
However ...
CLUB...
...we just hadn't noticed it yet...

THE END

Afterword

Speaking of rejections, there was a crazy idea I had where Inugami reverts back to his early, fainthearted emotional self and sorts through his feelings once a month (a.k.a. "girl day"). The pool incident classroom arbitration happens to coincide with that day, so Tento takes over Abaku's role and struggles his way through.

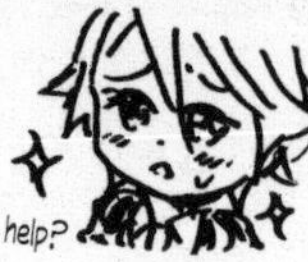
Abaku Girl Day version
(a.k.a. Abako)
Tento, please help?
I just can't do it...!

There are other such examples of material I wanted to write but couldn't for various reasons. There were also stories and scenes I didn't want to write but had to for the sake of plot progression.

Honestly, around the time of the Civil Trial Arc, I was almost thinking about how painful it was to write manga. (Because I was struggling.)

Volume 2 thoroughly taught me the difficulties of manga. All of you who picked up a copy, thank you so much!!

Only one volume of this tale remains...! What is the greatest Classroom Arbitration to strike 6-3...?! What is the truth behind the **Bloody Classroom Session**...?! Please look forward to volume 3, where all will be revealed!!!

Hm...? It's going to be the final volume already? Isn't that fast...? Ropapapapa... For sure, it could be said that a three-volume series is short, but from a different angle, think about how easy it is to collect the complete set, ropapapa... Oh, by the way, *ropapapapa* is Inugami's original laugh, which was also rejected. This one is honestly something I nixed myself after two seconds of thinking about it...
I pray that we shall meet again in volume 3!!

Ropapapapapa...

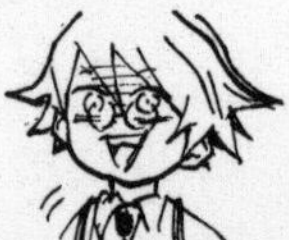

Nobuaki Enoki

COURT IS NOW IN SESSION

Hi! Thank you for reading *School Judgment: Gakkyu Hotei*! There are quite a few instances in this series where knowledge of the Japanese language is a key part of understanding the cases and extra pages, so I would like to take the time to explain some of this to you!

School Sign (p. 10)	The sign on the post says, "Tenbin Elementary."
Tsundere (p. 15)	A tsundere is someone who acts really mean and abrasive towards the person they like but will occasionally show their sweet side.
証 (*sho*) (kanji on witness stand, p. 18)	This kanji means "evidence." It is also used in the word 証人 (*shonin*), which means "witness." This sign refers to the witness stand.
裁 (*sai*) (kanji on judge's stand, pgs. 19, 55)	This kanji comes from the word 裁判所 (*saibansho*), which means "courthouse."
Chalkboard (p. 27)	The writing on the chalkboard says, "Wednesday, June 2nd. Classroom helpers: Akasu and Namae."
月の予定 (*tsuki no yotei*) (kanji on bulletin board, p. 53)	The kanji means "monthly schedule." One may find notices about Classroom Arbitration Sessions and other class events on this board.
Sarutobi (p. 55)	Sarutobi's name has the word for monkey, 猿 (*saru*), in it. This alludes to both the fact that he is a ninja and is most likely named after the legendary ninja Sarutobi Sasuke, as well as his role in the story as the monkey figure.

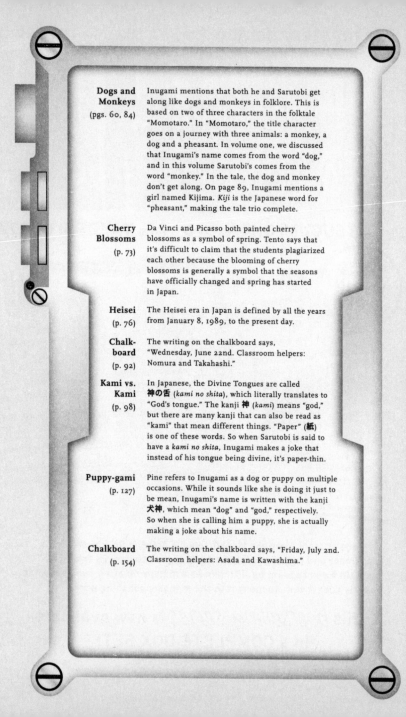

Dogs and Monkeys
(pgs. 60, 84)

Inugami mentions that both he and Sarutobi get along like dogs and monkeys in folklore. This is based on two of three characters in the folktale "Momotaro." In "Momotaro," the title character goes on a journey with three animals: a monkey, a dog and a pheasant. In volume one, we discussed that Inugami's name comes from the word "dog," and in this volume Sarutobi's comes from the word "monkey." In the tale, the dog and monkey don't get along. On page 89, Inugami mentions a girl named Kijima. *Kiji* is the Japanese word for "pheasant," making the tale trio complete.

Cherry Blossoms
(p. 73)

Da Vinci and Picasso both painted cherry blossoms as a symbol of spring. Tento says that it's difficult to claim that the students plagiarized each other because the blooming of cherry blossoms is generally a symbol that the seasons have officially changed and spring has started in Japan.

Heisei
(p. 76)

The Heisei era in Japan is defined by all the years from January 8, 1989, to the present day.

Chalkboard
(p. 92)

The writing on the chalkboard says, "Wednesday, June 22nd. Classroom helpers: Nomura and Takahashi."

Kami vs. Kami
(p. 98)

In Japanese, the Divine Tongues are called 神の舌 (*kami no shita*), which literally translates to "God's tongue." The kanji 神 (*kami*) means "god," but there are many kanji that can also be read as "kami" that mean different things. "Paper" (紙) is one of these words. So when Sarutobi is said to have a *kami no shita*, Inugami makes a joke that instead of his tongue being divine, it's paper-thin.

Puppy-gami
(p. 127)

Pine refers to Inugami as a dog or puppy on multiple occasions. While it sounds like she is doing it just to be mean, Inugami's name is written with the kanji 犬神, which mean "dog" and "god," respectively. So when she is calling him a puppy, she is actually making a joke about his name.

Chalkboard
(p. 154)

The writing on the chalkboard says, "Friday, July 2nd. Classroom helpers: Asada and Kawashima."

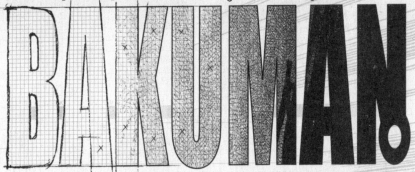
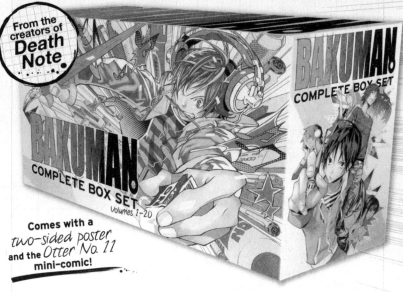

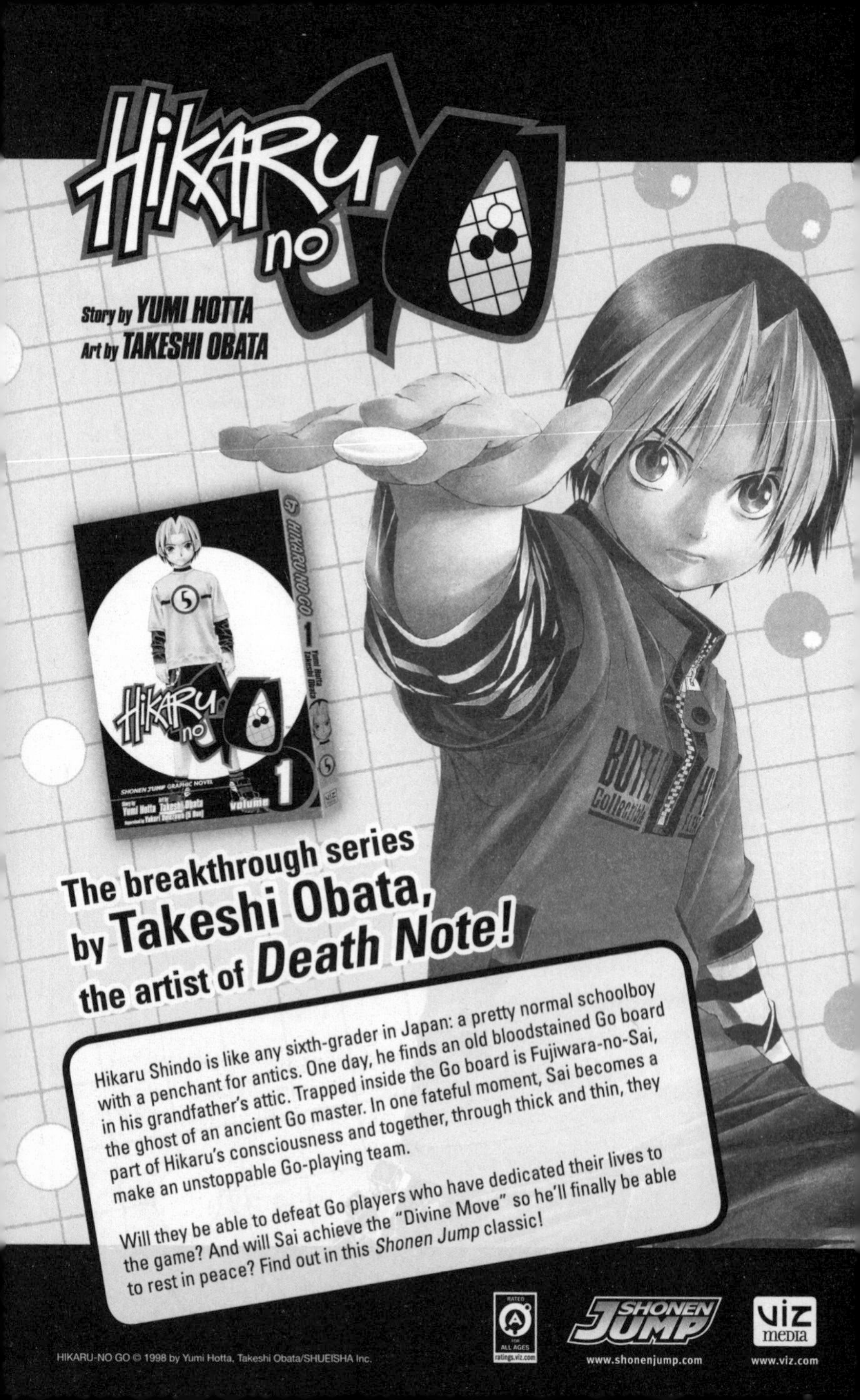
HIKARU no GO
Story by YUMI HOTTA
Art by TAKESHI OBATA
The breakthrough series by Takeshi Obata, the artist of Death Note!
Hikaru Shindo is like any sixth-grader in Japan: a pretty normal schoolboy with a penchant for antics. One day, he finds an old bloodstained Go board in his grandfather's attic. Trapped inside the Go board is Fujiwara-no-Sai, the ghost of an ancient Go master. In one fateful moment, Sai becomes a part of Hikaru's consciousness and together, through thick and thin, they make an unstoppable Go-playing team.
Will they be able to defeat Go players who have dedicated their lives to the game? And will Sai achieve the "Divine Move" so he'll finally be able to rest in peace? Find out in this Shonen Jump classic!
HIKARU-NO GO © 1998 by Yumi Hotta, Takeshi Obata/SHUEISHA Inc.
www.shonenjump.com
www.viz.com

YOU'RE READING THE WRONG WAY!

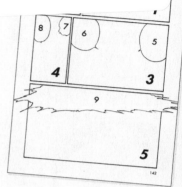

School Judgment: Gakkyu Hotei

reads from right to left, starting in the upper-right corner. Japanese is read from right to left, meaning that action, sound effects and word-balloon order are completely reversed from English order.

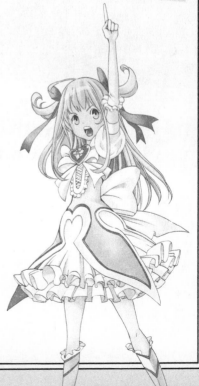